Transformative AI Practices for Personalized Learning Strategies

Lydia Kyei-Blankson
Illinois State University, USA

Esther Ntuli
Idaho State University, USA

IGI Global
Scientific Publishing
Publishing Tomorrow's Research Today

Vice President of Editorial	Melissa Wagner
Director of Acquisitions	Mikaela Felty
Director of Book Development	Jocelynn Hessler
Production Manager	Mike Brehm
Cover Design	Phillip Shickler

Published in the United States of America by
IGI Global Scientific Publishing
701 East Chocolate Avenue
Hershey, PA, 17033, USA
Tel: 717-533-8845
Fax: 717-533-7115
Website: https://www.igi-global.com E-mail: cust@igi-global.com

Library of Congress Cataloging-in-Publication Data

Names: Kyei-Blankson, Lydia, editor. | Ntuli, Esther, 1976- editor.
Title: Transformative AI practices for personalized learning strategies / edited by Lydia Kyei-Blankson, Esther Ntuli.
Description: Hershey, PA : IGI Global Scientific Publishing, [2025] | Includes bibliographical references and index. | Summary: "This book explores the best methods for leveraging Generative AI to create personalized and adaptive learning experiences, foster student motivation and comprehension, and address ethical considerations"-- Provided by publisher.
Identifiers: LCCN 2024054532 (print) | LCCN 2024054533 (ebook) | ISBN 9798369387443 (hardcover) | ISBN 9798369387450 (paperback) | ISBN 9798369387467 (ebook)
Subjects: LCSH: Artificial intelligence--Educational applications.
Classification: LCC LB1028.43 .T735 2025 (print) | LCC LB1028.43 (ebook) | DDC 371.33/463--dc23/eng/20250304
LC record available at https://lccn.loc.gov/2024054532
LC ebook record available at https://lccn.loc.gov/2024054533

British Cataloguing in Publication Data
A Cataloguing in Publication record for this book is available from the British Library.

Table of Contents

Detailed Table of Contents

At its core, AI in education aims to personalize learning, streamline administrative tasks, and foster more efficient, engaging educational interactions. Technology's ability to process vast amounts of data, recognize patterns, and generate insights can significantly improve both student outcomes and teacher effectiveness. By analyzing students' interactions, progress, and assessments, AI can identify strengths and weaknesses, adapting lessons and resources to better suit each learner. For instance, intelligent tutoring systems use algorithms to provide customized feedback and support, enhancing students' grasp of subjects and addressing gaps in their understanding more effectively than generic instruction.AI also contributes significantly to automating administrative tasks, which can alleviate some of the burdens on educators. Furthermore, AI fosters greater engagement and interactivity in the classroom. Educational tools powered by AI, such as virtual assistants and chatbots immediate help and resources to students, facilitating a more interactive learning experience.

D. Suresh, Meenakshi College of Engineering, Chennai, India
P. Lokesh, Meenakshi College of Engineering, Chennai, India
B. Yamini, SRM Institute of Science and Technology, India
B. Yuvasri, R.M.K. College of Engineering and Technology, India
V. Sathya, Vel Tech Rangarajan Dr. Sagunthala R&D Institute of Science and Technology, Chennai, India
P. Girija, Vel Tech Rangarajan Dr. Sagunthala R&D Institute of Science and Technology, Chennai, India
Subramanian R. Siva, R.M.K. College of Engineering and Technology, India

Education systems adopting technological solutions, Artificial Intelligence (AI) is making its ways into becoming a game changer in delivering learner centered approaches to learning. This questionnaire focuses on the promotion of effective learning plans using artificial intelligence to improve learning experiences as they are made to suit the learner. They are adaptive learning system which change content on the basis of performance, intelligent tutor system, and big data analytical system which provides solutions. Those include machine learning, NLP, and computer vision technologies that play an essential role in such developments. Although a number of positive case studies, across K-12, higher education, and corporate training indicate improvements, issues persist such as data privacy, equity and algorithm bias. The paper is wrapped up with the guidelines on the implementation of AI in education and suggestion of the prospects for further research.

Rohit Yadav, IILM University, Greater Noida, India
Mohit Yadav, O.P. Jindal Global University, India
Geshwaree Huzooree, Edinburgh Napier University, UK
Ali Najeeb, Qasim Ibrahim School of Business, Villa College, Maldives
Asanga Ranasinghe, Postgraduate Institute of Management, University of Sri Jayewardenepura, Sri Lanka

AI-powered personalized learning holds the potential to revolutionize education by tailoring content to meet the diverse needs of learners. However, for such systems to be truly effective, they must prioritize accessibility and inclusivity, ensuring equitable opportunities for all students, regardless of ability, background, or resources. This chapter explores the role of AI in personalized learning, focusing on the importance of designing systems that are both accessible and inclusive. It examines key issues such as algorithmic bias, data privacy, and the digital divide, offering strategies to

bias, and equitable access must be addressed to ensure responsible implementation. Future trends, including the integration of immersive technologies like Virtual Reality (VR) and predictive analytics, highlight AI's potential to revolutionize education. By navigating ethical considerations and fostering transparency, generative AI can become a powerful ally in creating inclusive, engaging, and student-centered learning environments.

Generative AI for assessment and feedback is transforming the way educators evaluate and enhance student learning in higher education. This study investigates the adoption of Generative AI (Gen AI) by faculty members in the Middle East to assess student performance. Specifically, it explores how teachers utilize Gen AI tools, the factors driving their adoption, and the interrelationships among these factors. Data was collected from early adopters of Gen AI using the snowball sampling method, focusing on their application of Gen AI in teaching, frequent tool usage, and assessment practices. The study also incorporates advanced preprocessing, feature extraction using Particle Swarm Optimization (PSO), and feature selection using the Remora Optimization Algorithm (ROA) to prepare the dataset for analysis. Further, the use of Convolutional Neural Networks (CNNs) for generating, categorizing, and grading assignments, as well as assessing student performance, is explored.

Teaching and learning methodologies are being completely transformed by new developments in educational technology. The way that individual courses and instructional units are designed in the classroom will be significantly impacted by

findings reveal that Generative AI facilitates personalized learning experiences, automates content generation, and provides immediate feedback, thereby transforming traditional educational practices. However, the study also highlights significant ethical challenges, including data privacy, algorithmic bias, and equity concerns. The conclusions emphasize the necessity of developing robust ethical frameworks to guide the responsible use of AI in education, ensuring that its benefits are equitably distributed while minimizing potential harms.

This chapter discusses the enhanced individualisation of learning in relation to AI and presents a deeper look at the prospects, obstacles, and ethical issues relating to AI based learning technologies. Thus, this aims to reveal how AI affects the nature of the models of personalised learning and instructional adaptation in order to discuss the potential opportunities and challenges emerging from the implementation of technological tools in learning. This is all about generating academic debate on ethics of algorithmic decision-making regarding equity, privacy and accountability within education. However, based on the increased technological integration in the construction of learning contexts, the analysis should be sustainable concerning the moral issues as AI more actively tries to fit into the processes of learning contexts. This would mean there is a thrust towards human agency, autonomy and dignity in the emphasis even as technology becomes a mediating factor in education meaning that it must be innovations with ethical responsibilities.

This chapter explores the transformative potential of artificial intelligence (AI) in revolutionizing physical education (PE) within Vietnamese universities. Recognizing universities as crucial spaces for holistic student development and PE as essential for physical and mental well-being, it advocates for the timely integration of AI technologies. The chapter critically examines the current state of PE in Vietnamese higher education and highlights opportunities for enhancement through AI-driven solutions. Key applications discussed include AI-powered diagnostics for personalized fitness assessments, comprehensive progress-tracking systems, and intelligent decision-making tools to optimize curriculum design. It also explores cutting-edge technologies such as intelligent guidance systems, automated evaluation systems, and educational sports robots. By promoting strategic pedagogical reforms and embracing AI, this chapter envisions a future where PE in Vietnamese universities becomes more effective and empowers students to reach their full potential.

This chapter provides an in-depth analysis of the integration of Generative AI in education, highlighting its transformative potential for personalized learning, assessment, and administrative efficiency. The chapter explores current trends, theoretical underpinnings, and speculative future scenarios, emphasizing the ethical considerations and challenges, such as data privacy, fairness, and the digital divide. By offering actionable strategies, real-world case studies, and best practices, the chapter equips educators, administrators, and policymakers with the tools to leverage AI technologies effectively and ethically. The discussion culminates in a comprehensive roadmap for implementing AI to promote equity, enhance student engagement, and prepare learners for an AI-driven future.

This chapter explores the evolving role of educators in the context of increasing Artificial Intelligence (AI) integration in education. As AI transforms traditional teaching methods, educators will shift from knowledge dispensers to facilitators of personalized learning, higher-order thinking, and social-emotional development. The collaboration between teachers and AI holds significant potential for enhancing learning experiences through personalized instruction, data-driven insights, and improved classroom efficiency. However, this transformation also presents practical, social, and ethical challenges, such as the digital divide, algorithmic biases, and data privacy concerns. To harness the full potential of AI in education, robust professional development programs for teachers, ethical AI design, and equitable access to technology are essential. This chapter outlines the opportunities and

Preface

Traditional education systems have predominantly been designed around standardized curricula and uniform instructional methods, prioritizing a one-size-fits-all approach. While this model has successfully supported many learners throughout the years, it has also resulted in considerable disparities in student achievement. These gaps are particularly pronounced among students whose learning styles, cultural backgrounds, or specific needs diverge from conventional expectations. For these diverse learners, strategies such as differentiated instruction and personalized learning might provide effective solutions to enhance their educational experiences.

Personalized learning can be broadly defined as an instructional approach in which educators actively customize and adapt students' learning experiences to better fit their individual backgrounds, skills, preferences, and learning paces (U.S. Department of Education, 2017). This method emphasizes the importance of recognizing and addressing each student's unique needs and interests, enabling a more tailored educational experience. Central to personalized learning are elements such as adaptive learning technologies, which adjust content and assessments according to student performance, and individualized learning plans, which outline specific learning goals and pathways for each student. Additionally, personalized learning encourages student agency, allowing learners to set their own goals and take ownership of their educational journeys.

According to Bingham et al. (2018), personalized learning can manifest in a variety of formats including competency-based progression, where students advance upon mastering skills rather than adhering to a fixed schedule; differentiated instruction, which involves varying teaching strategies and assignments based on students' needs; and learner-driven pathways, where students have the flexibility to choose subjects and projects that align with their interests and career aspirations.

In contrast to traditional educational models that often overlook individual differences, personalized learning acknowledges the diverse characteristics of each learner. It recognizes that students possess varying learning styles, paces, and capacities for understanding. Within a personalized learning environment, students are empowered to take control of their educational experiences, leading to greater motivation, deeper engagement with the material, and ultimately, improved academic outcomes.

Traditionally, personalized learning has involved strategies such as differentiated instruction, adaptive assessments, and flexible learning paths that cater to individual strengths and weaknesses. However, the integration of artificial intelligence (AI) into these practices promises to elevate them even further. AI can facilitate real-time data analysis, enabling educators to monitor student progress and adapt their teaching methods more quickly and effectively. This technological advancement has the potential to create even more responsive and inclusive learning environments, fostering success for all students, regardless of their starting points.

Personalized learning is deeply rooted in several influential constructivist learning theories, which include Piaget's Cognitive Development theory (1952), Vygotsky's Social Learning theory (1978), and Gardner's Multiple Intelligences theory (1983). This educational approach seeks to transcend the traditional one-size-fits-all model by tailoring educational experiences to meet the unique needs, strengths, and interests of each learner (Pane et al., 2017). Research has demonstrated that personalized learning can lead to a wide range of positive outcomes. Notably, it can significantly enhance student motivation and engagement by providing students with a sense of autonomy in their learning processes (Walkington, 2013). Additionally, studies indicate that students in personalized learning environments often achieve greater academic gains compared to those in traditional classrooms (Pane et al., 2017). Furthermore, personalized learning is effective in narrowing achievement gaps among diverse student populations, including those with varying abilities and backgrounds (Basham et al., 2016). It also fosters the development of critical self-regulation and metacognitive skills, which are essential for lifelong learning (Zimmerman & Schunk, 2011).

The current renaissance of personalized learning is significantly bolstered by advances in artificial intelligence (AI). The integration of AI-driven tools into personalized learning strategies offers a transformative and innovative approach to education—one that effectively meets learners at their individual levels and adapts instruction according to their specific needs. AI enhances this process by collecting and analyzing vast quantities of student data, which generates insightful information that can inform instructional design. For instance, adaptive learning platforms leverage AI algorithms to adjust the difficulty and complexity of tasks according to each student's performance and progress. This ensures that learners are continually challenged but not overwhelmed, allowing them to operate within their optimal zone of development (VanLehn, 2011). These advanced technologies not only contribute to improved academic achievement but also promote essential skills like self-directed learning and metacognitive reflection.

Moreover, the incorporation of AI in education has fundamentally transformed the educational landscape, leading to revolutionary changes that were once considered unattainable. The growing presence of AI in educational settings is primarily driven by the increasing demand for customized learning experiences that accommodate the diverse profiles of students, including those with disabilities, English language learners, and gifted individuals. AI holds the potential to bridge these gaps by offering personalized learning paths that adjust to each student's unique requirements. It can also facilitate intelligent tutoring systems that provide real-time feedback, ensuring that students receive the support they need promptly. Additionally, AI generates data-driven insights that empower educators to make informed decisions regarding instructional strategies and interventions, ultimately enhancing the overall effectiveness of teaching and learning. This integration of AI represents a significant leap forward in the pursuit of equitable and effective educational practices for all learners.

AI-driven personalized learning represents a significant advancement in the way educators can deliver lessons, assess student progress, and provide tailored recommendations for both teachers and learners. By utilizing cutting-edge technologies, educators are increasingly able to adjust their traditional teaching methods and pedagogical frameworks to create unique learning experiences that cater to individual student needs. This approach promotes not only greater student engagement but also enhances overall efficiency and inclusivity in the learning environment (Luckin et al., 2016).

The implementation of AI technologies, which include machine learning algorithms, natural language processing, and intelligent tutoring systems, has shown remarkable potential in supporting differentiated instruction. These tools enable real-time feedback, allowing educators to identify and address learning gaps as they arise, thus fostering a more responsive educational framework (Holmes, Bialik, & Fadel, 2019). For example, intelligent tutoring systems can adapt the difficulty of the content based on a student's performance, providing a personalized learning pathway that enhances mastery of the material.

While the transformative potential of AI in education is significant, it is crucial to consider both its benefits and limitations thoughtfully. Implementing AI in educational settings requires a strong alignment with ethical standards and best pedagogical practices to ensure that the technology serves the interests of all students. Educators must be equipped with comprehensive training that enables them to integrate AI tools effectively into their curriculum and teaching strategies. Moreover, policy-makers play an essential role and must establish robust regulations that safeguard student data privacy while promoting equitable access to AI technologies in diverse educational institutions.

As AI continues to advance at an unprecedented rate, understanding its role in personalized learning becomes imperative. This understanding is essential for maximizing the benefits of AI while also addressing potential challenges, including ethical dilemmas and issues surrounding data privacy. The evolving landscape of AI in education will likely have profound implications for personalized learning strategies, making it crucial for educators, researchers, and policymakers to examine critically how AI can be utilized to create equitable and transformative learning experiences.

The book titled "Transformative AI Practices for Personalized Learning Strategies" provides an in-depth exploration of how AI is reshaping educational practices and examines the implications for educators and various student populations across diverse educational settings. This edited volume delves into both the possibilities that AI presents and the limitations it may entail regarding personalized learning. Featuring contributions from a diverse group of scholars, practitioners, and technologists, the book documents the role of AI in personalized education while outlining innovative strategies for harnessing AI in ways that empower learners, support educators, and foster inclusive and equity-driven educational environments. By critically assessing AI-driven educational practices, this book seeks to provide trustworthy insights for educators and decision-makers who are committed to leveraging AI's potential to create transformative learning experiences. The chapters collectively present a thorough examination of AI applications in personalized education, addressing best practices, challenges encountered, and potential future directions for research and implementation in this rapidly evolving field.

The chapters in this book delve into several important themes that explore the intersection of artificial intelligence (AI) and education, providing both theoretical insights and practical applications.

The themes addressed in the book include the following:

1. **Understanding AI in Education** – This theme offers a foundational overview of AI technologies, defining what AI is and how it is evolving. We examine various AI models and platforms that have been developed for educational settings, detailing their functionalities and potential to enhance teaching and learning processes. Topics such as machine learning, natural language processing, and data analytics will be discussed in the context of their relevance to educational practitioners.
2. **AI-Powered Instructional Tools and AI-Driven Adaptive Learning Systems** – Under this theme, we explore the diverse range of AI-powered instructional tools available today, including chatbots that provide instant feedback, adaptive learning platforms that personalize educational content, and virtual tutors that assist students in real-time. We will analyze how these tools adapt to individual learning styles and paces, providing tailored educational experiences that meet

the unique needs of each learner, thereby fostering more effective and engaging learning environments.

3. **Equity, Accessibility, Inclusion, and Data-Driven AI-Powered Education** – This theme emphasizes the critical need for AI implementation to be inclusive and equitable. We investigate how AI has the potential to either bridge or widen the educational disparities faced by marginalized student populations. The role of data analytics in creating individualized learning experiences is discussed, highlighting the importance of leveraging data to foster inclusive educational practices that cater to all learners, regardless of their socioeconomic backgrounds or learning abilities.
4. **Ethical Considerations in AI Education** – An examination of the ethical dilemmas associated with AI in education forms the core of this chapter. We address issues such as data privacy, the potential for algorithmic bias, and the complexities of student surveillance. The integration of AI into educational systems raises numerous ethical challenges that must be thoughtfully navigated to protect student rights and promote fairness. This section calls for rigorous discussions among educators and policymakers to ensure that AI technologies serve as facilitators of equitable educational opportunities, rather than as barriers.
5. **AI's Role in Teacher Support and Professional Development** – With this theme, we illustrate how AI tools can enhance educators' capabilities in providing targeted interventions, formative assessments, and ongoing professional development. By analyzing how AI can assist in real-time assessments of student performance and facilitate differentiated instruction, we highlight strategies for empowering teachers to create more effective learning experiences.
6. **Case Studies in AI-Driven Learning** – This theme provides compelling real-world examples of schools and educational institutions that have successfully integrated AI into their practices. We present case studies that illustrate the diverse ways AI can transform educational methodologies, including improvements in student engagement, retention rates, and learning outcomes. These examples will offer valuable insights into best practices and lessons learned from the field.
7. **Future Directions, Implications for Practice, and Policy Considerations** – The final theme examines emerging trends in AI and their implications for educational policy and practice. We explore how changes in technology may reshape curriculum design, teacher roles, and student learning experiences. Focusing on the evolving landscape of education, this section raises critical questions about the future of learning and how educators can adapt to these changes to better serve their students.

This volume aims to address the urgent need for an informed, evidence-based approach to integrating AI into educational frameworks. It is designed for a diverse audience, including educators, instructional designers, researchers, and policymakers who are seeking to comprehend and implement AI in meaningful, student-centered ways. As we embrace the transformative potential of AI, it is essential to remain critically engaged with the technology, ensuring it supports and enhances human relationships and pedagogical expertise rather than undermining them. We invite you to embark on a journey to explore the vast opportunities presented by AI in education, contributing to a future where technology enriches the learning experience. By envisioning an educational landscape where every learner has the opportunity to thrive—bolstered by the capabilities of intelligent, adaptive, and personalized AI—you will gain insights into creating equitable and engaging educational environments.

By the conclusion of this book, readers will not only have a thorough understanding of how AI can enhance personalized learning but will also be equipped with practical strategies and frameworks to effectively integrate these technologies into their educational practices. The ultimate goal is not to replace the invaluable role of human educators but to empower them with innovative tools that make learning more engaging, effective, and accessible for all students, ensuring successful outcomes in diverse educational settings.

REFERENCES

Bingham, A. J., Pane, J. F., Steiner, E. D., & Hamilton, L. S. (2018). *Informing progress: Insights on personalized learning implementation and effects.* RAND Corporation.

Gardner, H. (1983). *Frames of mind: The theory of multiple intelligences.* Basic Books.

Holmes, W., Bialik, M., & Fadel, C. (2019). *Artificial intelligence in education: Promises and implications for teaching and learning.* Center for Curriculum Redesign.

Luckin, R., Holmes, W., Griffiths, M., & Forcier, L. B. (2016). *Intelligence unleashed: An argument for AI in education.* Pearson Education.

Pane, J. F., Steiner, E. D., Baird, M. D., & Hamilton, L. S. (2017). *Informing progress: Insights on personalized learning implementation and effects.* RAND Corporation. DOI: 10.7249/RR2042

Selwyn, N. (2019). *Should robots replace teachers? AI and the future of education.* Polity Press.

U.S. Department of Education, Office of Educational Technology. (2017). *Reimagining the role of technology in education: 2017 National Education Technology Plan update.* https://tech.ed.gov/files/2017/01/NETP17.pdf

VanLehn, K. (2011). The relative effectiveness of human tutoring, intelligent tutoring systems, and other tutoring systems. *Educational Psychologist, 46*(4), 197–221. DOI: 10.1080/00461520.2011.611369

Walkington, C. (2013). Using adaptive learning technologies to personalize instruction for struggling students. *Journal of Educational Psychology, 105*(4), 932–945. DOI: 10.1037/a0031882

Zimmerman, B. J., & Schunk, D. H. (2011). *Self-regulated learning and academic achievement: Theoretical perspectives.* Routledge.

Acknowledgments

We would like to express our gratitude to all the reviewers who dedicated their time and expertise to provide insightful feedback. Their critical assessments, constructive suggestions, and encouragement played a vital role in enhancing the quality of this scholarly work, making it possible for us to bring it to fruition.

Thank you!

Our Reviewers:

Alesia Moldavan, Georgia Southern University, USA

Atanu Roy, The Neotia University, India

Elaine Foster, Idaho State University, USA

Jackie Kim, Georgia Southern University, USA

J. B. Oleet, Mississippi State University, USA.

P. Selvakumar, Nehru Institute of Technology, India

Usharani Bhimavarapu, Andhra Pradesh, India

Siva Subramanian, RMK College of Engineering and Technology, India.

Robert Terry, Georgia Southern University, USA

Rohit Yadav, IILM University, India

Sabyasachi Pramanik, Haldia Institute of Technology, India.

Thuc Chanh Dao, Vietnam National University, Vietnam

Chapter 1
Overview of Current AI Technologies in Education

Rajat B. Hubballi
New Horizon College of Engineering, Bangalore, India

P. Selvakumar
https://orcid.org/0000-0002-3650-4548
Department of Science and Humanities, Nehru Institute of Technology, Coimbatore, India

Ravikumar Seenivasan
https://orcid.org/0000-0002-8235-8051
Woxsen University, Hyderabad, India

Guru Basava Aradhya S.
https://orcid.org/0000-0002-3335-2681
Chandigarh School of Business, Chandigarh Group of Colleges, Mohali, India

N. Dinesh
https://orcid.org/0000-0002-0209-6988
FOM, CMS Business School, Jain University, Bangalore, India

Pramod Kumar Seelam
https://orcid.org/0009-0000-2114-3033
Dravidian University, Kuppam, India

ABSTRACT

At its core, AI in education aims to personalize learning, streamline administrative tasks, and foster more efficient, engaging educational interactions. Technology's ability to process vast amounts of data, recognize patterns, and generate insights can significantly improve both student outcomes and teacher effectiveness. By analyzing students' interactions, progress, and assessments, AI can identify strengths and weaknesses, adapting lessons and resources to better suit each learner. For instance, intelligent tutoring systems use algorithms to provide customized feedback and support, enhancing students' grasp of subjects and addressing gaps in their understanding more effectively than generic instruction.AI also contributes significantly to automating administrative tasks, which can alleviate some of the

DOI: 10.4018/979-8-3693-8744-3.ch001

burdens on educators. Furthermore, AI fosters greater engagement and interactivity in the classroom. Educational tools powered by AI, such as virtual assistants and chatbots immediate help and resources to students, facilitating a more interactive learning experience.

INTRODUCTION TO AI IN EDUCATION: ENHANCING TEACHING AND LEARNING

At its core, AI in education aims to personalize learning, streamline administrative tasks, and foster more efficient, engaging educational interactions. The technology's ability to process vast amounts of data, recognize patterns, and generate insights can significantly improve both student outcomes and teacher effectiveness. By analyzing students' interactions, progress, and assessments, AI can identify strengths and weaknesses, adapting lessons and resources to better suit each learner. For instance, intelligent tutoring systems use algorithms to provide customized feedback and support, enhancing students' grasp of subjects and addressing gaps in their understanding more effectively than generic instruction.AI also contributes significantly to automating administrative tasks, which can alleviate some of the burdens on educators. Furthermore, AI fosters greater engagement and interactivity in the classroom. Educational tools powered by AI, such as virtual assistants and chatbots, can offer immediate help and resources to students, facilitating a more interactive learning experience. These tools can simulate real-world scenarios, provide immersive learning environments through augmented reality (AR) and virtual reality (VR), and even facilitate collaborative learning experiences across different geographies. AI tools must be designed to complement and enhance human teaching rather than replace it, preserving the essential interpersonal elements of education. Embracing AI in education requires a balanced approach, combining technological advancements with a commitment to addressing ethical and practical concerns. This approach can help harness AI's full potential, ultimately enhancing the educational experiences and outcomes for students worldwide.

LEARNING MANAGEMENT SYSTEMS (LMS) WITH AI: PERSONALIZED LEARNING EXPERIENCES

Learning Management Systems (LMS) are pivotal in the modern educational landscape, providing platforms for managing, delivering, and tracking educational content and activities. The incorporation of Artificial Intelligence (AI) into LMS platforms marks a significant evolution, transforming them from basic repositories of instructional material into dynamic, responsive tools that offer personalized learning experiences. One of the most compelling features of AI-integrated LMS is their ability to deliver personalized learning paths. Traditional LMS platforms often offer static courses with a fixed progression, which may not accommodate the diverse needs and paces of learners(Baker, R.S., et al.,2022). AI-enabled LMS, however, can leverage data analytics to create adaptive learning pathways. By analyzing data from students' interactions with the platform, including quiz scores, time spent on topics, and engagement levels, AI algorithms can adjust the content delivery in real-time. This means that if a student excels in certain areas, the system can present more advanced material or supplementary resources to challenge them further. Conversely, if a student struggles with specific concepts, the LMS can provide additional support, remedial content, or alternative explanations to facilitate understanding.AI also enhances the customization of learning materials within LMS platforms. Instead of a one-size-fits-all approach(Black, P. et al., 2009), AI-driven systems can curate content based on individual learning preferences and needs. For instance, if a student shows a preference for visual learning, the LMS might prioritize video content and interactive simulations. If another student benefits more from textual content, the platform can adjust to offer detailed readings and explanations(Boden, M.A. 2018).

This level of customization helps address different learning styles and paces, making education more effective and engaging.This immediate response helps students understand their mistakes and learn from them promptly. Additionally, AI can generate detailed analytics for educators, highlighting patterns in student performance, identifying areas where students are struggling, and suggesting targeted interventions. These insights enable educators to refine their instructional strategies and provide more focused support, thereby improving overall educational outcomes. AI-powered LMS also facilitates enhanced engagement through interactive features. Chatbots and virtual assistants integrated within the LMS can offer instant answers to students' questions, provide guidance on navigating the platform, and offer additional resources based on students' queries. These tools can simulate conversations and provide personalized support, making the learning process more interactive and less dependent on the availability of human instructors. Ensuring that data is handled responsibly and in compliance with regulations is crucial. Additionally, there is the challenge of maintaining the balance between automation and the human element in education. While AI can provide valuable support and insights, it is essential to preserve the personal touch of teaching and the essential interpersonal interactions between educators and students. As AI technology continues to evolve, its integration into LMS platforms is likely to become more sophisticated, offering even more innovative solutions to meet the diverse needs of learners. Embracing these advancements while addressing the associated challenges can lead to a more tailored, effective, and engaging educational experience for students worldwide.

INTELLIGENT TUTORING SYSTEMS (ITS): AI-POWERED ADAPTIVE LEARNING

These systems integrate sophisticated algorithms and machine learning techniques to analyze student performance, predict learning challenges, and adapt educational content in real-time, thereby enhancing the efficacy and engagement of the learning process. Traditional educational methods often follow a standard approach, which may not cater to the varying needs of each student. ITS, however, utilize AI to assess a student's prior knowledge, learning style, and progress. By continuously monitoring interactions with the system, including responses to questions, time spent on tasks, and patterns in performance (Chen, C., et al.,2020), ITS can customize the content delivery to suit individual learning needs. For instance, if a student struggles with a particular concept, the system can provide additional explanations, practice exercises, or alternative instructional methods to reinforce understanding. Conversely, if a student demonstrates proficiency, the ITS can present more challenging material to stimulate further learning. Another significant advantage of ITS is their ability to deliver immediate, targeted feedback. In traditional classroom settings, students may have to wait for feedback on their assignments or assessments, which can hinder their learning progress. ITS address this issue by offering instant feedback on student responses, helping learners identify and correct mistakes as they occur. This immediate reinforcement supports the learning process by allowing students to understand their errors and adjust their approach in real-time. Furthermore, the system's adaptive capabilities ensure that the feedback is tailored to the individual's specific learning context, making it more relevant and effective. ITS also enhance the learning experience by incorporating adaptive problem-solving strategies (Bryant, J., et al.,2020).

The system's algorithms can identify common learning obstacles and deploy customized interventions to address them. For example, if a student consistently encounters difficulties with specific types of problems, the ITS can offer targeted practice sessions or alternative explanations that focus on these areas. This adaptive approach not only helps in overcoming learning barriers but also promotes a more efficient and personalized learning trajectory. The use of ITS in educational settings extends beyond individual learning to support collaborative and group learning experiences. Advanced ITS can facilitate group interactions by identifying students with complementary skills and interests, enabling collaborative problem-solving and peer-to-peer learning. Despite the numerous benefits, the deployment of ITS also presents certain challenges. Data privacy and security are paramount concerns, as these systems handle substantial amounts of personal and academic information. Additionally, while ITS offer valuable support, they should complement rather than replace human instructors (Celik, I., et al.,2022). The interpersonal skills, motivation, and emotional support provided by teachers are essential elements of the educational experience that AI cannot fully replicate. The integration of ITS into educational practices represents a significant leap forward in personalized and adaptive learning. By leveraging AI to offer customized instruction, immediate feedback, and adaptive problem-solving, ITS can significantly enhance learning outcomes and engagement. As technology continues to advance, ITS are likely to become even more sophisticated, offering more nuanced and effective support for diverse learning needs. Balancing these technological advancements with considerations for data security and the irreplaceable value of human interaction will be key to maximizing the benefits of ITS in education.

NATURAL LANGUAGE PROCESSING (NLP) IN EDUCATION: AUTOMATING GRADING AND FEEDBACK

Its application in education, particularly in automating grading and providing feedback, represents a transformative shift in how educational assessments are conducted. By leveraging NLP technologies, educational institutions can streamline assessment processes, reduce administrative burdens on educators, and enhance the timeliness and quality of feedback provided to students. One of the primary benefits of NLP in education is its ability to automate the grading of written assignments, essays, and open-ended questions. Traditional grading of such tasks often requires significant time and effort from educators, who must carefully read and assess each student's work. NLP algorithms, however, can analyze and evaluate text by comparing it against predefined criteria and rubrics. These systems use techniques such as semantic analysis and syntactic parsing to understand the context and content of the written material. For example, NLP can evaluate the coherence, relevance, and completeness of an essay (Chen, G., et al., 2015), providing a consistent and objective assessment that aligns with educational standards. This automation not only speeds up the grading process but also ensures uniformity in evaluation, reducing potential biases associated with human grading. Beyond grading, NLP enhances the feedback process by offering detailed, actionable insights to students. Automated feedback systems powered by NLP can provide real-time evaluations of written work, highlighting strengths and areas for improvement. For instance, these systems can identify grammatical errors, suggest stylistic improvements, and assess the logical flow of arguments. Furthermore (Dieterle, E., et al.,2022), advanced NLP systems can offer personalized feedback based on individual learning patterns and past performance. By analyzing a student's previous submissions and responses, NLP can tailor feedback to address specific recurring issues, thereby supporting targeted improvement and learning. NLP also facilitates more efficient handling of large volumes of student submissions. In educational environments with high student-to-teacher ratios, manually grading and providing feedback can be overwhelming. NLP-powered tools can manage and assess numerous submissions simultaneously, ensuring that all students receive timely and constructive feedback.

This scalability is particularly beneficial in large-scale assessments, online courses, and standardized testing environments, where human resources may be limited. However, the use of NLP in grading and feedback also raises several considerations. One key concern is the accuracy and reliability of automated systems. While NLP technology has advanced significantly, it is not infallible. Automated systems may struggle with nuances in language, context, and creativity, potentially leading to errors in grading or feedback. Ensuring the reliability of these systems requires continuous refinement of algorithms and rigorous testing. Additionally, there is the issue of data privacy and security, as automated grading systems process a significant amount of student data. Safeguarding this information and ensuring compliance with privacy regulations is crucial. Moreover, while NLP can greatly assist in grading and feedback, it is important to recognize the limitations of automation. Human judgment remains essential in assessing complex aspects of student work, such as creativity, originality, and nuanced understanding (Doewes, A. et al., 2021). NLP tools should be viewed as complementary to, rather than replacements for, human evaluators. Educators should use automated feedback as a supplement to their own insights and interactions with students, ensuring that the educational experience remains holistic and supportive. In conclusion, Natural Language Processing holds significant promise for automating grading and feedback in education, offering efficiency, consistency, and personalized support. By leveraging NLP technologies, educational institutions can enhance the assessment process, providing timely and detailed feedback that supports student learning and development. Balancing the benefits of automation with considerations for accuracy, data privacy, and the irreplaceable value of human judgment will be key to maximizing the effectiveness of NLP in educational assessments.

AI-DRIVEN CONTENT CREATION: GENERATING EDUCATIONAL MATERIALS AND ASSESSMENTS

Artificial Intelligence (AI) is increasingly transforming the landscape of educational content creation by automating the generation of instructional materials and assessments (Ersozlu, Z., et al, 2021). This advancement leverages sophisticated algorithms and machine learning models to produce high-quality, tailored educational content efficiently. By integrating AI into content creation processes, educators and institutions can benefit from a streamlined approach to developing diverse instructional resources, assessments, and personalized learning materials, ultimately enhancing the educational experience for students.AI-driven content creation encompasses a broad range of applications, from generating textbooks and lesson plans to designing quizzes and interactive exercises. For instance, AI algorithms can analyze curriculum standards, educational goals, and student performance data to create targeted lesson plans and instructional content. By adjusting content to meet the varying proficiency levels and learning styles of students, AI helps ensure that materials are both relevant and effective. In the realm of textbook and educational resource generation (Forsyth, S., et al., 2021), AI can assist in compiling and synthesizing information from a multitude of sources. Natural Language Processing (NLP) techniques enable AI to process and understand large volumes of text, extract key concepts, and organize content in a coherent manner.

This capability allows AI to draft textbooks, create study guides, and develop supplementary materials quickly and efficiently. Such automation not only accelerates content production but also facilitates the rapid updating of educational resources to reflect the latest developments and research in various fields. AI's role in creating assessments is equally transformative. Traditionally, developing assessments such as quizzes, tests, and exams required substantial time and effort from educators. AI-driven tools can automate this process by generating a wide variety of questions, including multiple-choice, short answer, and essay prompts, based on predefined learning objectives and content areas. These tools can also adapt assessments to the individual student's level of understanding, providing tailored questions that match their proficiency. For example, if a student demonstrates a strong grasp of basic concepts, the AI can generate more challenging questions to assess advanced understanding. Conversely, if a student is struggling (Friedman, L., et al.,2021), the AI can offer simpler questions to reinforce foundational knowledge. The use of AI in content creation also extends to the development of interactive and adaptive learning materials. AI-powered systems can design engaging educational games, simulations, and interactive exercises that cater to different learning preferences. By analyzing student performance data and feedback, AI systems can identify patterns and trends that inform the refinement of content. For example, if certain types of questions consistently lead to lower scores, AI can suggest adjustments to improve clarity or relevance. Similarly, AI can track how different types of instructional materials impact student learning and suggest modifications to enhance their effectiveness. This iterative approach ensures that educational content remains aligned with learning goals and responsive to student needs. While AI can produce content efficiently, it is essential to ensure that the generated materials are accurate, pedagogically sound, and free from bias. Human oversight remains crucial in reviewing and validating AI-generated content to ensure its suitability for educational purposes. Additionally, there is the challenge of maintaining the human touch in content creation.

VIRTUAL LEARNING ENVIRONMENTS (VLES) WITH AI: IMMERSIVE AND INTERACTIVE LEARNING

Virtual Learning Environments (VLEs) have become integral to contemporary education, offering a digital platform where students can engage with learning materials, collaborate with peers, and interact with educators. The integration of Artificial Intelligence (AI) into VLEs represents a significant advancement, transforming these platforms into dynamic, immersive, and highly interactive learning spaces. By leveraging AI technologies, VLEs can provide personalized learning experiences, enhance engagement through interactive features, and create realistic, immersive educational scenarios that go beyond traditional classroom settings.AI-powered VLEs enhance the personalization of learning by adapting to the unique needs and preferences of individual students. Through sophisticated data analytics and machine learning algorithms, these systems can analyze student interactions, performance, and behavior to tailor educational content and experiences. For instance, if a student struggles with specific concepts, the VLE can dynamically adjust the learning path, providing additional resources, practice exercises, or alternative explanations to address these challenges. The integration of AI also enhances the interactivity and engagement within VLEs. Traditional VLEs often rely on static content and limited interaction, which can lead to disengagement.

AI-driven VLEs, however, incorporate interactive elements such as virtual simulations, gamified learning experiences, and real-time feedback mechanisms (Gardner, J., et al.,2021). For example, AI can create interactive simulations that allow students to explore complex concepts in a virtual environment, such as conducting science experiments or exploring historical events. For example, VR can transport students to ancient civilizations, enabling them to explore historical sites and interact with virtual artifacts. Similarly, AR can overlay digital information onto physical objects, providing contextual information and enhancing the learning experience. These immersive technologies not only make learning more engaging but also provide students with experiential learning opportunities that are difficult to achieve in traditional classroom settings.AI also supports collaborative learning within VLEs by connecting students with peers and educators in innovative ways. AI-powered tools can facilitate group projects, discussions, and collaborative problem-solving by matching students with complementary skills and interests. For instance, AI can analyze students' strengths and preferences to form effective project teams or recommend discussion groups that align with their learning goals. Additionally, AI-driven chatbots and virtual assistants can provide real-time support and facilitate communication, helping students navigate the VLE and access resources more efficiently. These collaborative features foster a sense of community and teamwork, enhancing the overall learning experience (Godwin-Jones, R. 2021). Moreover, AI enhances the administrative and support functions within VLEs, making them more efficient and user-friendly. In conclusion, AI-driven Virtual Learning Environments represent a significant advancement in educational technology, offering personalized, immersive, and interactive learning experiences (Hammerness, K., et al., 2005). By leveraging AI technologies, VLEs can tailor educational content, enhance engagement through interactive features, and provide realistic, experiential learning opportunities. Addressing challenges related to data privacy and maintaining a balance between technology and human interaction will be key to maximizing the benefits of AI in virtual learning environments.

AI-POWERED STUDENT ANALYTICS: IDENTIFYING KNOWLEDGE GAPS AND LEARNING PATHWAYS

AI-powered student analytics represents a transformative advancement in educational technology, offering educators and institutions powerful tools to identify knowledge gaps and optimize learning pathways. Traditional assessment methods often provide limited insight into specific areas where students may be struggling. AI analytics, however, can process vast amounts of data from various sources, including test scores, assignments, participation metrics, and behavioral data. For instance, if a student consistently performs poorly on certain types of questions or topics, the AI can detect this pattern and highlight the specific knowledge gaps that need to be addressed (Holmes, W. et al., 2022). This targeted approach allows educators to focus their efforts on areas where students require the most support, rather than applying a broad, generalized strategy.AI-powered analytics also enable the creation of personalized learning pathways, tailored to each student's unique needs and progress. Traditional educational models often follow a fixed curriculum, which may not accommodate the diverse learning styles and paces of individual students. AI-driven systems, on the other hand, can continuously assess a student's performance and adapt learning materials accordingly. By analyzing data on a student's strengths, weaknesses, and learning preferences, AI can recommend specific resources, exercises, and instructional strategies that align with their individual needs. Furthermore, AI-powered analytics facilitate proactive interventions by identifying students who may be at risk of falling behind. By monitoring real-time data on student engagement, participation, and performance (Holstein, K., et al., 2019),

AI systems can flag early warning signs of potential issues. For example, a sudden decline in assignment completion rates or a drop in quiz scores might indicate that a student is struggling or disengaging. Educators can then use these insights to provide timely support, such as additional tutoring, targeted feedback, or adjustments to the learning environment. This proactive approach helps prevent small challenges from escalating into significant academic difficulties. The ability of AI to analyze and interpret large datasets also supports the development of data-driven instructional strategies. Educators can use insights from AI analytics to refine their teaching methods, design more effective learning activities, and tailor their instruction to better meet the needs of their students. For instance, if data shows that students generally perform better on interactive activities compared to traditional lectures, educators might choose to incorporate more hands-on, experiential learning opportunities (Kai, S., et al.,2018). This evidence-based approach enhances the overall effectiveness of instruction and contributes to improved learning outcomes.AI-powered student analytics also play a crucial role in supporting group and collaborative learning. By analyzing data on group interactions and performance, AI systems can identify patterns in group dynamics and collaboration effectiveness. This information can be used to form balanced groups, assign roles that align with each student's strengths, and facilitate more productive group activities. Additionally, AI can track and analyze peer feedback, helping to ensure that collaborative efforts are constructive and that all group members are contributing effectively. In conclusion, AI-powered student analytics represents a significant advancement in understanding and improving student learning. By identifying knowledge gaps, personalizing learning pathways, and supporting proactive interventions, AI provides valuable tools for enhancing educational outcomes. The ability to analyze and interpret large volumes of data enables more precise and effective teaching strategies, contributing to a more tailored and responsive educational experience. Chatbots and Virtual Assistants in Education: Enhancing Student Support tThe rise of chatbots and virtual assistants in education marks a significant advancement in providing student support and enhancing the overall learning experience. These AI-powered tools are transforming how institutions interact with students, offering real-time assistance, personalized guidance, and streamlined administrative processes. By integrating chatbots and virtual assistants into educational settings, institutions can deliver more responsive and efficient support, fostering a more engaging and accessible learning environment.

Chatbots and virtual assistants are increasingly used to address routine inquiries and provide immediate support, which helps alleviate the workload on administrative staff and educators. These AI systems are designed to handle a wide range of tasks, from answering frequently asked questions about course schedules, deadlines, and enrollment procedures to assisting with technical issues related to online platforms.

For instance, a chatbot integrated into a Learning Management System (LMS) can provide students with instant answers about assignment due dates, grading policies, or how to navigate the platform. This real-time support helps students find the information they need quickly, reducing frustration and ensuring that they can focus more on their studies rather than administrative details. By leveraging data on individual student interactions and preferences, these AI tools can provide tailored recommendations and support. For example, a virtual assistant could analyze a student's recent performance and suggest additional resources, such as supplementary readings, practice exercises, or tutoring sessions, based on their specific needs. Similarly, chatbots can guide students through course material by answering content-specific questions, providing explanations, and offering hints or feedback on exercises. This personalized approach helps students receive targeted support that aligns with their unique learning requirements and progress. In addition to individual support, chatbots and virtual assistants facilitate more effective communication between students and educators. These AI tools can serve as intermediaries, managing and routing student inquiries to the appropriate faculty or administrative staff. For instance, if a student has a question about a particular assignment, the chatbot can gather relevant details and forward the query to the instructor responsible. This streamlines communication, ensuring that inquiries are handled promptly and efficiently(Kaplan, R.M., et al.,2017). Furthermore, virtual assistants can schedule appointments, send reminders, and manage meeting logistics, making it easier for students to connect with their instructors and advisors. The integration of chatbots and virtual assistants also enhances student engagement and support through their availability and accessibility. Unlike traditional office hours or scheduled support sessions, AI-powered tools are available 24/7, providing assistance whenever students need it. This constant availability is particularly valuable in online or distance learning environments, where students may be participating in courses across different time zones. The ability to access support at any time can help address issues and questions that arise outside regular office hours, ensuring that students receive timely assistance and can continue their studies without interruption. Despite their numerous advantages, the deployment of chatbots and virtual assistants in education also presents challenges(Ke, Z., et al.,2019). Addressing challenges related to accuracy, data privacy, and the balance between AI and human interaction will be key to maximizing the benefits of these technologies. As AI continues to advance, chatbots and virtual assistants are likely to become even more integral to the educational landscape, providing innovative solutions to support student success and engagement.

AI-ENHANCED ACCESSIBILITY IN EDUCATION: SUPPORTING DIVERSE LEARNING NEEDS

Artificial Intelligence (AI) is fundamentally transforming how educational institutions address diverse learning needs by enhancing accessibility and providing tailored support for all students. As educational environments become increasingly inclusive, AI technologies play a critical role in breaking down barriers and ensuring that students with varying abilities and needs can fully engage in and benefit from educational opportunities. By leveraging advanced AI tools, educational systems can offer personalized learning experiences, adaptive technologies, and proactive support that cater to a wide range of learning differences. For example, a student with dyslexia may benefit from text-to-speech software that converts written material into spoken words, while a student with visual impairments might use screen readers and AI-powered image descriptions(Khosravi, H., et al.,2022). By customizing learning resources and strategies to meet individual needs, AI ensures that all students have access to the materials and support necessary for their success.AI also enhances accessibility through real-time translation and language support, breaking down language barriers and supporting non-native speakers or students with limited English proficiency. AI can also support students with cognitive disabilities by offering personalized prompts, reminders, and simplified content that aligns with their learning needs(Kulik, J.A., et al.,2016). These assistive technologies empower students to engage more effectively with educational content and participate more fully in classroom activities.

AI's role in accessibility extends to supporting students with mental health and emotional well-being needs as well. AI-powered tools can monitor and analyze behavioral and engagement data to identify signs of stress, anxiety, or disengagement. For instance, if a student shows patterns of declining performance or changes in participation, AI systems can alert educators to provide timely support and intervention. Additionally, AI-driven mental health applications can offer resources such as virtual counseling, mindfulness exercises, and stress management techniques, helping students manage their emotional well-being and maintain a positive learning experience.

The use of AI to support accessibility in education also involves enhancing the design of educational environments and tools. AI can analyze data on student interactions and preferences to inform the development of more accessible and user-friendly interfaces. For example, AI can identify design elements that may be challenging for students with visual impairments and suggest modifications to improve accessibility (Ma, W., et al.,2014). By incorporating feedback from diverse user groups, AI-driven design processes ensure that educational tools and platforms are inclusive and responsive to the needs of all students. Since AI systems often handle sensitive information about students' abilities and needs, it is crucial to safeguard this data and adhere to privacy regulations. Additionally, while AI can provide valuable support, it should complement rather than replace human interaction. In conclusion, AI-enhanced accessibility in education offers significant opportunities for supporting diverse learning needs and creating a more inclusive educational environment. By leveraging adaptive learning technologies, assistive tools, and real-time support systems, AI can provide personalized and effective solutions that address the unique needs of students.

GAME-BASED LEARNING WITH AI: ENGAGING AND EFFECTIVE LEARNING EXPERIENCES

Game-based learning, enhanced by Artificial Intelligence (AI), is revolutionizing education by making learning more engaging and effective through interactive and immersive experiences. By integrating AI into educational games, educators and developers can create dynamic learning environments that adapt to students' needs, provide instant feedback, and foster motivation through gamification. This approach not only enhances student engagement but also improves learning outcomes by combining the motivational aspects of games with educational content. For instance, if a student answers a question incorrectly or makes an error in a simulation, the AI can offer immediate explanations and guide them through the correct process. This instant feedback is crucial for reinforcing learning and promoting a deeper understanding of the material. Additionally (Maslej, N., et al., 2023), AI can track and analyze students' interactions and performance within the game, offering educators valuable insights into their progress and areas for improvement. This data-driven approach allows for more informed assessments and targeted instructional interventions. AI can enhance these motivational aspects by personalizing rewards and challenges based on individual student achievements and preferences. For example, a game might recognize a student's milestones and achievements, offering customized rewards or unlocking new levels that align with their interests and goals. AI can help manage and guide these collaborative activities by organizing groups based on students' strengths and needs, monitoring interactions, and providing feedback on group dynamics. This collaborative aspect of game-based learning helps develop essential social and interpersonal skills while reinforcing academic content (Sklar, M.B., et al.,2003).

Moreover, AI-powered game-based learning environments can create realistic and immersive scenarios that enhance experiential learning. By simulating real-world situations or historical events, educational games can provide students with hands-on experiences that deepen their understanding of complex concepts. For instance, a history game might allow students to explore ancient civilizations, interact with historical figures, and participate in key events. Similarly, a science game might simulate laboratory experiments, enabling students to test hypotheses and observe results in a virtual setting. These immersive experiences not only make learning more engaging but also provide opportunities for experiential learning that traditional classroom methods may not offer. Despite the numerous benefits, integrating AI into game-based learning presents several challenges. One major concern is ensuring the educational value of the games. While gamification can enhance engagement, it is essential that the educational content is effectively integrated and aligned with learning objectives. Developers must balance the entertainment aspects of games with the pedagogical goals to ensure that students achieve meaningful learning outcomes (Mousavinasab, E., et al., 2021). Additionally, there is the issue of accessibility and inclusivity. AI-powered educational games must be designed to accommodate diverse learning needs and abilities, providing equitable access and support for all students. Data privacy and security also pose significant considerations.

AI IN EDUCATION RESEARCH: EMERGING TRENDS AND FUTURE DIRECTIONS

Artificial Intelligence (AI) is rapidly transforming the field of education, leading to innovative research directions and shaping the future of teaching and learning. As AI technologies advance, researchers are exploring a range of emerging trends that promise to enhance educational practices, personalize learning experiences, and address diverse learning needs (Van Lehn, K. 2011). This exploration encompasses several key areas, including adaptive learning systems, intelligent tutoring, data-driven insights, and the ethical implications of AI in education. Understanding these trends and their potential impacts is crucial for advancing educational research and practice. By analyzing data from various sources—such as student performance, interaction patterns, and engagement levels—adaptive learning systems can provide personalized recommendations and adjust the difficulty of content in real-time. This customization aims to enhance student outcomes by ensuring that each learner receives instruction that aligns with their unique abilities and progress. Research in this area focuses on improving the accuracy and effectiveness of adaptive algorithms, as well as exploring how these systems can be integrated into diverse educational settings. These systems can address individual learning gaps, offer tailored explanations, and monitor progress to adjust instruction accordingly. Recent research is focusing on enhancing the sophistication of ITS by incorporating advanced natural language processing (NLP) capabilities, allowing for more natural and intuitive interactions between students and the system. Additionally, there is growing interest in exploring how ITS can support collaborative learning, foster critical thinking skills, and integrate with other educational technologies.

This data-driven approach enables researchers to identify patterns, predict trends, and gain insights into factors that influence student success. For instance, AI can reveal correlations between engagement levels and academic performance, helping educators design more effective interventions. Ongoing research is examining how to leverage these insights to inform instructional design, improve curriculum development, and support evidence-based decision-making in education. For example, AI-driven tools can provide real-time translations, text-to-speech functionalities, and adaptive interfaces that accommodate various accessibility requirements. Research in this area is focused on ensuring that AI solutions are equitable and effective in addressing the needs of all learners. This includes examining how AI can support students with cognitive, sensory, and physical impairments, as well as exploring the implications of AI for creating inclusive learning environments. Ethical considerations and the responsible use of AI in education are increasingly prominent in research discussions. As AI technologies become more integrated into educational settings, there are concerns about privacy, security, and bias. Researchers are investigating how to ensure that AI systems are transparent, accountable, and fair (Wiggins, G. 2015). This includes developing frameworks for ethical AI design, implementing robust data protection measures, and addressing potential biases in AI algorithms. For example, AI-powered VR simulations can offer students immersive environments for experiential learning, while AR applications can enhance classroom interactions with interactive digital content. Research in this area aims to evaluate the effectiveness of these technologies, explore their potential for enhancing engagement and learning outcomes, and identify best practices for their implementation. Moreover, AI research is increasingly focusing on the development of collaborative and social learning tools. AI technologies can facilitate group work, peer feedback, and collaborative problem-solving by analyzing group dynamics, providing real-time support, and guiding interactions.

ETHICS AND BIAS IN AI EDUCATION TECHNOLOGIES: ENSURING FAIRNESS AND TRANSPARENCY

As Artificial Intelligence (AI) technologies become increasingly integrated into education, addressing the ethical implications and biases inherent in these systems is crucial for ensuring fairness and transparency. However, their deployment also raises significant ethical concerns related to privacy, equity, and algorithmic bias. Addressing these issues is essential for building trust in AI technologies and ensuring that they serve all students equitably. For instance, if an adaptive learning system is trained on data from a specific demographic group, it might fail to adequately support students from other backgrounds. Similarly, automated grading systems that rely on biased data or flawed criteria may unfairly disadvantage certain students, leading to inaccurate assessments of their abilities (Winne, P.H. 2021). Ensuring that AI systems are trained on diverse, representative datasets and regularly audited for bias is crucial for mitigating these risks. Transparency is another critical ethical consideration in the development and implementation of AI education technologies. To address this issue, there is a growing emphasis on developing explainable AI (XAI) that provides clear, interpretable explanations of how decisions are reached. Ensuring transparency in AI systems allows stakeholders to scrutinize their functioning, identify potential biases, and make informed decisions about their use. Privacy and data security are also paramount ethical concerns in the realm of AI education technologies. AI systems often rely on collecting and analyzing sensitive information about students, including personal details, academic performance, and learning behaviors. Additionally, it is important to provide students with control over their own data, including the ability to access, correct, or delete information as needed.

For instance, AI tools should be accessible to students with disabilities and designed to accommodate various learning styles and preferences. Research and development in AI education must prioritize inclusivity, ensuring that technologies do not inadvertently reinforce existing inequalities or create new barriers for marginalized groups. Engaging with diverse stakeholders, including educators, students, and advocacy groups, can help identify and address potential equity issues. Developing and adhering to ethical guidelines and best practices for AI in education can help mitigate risks and promote responsible use. Incorporating lessons on AI ethics, data privacy, and digital citizenship into the curriculum can empower students to navigate and critically assess the use of technology in their learning experiences. Educators play a vital role in guiding students through these discussions and helping them develop the skills needed to engage with AI technologies responsibly, fairness, transparency (Zacamy, J. et al.,2022), and equity in educational practices. By focusing on reducing bias, increasing transparency, protecting privacy, promoting inclusivity, and establishing ethical guidelines, stakeholders can build trust in AI systems and ensure that they contribute positively to the educational experience.

TEACHER TRAINING AND AI LITERACY: PREPARING EDUCATORS FOR AI-DRIVEN CLASSROOMS

Teacher training and AI literacy are crucial for ensuring that educators can harness the potential of AI technologies to enhance teaching and learning while addressing the challenges these technologies present. Preparing educators for AI-driven classrooms involves a multifaceted approach that includes understanding AI technologies, implementing AI tools effectively, and fostering an environment where AI complements rather than replaces traditional teaching methods. Professional development programs should focus on demystifying AI, explaining how these technologies work, and showcasing their potential benefits and limitations. This foundational knowledge enables teachers to make informed decisions about which AI tools to use and how to leverage them to support their instructional goals. In addition to understanding AI technologies, teachers must also be trained in the effective implementation of AI tools in the classroom. This includes learning how to integrate AI systems with existing curricula, adapt lesson plans to incorporate AI-driven insights, and use AI tools to personalize learning experiences for students.

Training programs should provide practical guidance on how to use specific AI applications, such as setting up and managing adaptive learning systems, interpreting data from AI analytics, and utilizing intelligent tutoring systems to offer targeted support. Additionally, educators should be encouraged to critically evaluate AI tools and their effectiveness, ensuring that these technologies enhance rather than detract from the educational experience. Another crucial aspect of preparing educators for AI-driven classrooms is fostering a culture of collaboration and continuous learning (Zhai, X., et al.,2022). AI technologies and educational practices are constantly evolving, and teachers must be prepared to adapt and stay current with new developments. Professional learning communities, online forums, and collaborative workshops can provide ongoing support and opportunities for educators to share best practices, discuss challenges, and explore new AI tools and techniques. Encouraging a mindset of lifelong learning helps educators remain agile and responsive to changes in technology and pedagogy, ultimately benefiting their students. In addition to technical training, it is essential to support educators in developing a pedagogical approach that integrates AI in a meaningful and effective way. Training programs should emphasize how AI can be used to support personalized learning, provide timely feedback, and analyze data to inform instructional decisions, while still valuing the critical role of human interaction and mentorship. Educators should be encouraged to use AI to augment their teaching practices, fostering a balanced approach that leverages the strengths of both technology and personal engagement.

To ensure that teacher training programs are effective, it is important to involve educators in the development and evaluation of these programs. Educators' feedback can help identify the most relevant topics, preferred training formats, and potential challenges in implementing AI technologies. Collaboration with educational institutions, technology developers, and policy makers can help create training programs that are aligned with the needs of educators and the goals of AI integration in education. Additionally, providing ongoing support and resources, such as access to AI experts and technical assistance, can help educators overcome challenges and successfully integrate AI tools into their classrooms. Finally, addressing the digital divide and ensuring equitable access to AI training and resources is essential for preparing all educators for AI-driven classrooms. Disparities in access to technology and professional development opportunities can impact educators' ability to effectively use AI tools. Efforts should be made to provide training and resources to underserved schools and educators, ensuring that all teachers have the opportunity to develop AI literacy and benefit from AI technologies. By promoting equity in access to AI training, we can support a diverse range of educators and contribute to a more inclusive educational environment understanding

AI INTEGRATION IN CURRICULUM DESIGN: ENHANCING LEARNING OBJECTIVES AND OUTCOMES

Integrating Artificial Intelligence (AI) into curriculum design offers transformative potential for enhancing learning objectives and outcomes across educational settings. As educational institutions strive to prepare students for a rapidly evolving world, AI technologies can play a pivotal role in refining curriculum frameworks, personalizing learning experiences, and improving overall educational effectiveness. This integration involves leveraging AI to optimize curriculum content, assess learning outcomes, and support both educators and students in achieving educational goals. Understanding and harnessing AI's capabilities in curriculum design can lead to more dynamic, responsive, and effective educational practices. Educational AI tools can collect and analyze data from various sources, such as assessments, classroom interactions, and engagement metrics, to evaluate the effectiveness of curriculum components. By identifying patterns and trends in student performance, AI can help educators pinpoint areas where the curriculum may need adjustment or improvement. For instance, if data shows that students consistently struggle with a particular concept, educators can use these insights to modify instructional strategies, provide additional resources, or redesign curriculum components to better support learning. This data-driven approach allows for continuous refinement of the curriculum, leading to more targeted and effective teaching methods.AI technologies, such as natural language processing (NLP) and content generation algorithms, can assist educators in creating dynamic and engaging learning materials. For example, AI can help generate customized practice problems, interactive simulations, and multimedia resources that align with curriculum goals.

These AI-generated materials can enhance student engagement and provide diverse learning experiences that cater to different learning styles. Furthermore, AI can assist in curating and recommending high-quality educational resources from a vast pool of available content, ensuring that educators have access to relevant and up-to-date materials.AI integration in curriculum design also facilitates the implementation of formative and summative assessments. AI-powered assessment tools can automate the grading process, providing timely and objective feedback to students. Moreover, AI can analyze assessment data to generate insights into student learning progress and curriculum effectiveness. By identifying areas where students excel or struggle, AI can help educators adjust their teaching approaches and curriculum design to better meet learning objectives. Another significant advantage of AI in curriculum design is its ability to support and enhance collaborative learning. AI technologies can facilitate group work and collaborative projects by providing tools that manage group dynamics, track contributions, and offer feedback on group performance. Professional development programs should focus on equipping educators with the skills and knowledge needed to effectively incorporate AI into their curriculum design processes. This includes understanding how to leverage AI insights to inform instructional decisions, create personalized learning experiences, and develop innovative educational content. Second, ethical considerations and data privacy must be prioritized. AI systems in education often involve the collection and analysis of sensitive student data. Ensuring that AI tools adhere to strict data privacy regulations and ethical standards is crucial for protecting students' information and maintaining trust (Sugumaran K. M, D., et al., 2024).

CONCLUSION: THE FUTURE OF AI IN EDUCATION - OPPORTUNITIES, CHALLENGES, AND POSSIBILITIES

However, realizing these benefits requires careful consideration of the challenges and thoughtful strategies to address them. Understanding these dynamics is crucial for harnessing AI's full potential in enhancing educational outcomes and addressing the diverse needs of learners and educators alike. This level of personalization helps address the varied learning styles, paces, and preferences of students, leading to more effective and engaging learning experiences. By providing targeted support and resources, AI can help students overcome challenges, build on their strengths, and achieve their full potential. This personalized approach has the potential to transform traditional education, making it more responsive to each learner's unique requirements. Another promising opportunity lies in AI's ability to enhance educational content and instructional methods. AI-powered tools can assist in creating dynamic, interactive, and immersive learning materials, such as simulations, virtual reality experiences, and intelligent content generators (Zhang, H., et al.,2022). For example, AI technologies can offer real-time translation, text-to-speech functionalities, and adaptive interfaces to accommodate various learning requirements. This enhanced accessibility can help bridge gaps in educational opportunities and ensure that all students have equitable access to quality learning resources. AI systems are trained on data that may reflect existing biases, which can lead to unfair or discriminatory outcomes (Ramakrishnan T., et al.,2022). For example, biased data used in AI-driven assessments or personalized learning tools may result in inequitable support for certain groups of students.

Ensuring that AI systems are designed to be fair and unbiased involves using diverse and representative datasets, conducting regular audits, and implementing measures to mitigate bias. Addressing these challenges is essential for maintaining equity and fairness in AI-powered educational environments.AI technologies should be viewed as tools that support and augment educators' efforts rather than substituting them. It is important to strike a balance between leveraging AI's capabilities and maintaining the personal interactions and relationships that are crucial for effective teaching and learning. Educator training and professional development should emphasize how to integrate AI in ways that complement and enhance traditional teaching methods. Continued innovation in AI will drive the development of new tools and applications that can further enhance educational experiences. At the same time, ongoing research and dialogue will be necessary to address emerging challenges and refine the ethical guidelines for AI use in education.

CONCLUSION

AI technologies, including adaptive learning systems, intelligent tutoring systems, data analytics tools, natural language processing, and educational content generators, are driving significant advancements in how educational content is delivered, how student progress is monitored, and how educational outcomes are achieved. The ability to adapt in real time not only enhances student engagement but also supports a more inclusive approach to education, accommodating diverse learning needs and preferences. Intelligent Tutoring Systems (ITS) further exemplify AI's transformative impact on education by providing individualized instruction and feedback. ITS use AI to simulate one-on-one tutoring experiences, offering explanations, practice problems, and guidance tailored to each student's unique requirements. These systems are capable of identifying knowledge gaps, providing instant feedback, and adapting instructional strategies to meet specific learning needs. The integration of ITS into educational settings can significantly enhance learning outcomes by offering personalized support and fostering deeper understanding of complex concepts. By analyzing vast amounts of data from various sources, such as assessments, classroom interactions, and engagement metrics, AI can identify patterns and trends that inform instructional practices and curriculum design. These tools provide educators with a comprehensive view of student progress, helping them identify areas for improvement, tailor interventions, and refine teaching strategies to better support student success. Natural Language Processing (NLP) technologies are revolutionizing the way educators and students interact with educational content. NLP facilitates automated grading, feedback, and language translation, streamlining administrative tasks and enhancing communication. For instance. The use of NLP in education not only increases efficiency but also supports a more equitable learning environment by addressing language and accessibility challenges. AI's role in content creation and curriculum design is also noteworthy, with technologies enabling the generation of dynamic and engaging educational materials. AI can assist in creating customized practice exercises, interactive simulations, and multimedia resources that align with curriculum objectives. These tools help educators develop rich, varied content that caters to different learning styles and keeps students engaged. By automating content generation and curation, AI supports educators in delivering high-quality educational experiences and adapting to evolving educational needs. Despite these advancements, the integration of AI in education presents challenges that must be addressed to fully realize its potential. Additionally, ongoing research and dialogue are needed to refine AI technologies and address emerging challenges, ensuring that they contribute positively to educational outcomes and align with ethical standards. Continued innovation in AI will drive the development of more sophisticated tools and applications, further transforming the educational landscape.

REFERENCES

Akgun, S., & Greenhow, C. (2022). Artificial intelligence in education: Addressing ethicalchallenges in K-12 settings. *AI and Ethics, 2*(3), 431–440. DOI: 10.1007/s43681-021-00096-7 PMID: 34790956

Aleven, V., McLaughlin, E. A., Glenn, R. A., & Koedinger, K. R. (2016). Instruction based onadaptive learning technologies. In Mayer, R. E., & Alexander, P. A. (Eds.), *Handbook of research on learning and instruction* (pp. 522–560).

Mousavinasab, E., Zarifsanaiey, N., & Niakan Kalhori, R., S., Rakhshan, M., Keikha, L., & Ghazi Saeedi, M. (2018). Intelligent tutoring systems: A systematic review of characteristics, applications, and evaluation methods. *Interactive Learning Environments, 29*(1), 142–163. DOI: 10.1080/10494820.2018.1558257

Baker, R. S., Esbenshade, L., Vitale, J., & Karumbaiah, S. (2022). Using demographic data aspredictor variables: A questionable choice. https://doi.org/DOI: 10.35542/osf.io/y4wvj

Black, P., & Wiliam, D. (2009). Developing the theory of formative assessment. *EducationalAssessment, Evaluation andAccountability, 21*(1), 5–31. DOI: 10.1007/s11092-008-9068-5

Boden, M. A. (2018). *Artificial intelligence: A very short introduction.* DOI: 10.1093/actrade/9780199602919.001.0001

Bryant, J., Heitz, C., Sanghvi, S., & Wagle, D. (2020, January 14). How artificial intelligence will impact K-12 teachers. McKinsey. https://www.mckinsey.com/industries/education/ourinsights/how-artificial-intelligence-will-impact-k-12-teachers

Celik, I., Dindar, M., Muukkonen, H., & Järvelä, S. (2022). The promises and challenges ofartificial intelligence for teachers: A systematic review of research. *TechTrends, 66*(4), 616–630. DOI: 10.1007/s11528-022-00715-y

Chen, C., Park, H. W., & Breazeal, C. (2020). Teaching and learning with children: Impact ofreciprocal peer learning with a social robot on children's learning and emotive engagement. *Computers & Education, 150*, 103836. Advance online publication. DOI: 10.1016/j.compedu.2020.103836

Chen, G., Clarke, S., & Resnick, L. B. (2015). Classroom Discourse Analyzer (CDA): A discourseanalytic tool for teachers. Technology, Instruction. *Cognition and Learning, 10*(2), 85–105.

Khosravi, H., Buckingham, S., Guanliang, C., Conati, C., Tsai, Y., Kay, J., Knight, S., Martinez-Maldonado, R., Sadiq, S., & Gašević, D. (2022). *Explainable Artificial Intelligence in Education*. Science Direct., DOI: 10.1016/j.caeai.2022.100074

Dieterle, E., Dede, C., & Walker, M. (2022). The cyclical ethical effects of using artificialintelligence in education. AI & Society. https://link.springer.com/article/10.1007/s00146-

Doewes, A., & Pechenizkiy, M. (2021). On the limitations of human-computer agreement inautomated essay scoring. In *Proceedings of the 14th International Conference on Educational*

Englebart, D. C. (October 1962). Augmenting human intellect: A conceptual framework. SRI SummaryReport AFOSR-3223. https://www.dougengelbart.org/pubs/augment-3906.html

Ersozlu, Z., Ledger, S., Ersozlu, A., Mayne, F., & Wildy, H. (2021). Mixed-reality learningenvironments in teacher education: An analysis of TeachLivETM Research. *SAGE Open*, *11*(3), 21582440211032155. Advance online publication. DOI: 10.1177/21582440211032155

Forsyth, S., Dalton, B., Foster, E.H., Walsh, B., Smilack, J., & Yeh, T. (2021, May). Imagine a moreethical AI: Using stories to develop teens' awareness and understanding of artificial

Friedman, L., Blair Black, N., Walker, E., & Roschelle, J. (November 8, 2021) Safe AI in educationneeds you. Association of Computing Machinery BLOG@ACM,

https://cacm.acm.org/blogs/blog-cacm/256657-safe-ai-in-education-needs-you/fullte

Gardner, J., O'Leary, M., & Yuan, L. (2021). Artificial intelligence in educational assessment:"Breakthrough? Or buncombe and ballyhoo?". *Journal of Computer Assisted Learning*, *37*(5), 1207–1216. DOI: 10.1111/jcal.12577

Godwin-Jones, R. (2021). Big data and language learning: Opportunities and challenges. *Language Learning & Technology*, *25*(1), 4–19. http://hdl.handle.net/10125/44747

Hammerness, K., Darling-Hammond, L., & Bransford, J. (2005). *Preparing teachers for a changingworld: What teachers should learn and be able to do*. Jossey-Bass.

Holmes, W., & Porayska-Pomsta, K. (Eds.). (2022). *The ethics of artificial intelligence in education*. Routledge. DOI: 10.4324/9780429329067

Holstein, K., McLaren, B. M., & Aleven, V. (2019). Co-designing a real-time classroomorchestration tool to support teacher–AI complementarity. *Journal of Learning Analytics*, *6*(2). Advance online publication. DOI: 10.18608/jla.2019.62.3

Kai, S., Almeda, M. V., Baker, R. S., Heffernan, C., & Heffernan, N. (2018). Decision tree modeling of wheel-spinning and productive persistence in skill builders. *Journal of Educational Data Mining*, *10*(1), 36–71. DOI: 10.5281/zenodo.3344810

Kaplan, R. M., & Saccuzzo, D. P. (2017). *Psychological testing: Principles, applications, and issues*. Cengage Learning.

Ke, Z., & Ng, V. (2019). Automated essay scoring: A survey of the state of the art. In *Proceedings ofthe Twenty-Eighth International Joint Conference on Artificial Intelligence*, 6300–6308.DOI: 10.24963/ijcai.2019/879

Kulik, J. A., & Fletcher, J. D. (2016). Effectiveness of intelligent tutoring systems: A meta-analyticreview. *Review of Educational Research*, *86*(1), 42–78. DOI: 10.3102/0034654315581420

Ma, W., Adescope, O. O., Nesbit, J. C., & Liu, Q. (2014). Intelligent tutoring systems and learning outcomes: A meta-analysis. *Journal of Educational Psychology*, *106*(4), 901–918. DOI: 10.1037/a0037123

Maslej, N., Fattorini, L., Brynjolfsson E., Etchemendy, J., Ligett, K., Lyons, T., Manyika, J., Ngo,H., Niebles, J.C., Parli, V., Shoham, Y., Wald, R., Clark, J. and Perrault, R., (2023). The AIindex 2023 annual report. Stanford University: AI Index Steering Committee, Institute forHuman-Centered AI.

Merrill, S. (2020). In schools, are we measuring what matters? Edutopia. https://www.edutopia.org/article/schools-are-we-measuring-what-matters

Mousavinasab, E., Zarifsanaiey, N., R. Niakan Kalhori, S., Rakhshan, M., Keikha, L., & Ghazi Saeedi, M. (2021). Intelligent tutoring systems: A systematic review of characteristics,

Ramakrishnan, T., Mohan Gift, M. D., Chitradevi, S., Jegan, R., & Subha Hency Jose, P. Nagaraja, Rajneesh Sharma H.N., Selvakumar P., Sintayehu Mekuria Hailegiorgis, (2022). "Study of Numerous Resins Used in Polymer Matrix Composite Materials", Advances in Materials Science and Engineering, vol. 2022, Article ID 1088926, 8 pages, 2022. DOI: 10.1155/2022/1088926

Sugumaran, K. M. D., Pandiyarajan V., Y. B S, Selvakumar P. and M. S, (2024). “Analysis of Electromyography Signals for Control of Mechanical Prosthesis using Machine Learning Techniques,” 2024 2nd International Conference on Intelligent Data Communication Technologies and Internet of Things (IDCIoT), Bengaluru, India, 2024, pp. 1059-1067, DOI: 10.1109/IDCIoT59759.2024.10467707

Van Lehn, K. (2011). The relative effectiveness of human tutoring, intelligent tutoring systems,and other tutoring systems. *Educational Psychologist*, *46*(4), 197–221. DOI: 10.1080/00461520.2011.611369

Wiggins, G. (2015). Seven keys to effective feedback. ACSD. https://www.ascd.org/el/articles/sevenkeys-to-effective-feedback

Winne, P. H. (2021). Open learner models working in symbiosis with self-regulating learners: Aresearch agenda. *International Journal of Artificial Intelligence in Education*, *31*(3), 446–459. DOI: 10.1007/s40593-020-00212-4

Zacamy, J., & Roschelle, J. (2022). Navigating the tensions: How could equity-relevant research also beagile, open, and scalable? Digital Promise. http://hdl.handle.net/20.500.12265/159

Chapter 2
AI Driven Personalization in Education:
Transformative Practices and Emerging Trends

D. Suresh
Meenakshi College of Engineering, Chennai, India

P. Lokesh
Meenakshi College of Engineering, Chennai, India

B. Yamini
https://orcid.org/0000-0003-3531-108X
SRM Institute of Science and Technology, India

B. Yuvasri
R.M.K. College of Engineering and Technology, India

V. Sathya
Vel Tech Rangarajan Dr. Sagunthala R&D Institute of Science and Technology, Chennai, India

P. Girija
https://orcid.org/0009-0000-1691-8180
Vel Tech Rangarajan Dr. Sagunthala R&D Institute of Science and Technology, Chennai, India

Subramanian R. Siva
https://orcid.org/0000-0002-7509-9223
R.M.K. College of Engineering and Technology, India

ABSTRACT

Education systems adopting technological solutions, Artificial Intelligence (AI) is making its ways into becoming a game changer in delivering learner centered approaches to learning. This questionnaire focuses on the promotion of effective learning plans using artificial intelligence to improve learning experiences as they are made to suit the learner. They are adaptive learning system which change content on the basis of performance, intelligent tutor system, and big data analytical system which provides solutions. Those include machine learning, NLP, and computer vision

DOI: 10.4018/979-8-3693-8744-3.ch002

technologies that play an essential role in such developments. Although a number of positive case studies, across K-12, higher education, and corporate training indicate improvements, issues persist such as data privacy, equity and algorithm bias. The paper is wrapped up with the guidelines on the implementation of AI in education and suggestion of the prospects for further research.

1. INTRODUCTION

1.1 Personalized Learning

Personalized learning can be described as the educational approach education delivery system that is customized depending on the needs, abilities and inclinations of individual students (Grant, P., & Basye, D. 2014). As opposed to the regular teaching methodologies, where one approach is adapted for all, personalized learning adapts student data and preference-derived approaches. It takes into consideration things like speed, style and deficiency map for students to move at their own pace with emphasis being placed on difficult areas. The objective aimed at helping each learner to acquire as much knowledge as possible in the shortest time possible. There are many systems of personalized learning, which are as follows: adaptive learning systems; competency-based learning; and individualized learning plans. Fundamentally it seeks to provide the learner with control in determining and shaping their education processes. It increases interest because the content being passed becomes more relevant as well as the form, and thus increases the rate of learning. In addition, the technology also offers the advantage of closing gaps in students' education by due to the provision of differential learning for disadvantaged students (Basham et al 2016).

1.2 Overview of AI's Role in Education

AI is still growing into a ruling factor in education and has been seen as having a great impact on the provision of teaching learning services mainly through using of differentiated learning. Another benefit of the application of AI in education is that it has abilities in processing of big amounts of student data to find patterns of learning, students' strengths, and learning weaknesses (Grassini, S. 2023). By doing so, AI systems are able adapt learning materials in real time for students, which means that we can determine valuable insights for student learning. For example, in intelligent tutoring systems that support an adaptive learning environment assessments are made to be easy if the learner seems to struggle but they become challenging if the learner has been excelling (Xu et al 2022). Furthermore, AI applications such as conversational AI, NLPs, ML, and CV are facilitating the creation of 1: Many custom learning solutions. NLP, for instance, is applied in the design of chatbots and virtual tutors to enhance an interactive and personalized Student-Stakeholder interface (Saravanan et al 2023). On the other hand, the other forms of AI called the ML algorithms work on the analysis of student's progress and the consequent outcome prediction to provide opportunity and support or the redesigning of areas for improvement. Such technologies not only facilitate personalized education, but also help the teachers by with tasks such as grading and other related clerical workload which take most of the teacher's time away from students. Thus, AI is not limited to applying learning for learners but can be used in Intelligent Tutoring Systems (ITS), Virtual Reality Learning Environment, and as Assessment tools. All these innovations are contributing to the future of education these make education to become flexible, accessible and effective.

1.2 Objectives of the Survey Paper

The following survey paper is going to give overall perspective on the use of AI in the field of personalised learning. The objectives are threefold:

1. Exploring AI-driven personalized learning systems: More specifically, this paper will unearth how adaptive learning systems, ITS, and AI-based analytics are now making learning personal. Here, emphasis will be made to the process of these technologies, and examples of their use as well as the demonstrable effects on learner performance. 2. Analyzing the challenges and limitations: AI has enormous advantages in educational sector, it has also brought major obstacles, for example data protection, developing prejudices of AI, problems with equity and entrance. The following paper will critically analyse these challenges so that to give directions about the ethical and pragmatic issues concerning practitioners and policymakers. 3. Identifying future directions and research opportunities: Finally, the paper shall identify new trends in advancement in AI and its application in personalized learning, make some proposals to the practitioners and make suggestion on further development on the topic. These are: New technologies in artificial intelligence, their effects on learning contexts and environments and finally the general effects on learning in the future.

Thus, this survey paper to provide an elaborate account of change AI has brought to Personalized Learning, in addition to discussing strengths, weakness, opportunities, and threats in the nascent field. Through an analysis of the suggested key technologies, their usage, and their drawbacks, the paper seeks to support the existing discussion on the proper ways of AI implementation to foster learning for all students.

2. THEORETICAL BACKGROUND

2.1. Overview of Personalized Learning

Personalization is the focus of differentiation because students bring with them different needs, learning styles, and objectives. The main goal is to provide learning content, timing, and materials that target those needs. In contrast to the common traditional approach in which all learners are equally presented material at an equal pace, there is more variability in modalities, timing, and locations in personalized learning. Its key principles include:

Student-centered learning: Teaching and learning is individualized and all learn to be responsible for their own learning.

Flexibility in pace and approach: Students can cover content in their own pace and also since the content is presented in terms of modules and lessons, a student can skip a lesson and continue with the next one effortlessly.

Data-driven decision making: Instructional content is dynamic with feedback being provided real-time, with the content modifying depending on the learner's performance (Sudha at al 2024).

Competency-based progression: Through mastery, learners progress through a curriculum rather than being based on a set time table.

Individualization of instruction is intended to make it more interesting; provide better learning outcomes as well as the comprehension of the material in question and finally, increase a learner's motivation through addressing his or her learning profile.

Historical Context and Evolution

Personalized learning has been around from when students and educationists strived to break free from the traditional rote learning styles of the earlier eras. But the kind of learning that was an indication of possible differential treatment has drastically changed in their practical implication with the introduction of technology. In the late of the twentieth century a new concept came into the scenario called computer assisted instruction (CAI), which promised a more individualized approach to teaching. By the 1990s there was talk of personalised learning referring to software which differentiates the lesson depending on the learner's progress. The advancement of internet technology and other digital technologies in the beginning of the 21st century stimulated the continued progression of the subject, with resultant improved flexibility and interactivity of learning environments. Internet grows popularity and the latest incorporation of AI technologies further enhance the innovation of the practice and implementation of the personalized learning system.

2.2. Introduction to Artificial Intelligence (AI) in Education

Definition and Components of AI

AI is defined as the human brain's ability to replicate its capabilities in machines, tools that can think like human beings, learn, and solve problems, understand language, make decision, and comprehend what they learn among others. AI encompasses a range of technologies, including:

Figure 1. Artificial intelligence (AI) in education

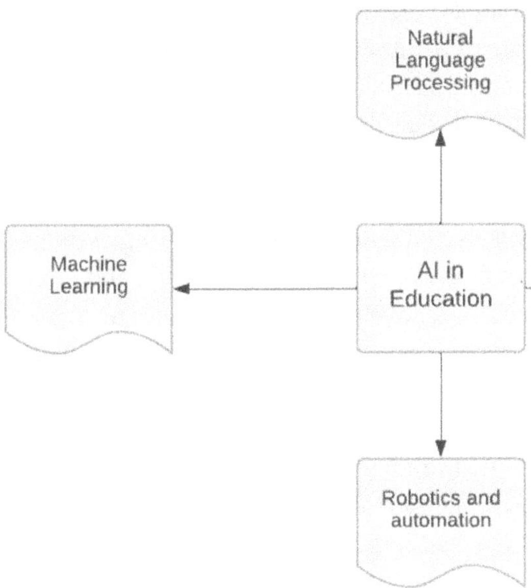

Machine Learning (ML): One of the categories of Artificial Intelligence where a system adapts to changes in its environment, and the more it is used, the better it becomes (Nithya et al 2023).

Natural Language Processing (NLP): Size and scope of knowledge that AI possesses about the human language (Solaimalai et al 2024).

Computer Vision (CV): A variation used to refer to the capacity of machines to understand and utilize info that is presented in picture, video or other related forms.

Robotics and automation: AI technologies used to design intelligent agents to able to act in the environment to accomplish tasks (Khang et al 2023).

In education these components are employed to develop such applications as adaptive learning environments, It IS or Intelligent Tutoring Systems, and analytics to foster learning and teaching.

Historical Perspective on AI in Learning

It is possible to note that the integration of AI and education started in the sixties of the previous century with the creation of ITS. In the 1980s and the 1990s, the use of AI in education was an area of computerised expert systems and rule-based procedures to tell students precisely what it is that they need to do when asked to complete a specific assignment. However, these systems were closed and mechanisms behind learning were quite often either overlooked or did not take into account the way human beings learn. The coming of the new century gave rise to a new means of automation known as machine learning. As a result of increased data processing capacity AI could diagnose trends in student performance on complements and provide more adequate assistance. Recently the use of AI in education has grown significantly because of the improvements in ML algorithm, availability of large data sets and better processing power. Hypothetical adaptive learning systems that rely on artificial intelligence to alter student performance feedback and guide the student. In the same way, technologies like conversational agents, such as chatbots or virtual assistants equip individuals to interact more with student learning materials in real time, increasing effectiveness.

AI evolution in education has started with basic rule based system and progresses to the more potent analytic systems that are being used in modern day education that targets to deliver personalized experiences for large student populations. Today, AI technologies are expanding in the learning environments including adaptive assessments, learning analytics, intelligent content delivery in K-12 schools as well as in colleges and universities and corporate training.

3. TRANSFORMATIVE AI PRACTICES IN PERSONALIZED LEARNING

3.1. Adaptive Learning Systems

In adaptive learning systems, artificial intelligence is applied in modifying the content to be delivered, its delivery frequency and its level of difficulty depending on the student's progress and learning competence. These systems provide feedback to students' answers to questions or tasks, and change themselves regarding delivery of subsequent materials. For instance, if a child fails to grasp concepts relating to a given chapter, it may provide worksheets, tutorials and explanatory notes. On the other hand, if the student is percentile high then the system offers higher level of tasks familiarize the student with the higher level outputs.

Adaptation occurs across multiple dimensions:

Content: Applications change the content of the material according to the knowledge of a student. For instance, learners may get different sets of examples or exercises or may get lesion in the form of video or text accordingly.

Pace: Group of students works step-by-step via the subject to ensure more time is spent on a complicated topic while a simple one is tackled briefly.

Difficulty: Operational flexibility signifies that the teaching learning activities reduce the level of challenge only when a student fails to perform to the expected standard and increase the level of difficulty when students are able to perform well.

3.2. Intelligent Tutoring Systems (ITS)

Functionality and Features

Computerised learning that employs artificial intelligence technology that can personally teach a learner in a class is commonly known as Intelligent Tutoring Systems (ITS). ITSs act almost like a real tutor; they can lead the students through a lesson, respond to questions or provide feedback immediately. These systems typically have several key features:

Interactive problem-solving: When completing problems, ITSs teach the student the problems while offering suggestions and solutions.

Immediate feedback: The answers to the questions are checked immediately allowing learners to rectify their misconceptions.

Personalized learning paths: The system adapts the future activities and lessons in accordance to the performance of the learner thus making students practice on concepts they have weak understanding on.

ITSs can be utilized in such a context as to accommodate topics in mathematics, science, and even language acquisition. For instance, Cognitive Tutor already implemented by Carnegie Learning, aims at helping students learn algebra by mimicking the students' thought processes and giving the feedback.

Impact on Student Learning Outcomes

Quite a number of scholars have clearly shown that ITSs enhance the learning of students. ITSs can improve learning, knowledge retention, and interest since they provide content more tailored to the learner's ability. Studies have proved that students who employ ITSs have higher results in their exams than those given conventional instructions. In addition, ITSs have well helped learners experiencing difficulties, as the computer does not require a call to a teacher.

Figure 2. Transformative AI practices in personalized learning

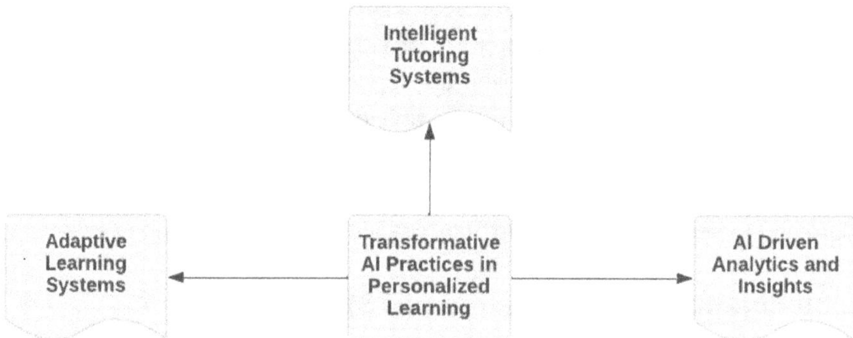

3.3. AI Driven Analytics and Insights

Data Collection and Analysis Methods

Instructors make use of AI driven analytics systems which capture students' data resulting from their performances in the learning platforms. This is in the form of quiz results, time taken on different activities, contribution during group discussions and forums, academic writing preferences and mathematical logic patterns. AI algorithms which follow up may then further analyze this data to discover such things as what concepts students find difficult, what incentivises them or how they learn.

Advanced analytics methods include: Predictive analytics: Students' outcomes for example, their ability to pass a certain course or exam, dropout rate etc is predicted by AI models, thus, teachers can make interventions early on. Learning analytics dashboards: Most of these dashboards offer real time information about students' performance, allowing the teacher to track progress and make data-based decisions.

AI powered systems also track and provide individual feedback to students, which inform the learner about different ways to enhance his performance. For instance, in language mastery, applications such as Grammarly wade through writing done in real-time and provide feedback on how the language could be written with better grammar, tone and flow. Likewise, recommendation systems provide other materials or experiences, linked with a student's learning history. An actual example of a recommendation system is the AI-driven course suggestions in Coursera, which assigns courses or individual learning modules based on user choices and the results that a user has achieved in the past. It makes education engaging and hence the learners are motivated, thereby what these systems of student centered approaches provide for the learners. Analytics and recommendation systems as powered by Artificial Intelligence do not only augment scholarly performance of students but also creates understanding for instructors to be able to modify delivery of instruction and other forms of learning activities to yield the intended learning outcomes.

Lastly, proactive and innovative technologies like adaptive learning systems, ITSs and big data analytics are revolutionising personalised learning. These technologies enhance the delivery of learning activities by offering real-time learning techniques that will enable students' participation, personal attention to teach, and ultimately enhancing the performance.

4. AI TECHNOLOGIES AND TOOLS FOR PERSONALIZED LEARNING

4.1. Machine Learning and Data Mining

ML and Data Mining are two advanced AI methods that are employed to make analysis of large amount of data relative to students with a view of identifying patterns of learning behaviors (Tiwari, R. 2023). Personalized learning here involves training of the ML models to observe what the students do in regards to learning content, what aspect challenges them and how they evolve to overcome such barriers. Other methods such as cluster analysis, classification, and regression seek to find out which group of students has similarities in learning needs or even can predict future performance.

For example:

One of the main advantages of clustering is that the implementation of this concept allows to determine, which types of actions (visual, auditory, or motoric) are most effective for each certain group of students. In classification algorithms assist in finding out the students who are most likely to drop out hence notifying early prompt action. Using the results of the regression analysis, it is possible to find out what a student is likely to do next based on what he or she does in the learning process, including time spent on tasks and attitude towards review. These models can be changed dynamically, meaning that they can become more accurately as more data is obtained. This makes it easier to recommend the right learning trajectories that could help learners achieve their best, with an added convenience of filling knowledge gaps.

When curriculum development needed to arise, the following are some of the applications that people used: Such a curricula has to be adaptive and dynamic and this is made possible through use of ML and Data Mining. It assigns student performance statistics to these technologies which in turn indicate which learning content or areas work best for that learner. This data driven approach helps educators make and refine changes to curricula as novelties are informed by students' feedback in real time, strongly implying that content remains relevant and personalised. For example, curriculum through AI can identify additional instruction tools for the students with lower comprehension levels or indicate additional instructional tools for gifted learners. Many learning platforms, employ ML algorithms to develop individual learning experiences and even change content depending on learners' performances in real time.

4.2. Natural Language Processing (NLP)

NLP therefore refers to the ability of machines to comprehend process and even produce human speech. Applications of NLP in education The most commonly employed application of NLP is the automated essay scoring and feedback (Das, S., & Das, D. 2024). These systems evaluate students' writing style, its syntax and its content; in effect giving timely feedback on quality of writings. They might evaluate almost everything from the general logical flow of the whole paper to specifics, like sources and arguments, the language used, and even students' imagination. Also, NLP tools will make it possible to analyse the writing styles and give writers' individual coaching tips, for instance, to use more different grammatical constructions or improve argumentation (Kalaiselvi et al 2024).

Chatbots and Conversational Agents for Student Support

NLP also helps to drive the chat and conversational agents, that is, the bots offer a real-time, student-centric support. These AIdriven systems replicate human interaction and can help the student answer questions through a subject, explain complex molecular concept and also help the student out by directing them to relevant source when required. These chatbots are especially helpful within large-cross settings such as colleges and universities where physical one on one communication might not always be possible.

Figure 3. AI technologies and tools for personalized learning

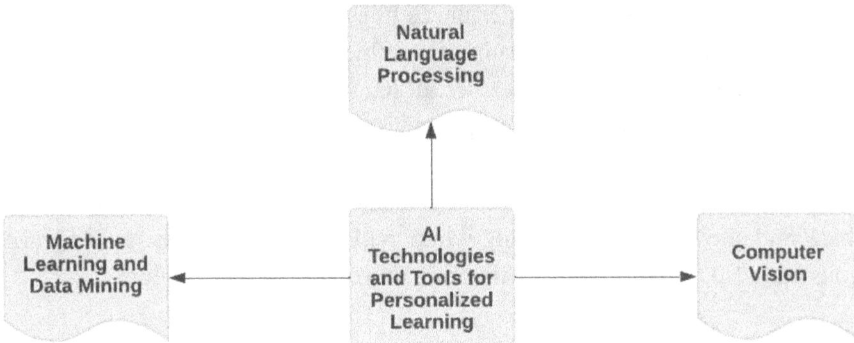

4.3. Computer Vision

Applications in Monitoring Engagement and Behavior

Computer Vision (CV) is the AI technique that permits the machine to compare the patterns of the light in the world. In reverse, monitoring of engagement and behaviour during digital or in person learning activities in personalized learning is well done through the application of CV. From facial expressions and gestures, from eyes movements, CV can know if the student is attentive, puzzled, or bored. For instance, an AI can use facial expressions of students during an online lesson to determine if a student needs help and the system itself will interject to help the student with clarification or to kindly remind him/ her that it's time for a break. This realtime analysis gives direction to learners and support them where they are most likely to require it.

Integration with Virtual and Augmented Reality

Computer vision is used in conjunction with Virtual Reality (VR) and Augmented Reality (AR) to provide individualised learning experience. In such situations, the use of 3D objects or simulations means that students can directly engage with what they are learning besides being a form of entertainment helping students learn through Handson activities (Aswini et al 2023). CV enables a student to move about an area, make gestures, to control some item or even environment naturally. For instance, to teach students about such features of the real world as molecular structures, historical events and other, it is possible to use applications that layer digital content on top of real-world surfaces. Applications such as Google Expeditions apply AR and VR to deliver Good classroom experiences to students by exposing them to what they can learn more details concerning the subject through an interactive method that is friendly to students (Sanjeera et al 2024). It is noteworthy to understand that Machine learning, NLP and Computer vision are the AI Technologies that are enhancing personalized learning even more (Pajila et al 2023). These tools allow the use of learning paths within learning management systems, allows real time feedback and allows for rich learning which will in turn lead to increased learning sessions and also to increased learning outcomes among the students.

6. CHALLENGES AND LIMITATIONS

6.1. Data Privacy and Security

With the integration of the AI powered systems entailing collection of massive data for education, issues to do with data privacy and security have arisen. This system takes data from individual learners and using different inputs including their likeness, writing style, behavioral patterns and academic performance records. This volume of data accumulation generates risk of violation and unauthorized access. Furthermore, the storage of such kind of information for long term raises serious issues concerning the entails uses of such information as well as who has access to it. In order to avoid these problems, countries have developed laws that would guard student information. These regulations apply to institutions of education and companies through the need to protect the administration of student data.

Best Practices for Safeguarding Student Information

Educational institutions and developers of AI systems can adopt several best practices to safeguard student information:

Data encryption: Some of the solution measures which can help prevent unauthorized access include encrypting student data in transit as well as encrypting data at rest.

Minimizing data collection: The platforms should collect only the information that is required for further personalization of learning, at the same time, ignoring any additional sensitive data.

Consent and transparency: Schools should ensure students and parents give express consent over collection of their data and ensure that users are informed on the uses of data collected.

Regular audits and updates: Security audit testing and the check and implementation of the latest software security can help forestall a data breach.

6.2. Equity and Access

Addressing Disparities in Access to AI Technologies

The first problem of AIdriven personalized learning is the inequality in the availability of AI technologies. Students in the low income or under developed areas don't get the necessary infrastructure for the AI tools like internet, advanced devices, or proper learning platforms. This result in creating a digital divide that compounds with the existing inequalities in education making young disadvantaged learners to be even more behind.

For instance, in the rural or in the remote areas schools may lack the infrastructure to put into practice smart learning systems endowed with advanced artificial intelligence. This implies that students in such areas cannot be given the same quality of learning experience as the students in well endowed region. Also, it also advances several arguments that learners with disabilities may encounter numerous difficulties if only AI systems are not developed for an inclusive purpose.

Strategies for Inclusive Implementation

To ensure equitable access to AI technologies, the following strategies can be implemented:

Infrastructure investment: Educational stakeholder must invest on infrastructure of internet and devices to enable all learners have access on AI supported tools. Opensource and affordable AI tools: Currently, there are relatively low cost or opensource platforms for learning AI which may reduce the barriers to distributing personalized education technologies. Inclusive design: Reflections indicate that it is possible to design AI systems where other input/output methods are provided to accommodate the learners with disabilities or alternatively, the systems can support accessible customization.

6.3. Accuracy and Bias

Risks of Algorithmic Bias

AI systems are aligned with systemic prejudice in that they further continue the negative impacts on the learning progress of students. Such biases emerge when machine is trained with data that do not reflect the diversity of students. For example, if the learning platform uses data from learners from well-off urban areas, it will be likely to make wrong prediction or suggestions for learners from other backgrounds. These include gender bias or race bias or ethnic bias that may make the system to treat different people differently depending on their gender, race, or ethnicity. For instance, in automated grading systems, cases where student's beneficiation was subjected to a low score because of deficiency of classifier training with samples coming from specific cultural or linguistic back grounds. Discriminatory bias in machine learning algorithms can reinforce existing patterns of inequality and thus put certain students at a disadvantage.

Ensuring Fairness in AI Systems

To address the issue of accuracy and bias in AI systems, developers and educators can implement several strategies:

Diverse and representative training data: Training data must contain the same variety in students as is observed in terms of their origin, location, and learning requirements. This, in return, fosters the development of algorithms that work with uniform precision and reliability across the different groups of people.

Bias detection and mitigation: It is important to issue a simple check list for periodic audits of the AI algorithms in order to flushing out the biases. Methods like putting into practice of fairness constraints or bias correction algorithms enables the system to perform fairly on all students.

Human oversight: Human educators must be involved in the decision making processes and not allow AI driven recommendations to be final. This allows you to prevent dependency upon the algorithms and make context-sensitive interferences.

Thus, the AI technologies helped in improving the aspect of personalized learning, However, the study also yielded findings that point to the negative impact of the technologies in use mainly with regards to data privacy, Equity, and Bias potentials. Solving these issues related to security development, accessibility, and eradicating bias in AI systems is crucial, so that learning is improved for each learner.

7. FUTURE DIRECTIONS

7.1. Emerging Trends in AI and Education

AI in education remains to be fluid with several other new trends emerging which are likely to transform the personalized learning. Incorporating Artificial Intelligence in learning is another emerging technology that has seen growth; the connection of AI with IoT gives birth to the AI of Things (AIoT). For instance, the

AIoT enabled classrooms can adapt lighting and temperature, and even the pacing of lessons and student activities analyzing data in real time. This in turn leads to learning settings that are fully dynamic with emphases on the individual learner needs and student need, thus improving on the issues of personalization. Instead, another trend is the use of artificial intelligence for immersive technologies including Virtual Reality (VR) and Augmented Reality (AR) for enhancing the learning capabilities in curriculum. With these technologies, students can sometimes get a better grasp on material they are being taught, such as science or history, because they are able to 'handle' an object or walk through an environment that are often more tangible in form. Furthermore, Ai driven lifelong learning platforms are emerging, to learn and unlearn activities that continue for a lifetime. These platforms use AI to introduce learning paths and material based on the use of needs, aims, and individual performance for the lifetime career.

Potential Impacts on Personalized Learning

The combination of these aforementioned trends will also augment the flexibility of the proposed model of personalized learning. AIoT and immersive technologies are likely to provide even better learning experience customization in the future that will adapt to realtime student actions and deliver rich, interactive, concrete context practices. The presence of the lifetime learning system indicates that people would spend a lifetime updating their learning and hence personalized learning would not be limited to school systems.

7.2. Recommendations for Practitioners

For educators and institutions looking to integrate AI into their learning environments, there are several key recommendations to consider:

1. Start Small: Introductions should therefore be done gradually and first with trials employing the tools in constraints areas like in selected subjects or classes using AI tutor systems. That makes it easier for educators to pilot the use of AI tools allowing them to understand how best to integrate it into the curriculum wholly.
2. Leverage DataDriven Insights: Clearly, the AI systems that teachers should adopt must give them insights about the performance of their students. This in turn helps educators to pinpoint where the students are weak or strong to enable them come up with better interventions.

3. Promote Teacher Technology Collaboration: AI should be an assistant and enhance human educators' work. Teachers should be engaged users and should use AI tools as supporting tools to apply in their teaching practices themselves. For instance, AI can mark assignments, set discussions, and monitors them keeping the teachers to other noble responsibilities of encouraging class discourse and supporting learners individually.
4. Invest in Professional Development: For AI to be integrated, the educators requires know-how on the AI systems, data analysis as well as incorporating AI into education. There is a need for a continued professional development by institutions bearing in mind that integration of AI should enable the educator to get the best results.
5. Focus on Inclusivity and Equity: Make sure the AI tools you use can be understood by students with disabilities and learners of color as well. AI's used by the institutions should have features that meet learning needs since these needs come in various types and levels.

7.3. Areas for Further Research

While AI has already transformed many aspects of personalized learning, there are several areas where further research is needed:

1. AI's Impact on LongTerm Learning Outcomes: Majority of the studies undertaken on AI in education have been interested in the short-term outcomes in learning engagement and assessments. Thus in the future, there is the need for researchers to conduct Longitudinal research in order to gain deeper insight about how effective AIdriven learning environments perform in enhancing student long term outcomes in terms of academic achievements and further training directions.
2. Bias and Fairness in AI Systems: Although much work has been done to detect bias in AI plus, there is more to be done to approach solutions to bias in learning systems. Further research should be conducted to understand how biases are introduced into individualised learning environments and how they might be reduced to achieve a better balance for students.
3. Ethical Implications of AI in Education: Since the use of artificial intelligence in education is expected to grow with time, issues of data privacy, how algorithms perform decision-making, and learners' freedom become issues of concern. There is need for future studies to tailor proper ethical standards for applying AI in learning environments as well as fashion practical recommendations on correct application of the AI data.

4. AI in Global and Cross Cultural Education: More empirical work is required to understand how proposed technologies can be implemented in multi-cultural as well as multi-lingual environments. AI supported systems that should encompass diverse obligatory educational patterns, language barriers, or cultural settings remain essential for making AI technologies positively impact learners from different countries.

In conclusion, current AI availability has undoubtedly managed to leave a durable mark in the domain of individualised learning; however prompt advancements are demanded. Teachers must begin adopting new trends, implement AI appropriately and concentrate on knowledge that can help to identify moral, cultural and pragmatic issues that AI causes in education.

8. CONCLUSION

In this survey paper, we also highlighted how one could utilize AI in redefining or redesigning personalized learning in school, college, university, and corporate settings. The following important discoveries note how; AIdriven tools like, The adaptive learning system, The intelligent tutoring systems- ITS, technology and the data analytics boost personalized education patterns by applying data that changes the content, rate, & feedback in real time AI driving tools and practices. Included examples illustrate how, on the positive side, costs would include aspects such as increased student involvement, enhanced learning productivity, and higher retention ratios. AI technologies like machine learning; natural language processing, and computer vision have continued to supplement the delivery of personalized learning; making it more flexible. However, it also has issues with concerns to data privacy, the distribution of AI, and issues with algorithms held. Meeting all these is paramount towards the achievement of the right use of artificial intelligence in education. The three conclusions derived from this research have important consequences for educators and institutions. While the use of AI can positively impact teaching and learning, it needs to be done effectively. Leaders of schools, universities and firms should focus on infrastructure development, providing equal opportunities for use of AI tools and state clearly how students' data is being collected and used. Furthermore, it is crucial to carry out further professional practice for educators to help them use AI in adapting education for each learner while keeping human involvement in check. Future research directions include the role of AI on students learning outcomes over the long time, the biases associated with AI algorithms and moral norms governing the use of AI in educating students. In this way, educators are capable of creating learning experiences that are relevant, acceptable and efficient to all students, mediated by AI.

REFERENCES

Aswini, J., Malarvizhi, N., Subramanian, S., & Gayathri, A. (2023). Augmented Reality and Virtual Reality in E-Governance: An Immersive Technology Applications and Its Challenges. In AI, IoT, and Blockchain Breakthroughs in E-Governance (pp. 138-153). IGI Global.

Basham, J. D., Hall, T. E., Carter, R. A.Jr, & Stahl, W. M. (2016). An operationalized understanding of personalized learning. *Journal of Special Education Technology, 31*(3), 126–136. DOI: 10.1177/0162643416660835

Das, S., & Das, D. (2024, March). Natural Language Processing (NLP) Techniques: Usability in Human-Computer Interactions. In 2024 6th International Conference on Natural Language Processing (ICNLP) (pp. 783-787). IEEE.

Grant, P., & Basye, D. (2014). *Personalized learning: A guide for engaging students with technology*. International Society for Technology in Education.

Grassini, S. (2023). Shaping the future of education: Exploring the potential and consequences of AI and ChatGPT in educational settings. *Education Sciences, 13*(7), 692. DOI: 10.3390/educsci13070692

Kalaiselvi, K., Shanmugam, R., Tamilselvan, S., Manikandan, S. P., & Rajasekar, P. (2024, July). Innovations in Natural Language Processing through Enhanced Linguistic Model Accuracy and Efficiency Using Advanced Reinforcement Learning Techniques. In *2024 Second International Conference on Advances in Information Technology (ICAIT)* (Vol. 1, pp. 1-5). IEEE. DOI: 10.1109/ICAIT61638.2024.10690717

Khang, A., Shah, V., & Rani, S. (Eds.). (2023). *Handbook of Research on AI-Based Technologies and Applications in the Era of the Metaverse*. IGI Global. DOI: 10.4018/978-1-6684-8851-5

Nithya, T., Kumar, V. N., Gayathri, S., Deepa, S., Varun, C. M., & Subramanian, R. S. (2023, August). A comprehensive survey of machine learning: Advancements, applications, and challenges. In *2023 Second International Conference on Augmented Intelligence and Sustainable Systems (ICAISS)* (pp. 354-361). IEEE. DOI: 10.1109/ICAISS58487.2023.10250547

Pajila, P. B., Sudha, K., Selvi, D. K., Kumar, V. N., Gayathri, S., & Subramanian, R. S. (2023, July). A Survey on Natural Language Processing and its Applications. In 2023 4th International Conference on Electronics and Sustainable Communication Systems (ICESC) (pp. 996-1001). IEEE.

Sanjeera, S. K., Jevin, J. A., Pajila, B., & Kumari, R. (2024). Exploring the Applications of Augmented Reality and Virtual Reality in Medicine: A Comprehensive Overview. Navigating the Augmented and Virtual Frontiers in Engineering, 212-222.

Saravanan, K., Prakash, R. B., Balakrishnan, C., Kumar, G. V. P., Subramanian, R. S., & Anita, M. (2023, December). Support Vector Machines: Unveiling the Power and Versatility of SVMs in Modern Machine Learning. In 2023 3rd International Conference on Innovative Mechanisms for Industry Applications (ICIMIA) (pp. 680-687). IEEE.

Solaimalai, G., Shanthi, J. M., Khabiya, P., Geetha, K., & Talele, G. (2024, April). Natural Language Processing in Virtual Assistants Current Approaches and Challenges. In *2024 International Conference on Science Technology Engineering and Management (ICSTEM)* (pp. 1-5). IEEE. DOI: 10.1109/ICSTEM61137.2024.10560644

Sudha, K., Balakrishnan, C., Anish, T. P., Nithya, T., Yamini, B., Subramanian, R. S., & Nalini, M. (2024). Data Insight Unveiled: Navigating Critical Approaches and Challenges in Diverse Domains Through Advanced Data Analysis. Critical Approaches to Data Engineering Systems and Analysis, 90-114.

Tiwari, R. (2023). The integration of AI and machine learning in education and its potential to personalize and improve student learning experiences. International Journal of Scientific Research in Engineering and Management, 7.

Xu, W., & Ouyang, F. (2022). A systematic review of AI role in the educational system based on a proposed conceptual framework. *Education and Information Technologies*, *27*(3), 4195–4223. DOI: 10.1007/s10639-021-10774-y

Chapter 3
Accessibility and Inclusivity in AI-Powered Personalized Learning

Rohit Yadav
https://orcid.org/0000-0002-7573-8005
IILM University, Greater Noida, India

Mohit Yadav
https://orcid.org/0000-0002-9341-2527
O.P. Jindal Global University, India

Geshwaree Huzooree
https://orcid.org/0000-0001-8076-6636
Edinburgh Napier University, UK

Ali Najeeb
https://orcid.org/0000-0003-4663-9347
Qasim Ibrahim School of Business, Villa College, Maldives

Asanga Ranasinghe
https://orcid.org/0009-0005-2846-0732
Postgraduate Institute of Management, University of Sri Jayewardenepura, Sri Lanka

ABSTRACT

AI-powered personalized learning holds the potential to revolutionize education by tailoring content to meet the diverse needs of learners. However, for such systems to be truly effective, they must prioritize accessibility and inclusivity, ensuring equitable opportunities for all students, regardless of ability, background, or resources. This

DOI: 10.4018/979-8-3693-8744-3.ch003

chapter explores the role of AI in personalized learning, focusing on the importance of designing systems that are both accessible and inclusive. It examines key issues such as algorithmic bias, data privacy, and the digital divide, offering strategies to mitigate these challenges. Additionally, it discusses the evolving regulatory landscape and the need for policies that foster equitable access to AI-driven educational tools. Looking ahead, the chapter highlights emerging innovations that promise to further enhance the accessibility and inclusivity of AI in education, ensuring that all learners can benefit from personalized, technology-enhanced learning experiences.

INTRODUCTION

Accessibility and inclusivity in education are critical to ensuring that all learners, regardless of their abilities, backgrounds, or circumstances, have equitable opportunities to learn and succeed. These principles are increasingly relevant as education systems worldwide embrace artificial intelligence (AI) to enhance teaching and learning experiences. AI-powered personalized learning systems promise to revolutionize education by tailoring content, pace, and delivery methods to individual learners' needs. However, the design and implementation of these systems should take into consideration diverse learner profiles, such as those with disabilities, linguistic challenges, and different levels of digital literacy. If not considered, it will be a source of inequity and exclusion for vulnerable groups (Cooper et al., 2021).

Accessibility is important because it eliminates barriers that prevent learners from engaging fully in learning activities. These barriers can be physical, such as inaccessible user interfaces, or digital, such as incompatibility with assistive technologies like screen readers or voice commands (Burgstahler, 2020). Inclusivity, however, is beyond accessibility; it is the guarantee that educational experiences are designed to reflect and respect the diversity of learners. This means that AI systems have to take into consideration the cultural relevance, language diversity, and socioeconomic differences (Holmes et al., 2019).

AI technologies, including adaptive learning algorithms, natural language processing, and computer vision, have demonstrated great potential for creating personalized and inclusive educational experiences. Such differences have ensured that adaptive learning systems can differ instruction to differently capable learners, as speech recognition allows accessibility for both vision and mobility disabled individuals (Kim & Rose, 2022). However, this will depend on AI having been designed by the very creators to prioritize issues of equity and inclusion from conception. This chapter discusses the challenges and opportunities related to accessible and inclusive AI-powered personalized learning systems, which provide insights into design strategies, ethical considerations, and policy implications (Lazar et al., 2015).

By discussing these themes, the chapter will be able to give educators, developers, and policymakers a comprehensive understanding of the steps needed to ensure that AI-driven education systems serve all learners equitably. It also brings into the forefront the issue of interdisciplinarity that would be needed to tackle such issues as bias in AI models, inequalities in the availability of technology, and ethical issues with the use of AI in education. Such conversations are vital to a future in which AI-based personalized learning unlocks its promise for democratizing education.

THE ROLE OF AI IN PERSONALIZED LEARNING

The advent of artificial intelligence was a revolution in education processes and offered tools and methods to craft learning experiences tailored to individual needs and preferences. AI supported forms of learning are data-driven and create customized educational content, pacing, and feedback. This model allows students to review content as needed, fill knowledge gaps, and also push more advanced learners ahead of traditional curricula (Zawacki-Richter et al., 2019). The AI can, using learner data analysis algorithms, find patterns and predict learner trajectory, making instructional strategies to be most effective for optimal learning results (Holmes et al., 2019).

The key technologies driving AI-powered personalized learning are adaptive learning platforms, natural language processing, and computer vision. Adaptive learning platforms dynamically adjust the educational content depending on the interactions of the learner, ensuring that the material is neither too challenging nor too mundane. For instance, systems like DreamBox and ALEKS use AI to assess learners' proficiency levels and provide tailored lessons, quizzes, and exercises (Kim & Rose, 2022). NLP tools, such as intelligent tutoring systems, enable personalized interaction by understanding and responding to the questions of learners in natural language, making education accessible to non-native speakers and learners with disabilities. Computer vision technology can also be used to analyze facial expressions and body language in order to assess learner engagement and provide feedback to instructors (Luckin et al., 2016).

AI further promotes inclusivity in education through the accommodation of diverse learning needs. For example, voice recognition technologies allow blind students to access digital content, and real-time language translation tools break down the linguistic barriers (Cooper et al., 2021). In addition, AI systems can detect and correct unconscious biases in instructional content so that learning materials are culturally relevant and inclusive. However, the success of AI in personalized learning depends on the ethical design and implementation of these technologies. Issues such as data privacy, algorithmic bias, and equitable access to AI tools remain significant challenges that must be addressed to ensure that AI-driven education benefits all learners (Wang & Molnar, 2023).

AI is transforming the way education is delivered and experienced by providing dynamic, data-driven solutions. It allows a shift from one-size-fits-all teaching methods to learner-centric approaches that empower individuals to take charge of their education. As research and innovation in AI-powered personalized learning continue to evolve, it is essential to prioritize accessibility, inclusivity, and ethical considerations to maximize its potential for improving educational equity worldwide (Zawacki-Richter et al., 2019).

Limitations of Current AI Technologies in Adapting to Complex Learner Profiles

Despite the advancements in artificial intelligence (AI) within educational contexts, current AI technologies exhibit significant limitations in adapting to complex learner profiles. A primary concern is the over-reliance on data-driven models, which often fail to capture the nuanced and individualized needs of diverse learners. This dependence can lead to a one-size-fits-all approach, neglecting unique learning styles or specific requirements of students who are underrepresented in the training data (Brand Education, 2024). Additionally, AI systems may struggle to interpret contextual factors such as student motivation, emotional states, and external challenges, which are crucial for effective personalized learning. The absence of human empathy and adaptability in AI-driven education can result in a lack of meaningful engagement and support for students, particularly those with unique learning needs (Aquarius AI, 2024). Furthermore, the potential for bias in AI algorithms poses a risk of perpetuating existing educational inequalities, as these systems might inadvertently favor certain groups based on the data they were trained on (AI for Social Good, 2024). Privacy concerns also arise due to the extensive data collection required by AI systems, leading to apprehension regarding the security and ethical use of sensitive student information (Aquarius AI, 2024). Collectively, these limitations underscore the necessity for a balanced integration of AI and human oversight in education to ensure that the diverse and complex needs of all learners are adequately addressed.

UNDERSTANDING ACCESSIBILITY IN AI-POWERED LEARNING

Accessibility in AI-powered learning refers to the designing and implementation of educational systems and tools that can be effectively used by all learners, including those with disabilities or other limitations. Accessibility ensures that technological advancements in education do not exclude individuals based on physical, sensory, cognitive, or situational barriers. As education becomes more and more dependent on AI-based solutions, issues of accessibility take on the characteristics of not just a technical issue but a moral question, given its direct relationship with the rights of learners to equity in education (Burgstahler, 2020).

Compatibility issues with assistive technologies represent the main source of barriers for access in both conventional and AI-enabled educational environments. For instance, visually impaired learners will rely on screen readers or Braille displays. However, such tools may not work effectively if the user interface is poorly designed or if content is not labeled properly. Learners with motor disabilities who rely on voice commands or adaptive hardware will find it hard to navigate systems that heavily depend on keyboard or mouse inputs (Cooper et al., 2021). Accessibility requires designing systems that are in tune with established standards like Web Content Accessibility Guidelines, which are very comprehensive in addressing the accessibility of digital content.

AI technologies can improve accessibility by offering solutions custom-made for individual needs. For example, speech recognition and text-to-speech technologies allow learners who are either hard of hearing or visually impaired to interact with educational content much better. Similarly, the same AI-powered real-time transcription and translation tools can support deaf and hard-of-hearing students or those in a multilingual classroom who encounter linguistic adversity (Kim & Rose, 2022). It supports learners where language diversity and literacy differences form an immense barrier to accessing education in low-resource environments.

With this, the issue is still, however, with the implementation of accessibility in AI-powered learning. The primary problem lies in the absence of diversified user needs within the training data sets. The biases and constraints within the data often find expression in the resulting AI systems. Training data is sometimes limited by an under-representation of examples for people with disabilities or other under-represented groups, meaning the needs of such users may not be met within these systems. This requires deliberate efforts to include diverse perspectives in the design and development process and ensuring that accessibility features are integrated from the outset rather than added as an afterthought (Holmes et al., 2019).

Another significant aspect to keep in mind is accessibility and privacy at a crossroads. Some of the accessibility features consist of facial recognition or emotion detection that gets sensitive information about the users. Although the tool may help many learn some content, it also brings concerns regarding security and consent over the data being collected. Balancing accessibility with great ethical practice pertaining to data will help build the trust and ensure that learners feel secure while using AI tools (Wang & Molnar, 2023).

Accessibility in AI-powered learning requires a holistic approach that involves the technical, social, and ethical dimensions. This does not only entail adherence to existing standards but also the creation of an inclusive culture in the development and deployment of educational technologies. By focusing on accessibility, educators, developers, and policymakers can tap into the full potential of AI to create learning environments that are equitable, inclusive, and empowering for all.

The integration of AI in educational platforms has significantly enhanced accessibility features, benefiting learners with disabilities. However, this advancement necessitates the collection and processing of substantial amounts of personal data, leading to a critical trade-off between enhancing accessibility and maintaining data privacy. AI-driven educational tools often gather sensitive information, including personal identifiers, behavioral patterns, and academic performance metrics, to tailor learning experiences effectively. While such data collection facilitates personalized learning, it also raises concerns about potential unauthorized access, data breaches, and misuse of information. For instance, a report highlighted that in 2022, there was a 20% increase in cyber threats targeting the global education sector compared to the previous year, underscoring the vulnerability of educational data systems (Havish, 2024).

Moreover, the implementation of robust accessibility features may require continuous monitoring and data analysis, potentially infringing on students' privacy rights if not managed properly. To mitigate these risks, it is imperative to establish transparent data governance policies that balance the need for accessibility with stringent privacy protections. Adhering to regulations such as the General Data Protection Regulation (GDPR) provides a framework for safeguarding personal data while leveraging AI to support learners with disabilities. By implementing measures like data encryption, access controls, and obtaining informed consent, educational institutions can uphold data privacy without compromising on the accessibility benefits that AI technologies offer (Smith, 2024).

AI has recently made significant strides in enhancing accessibility for learners with disabilities, leading to notable success stories. For instance, AI-powered applications like Microsoft's Seeing AI assist visually impaired students by describing their surroundings, reading text, and identifying objects, thereby facilitating greater independence in educational settings. Similarly, AI-driven speech recognition tools have been employed to support students with speech disabilities, providing real-time feedback and personalized language exercises to improve their communication skills.

Moreover, AI applications such as Voiceitt utilize machine learning algorithms to interpret the speech patterns of individuals with speech impairments, translating their words into clear text or speech, which enhances classroom participation.

These examples illustrate how AI technologies are actively transforming educational experiences, making learning more accessible and personalized for students with diverse needs.

INCLUSIVITY IN AI-POWERED LEARNING

Inclusivity in AI-powered learning means creating educational systems and tools that respect and address the diverse needs, backgrounds, and experiences of all learners. While accessibility focuses on removing barriers for learners with disabilities, inclusivity goes further by ensuring that AI-driven educational systems are designed to accommodate differences in cultural backgrounds, socioeconomic status, linguistic diversity, and learning styles. Inclusivity focuses on equity, striving for every learner to acquire the necessary equipment and chances for success without depending on where he or she started (Holmes et al., 2019).

AI systems have demonstrated notable shortcomings in accommodating linguistic and cultural diversity, leading to significant accessibility challenges. A prominent example is the failure of AI-powered speech recognition technologies to accurately interpret diverse accents and dialects. Studies have shown that these systems often struggle with regional accents, such as Southern or New York City accents in the United States, resulting in higher error rates and user frustration (Gillis, 2024). This limitation underscores a broader issue: AI models are frequently trained on data that lacks sufficient representation of linguistic diversity, leading to biases that disadvantage non-standard language users.

Moreover, AI language models like ChatGPT have encountered challenges in maintaining linguistic consistency. For instance, users in the UK reported instances where ChatGPT responded in Welsh instead of English, despite the users not understanding Welsh or being located near Wales. This glitch was attributed to errors in the voice transcription system, highlighting the difficulties AI systems face in accurately processing and responding to diverse linguistic inputs (Williams, 2024).

Additionally, AI translation tools often fall short in capturing cultural nuances and context, leading to misinterpretations. Experts argue that while AI can handle direct translations, it struggles with the subtleties of language that are deeply rooted in culture, which human translators navigate adeptly (Flood, 2024). These examples illustrate the critical need for more inclusive and representative data in AI training to ensure these systems can effectively serve a linguistically and culturally diverse global population.

The fundamental aspect of inclusivity is having AI systems not biased but created with the goal of serving learners in all walks of life. There are several sources through which bias can emerge in AI, such as unrepresentative datasets, poor design of algorithms, and the lack of diversity among developers and stakeholders involved in system creation. For instance, language models tend to favor dominant languages and dialects, thereby excluding or marginalizing speakers of less commonly used languages. Adaptive learning platforms trained on data from well-resourced schools may not account for the unique challenges learners face in underprivileged settings, such as lack of reliable internet access or limited exposure to digital tools (Kim & Rose, 2022). This calls for deliberate efforts to diversify training datasets, include underrepresented voices, and prioritize equity during the design and development of AI systems.

Tailoring education content also entails the tailoring of such educational content within the cultural and linguistic settings in which learners function. AI-enabled learning platforms could employ NLP and translation instruments to provide materials in multiple languages and accommodate classes composed of multilingual students and a learner population hailing from many backgrounds. Nevertheless, inclusiveness calls for much more than a translation; inclusivity involves tailoring education materials according to the cultures, traditions, and contexts prevalent in different learner groups. For example, an AI system implemented in a rural setting should include examples, scenarios, and challenges that are relevant to the local environment and lived experiences of learners (Zawacki-Richter et al., 2019).

An inclusive approach also takes into account the intersectionality of learners' identities. Many learners experience multiple layers of disadvantage, such as a student who is both economically disadvantaged and has a disability. The overlapping challenges identified should be something AI systems will learn to be sensitive to and solve. Customized learning sites that consider intersectionality can ensure differential resources for instance, ensure the availability of the materials for use when there is no stable internet access, incorporate captioning and transcript and sign language interpretation when necessary for learners who are deaf or hard of hearing (Burgstahler, 2020).

Moreover, another way inclusiveness cuts across ethical use of AI in education. AI systems will require developments where they are deployed such a way that they do not inadvertently exclude certain groups. For instance, systems monitoring learner engagement might fail when facial recognition fails to detect images produced by people with darker skin tones or other non-Western facial features. Similarly, systems that are highly dependent on user data for personalizing learning experiences should provide strong privacy protections to prevent alienation of learners from communities that have greater concerns about data security and surveillance (Wang & Molnar, 2023).

Collaboration among technologists, educators, policymakers, and communities is important for creating inclusive AI-powered learning environments. Co-design processes with learners from different backgrounds can be useful in determining the potential barriers that might be created and in making sure that the systems work well for everyone. In addition, inclusivity is a process of continuous monitoring and iteration that takes into consideration the emerging challenges and changing demographics of learners (Luckin et al., 2016).

Education can be used as a strong tool for the reduction of disparities and equity building by embedding inclusivity into the design and deployment of AI systems. Inclusive AI-powered learning can bridge gaps in access, improve outcomes for underrepresented groups, and empower all learners to reach their full potential.

DESIGNING FOR ACCESSIBILITY AND INCLUSIVITY IN AI SYSTEMS

Designing AI systems for accessibility and inclusivity requires an intentional approach that places the needs of diverse learners at the forefront of the development lifecycle. This process integrates principles of universal design for learning, user-centered design, and participatory design to create systems that are equitable, adaptable, and responsive. These approaches guarantee that AI-based education tools are able to meet a wide range of abilities, cultures, and styles of learning without favoring the narrow set of users (Burgstahler, 2020).

UDL principles can be a very good foundation in designing accessible and inclusive AI. UDL is defined as the way of providing representation, engagement, and expression means to suit multiple learning needs. For example, an AI-powered learning platform might include instructional content in text, audio, and video formats, to ensure accessibility by learners who may have differing sensory or cognitive preferences. It may also make tools such as real-time transcription and text-to-speech capabilities available for use by the deaf, hard of hearing, and visually impaired learner. Through such principles, AI systems can go beyond the mere accessibility standards to real inclusiveness in design (Meyer et al., 2014).

UCD further aids inclusiveness by actively involving end-users in the design process. Involving learners with disabilities, educators, and other stakeholders ensures that the system addresses real-world challenges and reflects the needs of its users (Seale, 2014). For instance, including feedback from visually impaired learners in the design of an AI-powered learning management system may identify gaps in navigation or compatibility with screen readers. UCD also prevents assumptions about user preferences or capabilities that may inadvertently exclude certain groups (Holmes et al., 2019).

Participatory design extends the principles of UCD by involving users as co-creators in the design and development of AI systems. This will make the users feel a sense of ownership, and developers can identify subtle barriers that are not immediately apparent. For instance, working with educators and students in under-resourced communities might reveal challenges with internet connectivity or lack of devices; this would enable developers to design offline-compatible features or lightweight applications that run on low-end hardware (Zawacki-Richter et al., 2019).

The elimination of algorithmic bias is another crucial dimension of building inclusion into AI systems. Algorithms trained on inappropriate or biased data might copy earlier inequalities and oppress certain groups. For instance, facial recognition algorithms might not be able to recognize individuals with darker skin tones if the datasets for the training are monochromatic (Gay, 2018). Similarly, language models may not assist learners who speak different dialects or lesser languages in natural language processing applications. These biases can be mitigated through the curating of diverse and representative datasets, regular auditing of algorithms for unintended disparities, and fairness-aware machine learning techniques that guarantee equitable outcomes (Kim & Rose, 2022).

Besides technical concerns, designing for accessibility and inclusion presents ethical issues. Privacy becomes a significant concern in the design of AI systems that collect sensitive user data for personalization purposes. Developers should have robust data protection measures, ensure informed consent, and minimize the amount of data collected to ensure a balance between personalization and user privacy. Transparent communication regarding how data is used and stored can help foster trust among learners and educators (Wang & Molnar, 2023).

Finally, iterative design and testing should be used to refine accessibility and inclusivity features. By continuously monitoring and accepting user feedback, developers are able to better assess and eliminate barriers as they are identified (Selwyn, 2022). Regular updates harmonize with changing accessibility standards and user needs ensure that these AI systems remain accommodating over time. For example, testing can be done at regular intervals using assistive technologies and diverse user groups in order to find compatibility issues or new requirements that need to be addressed (Cooper et al., 2021).

By embracing an overall, user-centric perspective, it is possible for developers to develop AI-based learning systems that are not only accessible but also inclusive, equitable, and empowering. Such systems have the potential to make education barrier-free for all learners.

AI BIAS AND ETHICAL CHALLENGES

With this, artificial intelligence systems are in a position to revolutionize learning, but all this is solely dependent on how their design and implementation are made with fairness, transparency, and integrity. Bias and ethical issues constitute significant risks against inclusivity and accessibility in AI-supported learning environments. These problems would be approached multifaceted: sources of bias would be determined and strategies put into place to neutralize the occurrence of these issues, as well as incorporating considerations of ethics during the processes of design and deployment (Holmes et al., 2019).

Understanding Bias in AI Systems

Bias in AI systems can be due to a variety of reasons, such as unrepresentative training data, flawed algorithm design, or the inadvertent introduction of subjective assumptions by developers. For instance, an AI system trained on datasets dominated by male or Western-centric examples may fail to accurately analyze or adapt to the needs of female learners or those from non-Western cultures. Such biases can therefore be perpetuated to create systemic inequities and disadvantage already marginalized groups (Wang & Molnar, 2023). In the case of educational contexts, for instance, bias in AI systems may appear as lower prediction accuracy for certain groups, culturally irrelevant content, or failure to accommodate diverse learning styles and abilities.

Strategies to Mitigate Bias include:

Ensuring bias in AI systems requires intention at several phases of the lifecycle. One specific method is diversifying training data sets and the populations the systems will serve in those contexts. This includes, for example, gathering data about demographics, cultural practices, and learning experiences. But then, it becomes a matter of gathering such information ethically using informed consent measures and adequate protective data policies with regard to individual privacy of the learners (Binns, 2022).

Algorithmic fairness techniques may also reduce the bias of an AI system. For example, developers can employ fairness-aware machine learning models, which can use constraints to guarantee equitable treatment across different groups. Regular audits on AI systems with respect to performance disparities can reveal unintended biases and guide corrective actions. Another important factor is transparency—developers should document the sources of their data, the design choices behind their algorithms, and any known limitations to enable scrutiny and build trust (Cooper et al., 2021).

Ethical Challenges in AI

Ethical challenges in AI-powered learning extend beyond bias to encompass issues such as data privacy, consent, accountability, and the potential for unintended harm. Most AI systems utilize large amounts of personal data to create personalized learning experiences, resulting in data security and misuse issues. For instance, a data breach or unauthorized sharing may reveal sensitive information about the learner's abilities or disabilities, or even his/her socioeconomic status (Kim & Rose, 2022). Thus, developers should be able to implement very stringent data protection measures, including encryption, anonymization, and very secure storage practices.

In general, transparency and accountability are needed for ethical AI. Users like learners, teachers, and even administrators need to know how these AI systems work and what they are based upon (Traxler & Smith, 2020). Explainable AI (XAI) techniques describe the decision-making process of an AI system with clear and understandable insights, building trust and the ability to dispute or override such decisions when deemed necessary (Holmes et al., 2019). Accountability mechanisms include clear policies regarding how errors or grievances can be addressed to ensure that stakeholders can seek redress if an AI system causes harm or operates unfairly.

The other ethical challenge is overreliance on AI systems in education. Though AI can augment and enhance learning experiences, it should not replace the role of educators or reduce human oversight. AI systems are tools and do not represent autonomy; use must, therefore always be coupled with human judgment and empathy. Policymakers and developers will need to reinforce the value that education holds above technological innovation alone (Wang & Molnar, 2023).

Shared Solutions in the Ethics of AI

It calls for joint cooperation among the stakeholders: the developer, the teacher, policymaker, and the learner themselves, if bias and ethics in AI were to be countered. Diverse stakeholder involvement in co-designing can alert one to bias and ethical issues in the earlier stages of product development. Data privacy and accountabilities can then be guided with the help of regulatory frameworks, standards, including the EU's General Data Protection Regulation (GDPR). Educational institutions also need to invest in educator and learner education and training about the nature and use of AI systems, enabling educators and learners to use the tools effectively and responsibly (Luckin et al., 2016).

AI systems can become more inclusive, fair, and beneficial to all learners if bias and ethical challenges are addressed proactively. These efforts will not only enhance the quality of AI-powered education but also work towards more universal goals such as equity, justice, and respect for human rights.

POLICY AND REGULATION FOR INCLUSIVE AI IN EDUCATION

Policies and regulatory frameworks would have to be strong to guide the development and deployment of inclusive AI systems in education so that fairness, accountability, and accessibility can be ensured. Yet, as profound as technological benefits appear to be for transforming education, their potential is only realizable if there is thoughtful governance prioritizing inclusivity, equity, and protection of learners' rights. Policymakers, educators, and technology developers need to collaborate in the development of frameworks that address the unique challenges posed by AI in educational contexts (Holmes et al., 2019).

The Need for Policy in Inclusive AI

AI technologies are not neutral by themselves; they reflect the values, biases, and assumptions embedded in their design. If left unregulated, AI systems can perpetuate existing inequities or create new barriers for marginalized learners without even knowing it. Policies must clearly define the fair, accessible, and ethical requirements for AI-powered education to ensure the implementation of standards in order to deal with issues such as algorithmic bias, data privacy, and the digital divide, wherein AI systems improve equity rather than exacerbate differences (Kim & Rose, 2022).

Accessible and Inclusive Standards

Policies should enforce accessibility standards like the Web Content Accessibility Guidelines (WCAG) or national legislation, for instance, the Americans with Disabilities Act (ADA). These accessibility standards guarantee AI-based learning platforms support learners with disabilities by requiring an integration of capabilities like support for screen readers, alternative text descriptions about images, and reflowable text. Regulations could also encourage research into assistive technologies like AI-related text-to-speech tools. Such tools could help learners with specific needs utilize these applications (Burgstahler, 2020).

Policies should extend to emphasizing cultural and linguistic diversity. Policies may, for example, require AI systems to support multilingual education through translation and transcription of less commonly spoken languages. Additionally, culturally responsive design should be encouraged to involve diverse lived experiences and values in content for educational purposes. Policymakers can encourage these practices by establishing standards for inclusivity in AI development and funding programs that support equal access to educational technology (Zawacki-Richter et al., 2019).

Data Privacy and Ethical Use

The use of AI in education at scale raises a number of issues related to data privacy and security. Policies should ensure that there are strong regulations on the collection, storage, and usage of data to protect sensitive learner information. For example, the General Data Protection Regulation in Europe is an excellent model to protect data, but it still maintains transparency and accountability. Educational institutions should be allowed to collect data only after having informed consent, and they must also give adequate information about what will be done with that particular data. Similarly, AI systems should have the integration of privacy-preserving technologies, such as encryption and anonymization, which will reduce risks (Wang & Molnar, 2023).

Ethical issues associated with AI use in decision-making also need to be addressed in policies. For example, in cases where AI systems are deployed to evaluate the performance of learners or suggest learning routes, there needs to be mechanisms for human intervention and appeal. Learners and educators should have the right to view and appeal AI-generated decisions, ensuring that these systems support rather than supplant human judgment. Regulatory frameworks should provide accountability measures, and developers and institutions must correct errors or biases that appear in AI-based tools (Binns, 2022).

Decreasing the Digital Divide

Systemic barriers to access must also be addressed through inclusive AI policies. Unequal access to technology and internet connectivity remains a major challenge, especially in low-income and rural communities. Investments in infrastructure like the broadband expansion will increase equity by supporting subsidies on devices and internet. Public-private partnerships are likely to play a central role in these gaps in the provision of learning resources so that all learners may benefit from AI-powered education (Luckin et al., 2016).

Global and Local Governance

The international level is witnessing efforts from organizations such as UNESCO and the OECD in the establishment of guidelines on AI in education, focusing on inclusivity and equity. Such frameworks offer national governments benchmarks while fostering cross-border cooperation. However, local governments need to adapt the guidelines to the unique cultural and educational contexts, thus making policies relevant and actionable at the community level (Zawacki-Richter et al., 2019).

National policies should also contain provisions for review and updating regularly. The challenges and opportunities presented by AI technologies change as the technology changes. Policymakers need to be nimble, updating regulations based on emerging research and feedback from stakeholders as issues arise. Public consultation processes can ensure that policies are responsive to the needs of learners, educators, and other stakeholders.

Promoting Ethical Innovation

Inclusive AI policies must regulate but also incentivize innovation. Governments can provide funding for research and development that focuses on the development of AI systems specifically designed for the underserved population. For example, grants and awards can support projects that design AI-powered tools for learners with disabilities or educational platforms in low-resource settings. In doing so, policymakers can foster a culture of ethical innovation that will promote the development of AI technologies to advance equity and inclusion (Burgstahler, 2020).

Policy and regulation are critical to ensuring that AI systems in education are accessible, inclusive, and equitable. Clear standards for accessibility, data privacy, bias, and systemic barriers will be established through policymaking, creating a framework that enables AI to enhance learning opportunities for all. Inclusive AI policies can open the way toward a more equitable and empowering educational landscape through collaboration and continuous refinement.

FUTURE DIRECTIONS AND INNOVATIONS IN AI-POWERED INCLUSIVE EDUCATION

The future of AI-powered education is in developing systems that adapt to the diverse needs of learners and actively foster inclusivity, equity, and accessibility on a global scale. Convergence of innovation in technology, pedagogy, and policy is expected to create personalized, culturally responsive, and universally accessible educational ecosystems. This section discusses the main areas likely to be advanced by AI and related technologies, and faces challenge and opportunity together in building education systems.

Advances in Adaptive Learning Technologies

Future adaptive learning systems will likely use more advanced AI algorithms that are capable of better understanding and predicting student needs. These systems will take advantage of the latest advances in machine learning, NLP, and real-time data analytics to provide highly personalized content. For example, AI can offer dynamic feedback during lessons, adjust the difficulty level of exercises based on a learner's progress, or identify knowledge gaps to offer targeted interventions. Such systems will be particularly beneficial for learners with disabilities or those requiring individualized support (Luckin et al., 2016).

Moreover, multimodal interfaces, like voice, gesture, and eye-tracking, will be integrated to provide more accessible interactions for learners with physical or sensory impairments. More advanced learning platforms will use AR and VR to create these immersive environments that capitalize on different learning preferences and abilities. For instance, simulations based on VR can be useful in imparting social skills among kids with autism in a controlled, low-stress environment (Holmes et al., 2019).

AI-Driven Cultural and Linguistic Adaptation

As AI systems expand their capabilities, they will deliver more culturally and linguistically relevant education. Future innovations in NLP and translation technologies will better facilitate real-time multilingual content delivery to learners, offering the delivery of materials in their native languages or dialects. Beyond translation, AI can fit instruction to the cultural norms, traditions, and values of specific learner communities for greater engagement and inclusivity (Zawacki-Richter et al., 2019).

This means that AI-powered systems can also bridge the gap for indigenous and minority languages that are often overlooked in mainstream education. The translation of these languages into digital format and inclusion in learning platforms enabled by AI can help preserve cultural heritage and offer equal learning opportunities to speakers of less commonly taught languages.

Accessibility Through Assistive Technology

The integration of AI in assistive technologies is further expected to increase the scope and effectiveness of accessibility tools in education. For example, the use of wearable AI devices with features such as haptic feedback and audio descriptions should support learners who have impairments in vision or hearing. Tools such as AI-powered automatic captioning, sign language recognition, and real-time transcription are already being done, and future systems will be even more accurate and usable (Burgstahler, 2020).

Additionally, advances in brain-computer interfaces (BCIs) could revolutionize accessibility for individuals with severe physical disabilities. BCIs that leverage AI to decode neural signals have the potential to enable direct communication with educational platforms, bypassing traditional input methods entirely. Such innovations will empower learners who might otherwise face insurmountable barriers to accessing education.

Ethical AI and Transparent Decision-Making

Future innovations will involve the development of ethical, transparent, and trustworthy AI systems. Explainable AI (XAI) technologies, which enable insights into the decision-making algorithms, will form an integral part of educational platforms. These tools will enable educators, learners, and parents to understand the reasons behind AI-driven recommendations or assessments, ensuring accountability and reducing bias (Kim & Rose, 2022).

Ethical AI systems would also emphasize techniques for data minimization and techniques for privacy, such as federated learning and differential privacy. By decreasing the amount of data collected, these systems reduce the potential compromise of learners' privacy while serving personalized experiences for them. Strong guidelines and robust frameworks will be collaborated on by both policymakers and developers to address these ethical implications of AI in education.

Global Collaboration and Equity-Focused Initiatives

The future of inclusive AI in education will heavily rely on collaborations between governments, educational institutions, technology companies, and nongovernmental organizations around the world. Partnership efforts will work to close the digital divide, investing in the infrastructure of technology, offering lower-cost access to devices and internet connection, and implementing equitable access and distribution of AI-powered tools. This will be supported by public-private partnerships that reach out to far-flung places and low-income regions (Wang & Molnar, 2023).

Thus, equity-focused initiatives will also encourage the co-design of AI systems with the involvement of the diverse stakeholder group, including the underrepresented communities. Involving these groups in the design process will make future AI systems better address some of the challenges brought forward by marginalized learners.

Cross-Disciplinary Applications and Emerging Technologies

Emerging technologies such as blockchain, the Internet of Things (IoT), and quantum computing will likely intersect with AI to enhance educational systems. Blockchain can be used to create secure, decentralized records of academic achievements, allowing learners to own and share their credentials across institutions and borders. IoT-enabled devices, such as smart classrooms and wearable sensors, could provide real-time data on learners' engagement and well-being, informing AI systems to optimize learning environments (Cooper et al., 2021).

Quantum computing, though in its infancy, will be capable of processing enormous amounts of educational data at a speed and accuracy never before achieved. This ability will open doors to new dimensions of predictive analytics that will help AI systems identify problems before they happen.

Sustainability and Inclusivity at Scale

Scaling AI systems to make them inclusive and sustainable will be the main focus of future innovations. AI-powered platforms should be designed to work in a variety of environments, including low-resource settings. This means that lightweight algorithms should be developed to work on low-cost devices and offline-compatible systems in areas with unreliable internet access. Sustainability efforts will also include reducing the environmental footprint of AI systems by optimizing energy consumption and using renewable energy sources (Zawacki-Richter et al., 2019).

The future of AI-powered inclusive education is one that holds immense promise and responsibility. Harnessing the latest technological advancement and prioritizing inclusivity, equity, and accessibility, it can empower the learner from the most diverse of backgrounds and abilities. This vision, however, demands continuous innovation and collaboration with unwavering dedication to ethical principles. As the fruits of such efforts begin to bear, AI can transform education into a true universal and inclusive endeavor.

CONCLUSION

The potential of AI in personalized learning is huge for revolutionizing education in the direction of working to provide each learner with an experience unique to the need of the learner. But that can be done only if such AI-powered learning systems, while conforming to the norms and standards of equity and fairness, are also designed and implemented within the framework of ethics. As explored throughout this chapter, inclusivity and accessibility must be foundational elements of AI in education, allowing all learners—regardless of background, abilities, or socio-economic status—to have access to personalized learning experiences.

The role of AI in personalized learning is growing, with developments in machine learning, natural language processing, and adaptive technologies providing opportunities for a more inclusive environment in education. AI can analyze enormous amounts of data and adjust content in real time, making it possible to have more personalized support for diverse learners, including people with disabilities, from marginalized communities, or with varied learning needs. However, the promise of AI is not without challenges. Algorithmic bias, unequal access to technology, and ethical dilemmas regarding data privacy are among the risks that must be addressed through intentional design, transparent policies, and inclusive practices.

Policy and regulation are important to ensure that the application of AI in education is ethical and equitable. Governments, educational institutions, and technology developers need to collaborate in developing robust frameworks that protect learners' rights, promote fairness, and reduce disparities in access to AI-powered tools. These frameworks should focus not only on the technology itself but also on the broader social, cultural, and economic factors that influence educational opportunities. Further, as the technology of AI is advancing, policies must be flexible enough to adapt to new challenges and innovations so that inclusive education remains at the forefront.

Future-looking, then, there is lots of promise on the horizon to further develop accessibility and inclusion in AI. Multimodal interfaces and AI-driven cultural adaptation, not to mention other forms of assistive technologies, help further break the barriers to learning. At the same time, there will be calls for ethical best practices in the AI industry-issues of transparency and accountability-as the industry can further build confidence in its solutions for users.

Inclusiveness through AI in education will therefore be more of a colaborative and dynamic process continued through continued dialogue among the educators, learners, policymakers, and technologists. While much has been achieved so far, more is yet to be realized to reach the aspirations toward an equitably and perfectly powered AI educational landscape. As these efforts play out, AI can be a powerful tool to bridge gaps in educational opportunity, empower learners, and foster a more inclusive and just educational environment for all.

REFERENCES

AI for Social Good. (2024). *Disadvantages of AI in Education.* Retrieved from https://aiforsocialgood.ca/blog/disadvantages-of-ai-in-education-limitations-and-challenges

Aquarius, A. I. (2024). *Disadvantages of AI in Education.* Retrieved from https://aquariusai.ca/blog/the-disadvantages-of-ai-in-education

Binns, R. (2022). Fairness in machine learning: Lessons from political philosophy. *Communications of the ACM, 65*(6), 40–48.

Brand Education. (2024). *How Artificial Intelligence Declines Personalized Learning.* Retrieved from https://brand.education/how-artificial-intelligence-declines-personalized-learning/

Burgstahler, S. (2020). *Creating inclusive learning opportunities in higher education: A universal design toolkit.* Harvard Education Press.

Cooper, H., Nye, B., Charlton, K., Lindsay, J., & Greathouse, S. (2021). The impact of artificial intelligence on educational equity. *Educational Technology Research and Development, 69*(3), 1023–1045.

Flood, A. (2024, November 11). 'It gets more and more confused': can AI replace translators? *The Guardian.* Retrieved from https://www.theguardian.com/books/2024/nov/11/it-gets-more-and-more-confused-can-ai-replace-translators

Gay, G. (2018). *Culturally Responsive Teaching: Theory, Research, and Practice.* Teachers College Press.

Gillis, A. S. (2024, October 3). How AI speech recognition shows bias toward different accents. *TechTarget.* Retrieved from https://www.techtarget.com/whatis/feature/How-AI-speech-recognition-shows-bias-toward-different-accents

Havish, K. L. (2024, January 14). *Data privacy and security in AI-powered education systems. The Financial Express.* Retrieved from https://www.financialexpress.com/jobs-career/education-data-privacy-and-security-in-ai-powered-education-systems-3363991/

Holmes, W., Bialik, M., & Fadel, C. (2019). *Artificial intelligence in education: Promises and implications for teaching and learning.* Center for Curriculum Redesign.

Kim, J., & Rose, K. (2022). Designing adaptive AI tools for equitable education. *Journal of Learning Analytics, 9*(2), 112–130.

Lazar, J., Goldstein, D. F., & Taylor, A. (2015). *Ensuring Digital Accessibility through Process and Policy*. Morgan Kaufmann.

Luckin, R., Holmes, W., Griffiths, M., & Forcier, L. B. (2016). *Intelligence unleashed: An argument for AI in education*. Pearson Education.

Luckin, R., Holmes, W., Griffiths, M., & Forcier, L. B. (2016). *Intelligence unleashed: An argument for AI in education*. Pearson Education.

Meyer, A., Rose, D. H., & Gordon, D. (2014). *Universal design for learning: Theory and practice*. CAST Professional Publishing.

Seale, J. K. (2014). *E-Learning and Disability in Higher Education: Accessibility Research and Practice*. Routledge.

Selwyn, N. (2022). *Digital Technology and the Future of Education: Critical Perspectives*. Routledge.

Smith, E. (2024, March 10). *Understanding GDPR and data privacy in AI educational tools. DEV Community*. Retrieved from https://dev.to/emmasmith/understanding-gdpr-and-data-privacy-in-ai-educational-tools-3po1

Traxler, J., & Smith, M. (2020). *Artificial Intelligence in Mobile and Ubiquitous Learning*. Springer.

Wang, S., & Molnar, A. (2023). Ethics in AI education: Balancing innovation and equity. *AI & Society, 38*(4), 765–780.

Williams, O. (2024, September 15). English ChatGPT users flummoxed by language glitch as bot turns Welsh. *Financial Times*. Retrieved from https://www.ft.com/content/8ebc9193-7578-40bc-b44a-282df01ae9a3

Zawacki-Richter, O., Marín, V. I., Bond, M., & Gouverneur, F. (2019). Systematic review of research on artificial intelligence applications in higher education: Where are the educators? *International Journal of Educational Technology in Higher Education, 16*(1), 1–27. DOI: 10.1186/s41239-019-0171-0

Chapter 4 Enhancing Student Engagement With Generative AI

Jackie HeeYoung Kim
https://orcid.org/0009-0005-5202-2978
Armstrong State University, Savannah, USA

Alesia Mickle Moldavan
https://orcid.org/0000-0001-7946-9028
Georgia Southern University, Savannah, USA

Robert Terry
https://orcid.org/0009-0000-1479-4823
Georgia Southern University, Savannah, USA

Cynthia C. Massey
https://orcid.org/0000-0001-5093-6016
Georgia Southern University, Savannah, USA

ABSTRACT

This chapter explores the impact of Artificial Intelligence (AI) on modern education, focusing on its potential to enable personalized learning. It offers educators practical strategies to use AI for tailoring instruction to diverse needs. The chapter examines AI's role in second language acquisition, where real-time feedback and adaptive exercises enhance engagement. It also discusses AI's role in advancing Universal Design for Learning (UDL) and supporting Individualized Education Programs (IEPs), making education more accessible for students with disabilities. Additionally, the chapter highlights how generative AI fosters creativity and critical thinking in writing, offering new ways for students to express ideas. AI encourages

DOI: 10.4018/979-8-3693-8744-3.ch004

collaboration through peer feedback, while also sparking ethical discussions about authorship and the role of technology in creative processes. The chapter concludes by emphasizing the significant shifts AI is driving in educational practices, underscoring its potential to reshape the future of learning.

INTRODUCTION

The emergence of Artificial Intelligence (AI) has significantly transformed the landscape of education. Educators at all levels are exploring AI's potential to address long-standing challenges, such as personalized and differentiated instruction, due to its interactive features that can track student learning profiles and provide instant feedback, making it a powerful tool for enhancing personalized learning experiences. Given its diverse capabilities, integrating AI into higher education holds great potential for personalizing learning (Wayne et al., 2019).

Personalized learning is conceptualized as a learning approach that aims to provide personalized learning experiences based on learners' needs, goals, and skills through current instructional technology (Shemshack et al., 2021). In particular, technology-facilitated personalized learning has become an important learning paradigm in the field of education (Shemshack et al., 2021). Moreover, growing evidence suggests that technology-facilitated personalized learning was more effective than traditional learning on students' learning (Zheng et al., 2022) and enhance motivation by fostering a deeper comprehension of subjects (Makhambetova et al., 2021).

While emerging AI technologies offer instructional assistance (e.g., via chatbots and robots) and provide teachers with valuable information to support pedagogical decision-making (e.g., learning analytics; Kim et al., 2022), researchers have noted a lack of connection between these technologies and their practical use in teaching. Chiu et al. (2023), after systematically reviewing the literature of 10 years (from 2012 to 2021) on AI integration across the four key educational domains—learning, teaching, assessment, and administration— emphasize that educators may not fully understand these technologies to apply them effectively. Additionally, they highlight that educators often lack awareness of AI's affordances for education and may be uncertain about its pedagogical implications. To address this gap, this chapter explores the pedagogical implications of AI in teaching and aims to bridge the disconnect between AI technologies and their affordance in education, focusing on the personalization aspect of education.

Therefore, this chapter aims to help practitioners understand the broader implications of AI in education by examining its significant applications happening in current educational settings. The discussion begins with AI's application in second language acquisition, highlighting how it can function as a teacher, tutor, and conversation partner by providing personalized exercises and real-time feedback. It then explores AI's role in supporting translation and formative assessment. The chapter also considers AI's contributions to Universal Design for Learning (UDL), particularly in enhancing personalized experiences for students with disabilities. Additionally, it examines AI's role in developing and monitoring Individualized Education Programs (IEPs) and its potential to revolutionize debate and critical thinking skills. Finally, the chapter outlines best practices for ensuring that AI's use in education remains both effective and ethical.

ENGAGING SECOND LANGUAGE LEARNING WITH AI

To date, second language (referred to hereafter as L2) education has utilized three AI tools to enhance personalized learning: commercialized AI tools, grant-funded AI tools, and recently Generative AI tools. Knowing about these three kinds of AI tools is important to understand how Generative AI tools can be transformative in L2 education. Before the rise of Generative AI tools, several AI-based tools, such as Duolingo, Rosetta Stone, Google Translate, ELSA Speak, and Anki, were utilized in L2 learning, focusing primarily on structured, rule-based approaches and machine learning techniques. These tools often prioritized grammar, vocabulary acquisition, pronunciation, and translation (Medium, 2020). Additionally, designated institutions and organizations in the United States are provided with resources and grants for researching and developing AI-driven personalized learning platforms with great potential to boost academic performance (Boninger et al., 2020; Williamson & Eynon, 2020).

However, while these AI-based tools and grant-funded platforms show promise, general consumers like teachers in regular school districts have difficulty accessing them due to high costs, and they are designed for specific institutions or programs, limiting their reach. This issue can create accessibility barriers, especially for learners outside of these specific institutions or those who cannot meet such platforms' financial, technical, or resource demands. In contrast, Generative AI tools like ChatGPT offer distinct advantages, particularly regarding accessibility and scalability. Another advantage is that Generative AI tools like ChatGPT benefit from rapid innovation cycles, as they are continuously updated based on real-time user feedback (Rospigliosi, 2023). This approach allows the tool to evolve quickly, incorporating new features or addressing any issues that may arise. Therefore, this section focuses on the transformative impact of Generative AI-powered education on foreign language learning rather than discussing other commercial and grant-funded AI platforms.

The major difference between older AI tools and Generative AI tools, such as ChatGPT, is that new AI tools use Natural Language Processing technologies, which have become game changers. With older AI tools, these robots could only follow strict instructions. If users asked to check spelling or help practice a new language, they would only look for specific things like certain words or rules. They did not understand much beyond the basics. With a new AI tool, a robot can understand everything users say and even have a back-and-forth conversation with users, like they are talking to a friend. NLP (Natural Language Processing) is what makes this possible. It helps computers understand language like humans do—listening for meaning (OpenAI, 2022), not just specific words or rules.

With its innovative capabilities, Generative AI has emerged as a pioneering technology for advancing personalized adaptive learning (Peng et al., 2019) through the fast-adjusting power, which can adaptively adjust teaching strategies timely based on real-time monitored changes in individual performance and personal development. It did not take long for L2 educators to recognize the significant potential of Generative AI tools in meeting key principles of second language acquisition, including comprehension, speaking, grammar, and fluency. These tools provide dynamic, adaptive support that aligns with effective language learning strategies, enabling tailored and engaging educational experiences.

Researchers like Meniado (2023) found that ChatGPT helps students improve their English by engaging in meaningful activities that are more relevant to their current interests and ability levels. These activities include understanding and producing language, learning language rules, and practicing fluency, which are essential dimensions of the principles of second language acquisition (Nation, 2007). ChatGPT effectively supports all these essential learning components.

ChatGPT makes the learning activities meaningful for students by offering iterative, interactive, and contextual responses. In particular, ChatGPT's iterative process of trial and error to improve or refine the outcomes tailors the learning experience to each individual's needs and preferences. For example, it can adapt to different proficiency levels, interests, and learning styles, making the practice of spoken and written English more aligned with learners' real-time needs. This personalized approach helps learners practice and enhance their language skills at the ability level at the time of practice, as noted in studies like Young & Shishido (2023).

ChatGPT could assist teachers in generating and refining lesson plans, exercises, and activities based on specific learning objectives in ESL/EFL classrooms (Alenizi et al., 2023; Tolstykh, & Oshchepkova, 2024; Ulla et al., 2023). These findings aligned with those of Meniado (2023), who also identified ChatGPT's potential to serve as both a lesson planner and an instructional material developer. ChatGPT can also support teachers in various aspects, such as preparing teaching materials (Jeon et al., 2023) and grading students' writing (Mizumoto & Eguchi, 2023). Therefore, this section will explore the advantages Generative AI offers in foreign language education, specifically examining its role as a machine translation tool, its potential as a writing tutor, and its capacity to enhance formative assessment in writing. We will analyze how the development of AI-driven translation tools impacts L2 education, how recent AI tutoring systems improve L2 students' writing proficiency, and how AI tools facilitate the delivery of effective formative feedback in L2 learning contexts. This discussion highlights the transformative capabilities of Generative AI in personalizing and optimizing foreign language instruction.

1.1. AI Translation Tools for Enhanced Writing Proficiency

Recently, Generative AI tools, particularly neural machine translation (NMT), have brought more transformative changes to the development of all language skills (speaking, reading, listening, and writing), primarily by fostering personalized learning experiences. NMT surpasses earlier translation tools by offering several distinctive advantages in foreign language education. Unlike statistical or rule-based systems, which often produce fragmented and rigid translations, NMT employs deep learning to generate more fluent and contextually accurate outputs (Bahdanau et al., 2015). Instead of translating word by word, it processes entire sentences or even paragraphs holistically, ensuring better grammatical and semantic coherence (Wu et al., 2016).

One of the most significant contributions of NMT tools, such as Google Translate (GT) and DeepL Translator, is their ability to personalize the learning process. For instance, when learners use these tools to develop their writing skills, they receive immediate translations and corrections that help them understand complex linguistic structures. Studies show that learners using Google Translate for foreign language writing tasks can see direct improvements in their written work, from paragraph-level construction to full-text translations (Chen, 2020). This immediate feedback allows students to identify their mistakes in specific areas (e.g., syntax, grammar, vocabulary), facilitating a more targeted approach to improvement (Chung & Ahn, 2021; Tsai, 2020), which is important for personalized learning. When learners use NMT outputs as a reference point for revising their work, personalized learning is further amplified, encouraging users to critically reflect on and evaluate their language use (Klímová et al.,2022; Lee, 2020).

DeepL Translator has emerged as a particularly effective tool for advancing personalized learning. In an experimental study, students were asked to summarize texts first in their native language, then in English without assistance, and finally using DeepL. This process enabled learners to compare their self-produced summaries with those generated by the tool, providing a clear and immediate way to identify their errors and weak points. Such a task structure allowed each learner to focus on specific areas where they needed improvement, whether it was expanding their vocabulary, improving grammatical accuracy, or structuring their ideas more coherently (Polakova & Klimova, 2023). The iterative nature of these tasks also supported the gradual development of writing skills, with learners gaining confidence in their ability to produce higher-quality work over time.

Moreover, these tools empower learners to engage with content at their own pace, a cornerstone of personalized learning. The United States National Education Technology Plan also emphasizes adjusting the learning pacing in personalized learning to optimize each learner's needs (U.S. Department of Education, 2017). Research shows that when students use tools like DeepL or GT, they improve their language proficiency and become more adept at identifying areas for improvement in their writing, such as correctly using articles or avoiding common lexical errors (O'Neill, 2019; Tsai, 2020). Identifying areas for improvement provides valuable insights into how the learning pacing should be adjusted. This reflective process, the principle of personalized learning, highlights specific language patterns, helping learners notice and correct mistakes.

However, several concerns regarding students' use of machine translation (MT) have been acknowledged, including doubts about output accuracy (Lee, 2022), feelings of guilt associated with MT use (Xu, 2021), and anxiety due to the lack of clear guidelines (Vinall & Hellmich, 2021). Language instructors consider presenting MT-generated texts as original work unethical (Groves & Mundt, 2021), and there is widespread concern that students may become overly dependent on MT, using it indiscriminately, which could hinder language learning (O'Neill, 2019). A key issue in improving students' writing is how they handle MT-generated content, as low-proficiency students are more likely to accept outputs without critically selecting better alternatives (Chung & Ahn, 2021). Additionally, researchers warn of the potential risk that MT use may diminish students' motivation to learn and engage with languages meaningfully (Urlaub & Dessein, 2022). Educators should be aware of these drawbacks of using MT in foreign language education and be proactive about the detrimental effects of MT use.

1.2. AI Tutor and Teaching Assistant for Writing Proficiency

The potential of AI tools is to become tutors and teaching assistants, which can offer guided instruction and scaffolding, major elements of personalized learning, in students' writing development process. Guided instruction and scaffolding help tailor educational experiences to meet individual students' needs (Cevikbas & Kaiser, 2022; Zuo et al., 2023). It aligns well with personalized learning principles. Through purposeful prompting, AI-enabled chatbots can act as a more knowledgeable other (John-Steiner & Mahn, 1996) that can provide comprehensible input (Krashen, 1982) to guide students along different stages of the writing process. Imran and Almusharraf

(2023) reviewed 30 articles examining the use of ChatGPT as a writing assistant and concluded that it can scaffold learners in generating drafts, brainstorming ideas, and summarizing research articles. It is especially effective for less motivated and shy students who are resistant to seek help because the automation of feedback delivery would offer foreign language writers a safe environment for experimental learning (Üstünbaş, 2024) and motivate them to engage in L2 writing practice more frequently, which improved students' writing output by suggesting effective wording and detecting logical inconsistencies (Kasneci et al., 2023).

Ljujić et al. (2023) also found the ChatGPT function of teaching assistance while comparing ChatGPT written essays with highly ranked students' essays. In another study, Kasneci et al. (2023) conducted a scoping review of the literature on the benefits of AI for writing instruction and reported that it can help train students on mundane writing processes. These findings underscore the transformative potential of AI tools in enhancing writing instruction and fostering personalized learning environments.

Despite the numerous advantages of AI tools, researchers have identified concerning side effects associated with the regular use of AI tools in writing. Studies indicate that overreliance on machine learning systems like ChatGPT is linked to diminished student motivation and commitment to learning (Krullaars et al., 2023), decreased cognitive abilities, reduced memory retention (Dergaa et al., 2023; Marzuki et al., 2023), and an increase in metacognitive laziness (Risko & Gilbert, 2016). Metacognitive laziness, driven by cognitive offloading, negatively impacts students' self-regulation and engagement in learning. Cognitive offloading occurs when learners depend on external tools, such as AI, to perform cognitive tasks, thereby reducing their active participation in metacognitive processes and leading to a habitual decline in internal cognitive monitoring and self-regulation. While cognitive offloading can help manage cognitive load, excessive reliance on AI may weaken students' ability to engage with learning materials independently over time (Risko & Gilbert, 2016).

Similarly, Krullaars et al. (2023) warn that over-reliance on AI tools can diminish students' motivation and engagement, as they may prioritize obtaining quick answers over meaningful learning. To address this issue, researchers advocate for a paradigm shift in writing curricula—from outcome-oriented to process-oriented approaches. Godwin-Jones (2022) emphasizes the need to reestablish instructional goals and desired outcomes through situated practice while critically conceptualizing the integration and advocacy of AI-enabled tools. This reexamination of educational objectives in writing should differentiate between contexts, such as writing for placement or summative assessment, versus process-oriented learning. Each context requires tailored objectives, and understanding how AI-enabled tools can support these varied goals remains a critical research area. Additionally, educators are encouraged to explore how AI can dynamically analyze and adapt teaching strategies in real-time based on monitoring individual learners' characteristics, performance, and personal development (Peng et al., 2019).

1.3. AI as a Formative Feedback Tool

Writing in a second language presents significant challenges for both students and instructors. In particular, teacher-provided feedback is crucial in enhancing L2 writing; however, delivering effective feedback requires substantial time and effort, especially when delivering the content to students with varying proficiency levels. Additionally, providing individualized support is often difficult due to constraints such as large class sizes, limited instructional time, and teacher shortages (Ferris & Hedgcock, 2014; Lee, 2020). Consequently, opportunities for students to engage in meaningful L2 writing practice may be restricted, limiting their skill development (Tsai, 2022).

Many educators have turned to AI tools as a solution for providing comprehensive and personalized feedback. The emergence of AI-powered writing tools, such as Grammarly, QuillBot, Copy.ai, WordTune, and ChatGPT, has expanded opportunities for skill development by offering students alternative avenues for receiving writing feedback (Marzuki et al., 2023; Zhao, 2022). Among these technologies, ChatGPT has been widely recognized for its capacity to generate formative assessments tailored to individual learners (Kohnke et al., 2023). In particular, the immediacy of feedback, a critical element of formative assessment, is made possible with ChatGPT, which provides instant and constructive feedback. This immediacy allows students to refine their writing skills through reflection and continuous improvement. Timely and precise feedback enhances student comprehension and motivation, reinforcing active engagement with learning materials (Crook et al., 2012).

Automated writing evaluation (AWE) tools such as Grammarly and Pigai have long supported students and educators by offering corrective feedback on written work. While traditional spelling and grammar checkers have been useful for identifying and rectifying errors, the advancement of Generative pre-trained transformers (GPT) and large language models (LLMs), such as ChatGPT-4 and PaLM 2, has introduced a new dimension to AWE capabilities. Advanced AI-driven technologies allow both learners and educators to track writing progress more effectively, offering insights into students' developmental trajectories (Hawanti & Zubaydulloevna, 2023). The rapid integration of AI into foreign language education is progressing at an accelerated rate, partly due to students' positive reception of ChatGPT-generated feedback. For instance, Üstünbaş (2024) conducted semi-structured interviews with five Turkish university students learning English writing and found that they perceived ChatGPT's corrective feedback as both beneficial and accessible. These findings highlight the potential of Generative AI to enhance language learning by offering timely and individualized support.

Beyond individualized feedback, the effectiveness of ChatGPT in providing formative feedback can be analyzed through theoretical frameworks, such as the dialogic feedback process proposed by Winstone and Carless (2020). This framework posits that interactive feedback fosters deeper understanding, enabling students to clarify expectations, seek guidance, and make meaningful progress. ChatGPT promotes this dialogic process by responding to student queries about various writing aspects, offering suggestions, and serving as an on-demand support tool. In this sense, ChatGPT functions as a reliable, always-available tutor, providing students with immediate and customized writing support throughout different stages of the writing process (Barrot, 2023). In addition to benefiting students, AI technologies have also contributed to the assessment practices of ESL/EFL instructors. Wang et al. (2024) found that ChatGPT generated more comprehensive feedback than human instructors, covering aspects of content, organization, and language. This suggests that AI could alleviate some of the workload associated with providing extensive writing feedback. Given these findings, an optimal approach would involve integrating AI tools with human expertise to ensure more balanced and effective feedback mechanisms in ESL/EFL writing instruction.

Despite the advantages of AI-assisted feedback, researchers have cautioned against its potential unintended consequences. One key concern is the presence of algorithmic bias, which may result in differential impacts on students from various backgrounds. AI-generated feedback, influenced by both statistical and societal biases, has the potential to either advantage or disadvantage certain social groups (Mitchell et al., 2021). Even when statistical bias is minimized, societal biases embedded in training data can persist, leading to unintended disparities in feedback quality. Consequently, educators should critically evaluate AI-generated responses and educate students on the potential biases inherent in AI-driven feedback systems. By fostering critical AI literacy, instructors can help students make more informed use of these technologies while mitigating risks associated with biased feedback.

FINDING A CREATIVE BEAT WITH AI WITHOUT LOSING ONE'S OWN DRUM

In discussions about the goals of education, creativity is often invoked. It appears in two primary forms: as applied creativity—typically framed as innovative problem solving—and as a more artistic ideal rooted in liberal education, which emphasizes the capacity to imagine new visions, stories, and concepts.

Before platforms like ChatGPT, DALL-E, and Midjourney emerged, this second kind of creativity was seen as one of the least automatable skills. In this domain, human ingenuity was believed to be safe from the encroachments of algorithmic AI, which was expected to disrupt repetitive, rule-based tasks. However, as Mollick (2024) notes, the rise of transformer-based AI systems upended these assumptions: "It is the jobs with the most creative tasks, rather than the most repetitive, that tend to be most impacted by the new wave of AI" (p. 97), leading to reactions like Maciejewska (2023)'s now-viral social media plea: "I want AI to do my laundry and dishes so that I can do art and writing, not for AI to do my art and writing so that I can do my laundry and dishes."

Mollick (2024) suggests that much of the discomfort surrounding AI's creative capabilities stems from a misunderstanding of creativity by those who see it as synonymous with novelty. However, Mollick argues that creativity can sometimes be better understood as recombination, where disparate ideas combine to make something new that is valued for its usefulness rather than its originality. He explains that such "breakthroughs happen when people connect distant, seemingly unrelated ideas" (p. 100), such as the Wright brothers combining their understanding of bicycle mechanics with observations of birds to solve the problem of powered flight (p. 100). By this logic, large language models (LLMs) like ChatGPT are inherently creative. They function as "connection machines" (p. 100), generating relationships between tokens that may appear unrelated to a human but are significant to the AI.

Mollick's (2024) observations primarily pertain to the problem-solving type of creativity. For instance, his colleagues at Wharton held a contest in which student teams pitched product ideas for college students. These student teams competed against ChatGPT 4.0, which also generated ideas for the challenge. The results were striking: "The students lost, and it wasn't even close . . . [Of] the 40 best ideas rated by judges, 35 came from ChatGPT" (p. 104). The AI-generated ideas were more likely to be deemed practical, innovative, and worthy of investment. Despite this success, Mollick also acknowledges important limitations. Without careful prompting, the AI tends to generate ideas that feel "same-y." This tendency likely arises from frequently repeating certain concepts in the training data. As a result, "As creative as the AI can be," Mollick notes, "most of its ideas will be mediocre" (p. 105). It is in recognizing that mediocrity can make humans shine.

When moving from business application to creative writing, a similar dynamic appears in the research of Doshi and Hauser (2024), who explored how using AI to help generate ideas for short stories affected perceptions of creativity. In their study, 293 participants wrote eight-sentence stories for a young adult audience, with genres and styles left to the writers' discretion. The participants were divided into three groups: one had no access to AI, another could request one AI-generated idea, and the third could request up to five AI-generated ideas. Among those with access to AI, 88.4% incorporated at least one AI-generated suggestion into their stories.

The researchers then asked 600 evaluators to assess these stories for creativity, using two metrics: novelty (originality) and usefulness (fit for the intended audience). Across the board, stories written with AI assistance scored higher in both dimensions, with those with access to up to five AI-generated ideas receiving the highest ratings. However, a drawback emerged: when the researchers evaluated the entire body of stories created, the stories written with AI assistance were significantly more similar to each other than those written by participants who worked without AI. This finding suggests that while AI can enhance individual creative outputs, overreliance on its suggestions risks homogenizing the results. The mediocrity can overwhelm.

The challenge, then, lies in leveraging AI's strengths—its ability to generate ideas and connect disparate concepts—without succumbing to its tendency to reinforce patterns. Researchers like Medeiros et al. (2024) suggest co-creativity to address this challenge. In this approach, humans collaborate with AI to refine ideas, introducing originality and critical engagement to counteract the risks of repetition. As Medeiros and colleagues note, "Low-quality AI assistance may, in fact, hinder human creativity [,] which highlights the importance of ensuring that AI-generated prompts" and the pedagogy surrounding them "are of high quality" (p. 18).

One way to foster this co-creative relationship is using story beats, which are broadly defined as the key plot points of a story, encompassing major actions, reactions, and moments of emotional growth. While the term is widely understood in many creative writing areas, especially screenwriting, it is rarely explicitly defined. Acosta (2023) uses the term "beat writing" to describe his process of mapping out a screenplay, a process of structuring by working through each of the beats in the narrative as an outline. He notes that this approach allows him to explore possibilities for each beat without "sacrificing [his] story or limiting [his] creativity" (p. 34). Importantly for this discussion, beat writing can also function as a collaborative tool, as Acosta illustrates through his experience co-writing a script: "We worked together to create a solid beat sheet, balancing originality with a useful understanding of the plot" (p. 22).

This approach to beat writing—structured, generative, and collaborative—makes it particularly well-suited for teaching creative writing with AI. By framing prompts around story beats, educators can help students engage critically with AI while maintaining their creative agency. For example, in a course one of the authors offered in comic book writing, students wrote scripts as their final project. These novice comic writers often struggled with structuring their stories. Previously, the author addressed this issue through one-on-one meetings to develop beat sheets. In the spring of 2024, however, the author introduced Generative AI as a collaborative tool using the following prompt:

For this exercise, you are an expert story coach who knows about American comic book scripts. I am working on a 20-page comic book script and want to develop my story beats using the three-act structure. I would like your help in breaking down the major story beats for each act and refining them. Let us have a Socratic-style discussion where you ask me questions to clarify my ideas, offer suggestions, and help me expand on each beat. Never start writing the script for me; instead, use questions to guide me to key ideas. Please keep the pacing of a 20-page comic script in mind, with the first act typically concluded by the sixth page, the second act extending to about page 14, and the comic concluding on page 20, while being open to adjustments based on the story's needs. Help me ensure that the beats balance action, dialogue, and visuals. Challenge me to think about how each beat connects to the story's overall theme and emotional resonance. Be willing to encourage me to be more creative, push for originality, and help me avoid overused tropes. Lastly, be iterative and willing to revisit beats that need further development.

This prompt encouraged students to engage critically and iteratively with AI, using it as a partner in the creative process rather than a replacement for their own ideas. After reviewing their AI sessions and discussing them in conferences, the author found that students were more satisfied with their scripts and more attuned to the nuances of storytelling. While anecdotal, the results that semester were promising: scripts felt more original, structurally sound, and aligned with the conventions of the genre than previous versions of the course.

By incorporating AI into frameworks like beat writing and fostering a critical, collaborative, and co-creative approach, educators can help students harness the creative potential of AI without losing their own perspective. In doing so, we can guide our students to find their creative beat with AI while ensuring they never lose the rhythm of their own drum.

SLOWING DOWN RHETORIC WHILE IMPROVING CRITICAL THINKING WITH AI

Public discourse often prioritizes speed over depth in a world increasingly shaped by artificial intelligence and algorithmic speed. Social media algorithms amplify polarizing arguments because they engender the most engagement, often fed by

Generative AI tools that churn out arguments in seconds. The resulting rhetorical dynamic fits what Kroll (2018) refers to as fast rhetoric, an approach "designed to settle disagreements quickly and efficiently" (p. 240) above all else, creating an adversarial model of argumentation. It may be helpful to imagine a debate model, in which two sides challenge each other with only one side able to 'win'. This model seeps into how many of our students imagine the idea of argumentation, illustrated by social media pundits shouting over each other and speaking as quickly as possible. However, while this emphasis on speed may fit the conditions our students encounter in real life, it often sacrifices the deliberation and empathy necessary for meaningful communication and compromise in the complex, fragmented reality of decision making.

One promising antidote to this is Kroll's counterargument for slow rhetoric, which "prioritizes thoughtful consideration of alternatives before moving to a conclusion or recommendation" (p. 242), a strategy in which rhetoricians don't immediately move to shut down arguments but array the possibilities at hand. At first, it may seem like a conflict to suggest that AI may help engender a slower, more considerate rhetorical framework when AI is often pitched in terms of increased efficiency, but through the deliberate application of a strategy called persona prompting, that may be possible. Persona prompting uses Generative AI to simulate diverse perspectives before it responds. By asking AI to adopt specific personas—such as a scientist, policymaker, or business executive—novice writers wanted to thoughtfully consider alternative perspectives can explore assumptions, counterarguments, and rhetorical strategies from multiple subjectivities. Used well, persona prompting can bridge the speed of AI and the depth of slow rhetoric, encouraging a more reflective, deliberate approach to argumentation. When combined with an applied analytic approach using Stephen Toulmin's model of argumentation, it provides a structured yet flexible framework for fostering critical thinking and ethical communication.

Toulmin's model dissects arguments into six components: claim, grounds, warrant, backing, qualifier, and rebuttal. The claim is supported by grounds (evidence), while warrants link the two, relying on shared assumptions. Backing reinforces warrants, qualifiers signal argument strength, and rebuttals address counterarguments (Karbach, 1987). These components do more than create logical structures. Recognizing them and their application encourages a reflective process that slows down the rhetor, asking them to consider the organization of the argument and the interaction between the parts. By compelling writers to consider not just what they are arguing but how and why, the model inherently promotes the kind of deliberate, empathetic argumentation that Kroll believes is the main benefit of slow rhetoric.

Persona prompting, with its ability to simulate diverse perspectives, can be used to bring the time-tested strengths of Toulmin's model into the AI era. The use of persona prompting, in which an imaginary subjectivity for the AI is created using ideological, demographic, and contextual information, can combine productively with Toulmin's framework and help students explore how arguments shift and develop to reflect those different perspectives.

Consider a classroom exercise on climate policy. Students might prompt AI to simulate the personas of a climate scientist, a policymaker, and a business executive, defining each aspect of the personas in question to more deliberately understand the background and goals of each rhetorical position. Each persona introduces distinct warrants and grounds: the scientist emphasizes ecological data, the policymaker weighs societal impact, and the executive considers economic feasibility. These variations help students uncover implicit assumptions and refine their arguments to address diverse viewpoints.

While persona prompting adds depth to Toulmin's analysis, slow rhetoric provides a broader philosophical framework. Slow rhetoric, as Kroll (2018) describes it, prioritizes deliberation, reflection, and empathy. It challenges the "win-or-lose push to decide or convince" (p. 240) that characterizes fast rhetoric's debate-like paradigm and instead it emphasizes sustained engagement, encouraging writers to consider alternatives and address complexity, to consider arguments from multiple perspectives. Toulmin's qualifiers and rebuttals are natural allies in this effort to consider these alternatives. Considering how qualifiers limit the way that arguments are structured and recognizing how rebuttals require anticipating and addressing counterarguments push students to move beyond adversarial approaches, fostering a rhetorical style rooted in empathy and reflection, especially when they are working through personas they have designed and guided the AI to assume. The rhetorical dynamic shifts from winning to losing and instead becomes a way to perceive the possibilities open to each rhetorical situation to each rhetor they have created.

Because of this interaction between imagining a rhetor and analyzing an argument, one of the most compelling benefits of using persona prompting is its potential to develop what psychology refers to as Theory of Mind (ToM)—the ability to understand other's mental states. Pathee and Williamson (2014) argue that ToM is crucial for first-year composition, enabling students to address "seemingly 'false' beliefs that arise from differences in social, cultural, political, and economic backgrounds" (p. 96). Toulmin analysis, mainly focusing on warrants and rebuttals across multiple personas and their arguments, provides a practical platform for fostering this skill while pushing students away from the too-quick assumptions of fast rhetoric.

Using persona prompts, students can practice adopting different perspectives and identifying where their assumptions clash with those of their audience. For example, a student writing about renewable energy might realize their argument assumes universal trust in scientific data. By engaging with personas prioritizing economic or cultural concerns, they refine their warrants to better connect with those audiences. This process not only improves rhetorical effectiveness by slowing down the writer's assumptions but also cultivates empathy and cultural awareness.

Integrating Toulmin analysis, slow rhetoric, and persona prompting offers a rich framework for classroom practice. One example exercise begins with students constructing an argument on a subject they are passionate about and then analyzing their own argument using the Toulmin components. With this understanding of their own argument in place, they can work with Generative AI to develop different personas that may disagree with their position and then ask the AI to generate arguments that conflict with theirs from the perspective of those personas. For each argument generated, the students then analyze how the grounds, warrants, and rebuttals differ, pushing them into the slow rhetorical stance of considering these different perspectives.

This iterative process encourages critical thinking and reflection, aligning with Kroll's (2018) assertion that "it's not sufficient... to teach students slower forms of argumentation as alternatives to fast rhetoric: they also need to acquire habits of mind that foster the values of slow living" (p. 249). Applying Toulmin's model, enriched by slow rhetoric and persona prompting, equips students to construct nuanced, empathetic arguments. It bridges the gap between AI-driven speed and human-centered deliberation, offering a framework for argumentation that values complexity, reflection, and connection. In the classroom, these practices may do more than teach students how to argue—they may teach them how to think critically and communicate ethically. In a world drowning in the consequences of fast rhetoric, that kind of deliberation might be a very vital skill.

AI AND UNIVERSAL DESIGN FOR LEARNING

AI analyzes large amounts of data, identifies patterns, and tailors learning to individual students, enabling personalized learning that continuously adjusts based on performance, preferences, and needs (Kasneci et al., 2023; Katiyar et al., 2024). These tools are particularly valuable for diverse learners as some students may require more time to master certain concepts, while others might need content presented in a different format (McMahon & Firestone, 2024). AI can accommodate these needs by adjusting the pace of instruction, providing alternative explanations, and offering additional practice opportunities tailored to each student's needs (Katiyar et al., 2024).

AI and UDL Principles

The UDL framework encourages educators to create inclusive learning environments that address the diverse needs of all students. AI can strengthen UDL core components, which include multiple means of engagement, representation, and expression (CAST, 2018; Meyer et al., 2014).

1. **Multiple Means of Engagement:** AI can personalize content delivery to keep students engaged. For example, AI can analyze student's engagement levels and suggest different activities or content formats (videos, interactive simulations, games) that are more likely to capture their interest. A student who is disengaged during traditional lectures might benefit from an AI-recommended interactive learning module (Saborio-Taylor & Rojas-Ramirez, 2024).
2. **Multiple Means of Representation:** AI can support diverse learners by suggesting ways to present information in various formats. For instance, text-to-speech technology, which is often AI-driven, allows students with visual impairments or reading difficulties to access written content through audible versions (Saborio-Taylor & Rojas-Ramirez, 2024). Similarly, AI can translate text into multiple languages or simplify complex language, making content more accessible to English language learners and students with disabilities or those who need additional support (McMahon & Firestone, 2024; Saborio-Taylor & Rojas-Ramirez, 2024).
3. **Multiple Means of Expression:** AI empowers students to demonstrate knowledge in ways that align with their strengths, such as students with speech impairments might use AI-powered speech-to-text tools to participate in discussions or complete assignments (Saborio-Taylor & Rojas-Ramirez, 2024). AI can also offer alternative assessment like visual storytelling or interactive quizzes, allowing students to express understanding in a way that suits them best.

AI-Powered Assistive Technologies

AI-powered assistive technologies change how students access education by enhancing communication, learning, and assessment. For students with communication challenges, such as speech or language difficulties, tools like the app *Vocable* (n.d.) help non-verbal students with physical limitations communicate by predicting and suggesting words or phrases based on context, capturing head nods to select responses.

In learning, AI tools like *WolframAlpha* (n.d.) support students across subjects by offering step-by-step solutions and simplifying complex topics with clear, structured explanations (McMahon & Firestone, 2024). Similarly, the web-based tool

Read&Write integrates AI-powered features like text-to-speech, speech-to-text, and content simplification to increase engagement and improve outcomes by presenting information in multiple formats and allowing students to choose how they demonstrate knowledge (Dawson et al., 2018; Texthelp, 2024).

AI can also strengthen assessment by offering formats aligned with individual abilities, such as oral or video-response options for students with expression difficulties, or screen reader-compatible assessments for visually impaired students (Hyatt & Owens, 2024; Swiecki et al., 2022). These tools provide equitable opportunities for all students to demonstrate their knowledge.

Emerging Trends in AI and UDL Integration

One emerging trend in education is the use of AI to create engaging and interactive learning experiences. Virtual and augmented reality, powered by AI, such as zSpace (n.d.), offer immersive environments where students can explore academic concepts in a hands-on manner. These simulations make learning more accessible for students with varying learning approaches and needs by allowing them to interact with and manipulate objects in a way that might be difficult or impossible in a physical classroom (Carreon et al., 2022). AI-driven virtual and augmented reality tools align well with the UDL framework, offering diverse means of engagement, representation, and expression.

Challenges in AI Adoption for UDL

While there are many ways AI can help further the goals of UDL, there are several that must be addressed for this to take place effectively:

1. Many educators are not adequately trained in AI applications (Pujeda, 2023). This deficiency can lead to educators being hesitant to use tools or the wrong application.
2. AI systems can inadvertently support current biases ingrained in their training data, resulting in unfair outcomes (Baker & Hawn, 2021). For example, if an AI tool is trained on non-representative data, inequities in the education system could continue.

Long-Term Impacts of AI and UDL

AI has the potential to make education more accessible to student through a customized learning experience that meets their individual needs, abilities, and interests. As AI continues to evolve, it can lead to a more inclusive educational setting where all students, regardless of their abilities or backgrounds, have equal access to high-quality education. Moreover, AI can positively impact educational inequities. By providing personalized learning support, AI can help teachers close achievement gaps, particularly for students who have historically been underserved by traditional educational models. AI's ability to offer real-time feedback and data-driven insights can also lead to more effective and timely interventions, ensuring that students receive the help they need. This proactive approach to education could significantly improve student outcomes.

AI AND IEPS: REVOLUTIONIZING INDIVIDUALIZED EDUCATION PROGRAMS

AI shows great promise in impacting Individualized Education Programs (IEPs; Rakap & Balikci, 2024). Mandated by the Individuals with Disabilities Education Act (IDEA), IEPs provide individualized plans for students with disabilities, but are time-intensive and complex, placing significant burdens on educators (IDEA, 2004; Mosher et al., 2024). AI can streamline this process by automating data collection and analysis, reducing errors, and enabling real-time progress tracking and adjustments, making IEPs more efficient and effective (Woolverton & Pollastri, 2021; Yuan & Barnett, 2024).

Using AI to Enhance PLAAPF Statements in IEPs

Present Levels of Academic Achievement and Functional Performance (PLAAFP) statements guide the IEP team to set appropriate measurable and achievable goals tailored to the student's needs. PLAAFP statements include a synthesis of data from standardized tests and classroom assessments to provide insights into a student's strengths and needs (Johnston et al., 2024; Yuan & Barnett, 2024). By synthesizing data from multiple sources, AI ensures that PLAAFP statements are accurate and comprehensive, reducing human error and allowing educators to create IEPs that better reflect a student's abilities (Rakap & Balikci, 2024; Yuan & Barnett, 2024). This approach creates a stronger foundation for meaningful IEP goals (Mosher et al., 2024).

AI-Assisted SMART Goals in IEPs

SMART (Specific, Measurable, Achievable, Relevant, and Time-bound) goals provide clear, actionable objectives that guide the student's educational progress and inform instruction. AI can enhance SMART goals by analyzing a student's current performance and generating individualized goals that align with their specific abilities and needs (Rakap & Balikci, 2024). Through data-driven analysis from multiple sources, AI can help teachers create goals that are not only specific and measurable but also realistically achievable within a set timeframe and based on appropriate standards (Johnston et al., 2024; Yuan & Barnett, 2024). This approach enables educators to create precise and responsive goals for each student (Mosher et al., 2024). By streamlining this process, educators can focus on meaningful interventions and support for students with disabilities.

Specially Designed Instruction (SDI) and AI

SDI, mandated by IDEA, tailors content, methods, and delivery to meet the unique needs of students with disabilities and support progress toward their individualized goals (Benninghof, 2020; IDEA, 2004). Effective SDI involves strategies such as breaking complex skills into manageable steps, scaffolding instruction with temporary supports, and building on prior knowledge through explicit modeling and guided practice. AI enhances SDI by analyzing real-time data to recommend precise instructional adjustments, such as task prioritization, visual supports, and specific feedback tailored to students' progress. For example, AI can help educators sequence tasks from simple to complex or provide diagnostic insights to guide meaningful practice. By integrating AI, teachers can deliver adaptive, data-driven instruction that aligns with IEP goals, create equitable learning opportunities, and, ultimately, improve student learning outcomes (Benninghof, 2020).

Improving Transparency and Understanding in the IEP process

Collaboration is integral to the IEP process, requiring input from educators, parents/guardians, students and other related stakeholders. AI-driven tools strengthen this collaboration by providing real-time updates and generating data-driven reports for stakeholders (Johnston et al., 2024). For example, an AI-driven platform can send progress reports to parents, highlighting achievements and areas for growth, thus fostering active involvement and stronger educator-parent partnerships (Johnston et al., 2024)

AI also promotes a more inclusive IEP process by giving students a voice in their education. Through interactive surveys or digital journals, students can share information such as their transition goals and preferences, ensuring IEP reflects their strengths, interests, and aspirations (Rakap, 2024). Also, AI tools simplify the IEP process for parents and students by presenting progress through clear visualizations, such as graphed data with clearly indicated timelines (Massey et al., 2024), helping all stakeholders understand performance relative to goals (Johnston et al., 2021). This transparency builds trust and ensures that the IEP process is a team effort.

Timeliness in Data-Driven Adjustments and Interventions

AI-powered predictive analytics can analyze vast datasets, including academic performance, attendance, and behavior, to identify early warning signs of learning difficulties (Woolverton & Pollastri, 2021). For example, AI might detect patterns like consistent struggles with reading comprehension or disengagement during class, flagging these isSues for educators to address early and prevent further setbacks.

Once difficulties are identified, AI can provide tailored recommendations, Such as additional practice problems, tutoring, or alternative teaching strategies. This proactive approach helps educators address challenges quickly, improving student outcomes and eliminating learning barriers.

Ethical Considerations in Predictive Analytics

While predictive analytics offers many benefits, it also raises ethical concerns. AI systems may misinterpret data, leading to false positives or negatives in identifying learning difficulties. To address this risk, combining AI insights with human judgment, and training educators to use AI effectively is essential (Khreisat et al., 2024).

Data privacy in special education is another critical isSue, as predictive analytics relies on large datasets (Khreisat et al., 2024). Teachers must fully anonymize data and schools must implement strong data protection meaSures to safeguard students' information and respect privacy rights. Transparency in how AI makes predictions is vital for building trust among educators, parents, and students.

AI Integration in IEPs

Through the development of IEPs, AI is making the typically lengthy process more efficient. Teachers can create PLAAFP statements and SMART goals as well as customized student accommodations with the help of AI-powered tools designed to meet individual student needs. Through data analysis, automation, and personalized recommendations, AI decreases teacher workload, allowing them to devote more time to direct student engagement. It is essential that AI functions as a collaborative aid that improves teachers' professional expertise while avoiding any substitution for their professional judgement.

Challenges and Considerations

While AI can strengthen the IEP process, challenges remain. Educators need training to effectively use these tools. Cost can be prohibitive for some schools, requiring policymakers to prioritize funding. Ethical concerns, including privacy, data security, and bias, require safeguards and audits to ensure trust and equity.

Strategies for Addressing Challenges

Potential strategies to overcome challenges:

1. Provide training on effective and ethical AI use.
2. Advocate for funding to ensure equitable AI access.
3. Set clear guidelines for privacy, security, and bias audits.
4. Ensure appropriate stakeholders review AI recommendations.

Future Directions

AI's long-term impact on special education could be profound, enabling more accurate assessments, personalized learning, and timely interventions to close achievement gaps and promote equity. Achieving this potential requires collaboration among educators, administrators, and policymakers, along with investments in technology, training, and ethical standards to ensure AI tools are accessible and effective for all students.

MAKING CONTENT MEANINGFUL AND RELEVANT WITH AI

AI can enhance the relevance and meaning of educational content by tailoring it to students' unique backgrounds, strengths, and learning needs (Roll & Wylie, 2026). For instance, personalized learning systems and AI tools can provide instruction for mixed-ability and diverse classrooms. AI can help customize information texts by adjusting language complexity, incorporating culturally relevant examples, and connecting topics that resonate with students' experiences. In science labs, AI can generate personalized experiments that align with students' interests and prior knowledge, making abstract concepts more tangible and engaging. Similarly, AI can adapt mathematics story problems to reflect real-life scenarios students encounter, such as financial literacy or environmental issues. Using AI to generate real-world applications of concepts provides students with opportunities to see the practical implications of their learning while also increasing student engagement. Furthermore, AI can scaffold lessons that promote AI-assisted human-centric reasoning and knowledge development (Relmasira et al., 2023). This section explores practical ways AI tools can be used to enhance learners' experiences, demonstrating the potential of AI to support student engagement and enhance content application.

Tailoring Learning Content to Meet Diverse Needs

Effective learning experiences prioritize the alignment of learning objectives and content with students' interests, cultural contexts, and prior knowledge. Research underscores that when instructional materials are designed to reflect students' individual backgrounds and experiences, learners are more likely to perceive the relevance of their studies, increasing their motivation and engagement (Gay, 2018). This alignment not only enhances comprehension but also fosters a sense of belonging and validation in the classroom. Students who see themselves reflected in their learning environments are more likely to take ownership of their educational journeys, becoming active participants in the learning process (Tomlinson, 2014).

AI tools can tailor learning experiences to meet diverse needs and customize instructional materials. AI platforms like Diffit can be used by educators to adjust the complexity of informational texts, ensuring accessibility for students with varying reading abilities. For example, an educator can input text from an article, website, or video into Diffit and generate content tailored to specific reading levels in multiple languages. Beyond mere simplification, the platform aligns the customized text with state grade-level standards, ensuring academic rigor. Educators can further scaffold the content by modifying the text length, adding visuals or diagrams, and incorporating key vocabulary with definitions and images, thus catering to students' differentiated learning needs.

Moreover, Diffit and similar AI tools can support deeper comprehension by creating student-ready resources, such as graphic organizers, note-taking guides, and summaries with key takeaways. These features scaffold the reading process and equip students with strategies for understanding and synthesizing information. By adjusting vocabulary and sentence structure, AI enables students to access complex concepts without compromising the depth of learning objectives. This adaptive approach empowers teachers to scaffold learning effectively, offering personalized support that fosters student confidence and mastery.

Cultural Relevance and Inclusion

In addition to linguistic and general differentiation modifications, AI can enhance cultural relevance by embedding contextually meaningful examples into lessons. Tools like MagicSchool.ai exemplify how AI can be used to recommend culturally relevant scenarios based on student's interests. For instance, MagicSchool.ai has a "Make it Relevant!" tool that generates ideas on ways to make content being taught relevant to students' interests and backgrounds. Educators can identify a grade level, a topic or standard they are teaching, and describe their students' interests. The AI output suggests ideas for classroom activities or projects that incorporate relevant interests. By integrating relevant examples that reflect students' lived experiences, AI-enhanced lessons can create a more inclusive and engaging learning environment (Eguchi et al., 2021). For instance, when teaching a lesson on ecosystems, AI can tailor the curriculum to include examples of flora and fauna from a student's local environment, making abstract concepts more tangible and relatable. This alignment with students' lived experiences not only increases engagement but also highlights the connections between academic content and the world students inhabit.

Cultural relevance in education provides opportunities to validate students' identities and fosters a sense of belonging in the classroom (Gay, 2018). AI tools can assist educators in integrating culturally significant narratives, histories, or practices into lessons, thereby affirming the diverse backgrounds of their students. For example, a social studies lesson might explore migration patterns using stories from the students' communities, or a mathematics lesson might contextualize data analysis using statistics related to local environmental or economic issues. These examples demonstrate how culturally responsive AI-driven content can bridge the gap between students' in-school and out-of-school experiences, increasing their engagement and motivation to learn.

In the context of a second-grade classroom with a mathematics focus on addition and subtraction, educators can incorporate examples or stories that resonate with the diverse cultural identities of their students. Magicschool.ai has a "Math Story Word Problems" tool that can customize mathematics story word problems based on a grade level, mathematics standards, and story topic. For instance, if a local agricultural community has an upcoming Harvest Fair selling fruits and vegetables, example second-grade story word problems can be created to foster conversations about addition and subtraction while also encouraging students to share stories about their experiences with the Harvest Fair or related tasks that relate to their involvement in agriculture. In this example, culturally responsive teaching practices bridge gaps in understanding and engagement while creating an inclusive learning environment where learners can connect meaningfully with the context (Ladson-Billings, 1995, 2014).

Moreover, AI's ability to process large datasets enables it to recommend resources and instructional strategies that align with culturally responsive teaching practices. By personalizing content to reflect cultural nuances, educators can challenge biases and promote equity in the classroom. Research shows that when students see their cultures and experiences reflected in the curriculum, their academic performance, self-esteem, and interest in learning improve significantly (Ladson-Billings, 1995). Integrating AI tools into lesson planning offers educators a scalable way to deliver culturally relevant content while maintaining high academic standards. This innovation represents a critical step toward creating equitable, inclusive, and effective educational experiences for all learners.

Bridging School and Real-World Experiences with AI

Additionally, AI can be leveraged to connect academic content with real-world applications, making learning more meaningful and relevant. By generating personalized experiments and scenarios, AI can bridge the gap between abstract theory and practical application (Huang et al., 2023). For example, Magicschool.ai offers a "Real World Connections" tool that generates application examples associated with grade level and learning objectives. A student interested in environmental science might be provided a lab activity that simulates the effects of pollution on their local waterways, using data and scenarios drawn from their specific geographic context and prior knowledge. Such personalization enables learners to relate academic concepts directly to their lived experiences, fostering deeper engagement and understanding.

AI-driven tools can also provide opportunities to explore topics aligned with their student preferences and passions while creating learning experiences that are both academically rigorous and personally meaningful. For instance, an AI tool might design a physics experiment for a student who enjoys sports, exploring the principles of motion and energy by analyzing a soccer ball's trajectory. These connections between academic content and personal interests help students see the practical value of their learning, encouraging them to actively engage with challenging material. Research consistently demonstrates that when students perceive their studies as relevant to their lives, their motivation, persistence, and performance improve significantly (Ryan & Deci, 2020).

Additionally, AI tools can support project-based learning by simulating real-world problem-solving scenarios. For example, students could use AI to model the impact of urban planning decisions on traffic flow or the effects of renewable energy solutions on carbon emissions. These projects not only provide hands-on experience with real-world challenges but also promote the development of critical thinking, collaboration, and data literacy skills. Through these applications, AI helps students forge stronger connections between their in-school learning and out-of-school experiences, empowering them to see themselves as capable problem-solvers and active contributors to their communities.

CONSIDERING AI BEST PRACTICES FOR STUDENT ENGAGEMENT

With the increasing recognition of AI tools for enhancing efficiency and customizing outputs to meet students' learning needs, it is important for AI users also to consider best practices and ethical implications (Nguyen et al., 2013). The rapid advances in AI have made it easier to use specific tools that incorporate students' prior experiences, backgrounds, assets, and interests to tailor curriculum, activities, and assessments. These advancements, as discussed throughout this chapter, can foster meaningful and relevant connections, thereby increasing student interest and engagement (Wang et al., 2024). However, users of AI must maintain a critical perspective when reviewing AI-generated output and consider the ethical ramifications of AI use (Zimmerman, 2018). This section shares research and recommendations for best practices for navigating AI tools while prioritizing ethical considerations to safeguard vulnerable students from the potential risks associated with AI in educational platforms.

AI as a Starting Point

Recognizing that AI serves as a starting point, not a final solution, is crucial. This understanding underscores the importance of rigorous review, including checks for bias and accuracy. Algorithms for AI reflect the values of their developers, which alludes to biases being easily infiltrated into AI output (Hrastinski et al., 2019; Stahl & Wright, 2018). Even though there are different types of biases and ethical challenges with AI applications, it is important to recognize how bias and discrimination play a role. For instance, gender in AI-based platforms reveals how gender-specific language perpetuates societal biases and gender-specific stereotypes (Miller et al., 2018). Similarly, racial biases are also associated with problematic AI facial recognition systems (Murphy, 2019). Thus, there is a potential to have predictive output to perpetuate existing biases and prejudices of social discrimination (Akgun & Greenhow, 2022). Furthermore, efforts to personalize content, such as aligning a read-aloud or mathematics story word problem with students' cultural backgrounds, must be carefully examined to ensure that these connections do not perpetuate inaccuracies, reinforce stereotypes, or further marginalize certain groups.

To ensure the legitimacy of AI output, educators should be equipped with the skills to cross-check information against reliable and diverse sources. It might be necessary to involve cultural experts or advisors and domain specialists to review the output and validate the information. This validation can be especially important for topics that may be sensitive or in question to avoid perpetuating misinformation. It can also be helpful to analyze the contextual relevance of the AI output, with considerations for how the information aligns with the context of use, such as the classroom. Should AI output appear to generalize, extra critique is warranted to ensure information does not misrepresent groups.

To further mitigate these concerns, educators and developers can also adopt proactive strategies, such as implementing diverse and representative training data, regularly auditing AI systems for biased outputs, and promoting transparency in algorithmic decision-making. By fostering AI literacy among educators and their students, users can be empowered to critically evaluate AI-generated content, ensuring that it serves as a tool for enhancing equity rather than reinforcing systemic biases. Moreover, encouraging interdisciplinary collaboration between developers, ethicists, and educators can further support the development of AI applications that align with principles of fairness, inclusivity, and responsible innovation.

Building AI Literacy Skills

To combat ethical challenges associated with AI, intentional efforts must be made to empower users with AI literacy. According to Wang and Lester (2023), AI literacy comprises three key components: understanding AI capabilities, utilizing AI for problem-solving, and applying AI in sociocultural contexts. Effective use of AI requires technical expertise that includes knowledge of its limitations, applications, and ethical considerations. Additionally, users must develop skills to employ AI efficiently, effectively, and ethically. Sociocultural considerations, such as traditions and norms within specific contexts, should also inform AI application. When these AI literacy skills are recognized and supported with evidence-based pedagogies, users can leverage these skills to critique AI output and identify potential biases.

Touretzky et al. (2019) emphasized the importance of fostering AI awareness across K-12 education. In elementary school, students should gain foundational knowledge about AI and examine how AI influences their daily lives, including its potential future contributions. Students should engage in activities that promote critical thinking about the societal impacts of AI technologies, exploring both their benefits and potential drawbacks. By middle school, students should delve into the historical parallels between industrial revolutions and the current advancements driven by AI. At the high school level, students should cultivate the ability to critically evaluate new AI technologies, assess their societal implications, and articulate their potential impacts.

To mitigate biases in AI, users should be made aware of AI tools' limitations and critically assess areas that might be prone to bias or gaps in knowledge. Actively involving marginalized groups in the co-creation of AI tools and content can enhance the inclusivity and functionality of AI tools, leading to more editable outcomes. Furthermore, users should be educated on designing prompts that avoid presupposing cultural norms or experiences. For instance, rather than assuming a singular viewpoint, we can ask, "How do different cultures approach [topic]? Provide diverse perspectives." This prompt allows for a broader, more inclusive understanding. Additionally, framing discussions with questions like, "What are multiple ways people around the world experience [event, tradition, or practice]?" ensures that AI-generated responses acknowledge global diversity. In educational settings, prompts such as "How can teachers frame discussions on [topic] in a way that is inclusive and respectful of all cultural backgrounds?" and "What are some equitable ways to assess student understanding that account for diverse cultural knowledge and learning preferences?" can help educators create more inclusive classrooms. In the realm of AI ethics, a question like "How can AI-generated content be designed to reflect global perspectives rather than a single dominant culture?" can promote diverse, innovative ideas. By incorporating such prompts, we can foster more thoughtful, culturally responsive interactions with AI and ensure that digital tools and educational practices are inclusive and equitable.

Privacy and Data Protection

The rise of AI has heightened public concerns about student privacy and data protection (Huang, 2023). AI technologies, while offering innovative tools to enhance teaching and learning, also introduce risks such as data trafficking, surveillance, and security breaches, which can compromise sensitive information. Addressing these risks requires a proactive approach to data management and a robust understanding of ethical considerations in AI use. Educators and institutions must establish clear policies to ensure data security and minimize exposure to potential vulnerabilities.

One effective strategy to safeguard student privacy is using anonymized data when using AI tools. Rather than including identifiable details, such as students' names or demographic information, users should substitute genetic identifiers, such as "Student A" or "Student 14." By anonymizing data, educators can mitigate the risk of reidentification and protect the integrity of private information. Additionally, data sharing should be strictly limited to what is necessary for achieving specific educational objectives. By sharing only essential data, the potential for misuse or unauthorized access is significantly reduced, thereby fostering a safer environment for both students and teachers.

Another important consideration is the use of simulated or "fake" data for training and testing AI models. When realistic but non-sensitive data is employed, educators can explore AI applications without jeopardizing privacy. This approach allows for meaningful experimentation while ensuring that no actual student information is at risk. However, it is critical that the simulated data closely mirrors real-world scenarios to ensure the reliability and applicability of the AI systems in educational contexts.

By integrating these practices into AI adoption, educators can take a responsible and ethical stance in protecting student privacy and data security.

REFERENCES

Acosta, M. D. (2023). *Sixteen weeks to fade out: A practical guide to screenwriting*. UNC Press Books.

Akgun, S., & Greenhow, C. (2022). Artificial intelligence in education: Addressing ethical challenges in K–12 settings. *AI and Ethics*, *2*(3), 431–440. DOI: 10.1007/s43681-021-00096-7 PMID: 34790956

Alenizi, A., Farzaneh, P., Ulla, S., & Yeh, L. (2023). ChatGPT and its potential in lesson planning and educational activities. *Journal of Language Teaching and Technology*, *14*(3), 56–73.

Bahdanau, D., Cho, K., & Bengio, Y. (2015). Neural machine translation by jointly learning to align and translate. *arXiv preprint arXiv:1409.0473*. https://doi.org//arXiv.1409.0473DOI: 10.48550

Baker, R. S., & Hawn, A. (2021). Algorithmic bias in education. *International Journal of Artificial Intelligence in Education*, *32*(4), 1052–1092. DOI: 10.1007/s40593-021-00285-9

Barrot, J. S. (2023). Using ChatGPT for second language writing: Pitfalls and potentials. *Assessing Writing*, *57*, 100745. DOI: 10.1016/j.asw.2023.100745

Benninghof, A. M. (2020). *Specially designed instruction: Increasing success for students with disabilities*. Routledge.

Boninger, F., Trentin, G., & Wright, B. (2020). Enhancing second language learning through AI-driven platforms. *Journal of Educational Technology*, *32*(3), 147–158. DOI: 10.54850/jrspelt.7.39.003

Carreon, A. C., Smith, S. J., Mosher, M., Rao, K., & Rowland, A. (2022). A review of virtual reality intervention research for students with disabilities in K-12 settings. *Journal of Special Education Technology*, *37*(1), 82–99. DOI: 10.1177/0162643420962011

CAST. (2018). *UDL and the learning brain*. https://www.cast.org/products-services/resources/2018/udl-learning-brain-neuroscience

Cevikbas, M., & Kaiser, G. (2022). Promoting personalized learning in flipped classrooms: A systematic review study. *Sustainability (Basel)*, *14*(18), 11393. DOI: 10.3390/su141811393

Chen, W. (2020). Using Google Translate in an authentic translation task: The process, refinement efforts, and students' perceptions. *Current Trends in Translation Teaching and Learning in English*, *7*, 213–238.

Chiu, T. K. F., Xia, Q., Zhou, X., Chai, C. S., & Cheng, M. (2023). Systematic literature review on opportunities, challenges, and future research recommendations of artificial intelligence in education. *Computers and Education: Artificial Intelligence, 4*, 100118. DOI: 10.1016/j.caeai.2022.100118

Chung, S., & Ahn, S. (2021). The effect of using machine translation on linguistic features in L2 writing across proficiency levels and text genres. *Computer Assisted Language Learning, 35*(9), 2239–2264. DOI: 10.1080/09588221.2020.1871029

Crook, A., Mauchline, A., Maw, S., Lawson, C., Drinkwater, R., Lundqvist, K., Orsmond, P., Gomez, S., & Park, J. (2012). The use of video technology for providing feedback to students: Can it enhance the feedback experience for staff and students? *Computers & Education, 58*(1), 386–396. DOI: 10.1016/j.compedu.2011.08.025

D. (2024). Ethical implications of AI integration in educational decision making: Systematic review. *Educational Administration: Theory and Practice, 30*(5), 8521–8527. https://doi.org/DOI: 10.53555/kuey.v30i5.4406

Dawson, K., Antonenko, P., Lane, H., & Zhu, J. (2018). Assistive technologies to support. students with dyslexia. *Teaching Exceptional Children, 51*(3), 226–239. DOI: 10.1177/0040059918794027

Dergaa, I., Chamari, K., Zmijewski, P., & Saad, H. B. (2023). From human writing to artificial intelligence generated text: Examining the prospects and potential threats of ChatGPT in academic writing. *Biology of Sport, 40*(2), 615 622. DOI: 10.5114/biolsport.2023.125623

Doshi, A. R., & Hauser, O. P. (2024). Generative AI enhances individual creativity but reduces the collective diversity of novel content. *Science Advances, 10*(28), eadn5290. Advance online publication. DOI: 10.1126/sciadv.adn5290 PMID: 38996021

Eguchi, A., Okada, H., & Muto, Y. (2021). Contextualizing AI education for K-12 students to enhance their learning of AI literacy through culturally responsive approaches. *Kunstliche Intelligenz, 35*(2), 153–161. DOI: 10.1007/s13218-021-00737-3 PMID: 34376922

Ferris, D., & Hedgcock, J. S. (2014). *Teaching L2 composition: Purpose, process, and practice* (3rd ed.). Routledge.

Gay, G. (2018). *Culturally responsive teaching: Theory, research, and practice* (3rd ed.). Teachers College Press.

Godwin-Jones, R. (2022). Partnering with AI: Intelligent writing assistance and instructed language learning. *Language Learning & Technology*, *26*(2), 5–24. 10125/73474

Groves, M., & Mundt, K. (2021). A ghostwriter in the machine? Attitudes of academic staff towards machine translation use in internationalized higher education. *Journal of English for Academic Purposes*, *50*, 1–11. DOI: 10.1016/j.jeap.2021.100957

Hawanti, S., & Zubaydulloevna, K. M. (2023). AI chatbot-based learning: Alleviating students' anxiety in the English writing classroom. *Bulletin of Social Informatics Theory and Application*, *7*(2), 182–192. DOI: 10.31763/businta.v7i2.659

Hrastinski, S., Olofsson, A. D., Arkenback, C., Ekström, S., Ericsson, E., Fransson, G., Jaldemark, J., Ryberg, T., Öberg, L., Fuentes, A., Gustafsson, U., Humble, N., Mozelius, P., Sundgren, M., & Utterberg, M. (2019). Critical imaginaries and reflections on artificial intelligence and robots in postdigital K-12 education. *Postdigital Science Education.*, *1*(2), 427–445. DOI: 10.1007/s42438-019-00046-x

Huang, A. Y. Q., Lu, O. H. T., & Yang, S. J. H. (2023). Effects of artificial intelligence–enabled personalized recommendations on learners' learning engagement, motivation, and outcomes in a flipped classroom. *Computers & Education*, *194*, 104684. DOI: 10.1016/j.compedu.2022.104684

Huang, S. (2023). Ethics of artificial intelligence in education: Student privacy and data protection. *Science Insights Education Frontiers*, *16*(2), 2577–2587. DOI: 10.15354/sief.23.re202

Hyatt, S. E., & Owens, M. B. (2024). Using universal design for learning and artificial intelligence to support students with disabilities. *College Teaching*, •••, 1–8. DOI: 10.1080/87567555.2024.2313468

Imran, A., & Almusharraf, N. (2023). Exploring the use of ChatGPT as a writing assistant: A review of 30 studies. *Journal of Educational Technology and Research*, *17*(3), 45–58.

Individuals with Disabilities Education Act, 20 U.S.C. § 1400. (2004).

Jeon, J., Lee, S., & Choi, S. (2023). A systematic review of research on speech-recognition chatbots for language learning: Implications for future directions in the era of large language models. *Interactive Learning Environments*, *32*(8), 4613–4631. DOI: 10.1080/10494820.2023.2204343

John-Steiner, V., & Mahn, H. (1996). Sociocultural approaches to learning and development: A Vygotskian framework. *Educational Psychologist*, *31*(3–4), 191–206. DOI: 10.1080/00461520.1996.9653266

Johnston, S. S., Jameson, J. M., O'Keeffe, B. V., & Raines, A. (2024). Teaching in the era of artificial intelligence: Reimagining activities and assignments in preservice special education teacher education programs. *Journal of Special Education Preparation*, *4*(2), 38–50. DOI: 10.33043/5z5b435y

Karbach, J. (1987). Using Toulmin's model of argumentation. *Journal of Teaching Writing*, *6*(1), 81–92.

Kasneci, E., Sessler, K., Kuchemann, S., Bannert, M., Dementieva, D., Fischer, F., Gasser, U., Groh, G., Gunnemann, S., Hullermeier, E., Krusche, S., Kutyniok, G., Michaeli, T., Nerdel, C., Pfeffer, J., Poquet, O., Sailer, M., Schmidt, A., Seidel, T., & Kasneci, G. (2023). ChatGPT for good? On opportunities and challenges of large language models for education. *Learning and Individual Differences*, *103*, 102274. DOI: 10.1016/j.lindif.2023.102274

Kasneci, G., Hübner, G., & Pizzolato, L. (2023). Leveraging AI for L2 writing development: Improving written output through automated feedback. *International Journal of Language Education*, *31*(2), 110–123.

Katiyar, N., Awasthi, V. K., Pratap, R., Mishra, K., Shukla, N., Singh, R., & Tiwari, M. (2024). AI-driven personalized learning systems: Enhancing educational effectiveness. *Educational Administration: Theory and Practice*, *30*(5), 11514–11524. DOI: 10.53555/kuey.v30i5.4961

Kim, J., Lee, H., & Cho, Y. H. (2022). Learning design to support student-AI collaboration: Perspectives of leading teachers for AI in education. *Education and Information Technologies*, *27*(5), 6069–6104. DOI: 10.1007/s10639-021-10831-6

Klímová, B., Pikhart, M., Benites, A. D., Lehr, C., & Sanchez-Stockhammer, C. (2022). Neural machine translation in foreign language teaching and learning: A systematic review. *Education and Information Technologies*, *28*(1), 663–682. DOI: 10.1007/s10639-022-11194-2

Kohnke, L., Munoz, E., & Gero, S. (2023). ChatGPT and its role in providing reliable explanations for language learners. *Language Learning & Technology*, *27*(1), 22–39.

Krashen, S. D. (1982). *Principles and practice in second language acquisition*. Pergamon Press.

Kroll, B. M. (2018). Not so fast: The virtues of slow rhetoric. In Chambers, J., & Gearhart, S. (Eds.), *Reversing the cult of speed in higher education* (pp. 239–251). Routledge. DOI: 10.4324/9781315113555-15

Krullaars, Z. H., Januardani, A., Zhou, L., & Jonkers, E. (2023). Exploring initial interactions: High school students and generative AI chatbots for relationship development. In *Mensch und Computer 2023-Workshopband* (pp. 10–18420). Gesellschaft für Informatik eV. https://doi.org/DOI: 10.18420/muc2023-mci-src-415

Ladson-Billings, G. (1995). Toward a theory of culturally relevant pedagogy. *American Educational Research Journal, 32*(3), 465–491. DOI: 10.3102/00028312032003465

Ladson-Billings, G. (2014). Culturally relevant pedagogy 2.0: A.k.a. the remix. *Harvard Educational Review, 84*(1), 74–84. DOI: 10.17763/haer.84.1.p2rj131485484751

Lee, S. M. (2020). The impact of using machine translation on EFL students' writing. *Computer Assisted Language Learning, 33*(3), 157–175. DOI: 10.1080/09588221.2018.1553186

Lee, S. M. (2022). An investigation of machine translation output quality and the influencing factors of source texts. *ReCALL, 34*(1), 81–94. DOI: 10.1017/S0958344021000124

Ljujić, B., Miljković, J., & Grozdić, V. (2023). ChatGPT and academic writing in higher education. In Radulović, M., & Trajković, M. (Eds.), *Towards a more equitable education: From research to change* (pp. 104–109). Institute for Educational Research.

Maciejewska, J. (2024, March 29). *You know what the biggest problem with pushing all-things-AI is?* https://x.com/AuthorJMac/status/1773679197631701238

Makhambetova, A., Zhiyenbayeva, N., & Ergesheva, E. (2021). Personalized learning strategy as a tool to improve academic performance and motivation of students. *International Journal of Web-Based Learning and Teaching Technologies, 16*(1), 1–17. DOI: 10.4018/IJWLTT.286743

Marzuki, S., Widiati, U., Rusdin, D., Darwin, R., & Indrawati, I. (2023). The impact of AI writing tools on the content and organization of students' writing: EFL teachers' perspective. *Cogent Education, 10*(2), 2236469. DOI: 10.1080/2331186X.2023.2236469

Massey, C. C., Kuntz, E. M., Peltier, C., Barczak, M. A., & Crowson, H. M. (2024). Manipulating graph elements to assess preservice special educators' evaluation of progress monitoring data. *International Journal for Research in Learning Disabilities, 7*(1), 27–39. DOI: 10.28987/ijrld.7.1.47

McMahon, D., & Firestone, J. (2024). Remixing special education practices with artificial intelligence: UDL, EBP, and HLPs. *Journal of Special Education Preparation, 4*(2), 66–76. DOI: 10.33043/3dq2d32d

Medieros, K., Cropley, D. H., Marrone, R. L., & Reiter-Palmon, R. (2024, October 16). Human-AI co-creativity: Does ChatGPT make us more creative? *PsyArXiv Preprints*. https://doi.org/DOI: 10.31234/osf.io/98hdk

Meniado, J. C. (2023). ChatGPT and the four components of meaningful and productive English Language acquisition. *Journal of Language Learning and Teaching*, *15*(2), 123–145.

Meyer, A., Rose, D. H., & Gordon, D. (2014). *Universal design for learning: Theory and practice*. CAST Professional Publishing.

Miller, F. A., Katz, J. H., & Gans, R. (2018). The OD imperative to add inclusion to the algorithms of artificial intelligence. *OD Practitioner*, *5*(1), 6–12.

Mitchell, S., Potash, E., Barocas, S., D'Amour, A., & Lum, K. (2021). Algorithmic fairness: Choices, assumptions, and definitions. *Annual Review of Statistics and Its Application*, *8*(1), 141–163. Advance online publication. DOI: 10.1146/annurev-statistics-042720-125902

Mizumoto, A., & Eguchi, M. (2023). Exploring the potential of using an AI language model for automated essay scoring. *Research Methods in Applied Linguistics*, *2*(2), 100050. DOI: 10.1016/j.rmal.2023.100050

Mollick, E. (2024). *Co-intelligence: Living and working with AI*. Penguin Random House.

Mosher, M. A., Dieker, L. A., & Hines, R. (2024). The past, present and future use of artificial intelligence in teacher education. *Journal of Special Education Preparation*, *4*(2), 6–17. DOI: 10.33043/8aa9855b

Murphy, R. F. (2019). Artificial intelligence application to support K–12 teachers and teaching: A review of promising application, challenges, and risks. *Perspective*, 1–20. DOI: 10.7249/PE315

Nation, I. S. P. (2007). *The four strands*. Cambridge University Press. DOI: 10.2167/illt039.0

Nguyen, A., Ngo, H. N., Hong, Y., Dang, B., & Nguyen, B. P. T. (2023). Ethical principles for artificial intelligence in education. *Education and Information Technologies*, *28*(4), 4221–4241. DOI: 10.1007/s10639-022-11316-w PMID: 36254344

O'Neill, E. (2019). Training students to use online translators and dictionaries: The impact on second language writing scores. *International Journal of Research Studies in Language Learning*, *8*(2), 47–65. DOI: 10.5861/ijrsll.2019.4002

Open, A. I. (2022). *Introducing ChatGPT*.https://openai.com/blog/chatgpt

Panthee, R., & Williamson, O. (2014). Stasis and theory of mind for first year composition: A transdisciplinary exploration. *Journal of Global Literacies, Technologies, and Emerging Pedagogies*, *2*(2), 96–116.

Peng, H., Ma, S., & Spector, J. M. (2019). Personalized learning: An emerging pedagogical approach enabled by a smart learning environment. *Smart Learning Environments*, *6*(9), 9. Advance online publication. DOI: 10.1186/s40561-019-0089-y

Polakova, P., & Klimova, B. (2023). Using DeepL translator in learning English as an applied foreign language – An empirical pilot study. *Heliyon*, *9*(8), e18595. DOI: 10.1016/j.heliyon.2023.e18595 PMID: 37520995

Pujeda, J. R. A. (2023). A systematic review on teachers' digital competencies on the adoption of artificial intelligence in enhancing learning experiences. *International Journal of Research and Innovation in Social Science*, *7*(12), 373–383. DOI: 10.47772/IJRISS.2023.7012031

Rakap, S. (2024). Chatting with GPT: Enhancing individualized education program goal development for novice special education teachers. *Journal of Special Education Technology*, *39*(3), 339–348. DOI: 10.1177/01626434231211295

Rakap, S., & Balikci, S. (2024). Enhancing IEP goal development for preschoolers with autism: A preliminary study on ChatGPT integration. *Journal of Autism and Developmental Disorders*. Advance online publication. DOI: 10.1007/s10803-024-06343-0 PMID: 38625490

Relmasira, S. C., Lai, Y. C., & Donaldson, J. P. (2023). Fostering AI literacy in elementary science, technology, engineering, art, and mathematics (STEAM) education in the age of generative AI. *Sustainability (Basel)*, *15*(18), 13595. DOI: 10.3390/su151813595

Risko, E. F., & Gilbert, S. J. (2016). Cognitive offloading. *Trends in Cognitive Sciences*, *20*(9), 676–688. DOI: 10.1016/j.tics.2016.07.002 PMID: 27542527

Roll, I., & Wylie, R. (2016). Evolution and revolution in artificial intelligence in education. *International Journal of Artificial Intelligence in Education*, *26*(2), 582–599. DOI: 10.1007/s40593-016-0110-3

Rospigliosi, P. (2023). Adapting to the future: How AI tools like ChatGPT are reshaping learning accessibility and flexibility. *Educational Policy and Practice Journal*, *25*(4), 300–315. DOI: 10.54321/epj.2023.004

Ryan, R. M., & Deci, E. L. (2020). Intrinsic and extrinsic motivations: Classic definitions and new directions. *Contemporary Educational Psychology*, *25*(1), 54–67. DOI: 10.1006/ceps.1999.1020 PMID: 10620381

Saborío-Taylor, S., & Rojas-Ramírez, F. (2024). Universal design for learning and artificial intelligence in the digital era: Fostering inclusion and autonomous learning. *International Journal of Professional Development. Learners and Learning*, *6*(2), ep2408. Advance online publication. DOI: 10.30935/ijpdll/14694

Shemshack, A., Kinshuk, , & Spector, J. M. (2021). A comprehensive analysis of personalized learning components. *Journal of Computers in Education*, *8*(1), 1–19. DOI: 10.1007/s40692-021-00188-7

Stahl, B. C., & Wright, D. (2018). Ethics and privacy in AI and big data: Implementing responsible research and innovation. *IEEE Security and Privacy*, *16*(3), 26–33. DOI: 10.1109/MSP.2018.2701164

Swiecki, Z., Khosravi, H., Chen, G., Martinez-Maldonado, R., Lodge, J. M., Milligan, S., Selwyn, N., & Gašević, D. (2022). Assessment in the age of artificial intelligence. *Computers and Education: Artificial Intelligence*, *3*, 100075. DOI: 10.1016/j.caeai.2022.100075

Texthelp. (n.d.). Read&Write. https://www.texthelp.com/products/read-and-write-education/

Tolstykh, O. M., & Oshchepkova, T. (2024). Beyond ChatGPT: Roles that artificial intelligence tools can play in an English language classroom. *Discover Artificial Intelligence*, *4*(1), 60. DOI: 10.1007/s44163-024-00158-9

Tomlinson, C. A. (2014). *The differentiated classroom: Responding to the needs of all learners* (2nd ed.). ASCD.

Touretzky, D., Gardner-McCune, C., Martin, F., & Seehorn, D. (2019). Envisioning AI for K-12: What should every child know about AI? *Proceedings of the AAAI Conference on Artificial Intelligence*, *33*(01), 9795–9799. DOI: 10.1609/aaai.v33i01.33019795

Tsai, S. C. (2020). Chinese students' perceptions of using Google Translate as a translingual CALL tool in EFL writing. *Computer Assisted Language Learning*, *35*(5-6), 1250–1272. DOI: 10.1080/09588221.2020.1799412

Ulla, S., & Yeh, L. (2023). Harnessing the power of ChatGPT for ESL/EFL instruction: A critical review. *Innovations in Educational Technology*, *10*(2), 145–159. DOI: 10.5539/elt.v17n5p41

Urlaub, P., & Dessein, E. (2022). Machine translation and foreign language education. *Frontiers in Artificial Intelligence*, *5*, 936111. DOI: 10.3389/frai.2022.936111 PMID: 35937139

U.S. Department of Education. (2017). *Reimagining the role of technology in education: 2017 National Education Technology Plan update*. https://tech.ed.gov/files/2017/01/NETP17.pdf

Üstünbaş, A. (2024). The role of AI feedback in promoting experimental learning in L2 writing: A case study of ChatGPT. *Language Learning & Technology*, *28*(1), 34–48.

Vinall, K., & Hellmich, E. A. (2021). Down the rabbit hole: Machine translation, metaphor, and instructor identity and agency. *Second Language Research & Practice*, *2*(1), 99–118. 10125/69860

Wang, L., Chen, X., Wang, C., Xu, L., Shadiev, R., & Li, Y. (2024). ChatGPT's capabilities in providing feedback on undergraduate students' argumentation: A case study. *Thinking Skills and Creativity*, *51*, 101440. DOI: 10.1016/j.tsc.2023.101440

Wang, N., & Lester, J. (2023). K-12 education in the age of AI: A call to action for K-12 AI literacy. *International Journal of Artificial Intelligence in Education*, *33*(2), 228–232. DOI: 10.1007/s40593-023-00358-x

Wang, X., Pang, H., Wallace, M. P., Wang, Q., & Chen, W. (2024). Learners' perceived AI presences in AI-supported language learning: A study of AI as a humanized agent from community of inquiry. *Computer Assisted Language Learning*, *37*(4), 814–840. DOI: 10.1080/09588221.2022.2056203

Wayne, H., Bialik, M., & Fadel, C. (2019). *Artificial intelligence in education: Promises and implications for teaching and learning*. Center for Curriculum Redesign.

Williamson, B., & Eynon, R. (2020). The role of AI-driven translation tools in language learning and teaching. *Computers & Education*, *74*(1), 112–124.

Winstone, N., & Carless, D. (2019). *Designing effective feedback processes in higher education: A learning-focused approach* (1st ed.). Routledge. DOI: 10.4324/9781351115940

WolframAlpha. (n.d.). I. https://www.wolframalpha.com/

Woolverton, G. A., & Pollastri, A. R. (2021). An exploration and critical examination of how "Intelligent classroom technologies" can improve specific uses of direct student behavior observation methods. *Educational Measurement: Issues and Practice*, *40*(3), 7–17. https://psycnet.apa.org/doi/10.1111/emip.12421. DOI: 10.1111/emip.12421

Wu, Y., Schuster, M., Chen, Z., Le, Q. V., Norouzi, M., Macherey, W., . . . Dean, J. (2016). Google's neural machine translation system: Bridging the gap between human and machine translation. *arXiv preprint arXiv:1609.08144*. https://doi.org// arXiv.1609.0814DOI: 10.48550

Xu, J. (2021). Google Translate for writing in a Japanese class: What students do and think. *The Journal of the National Council of Less Commonly Taught Languages*, *30*, 136–182.

Young, A., & Shishido, K. (2023). Unlocking the potential of generative AI for language learning: The case of ChatGPT in EFL contexts. *Frontiers in Education*, *8*, 789–802.

Yuan, C., & Barnett, J. E. H. (2024). Developing quality IEP goals in the age of artificial intelligence. *Teaching Exceptional Children*, *20*(10), 1–11. DOI: 10.1177/00400599241239311

Zhao, X. (2022). Leveraging artificial intelligence (AI) technology for English writing: Introducing Wordtune as a digital writing assistant for EFL writers. *RELC Journal*. Advance online publication. DOI: 10.1177/00336882221094089

Zheng, L., Long, M., Zhong, L., & Gyasi, J. F. (2022). The effectiveness of technology-facilitated personalized learning on learning achievements and learning perceptions: A meta-analysis. *Education and Information Technologies*, *27*(8), 11807–11830. DOI: 10.1007/s10639-022-11092-7

Zimmerman, M. (2018). *Teaching AI: Exploring new frontiers for learning*. International Society for Technology in Education. zSpace (n.d.). https://zspace/com

Zuo, M., Kong, S., Ma, Y., Hu, Y., & Xiao, M. (2023). The effects of using scaffolding in online learning: A meta-analysis. *Education Sciences*, *13*(7), 705. DOI: 10.3390/educsci13070705

Chapter 5
Generative AI for Personalized Learning Content Creation

Rohit Yadav
https://orcid.org/0000-0002-7573-8005
IILM University, Greater Noida, India

Geshwaree Huzooree
https://orcid.org/0000-0001-8076-6636
Edinburgh Napier University, UK

Mohit Yadav
https://orcid.org/0000-0002-9341-2527
O.P. Jindal Global University, India

Damith Sanjaya Kumara Gangodawilage
https://orcid.org/0000-0001-7968-6284
Qasim Ibrahim School of Business, Villa College, Male, Maldives

ABSTRACT

Generative AI has emerged as a transformative force in personalized learning, offering unprecedented opportunities to tailor educational content to individual needs. By leveraging advanced algorithms and data analysis, AI systems can dynamically generate customized materials, provide adaptive feedback, and foster student engagement. This chapter explores the intersection of generative AI and personalized learning, discussing its techniques, tools, and applications in creating immersive and adaptive educational experiences. Key benefits include enhanced learning outcomes, efficiency, and scalability. However, challenges such as data privacy, algorithmic bias, and equitable access must be addressed to ensure responsible implementation.

DOI: 10.4018/979-8-3693-8744-3.ch005

Future trends, including the integration of immersive technologies like Virtual Reality (VR) and predictive analytics, highlight AI's potential to revolutionize education. By navigating ethical considerations and fostering transparency, generative AI can become a powerful ally in creating inclusive, engaging, and student-centered learning environments.

1. INTRODUCTION

Generative AI is a form of artificial intelligence that involves creating new content in the form of text, images, audio, and even video, based on input data. It is unlike the traditional AI models, which are designed to classify or predict outcomes from existing datasets, whereas generative models try to generate novel data by learning the underlying patterns and structures within the input. The key techniques in generative AI include GANs, VAEs, and transformer-based models such as GPT (Generative Pre-trained Transformer) and BERT (Bidirectional Encoder Representations from Transformers). Such models have changed the face of art, content creation, and natural language processing, respectively (Goodfellow et al., 2014; Vaswani et al., 2017).

The most outstanding feature of the generative AI is that it can create content, which would simulate human-like creativity, such as generating coherent paragraphs of text, creating synthetic images, or composing music, and, therefore, distinguished from traditional methods of machine learning, which mostly focus on discriminative tasks such as classification or regression (Radford et al., 2021). The sophistication of these AI systems over the last few years has been to create increasingly high-quality outputs, even mimicking human behavior, style, and reasoning. For example, the GPT models by OpenAI have proven remarkable capabilities in natural language generation, including contextual relevance and coherence even for very complex subjects.

There is huge potential in applying generative AI to personalized learning content creation. AI can help in the creation of customized learning materials for students, so that the content is adapted to the individual's learning style, preferences, and pace. Generative AI can generate new content dynamically based on data about how students interact with the material, filling gaps in knowledge and providing personalized explanations. This resonates with the overall trend in education toward personalized learning, which focuses on addressing the individual needs of every learner (Brusilovsky & Millán, 2007). As generative AI technologies become increasingly accessible, educators and developers are now working to harness these systems for scalable, efficient, and customized learning experiences.

2. THE ROLE OF PERSONALIZED LEARNING IN EDUCATION

Personalized learning is one of the recent focuses in contemporary education because it can cater to the diverse needs of learners. Unlike traditional approaches, which focus on a one-size-fits-all approach, personalized learning emphasizes tailoring the educational experience to the individual strengths, weaknesses, preferences, and pace of each student. This would allow students to engage with content that is aligned with their learning style, hence improving motivation and enhancing learning outcomes. Personalized learning usually consists of adaptive learning technologies that alter the course of the instruction path by constantly assessing students' progress; hence, there is a much more dynamic and responsive learning environment as suggested by Pane et al., 2015.

Another potential benefit of personalized learning is increasing student engagement. Personalized learning allows students to have experiences tailored to their interests and abilities and promotes greater autonomy and motivation on the part of the student as suggested by Walkington, 2013. For example, they can follow subjects of interest or proceed with material at their own comfortable rate of understanding. This tailored strategy also not only aids students in achieving greater insight but also fosters the necessity of self-directed learning; an essential trait for lifelong learning (Siemens, 2013). Furthermore, research has demonstrated that personalized learning reduces achievement gaps mainly for students who would have otherwise fallen prey to the pitfalls of traditional classroom teaching; such individuals include students with disabilities or those belonging to diverse linguistic backgrounds (Mandinach & Gummer, 2016).

However, implementing personalized learning is not without challenges. One of the main issues relates to the time and resources that are required to produce learner-specific content for every student. Teachers are important to learning, but are not equipped in large numbers with the ability to create unique paths for each student to learn. Additionally, the underpinning of personalized learning: data collection that works, creating content, and monitoring tools; is resource-hungry as well (Hattie, 2012). Equity and access are of further concern because the exploited students of disadvantaged backgrounds will not possess such facilities or support to take full advantage of such learning experiences.

These challenges are well within their reach with the advent of high-end AI technologies. Generative AI promises to make such content creation and adaptation processes automatic so that more efficient scaling of personalized learning can be done within classrooms. AI can scan huge amounts of student data, including performance on assessments, interaction with learning materials, and preferences, to create personalized content in real time. This supports not only individualized learning but also allows rapid adjustment of the curriculum based on the student's changing needs (VanLehn, 2011). In utilizing generative AI for personalization in learning, educators will then be able to offer excellent and more engaging experiences based on students' individual learning capabilities.

3. HOW GENERATIVE AI MAY SUPPORT PERSONALIZED LEARNING CONTENT

This is a technique that uses AI to revolutionize personalized learning content by adjusting education content based on a student's individual needs dynamically. Traditional educational material typically is delivered in a one-size-fits-all manner. Thus, such a delivery system is not well suited to address all students' individual learning styles, paces, and preferences. Generative AI, on the other hand, can create content that not only is tailored but also is sensitive to a student's individual journey of learning. The use of large-scale data analysis, machine learning models, and natural language processing allows generative AI systems to create custom instructional materials like text, quizzes, practice problems, and even multimedia content that better align with the student's current level of understanding and preferred learning methods (Luckin et al., 2016).

Generative AI, on the personalized learning front, provides one of its most important strengths through the ability to modify content on the basis of real-time data from the students. The platform can track student progress, recognize knowledge gaps, and modify the content based on that. For example, if a student struggles with a particular concept, generative AI can create supplementary materials, such as simplified explanations or additional practice exercises, to help the student master the topic (Woolf, 2010). Conversely, if a student is excelling in a subject, the AI can provide more advanced materials to challenge and further engage them. This dynamic adaptability creates a much more personalized learning experience than the static content offered in traditional textbooks, which are either too difficult or not challenging enough for different learners.

Generative AI can further support differentiated instruction, which is crucial in heterogeneous classrooms. By producing content that aligns with diverse learning needs and styles, AI can offer differentiated resources that could be suitable for visual, auditory, kinesthetic, or text-based learners. For example, if a student is a visual learner, AI could provide diagrams, interactive simulations, or videos to support their learning. If the student is an auditory learner, AI may create audio explanations or podcasts. This way, students can approach content in the manner that is most conducive to their learning style (Rose & Meyer, 2002). In addition, AI systems can give personalized feedback. This helps students not only know what they are doing right but also where they should improve.

Interactivity is another feature that AI improves in personalized learning. AI-powered tutors, chatbots, and interactive simulations keep the student interacting with the subject matter continuously. These systems can provide instant feedback, clarifications, and personalized hints, simulating the support a student would receive from a human tutor. For instance, generative AI systems can help students in solving problems by giving context-specific prompts or suggesting alternative methods for approaching a problem (VanLehn, 2011). The continuous interaction between the student and the AI can help increase motivation and also maintain long-term engagement, because they are going to get answers right away as queries and a more interactive learning environment.

Generative AI can further be used in helping create diverse and rich assessment tools. Since traditional assessments feature mainly fixed tests or quizzes, the generative AI can assist in creating customized quizzes, tests, and assignments based on the student's history of learning. These evaluations may differ in terms of difficulty and format, making sure they are both relevant to what the student has learned and reflecting their progress in some periods. AI systems can also generate formative assessments that give immediate feedback, so educators can identify areas that need more focused attention and adjust instruction accordingly. This ability to continually assess and adjust for each student's performance is what keeps the students on the right track, thereby deepening their understanding of the material. Shute and Kim (2014) states this.

Moreover, the potential of generative AI to produce dynamic and customized content at scale solves the issue of creating individualized learning material for a number of students. In a traditional classroom, the instructor cannot prepare and tailor learning materials for each student in the class, especially in a diverse classroom. Generative AI automates much of this process, allowing educators to focus on higher-level teaching tasks such as mentoring, guiding discussions, and providing personalized support. This scalability is so valuable in distance learning or the large classroom, since the teacher usually cannot give an individualized, one-on-one attention due to time and resource availability (Pellegrino et al., 2014).

In summary, generative AI enhances personalized learning content by facilitating the creation of adaptive, responsive, and variable materials that tailor to the needs of individual learners. The generative AI system continuously analyzes data about student progress and preferences. As a result, it dynamically adjusts the content, offers differentiated resources, provides real-time feedback, and generates assessments reflecting students' unique learning journeys. With its increased integration into educational technology, generative AI may make personalized learning more efficient, engaging, and accessible to all students.

4. TECHNIQUES AND TOOLS IN GENERATIVE AI FOR CONTENT CREATION

Generative AI uses a range of advanced techniques to generate customized and dynamic educational content, providing powerful tools for content creators in the education sector. Among the most widely used methods in generative AI for content creation are text generation models, image generation models, and interactive media generation tools, all of which have specific applications in developing personalized learning materials. These techniques facilitate content that could be dynamically made appropriate to learning needs, presenting an opportunity to more engagingly provide more relevant, better-tailored educational experience.

Text Generation Models

One of the most prominent techniques in generative AI for content creation is the use of text generation models such as OpenAI's GPT (Generative Pretrained Transformer), BERT (Bidirectional Encoder Representations from Transformers), and T5 (Text-to-Text Transfer Transformer). These models can generate coherent and contextually relevant text based on minimal input, making them highly effective in creating educational content, ranging from textbook explanations to personalized practice problems and adaptive assessments.

For example, GPT models can create instructional material in the form of summary or explanation or even fully developed chapters based on specified topics or keywords. The power of these models rests within their ability to change content based on the contextual information they are provided, thus potentially allowing for personalized lessons and exercises to be created, even enabling conversation-style feedback. The student struggling with a concept can be given simpler explanations or alternative examples, whereas students performing well in a subject may be given more challenging material that matches their level of understanding (Brown et al., 2020). Similarly, it can be used to create quiz or assessment questions whose difficulty level changes according to the learner's most current level of mastery so that the content should always be relevant and challenging enough.

Visualization Content Generation

The ability of generative AI to generate visual content is also important for creating engaging and accessible educational content. GANs and VAEs are two popular methods used for image, diagram, and infographic generation in personalized learning. GANs function by generating images using a two-part model: the generator that produces images and the discriminator that assesses the authenticity of those images. This way, AI can generate highly realistic and contextually relevant images based on text input or other parameters (Goodfellow et al., 2014).

AI technologies, in teaching and educating, provide techniques to generate visual content, such as illustrations, graphs, and diagrams, but targeted towards a specific topic matter. For instance, during a lesson on biology, an AI tool can create diagrams of the human digestive system with a level of detail that responds to the student's knowledge level. In mathematics or physics, AI can also generate problem sets with corresponding visual representations to better help students understand abstract concepts. Moreover, the AI-generated visual aids can be adjusted according to the different learning styles of a student, who may benefit more from 3D models, flowcharts, or detailed scientific illustrations.

More than static images, AI can also create interactive visuals and simulations. For example, tools such as DeepArt and Runway ML take the form of AI to turn text descriptions into visual art or other forms of visual representations that allow educators to create engaging, interactive content, such as virtual tours or educational simulations, in which students learn by experience rather than by observation (El-gammal et al., 2017). Interactive Visual Tools

The ability of interactive visual tools can go a long way in explaining complex scientific phenomena or historical events in a richer way to different learning preferences.

Creation of Audio and Video Content Generative AI is also finding influence in the creation of audio and video content. Text-to-speech (TTS) models, such as Google's WaveNet or OpenAI's Jukedeck, have been integrated into educational platforms to generate spoken content that enhances learning for auditory learners. These AI-driven tools can convert textual content into natural-sounding speech, allowing learners to access material in audio form. This is helpful to students with visual impairments or those who learn better through their ears, so they can study anywhere, anytime, or even multi-task (Kumar et al., 2018).

The other role that generative AI plays is in the production of educational videos. For instance, AI systems can create video lectures by converting written material into video-based lessons, adding relevant visuals, animations, or even AI-generated instructors that walk students through the content. These tools can be particularly effective in online learning environments, where instructors may not be able to provide face-to-face interaction with every student. The AI-generated video content can be designed according to the needs of individual learners regarding the pace and depth, modifying the level of material complexity, and even embedding quizzes and other interactive features within the videos for higher engagement purposes (Sundararajan et al., 2019).

Interactive Learning Tools and Chatbots

Generative AI is changing the way students interact with the learning material beyond content creation. AI-powered chatbots and ITS are increasingly providing personalized assistance, offering tailored feedback, and engaging students in meaningful interactions. These systems use NLP and machine learning techniques to understand and respond to student queries, providing explanations, hints, and encouragement based on the student's current level of understanding.

For instance, chatbots may be used in generating responses to questions raised by students; their language would depend on the student's background knowledge about the topic. This is aside from answering questions because AI-based tutoring systems can even help guide the student through complicated problem-solving steps, offering individualized hints or breaking problems down into smaller steps. These systems can provide immediate feedback and suggest more resources or practice based on learner performance (VanLehn, 2011). The constant interactivity and personalized support provided by these systems make the learning process more interactive and dynamic.

Tools and Platforms for Content Creation

Several tools and platforms have emerged that support the use of generative AI for content creation in education. For example, Khan Academy utilizes AI to deliver exercises and personalized feedback to the student, whereas other platforms like ScribeSense and Lumi apply AI for helping in developing interactive learning content. Moreover, other platforms like Coursera and edX are now also embracing generative AI to develop adaptive quizzes, discussion prompts, and additional course material for MOOCs. These platforms provide AI-driven solutions that can automatically adjust course content, quizzes, and feedback based on the learner's progression.

Companies like OpenAI and Hugging Face also provide accessible AI models through APIs, allowing developers and educators to integrate generative AI into their own learning platforms. These tools provide the flexibility to create highly customized educational content, ranging from simple text generation to more complex interactive media and assessments.

Generative AI in education is helping transform content generation with tools capable of generating highly personalized text, images, videos, and other interactive content geared towards individualized learning needs. Such techniques as the use of text generation models, GANs, TTS systems, and even AI-powered chatbots can facilitate dynamic, adaptable, and more engaging content aligned with diverse preferences for learning. These innovations are not only enabling the scaling of personalized learning but also helping make educational resources more high-quality and rich - accessible, relevant, and engaging for students of all ages.

5. BENEFITS AND IMPACT OF GENERATIVE AI ON LEARNING OUTCOMES

The use of generative AI in the education sector is likely to considerably improve learning results by offering more personalized educational resources, improving engagement, and giving continuous support to students. One of the most profound benefits of generative AI is its ability to create highly personalized learning experiences that can cater to the diverse needs, learning styles, and paces of students. Using data-driven algorithms to assess the students' progress, learning preferences, and challenges, AI can create content that adapts in real time to ensure that students are always challenged but not overwhelmed, which enhances both retention and comprehension (Pane et al., 2015). For example, if a student is weak on a particular topic, generative AI can give him or her easier explanations or more practice problems that would fill the gap in understanding, whereas advanced learners can be given deeper, more complex material to ensure an optimal learning experience for all (Walkington, 2013).

The instant, personalized feedback from generative AI is another important benefit that directly impacts learning outcomes. Unlike traditional classroom settings, where students often have to wait for feedback on assignments or tests, AI-powered systems can provide immediate feedback, helping learners to quickly identify areas of improvement. This real-time feedback loop allows students to adjust their learning strategies promptly, reinforcing positive learning behaviors and correcting misconceptions early. For example, AI-driven content like adaptive quizzes or problem-solving exercises can be customized according to a student's performance so that the content stays relevant and challenging enough for the student to continually improve (Shute & Kim, 2014).

More importantly, the use of generative AI is likely to help in the establishment of a more interactive learning environment that ensures the motivation and attention of the students. It involves AI-generated multimedia content in the form of visual aids, interactive simulations, and even AI-driven avatars. In such an instance, learning can be much more engaging and enjoyable compared to reading static content. Such interactivity may explain very complex concepts more easily and make them digestible. For instance, AI-generated virtual labs, in which students can experiment with scientific concepts in a simulated environment, allow learners to experience hands-on learning without the constraints of physical resources (Woolf, 2010).

This level of engagement is especially important for students who might otherwise struggle to maintain focus or motivation in a conventional learning environment.

Moreover, scalable generative AI helps apply personalization at scale in a way that better availability of quality education resources could reach a broader mass of learners. For example, AI may allow the massification of producing adaptive learning paths tailored to big chunks of learners at once - tasks that, performed manually by teachers and instructors, could be incredibly costly in time. This scalability of personalized learning makes it possible to reach a wider audience, especially in online education settings or large classrooms where the attention from educators may be limited (Pellegrino et al., 2014). AI ensures that every student gets customized instruction according to their needs, regardless of the class size or institutional resources.

Another great impact of generative AI is that it has the potential to help bridge educational gaps. For students struggling on specific topics, generative AI can create supplementary content addressing their specific difficulties. This would particularly be of help to the learners who require additional support such as those who may have a learning disability or even those without one-on-one tutoring (Mandinach & Gummer, 2016). With further adaptation, AI generative content might have the ability to adapt to provide alternative learning supports-such as having text-based summaries for visual-based learners or generative interactive simulation for kinesthetic learners. Hence, with high customization, everyone learns something while having content tailor fit to meet unique educational needs that are individual based.

Another attribute of using the generative AI is increased levels of student engagement and autonomy in learning. Since the AI-powered systems allow students to be more proactive in their learning, students can develop self-regulated learning by monitoring their own progress and pace, making learning goals, and perusing content on their own. This freedom enables a stronger sense of ownership in students over their education and avails them of crucial skills such as time management, problem-solving, and independent learning (Siemens, 2013). As a result, the students become more confident and motivated towards their academics, which finally leads to a better overall outcome in learning.

In a nutshell, the benefits of integrating generative AI into education lie directly in influencing the learning outcome. Generative AI offers personalized content and real-time feedback and creates an environment that makes learning more interactive and engaging for the students. The scalability of AI allows personalized learning to be implemented across diverse educational settings, ensuring that students of all backgrounds and abilities have access to high-quality, tailored educational experiences. As generative AI continues to evolve, its potential to enhance learning outcomes will only increase, making it an essential tool in the future of education.

6. CHALLENGES AND ETHICAL CONSIDERATIONS

While the possible applications of generative AI in educational content creation are highly promising, many challenges and issues must be weighed and addressed when considering its adoption to ensure both responsible and effective practice. These problems include data security and privacy and the possibility that AI-generated content contains bias, alongside the impact it has on roles for educators and students. These are some of the issues that need to be addressed so that generative AI enhances education in a fair, equitable, and ethical manner.

Data Privacy and Security

The most significant challenge in integrating AI into education is the issue of data privacy and security. Generative AI systems require access to vast amounts of student data, including learning progress, behavioral patterns, and sometimes even personal information. This raises privacy concerns over students, especially when dealing with sensitive information. Educational institutions must ensure that data is collected and used in compliance with privacy regulations such as the Family Educational Rights and Privacy Act (FERPA) in the United States or the General Data Protection Regulation (GDPR) in Europe. The wrong use, unapproved access, and inappropriate handling of a student's personal information may put the individual's trust at stake, create serious legal implications, and even be used for stealing identities.

In addition, the implementation of AI in learning models raises the issue of the security of data storage and processing systems. The widespread use of cloud-based environments and third-party vendors of AI services makes it critical for educational institutions to develop strong security protocols that will protect students' data from cyber attacks or espionage surveillance, thus ensuring secure data management practices are employed to avoid such breaches that may lead to a violation of the rights of students and instructors (Cios et al., 2017).

Bias and Fairness in AI

Another critical challenge is that AI algorithms might be biased and unfair. Generative AI systems are trained on large datasets. If those datasets are not representative of the diverse student population, AI-generated content may only reinforce existing biases, perpetuate stereotypes, and disadvantage certain groups of students. For instance, if the training data is predominantly content from one geographic region or cultural context, the AI may generate materials that are biased or irrelevant to students from other backgrounds. Data goes only as good as the training models. It is a self-perpetuating bias: it is based on gender, race, and other socioeconomic biases which would end up in being reflected in an AI system by way of an educational content being developed in that AI. Therefore, one has to really be very particular in the way an AI is designed to meet fairness, inclusion, and access to education among all students. This would demand training on various, diverse representative datasets and the constant evaluation of the system for biases in content generation. Educators and AI developers should collaborate to make sure that the educational materials created by AI are fair and not used to promote discriminatory practices or increase educational disparities (O'Neil, 2016). Equitable AI content development also encompasses questions of accessibility to students with impairments as well as how the content could be usable and understandable for learners with different learning needs.

Too Much Dependence on AI and the Role of Teachers

This widespread use of AI in personal learning also sparks concerns about a too much dependency on technology to replace human educators. The ability of AI to offer significant advantages in terms of personalization of content and immediate feedback is not able to replace the human touch often critical in effective teaching. Teachers are important providers of emotional support, motivation, and complex needs that go beyond academic performance such as mental health and social-emotional development. Excessive dependency on AI tools could result in less human-to-human interaction and could hence be detrimental to student learning experiences and well-being.

This aside, AI has inherent limitations in relating to the implicit, subtle learning processes of the human mind. It cannot comprehend the nuances or sense the nonverbal expressions that might occur to a teacher for instant attention to. Hence, education still requires that educator's balanced hybrid model; that is to say, that AI tools merely complement and facilitate the educator's role rather than supplant the latter (Selwyn, 2019).

Accessibility and Equity

There are some concerns about the accessibility and equity of AI in scaling personalized learning. AI-powered systems may be helpful for providing unique learning experiences; however, all students do not have equal access to the technological tools and resources that would benefit from AI in education. For example, low-income or rural students may lack the high-quality internet connections, personal devices, or AI-driven educational platforms that might be beneficial to them. This digital divide could worsen inequalities in education as students who are not exposed to these resources get left behind. The first step toward ensuring that AI contributes to educational equity rather than worsening disparities is to ensure access to AI tools by all students regardless of their socio-economic background or geographic location (Eynon & Malmberg, 2020).

Additionally, AI-generated content also needs to be accessible for students with disability conditions. Any AI-based educational tool designed must focus on accessibility features that enable the use of content by students with visual, auditory, cognitive, or physical impairments. This includes access to text-to-speech functions, ensuring that visual content is provided with alternative text that describes it, and developing AI systems to improve accommodation of diverse abilities of learners (Burgstahler, 2015).

Ethical Use of AI-Generated Content

There is also an increasing concern regarding the ethical use of AI-generated content. As AI systems become more advanced in generating educational material, there's a possibility of generating content that does not always align with the goals of education; the generated content may be misleading, or even contains false or harmful information. AI, while able to produce large volumes of content in the shortest time, should not mean that educators fail to scrutinize and verify material produced by AI before it finds its way into the classroom. Inaccurate or inappropriate content may have serious consequences for students' learning experiences and may inadvertently promote misinformation.

Another need for this is that with the increased integration of AI tools into educational systems, there is a requirement to establish clear ethical guidelines on the use of AI in content creation. This includes setting boundaries on how AI should be used in the classroom, ensuring transparency in how AI systems are designed and implemented, and considering the long-term consequences of relying on AI for educational decision-making (Binns, 2018).

The integration of generative AI in educational content creation offers tremendous promise for enhancing personalized learning, but it also brings forth several challenges and ethical considerations that must be carefully managed. Data privacy, bias, the role of educators, accessibility, and the ethical use of AI-generated content are critical issues that need to be addressed to ensure that AI enhances education in a fair, secure, and responsible manner. Addressing these challenges proactively will ensure that educators, policymakers, and developers work together to harness the full potential of AI while mitigating its risks and ensuring that AI benefits all students equitably.

7. IMPLICATIONS OF GENERATIVE AI IN PERSONALIZED LEARNING: PRACTICAL, SOCIAL, AND ETHICAL CONSIDERATIONS

The massive penetration of generative AI into teaching environments presents a myriad of practical, social, and ethical implications that need to be scrutinized diligently so as to unleash the full benefit of the positive impact while dampening the negative consequences. Such implications include the teaching approach, the student participation, and aspects of the society-at-large, as well as the moral obligations from using advanced AI technologies within learning environments.

Practical Implications

On a practical level, the use of generative AI in personalized learning brings about significant efficiencies and scalability. AI-powered systems can generate tremendous amounts of learning content and adapt it in real time to fit the needs of individual students, allowing for an unprecedented level of personalization in education. This shift can bring about drastic differences in time and effort to which educators may use in planning lesson, assessment, and feedback tools. It may allow the educator time to do emotionally and socially relevant support work in guiding critical thinking and in organizing collaborative learning situations while leaving individualized repetitive, and boring teaching for AI to tackle (Holmes et al., 2019).

However, the widespread adoption of generative AI also requires substantial investment in infrastructure, teacher training, and system integration. Educational institutions need to ensure that both teachers and students are adequately equipped to use AI-powered tools. This includes providing training on how to interpret and use AI-generated content, understanding the limitations of AI, and fostering critical thinking to prevent over-reliance on technology. Moreover, the digital divide is a concern because schools with limited resources will not be able to implement AI systems effectively, thereby increasing educational inequalities between well-funded and underfunded institutions (Eynon & Malmberg, 2020).

Social Implications

The social implications of generative AI in education are wide-ranging, especially concerning accessibility, equity, and the potential for social stratification. AI could democratize education by providing more personalized learning experiences to a larger number of students, regardless of their geographical location or socioeconomic status. In theory, AI can level the playing field for underserved communities by offering high-quality educational content that adapts to individual needs. In practice, however, there is a significant risk that the digital divide could widen existing gaps. Students in low-income regions or rural areas may not have the same access to the necessary technologies or high-speed internet connections required to benefit from AI-powered educational tools, which could perpetuate or even exacerbate existing educational inequalities (Selwyn, 2019).

The use of AI in education can have a deep impact on the interaction of students with each other and with educators. As AI becomes an increasingly important entity in content delivery and feedback, face-to-face student-teacher contact may be minimal, which has a negative influence on the building of social skills and emotional quotient. Human relationship is the key in developing empathy, communication, and collaboration skills all of which have been proven important for success not only in learning but also outside the classroom, in the workforce. A balance should thus be struck between the elaborate use of AI-driven personalized learning and the need for socializing, group learning, and emotional support from the human educator (Koller et al., 2013).

Similarly, the impact of AI on student behavior and student interaction inside educational environments is also in question. A loss of creative thinking skill and inability to think critically could be seen as an effect if dependence upon AI for learning increases among students. AI systems, by their nature, tend to work within predefined frameworks and algorithms, which may potentially narrow the scope of intellectual exploration for students. Thus, the educational framework should be designed in such a way that it promotes curiosity, problem-solving, and critical thinking so that AI becomes a tool to enhance rather than replace these cognitive skills (Mandinach & Gummer, 2016).

Ethical Implications

The ethical connotations of applying generative AI in education cut across several avenues, including that of data security, bias issues, and its role in designing educational outcomes. The first principle is the case of handling information about students themselves. Since personalized learning depends fundamentally on large collection of data regarding students, there raise serious questions to be answered before the implementation-questions regarding handling, storage, and use. It is essential to ensure that students' data is dealt with in a manner that is secure, transparent, and ethical. More vigorous policies and rules are also needed over the use of AI in education to ensure strict adherence to privacy laws such as FERPA and GDPR.

Otherwise, the threat of data breaches, unauthorized access, or even exploitation of the most sensitive information about a student would be prevalent (Cios et al., 2017).

Another ethical concern is that bias may be locked into AI algorithms. Generative AI systems are only as good as the data they are trained upon, and in the event the training data does reflect societal imbalances or biases, the AI may well end up perpetuating those imbalances in the content it generates in the educational system. For example, AI-generated learning materials can potentially favor particular cultural norms, languages, or viewpoints at the expense of others, which might disadvantage marginalized members or create unfair conditions in the education given. AI developers and educators should thus collaborate to make the algorithms of generative AI neutral and equitable so as not to hold any biases and to represent diversity and social justice (O'Neil, 2016).

The ethical question of the role of AI in decision-making in education remains unsolved. The more AI is entrusted with assessing student progress, determining learning paths, and making recommendations, the more it threatens to undermine professional judgment. Teachers have insights into their students' needs, personalities, and social contexts that no AI system can fully replicate. While AI can personalize content and evaluations, it's also important that human educators play a role in making decisions impacting the well-being of students as well as the general educational experiences. AI must be seen as a supplement, not a substitute, for teacher judgment and expertise (Woolf, 2010).

Last but not least, there are broader concerns of society and philosophy about increasing reliance on AI in our daily lives. With AI becoming more integrated into education and other sectors, questions are raised about the long-term impact of AI on human development, job markets, and societal norms. Will widespread use of AI lead to a future where human workers are replaced by machines, and human creativity is diminished? Or can AI be harnessed to create new opportunities for learning and innovation? These are very important ethical questions that require thoughtful consideration and proactive engagement from policymakers, educators, and society at large (Binns, 2018).

The practical, social, and ethical implications of generative AI in personalized learning must be carefully navigated to ensure that AI benefits all students equitably and responsibly. While AI has the potential to revolutionize education by providing personalized, scalable, and engaging learning experiences, it also raises important questions regarding data privacy, bias, accessibility, and the role of human educators. Clear regulations, thoughtful implementation, and ongoing evaluation will be key to ensuring that AI contributes positively to the educational landscape. By taking into account these implications, society can utilize the power of generative AI to improve learning outcomes while reducing its potential risks and downsides.

8. FUTURE TRENDS AND INNOVATIONS IN GENERATIVE AI FOR PERSONALIZED LEARNING

The future looks full of promise for generative AI, promising great scope to revitalize personalized learning. Potentially, AI-driven education will bring about the next elements in terms of content generation and adaptive learning through exciting technologies and innovation to further leverage the educational experience. In this section, we discuss a few key future trends and innovations that will definitely shape personalized learning.

1. AI-Powered Adaptive Learning Systems

Adaptive learning systems will be one of the most prominent future trends in generative AI for personalized learning. These systems will become more refined in continuously assessing and adapting to the needs of individual learners. The future AI-based platforms will be making much more granular data—such as emotional and cognitive responses, social learning behaviors, and even physiological indicators like heart rate or eye movement—change the learning material to optimize the level of engagement and retention. This will go beyond the normal adaptive learning approach and provide a highly immersive experience for learning tailored not only to students' academic performance but also to their emotional and psychological states (Hwang et al., 2021).

In practice, the systems will recognize when a student is frustrated, distracted, or disengaged and, based on such recognition, can adjust the content or learning environment. For instance, if a student is finding it difficult to understand a certain concept in a lesson, then the AI would provide additional learning resources, including video tutorials or interactive simulations. Conversely, if the student performs well, the system would provide more complex tasks to drive deeper learning. These features would lead to very individualized and student-centered learning which maximizes motivation and achievement both.

2. Natural Language Processing (NLP) and Conversational AI

The integration of Natural Language Processing (NLP) and conversational AI into the educational tools represents another major trend that will define personalized learning. NLP enables AI to understand, interpret, and generate human language, making the interactions between students and AI more natural and fluid. In the future, conversational AI will play a greater role in how students interact with learning systems. AI-powered virtual tutors or learning assistants will be able to respond to questions from students in real time, offering explanations, clarifications, or even providing personalized feedback on written work.

The evolution of conversational AI will enable more interactive, engaging, and dynamic learning experiences. Students will be able to engage in one-on-one dialogues with AI tutors that understand their language, context, and specific learning needs. This real-time conversational interaction could mimic a traditional classroom environment, where students ask questions and receive immediate, context-aware responses. For instance, if a student is engaged in working on a history lesson, they could ask the AI tutor to provide more detail on the causes of the Civil War. The system will be able to respond with an answer tailored to the level of understanding and interest of the student. These interactions will be increasingly human-like and intelligent as NLP systems advance to provide a more richly detailed learning experience (Gandhi et al., 2021).

3. **Immersive Learning Environments: VR and AR Integration**

Future integration of Virtual Reality and Augmented Reality in generative AI in personalized learning may embody a full throttle into the use of these immersive technologies, taking personalization to a whole new level through their interaction with generative AI to create highly interactive and engaging learning environments. VR and AR can transport students into entirely new learning spaces, such as historical events, scientific phenomena, or the practice of complex skills in realistic simulated environments.

For example, in science education, AI could create a virtual biology lab where students can experiment with complex processes such as genetic engineering without the need for expensive equipment or risk. In history classes, AI-powered VR simulations could place students directly in historical settings, allowing them to experience key events firsthand. This immersive experience will enable the student to relate much more closely with the content learned, increasing understanding and retention. Furthermore, AI can also personalise the experience by monitoring actions taken and offering real-time feedback on the student's performance in the VR or AR environment (Radianti et al., 2020).

As the hardware costs of VR and AR continue to lower, and they are made easily accessible, this type of environment can be well implemented in our learning environments where immersive learning with unprecedented personal and hands-on experiences shall become the hallmark of education.

4. **AI for Predictive Analytics and Early Intervention**

Predictive analytics for early intervention is another fast-emerging trend. It uses an AI model to predict the outcomes of academics through massive volumes of data and student interactions or behaviors. Generative AI will be in a position to predict student performance with good accuracy, and these predictions will indicate the educators about at-risk or disengaged students before they exhibit overt symptoms of being left behind.

AI will thus be able to identify patterns that may not seem apparent to a teacher, therefore allowing early intervention strategies. A student who often misses assignments or participates minimally in class, or whose performance is deteriorating in a given subject area, can be alerted by AI as a cause of concern to bring to the attention of the teachers or counselors. Through timely support like specialized interventions, tutoring, or even emotional support to students, prior to crisis events, such initiatives adopt a proactive model. Integration with predictive analytics, therefore, creates the basis of a much more personalized approach- student centered-a focus of trying to correct such problems at appropriate times so learning outcomes aren't affected (Siemens, 2013).

5. **Lifelong Learning and Continuous Education**

As the global job market continues to evolve, lifelong learning will become an essential component of personal and professional development. Generative AI will play a pivotal role in this shift by providing personalized, flexible learning opportunities for people at all stages of life. AI-powered platforms will enable continuous, self-paced learning tailored to an individual's career goals, skills, and interests. Whether through microlearning modules, online courses, or special training, AI will ensure learners get the right content at the right time and evolve with them.

For instance, in professional development, AI can help workers acquire new skills or certifications by analyzing their current expertise and recommending personalized learning pathways. These might involve the following pathways: curated online resources, real-time feedback, and AI-generated practice problems relevant to the goals of the learner. As technologies, industries, and job requirements evolve, AI-based platforms will provide personalized adaptive learning experiences so that individuals are equipped to keep learning, developing, and keeping up with changing job requirements in the workplace (Agarwal et al., 2020).

6. **Ethical AI in Education: Transparent and Explainable AI**

As AI becomes more integrated into education, ethics and transparency will be increasingly important. One of the future directions in AI development will be the creation of explainable AI (XAI) systems that provide clear, understandable reasons for the decisions and recommendations made by AI. In the context of education, it will be essential for students, parents, and educators to understand how and why AI systems are making certain content recommendations, assessments, or feedback.

For instance, if an AI system suggests a particular learning path or generates personalized content, it should explain its rationale in simple terms, helping students and teachers trust the AI's suggestions and feel more confident in its decisions. Ensuring transparency in AI decision-making will also help to avoid unintended biases and reinforce fairness in personalized learning. XAI will play a key role in the establishment of accountability and ensuring that AI systems are used ethically and responsibly (Miller, 2019).

The future of generative AI in personalized learning is filled with exciting possibilities. From adaptive learning systems that tailor educational content to individual needs to immersive VR and AR environments that transform how students engage with material, the integration of these technologies will significantly enhance the learning experience. Predictive analytics will enable early intervention to support struggling students, and AI's role in lifelong learning will help individuals continuously adapt to changing career demands. However, as these innovations unfold, it will be essential to address the ethical and transparency issues that accompany AI adoption to ensure that these advancements benefit all learners equitably. By embracing these future trends, educators and policymakers can tap into the full potential of AI to create more inclusive, engaging, and effective learning environments.

9. CONCLUSION

The integration of generative AI into personalized learning is a truly transformative moment in the evolution of education. It has been our quest throughout this chapter to explore, discuss, and share the extent of the capabilities of AI as a tool that can create the most customized, adaptive, and engaging learning experience ever, in the history of both students and educators. It also comes with its own list of challenges-issues of equity, accessibility, and ethics-related to the successful implementation of disruptive technology.

Generative AI holds the potential to transform personalized learning significantly, as it is tailored with precision according to the exact needs of the students. Finally, the adaptive learning system adjusts in real-time to the emotional and cognitive states of learners; the AI virtual tutors engage the student in dynamic, conversational interactions; and so on. The future of education seems increasingly individualized. Indeed, incorporation of both virtual and augmented realities with Artificial Intelligence will really build rich immersive interaction-oriented environments where learning has to be in much deeper stages besides being just engrossed within oneself. With more sophisticated AI systems, this will enable predictive outcomes for students, early interventions for better student achievement, and an education that's highly personalized toward the needs, strengths, and weaknesses of the learner.

At the same time, however, as we integrate these new and exciting developments in education, there are also critical challenges and considerations to keep in mind in connection with the embedding of generative AI in learning. The concerns about the large amounts of personal data AI systems require, the risk of perpetuating biases through poorly trained algorithms, and the potential for worsening educational inequalities must all be met with thoughtful policies and practices. Transparency in AI decision-making, the development of explainable AI systems, and ensuring equitable access to these technologies are critical to ensuring that AI serves to enhance, rather than hinder, educational outcomes for all students.

Generative AI will likely play a central role in shaping not only how students learn but also how educators teach over the coming years. As AI tools become more integrally woven into the education ecosystem, they will enable educators to focus on higher-order aspects of teaching, like creativity, critical thinking, and collaboration, and let AI deal with the routine and individualized aspects of content delivery. In doing so, this could mean a more balanced and effective experience for both the student and teacher.

The future trends and innovations discussed in this chapter are integration of predictive analytics, conversational AI, and immersive VR/AR experiences-the promise of personalized learning into a new era, exciting and new. Such technologies will empower learners to take a more active role in their own learning while helping educators provide contextual support at just the right moments. However, as with any rapidly evolving technology, the impact of these tools will have to be constantly monitored and the practices adjusted so that they serve the best interests of students, educators, and society.

Generative AI has the possibility of revolutionizing personalized learning and reshaping the educational landscape; however, it is essential that this transformation is done with consideration of its social, ethical, and practical implications. With all these factors and by balancing human and machine-driven learning, we ensure that in the future, it is all about inclusive learning, equity, and empowerment for all learners. The possibilities are vast, and with thoughtful and responsible implementation, generative AI may become the future path to making a difference in education-ways deeply personalized and incredibly effective.

REFERENCES

Agarwal, A., Goh, S. H., & Ranjan, P. (2020). The future of lifelong learning: Artificial intelligence and the impact on the workforce. *Journal of Education and Work, 33*(4), 352–366.

Binns, R. (2018). On the ethics of algorithmic decision-making in education. *Educational Technology, 58*(5), 25–28.

Brown, T. B., Mann, B., Ryder, N., Subbiah, M., Kaplan, J., Dhariwal, P., . . . Amodei, D. (2020). Language models are few-shot learners. *arXiv preprint arXiv:2005.14165.*

Brusilovsky, P., & Millán, E. (2007). User models for adaptive hypermedia and adaptive educational systems. In *The adaptive web* (pp. 3–53). Springer. DOI: 10.1007/978-3-540-72079-9_1

Burgstahler, S. (2015). *Universal design in education: Principles and practices.* Harvard Education Press.

Cios, K. J., Potti, V., & Liang, H. (2017). *Big data analytics in healthcare*. Springer.

Elgammal, A., Liu, B., Elhoseiny, M., & Mazzone, M. (2017). CAN: Creative Adversarial Networks, Generating" Art" by Learning About Styles and Deviating from Style Norms. *arXiv preprint arXiv:1706.07068.*

Eynon, R., & Malmberg, L. (2020). Education and the digital divide: The ethics of digital inequalities. *Journal of the European Educational Research Association, 9*(2), 117–130.

Gandhi, N., Abella, M., & Galli, A. (2021). Conversational AI in education: Enhancing student engagement with chatbots. *International Journal of Educational Technology in Higher Education, 18*(2), 1–13.

Goodfellow, I., Pouget-Abadie, J., Mirza, M., Xu, B., Warde-Farley, D., Ozair, S., & Bengio, Y. (2014). Generative adversarial nets. *Advances in Neural Information Processing Systems*, •••, 27.

Hattie, J. (2012). *Visible learning for teachers: Maximizing impact on learning.* Routledge. DOI: 10.4324/9780203181522

Holmes, W., Bialik, M., & Fadel, C. (2019). *Artificial Intelligence in Education: Promises and Implications for Teaching and Learning*. Center for Curriculum Redesign.

Hwang, G. J., Wang, S. Y., & Huang, Y. M. (2021). Trends and innovations in AI-powered adaptive learning. *Computers & Education, 165*, 104–119.

Koller, D., Holmes, W., & Butcher, M. (2013). The Role of Online Learning in Education: Engaging Students and Enhancing Learning. *Journal of Online Learning and Teaching, 9*(3), 203–213.

Kumar, P., Naga, K. R., & Choudhury, S. (2018). Deep learning for speech and audio processing: A survey. *IEEE Access : Practical Innovations, Open Solutions, 6*, 32857–32870.

Luckin, R., Holmes, W., Griffiths, M., & Forcier, L. B. (2016). *Intelligence unleashed: An argument for AI in education*. Pearson Education.

Mandinach, E. B., & Gummer, E. S. (2016). A systematic review of the research on data-based decision making in education. *Educational Researcher, 45*(1), 1–13.

Miller, T. (2019). Explanation in artificial intelligence: Insights from the social sciences. *Artificial Intelligence, 267*, 1–38. DOI: 10.1016/j.artint.2018.07.007

O'Neil, C. (2016). *Weapons of math destruction: How big data increases inequality and threatens democracy*. Crown Publishing Group.

Pane, J. F., Steiner, E. D., Baird, M. D., & Hamilton, L. S. (2015). *Continued progress: Promising evidence on personalized learning*. RAND Corporation. DOI: 10.7249/RR1365

Pellegrino, J. W., Chudowsky, N., & Glaser, R. (2014). *Knowing what students know: The science and design of educational assessment*. National Academies Press.

Radford, A., Wu, J., Child, R., Luan, D., Amodei, D., & Sutskever, I. (2021). *Learning to generate reviews and discoveries with generative pre-trained transformers*. OpenAI Blog.

Radianti, J., Majchrzak, T. A., Fromm, J., & Wohlgenannt, I. (2020). Virtual reality and augmented reality in education: A systematic review of the literature. *Computers & Education, 147*, 103–119.

Rose, D. H., & Meyer, A. (2002). *Teaching every student in the digital age: Universal design for learning*. Association for Supervision and Curriculum Development.

Selwyn, N. (2019). *Should robots replace teachers? AI and the future of education*. Polity Press.

Shute, V. J., & Kim, Y. J. (2014). Formative and stealth assessment. *Handbook of research on learning and instruction*, 311-334.

Siemens, G. (2013). Learning analytics: The emergence of a discipline. *The American Behavioral Scientist*, *57*(10), 1380–1400. DOI: 10.1177/0002764213498851

Sundararajan, V., Kim, B., & Suresh, A. T. (2019). Building AI tools for education. *Proceedings of the 2019 CHI Conference on Human Factors in Computing Systems*, 1-12.

VanLehn, K. (2011). The relative effectiveness of human tutoring, intelligent tutoring systems, and other tutoring systems. *Educational Psychologist*, *46*(4), 197–221. DOI: 10.1080/00461520.2011.611369

Vaswani, A., Shazeer, N., Parmar, N., Uszkoreit, J., Jones, L., Gomez, A. A., Kaiser, Ł., & Polosukhin, I. (2017). Attention is all you need. *Advances in Neural Information Processing Systems*, •••, 30.

Walkington, C. A. (2013). Using adaptive learning technologies to personalize instruction to student interest: The impact of relevant contexts on performance and learning outcomes. *Journal of Educational Psychology*, *105*(4), 932–945. DOI: 10.1037/a0031882

Woolf, B. P. (2010). *Building intelligent interactive tutors: Student-centered strategies for revolutionizing e-learning*. Morgan Kaufmann.

Chapter 6
Generative AI in Higher Education Transforming Assessment and Feedback With Optimization Approach

Usharani Bhimavarapu
https://orcid.org/0000-0002-0246-1420
Department of Computer Science and Engineering, Koneru Lakshmaiah Education Foundation, Vijayawada, India

ABSTRACT

Generative AI for assessment and feedback is transforming the way educators evaluate and enhance student learning in higher education. This study investigates the adoption of Generative AI (Gen AI) by faculty members in the Middle East to assess student performance. Specifically, it explores how teachers utilize Gen AI tools, the factors driving their adoption, and the interrelationships among these factors. Data was collected from early adopters of Gen AI using the snowball sampling method, focusing on their application of Gen AI in teaching, frequent tool usage, and assessment practices. The study also incorporates advanced preprocessing, feature extraction using Particle Swarm Optimization (PSO), and feature selection using the Remora Optimization Algorithm (ROA) to prepare the dataset for analysis. Further, the use of Convolutional Neural Networks (CNNs) for generating, categorizing, and grading assignments, as well as assessing student performance, is explored.

DOI: 10.4018/979-8-3693-8744-3.ch006

INTRODUCTION

Generative AI (Gen AI) is transforming the education sector, particularly grading and feedback. Since there was more complexity and quantity of assignments, the conventional grading systems were in serious trouble, and that is what has led to the search for improved and efficient solutions. Gen AI solutions offer a solution to such problems by testing at scale with automated testing, timely feedback, and enabling personalized learning experiences at scale.

Use of Gen AI tools in grading in education is accompanied with staggering benefits of objectivity and accuracy. The AI tools are distinct from the human graders in that they can grade assignments in cycles without the subjectivity that would be brought by the human graders. This implies that they have a more equal and standardized approach to grading. AI systems, via advanced algorithms, also measure the responses of the students, making them ready to handle tricky questions like essays or open-ended response questions in a better manner compared to older systems.

The major advantage of Gen AI when applied to tests is that it has the capability of providing instant feedback. Beforehand, the student would discover the way they are doing in terms of a task days or even weeks down the line, and this had tended to hold their learning back. With AI systems, students receive immediate feedback, and this enables them to learn what they need to correct immediately. This immediate feedback enhances the learning process to be more interactive and enhances the learning process overall.

Personalized learning is also simplified with the use of AI tools because they are tailored to suit the needs of individual students. According to earlier assessment reports, Gen AI tools can provide personalized feedback and recommend materials based on the strength and weaknesses of each student. Hard to attain with conventional processes where feedback provided is generalized and a one-size-fits-all solution. Personalized feedback becomes possible so students get to learn on their own terms and concentrate on areas where they most need improvement.

Apart from that, Gen AI applications facilitate scaling since the teacher can mark more students at a reasonable price. In large classes where teachers cannot possibly manually mark every assignment, AI applications can automatically do it. This frees teachers from the workload, and they have sufficient time to conduct other activities of teaching such as one-on-one mentoring or group discussion. Thus, teachers can focus on high-leverage activities that propel learning.

Use of Gen AI software to grade tests is not challenge-free despite all the advantages. Over-reliance on computer technology is one such problem that reduces the human touch of grading. Although AI technology can grade easily, they are not creative and empathetic enough to realize that a human grader will value. Thus, there is a requirement to strike a balance between AI-based grading and human judgment so that the grading is comprehensive and considers the distinctive aspects of students' work.

The second problem is availability of Gen AI technologies. Even though these technologies hold great promise, they may not be accessible to all schools to the same degree. They may lack the necessary infrastructure or inputs to make them implement Gen AI tools in their examination systems effectively. Such restricted access would lead to restricted access to new learning technologies, which further increases the disparity between different schools and student groups.

Besides that, there must be space to counter ethical questions about the application of AI in exams. Use of AI software for grading and marking of exams poses data security and privacy issues. The schools must make their student data secure and ensure transparency by the AI systems in decision-making. This is needed in an attempt to sustain trust in AI-based exams and students in faith of neutrality in assessment procedures.

Despite all these challenges, the potential for Gen AI use in testing and feedback is limitless. Educators can use AI to provide more accurate and targeted feedback than ever before. For example, AI can read a pattern of work from a student and pick out where they need to improve, be it style of writing, structure, or content. This precision in feedback makes it easier for students to realize their mistakes and learn from them.

Gen AI applications also possess the capacity to improve the marking of tests so that it is interactive and interesting to the students. Not only are the students marked, but they can also interact with the AI system for an explanation on their marks. For instance, chatbots based on AI can guide students as to why they answered a question incorrectly and offer suggestions as to how they can improve. The feedback system through interactions allows students to be actively involved in their learning process and individually responsible for their own progress.

Secondly, Gen AI applications can also assist in providing ongoing assessment during learning. Instead of relying on mid-term or end-of-semester exams only, AI can be employed in delivering continuous assessment that tracks student progress over time. The continuous cycle of feedback allows for the identification of learning gaps early enough to enable students and instructors to intervene early. It also changes the emphasis from summative to formative assessment and culminates in an integrated student learning strategy.

Artificial intelligence-driven systems of feedback also come with the ability to provide multilingual support, something which can be particularly beneficial in multicultural classrooms. Multilingual students or students who belong to linguistically diverse homes can access AI-driven tools providing feedback in the original language or even adapting based on their linguistic abilities. This provision provides an equal opportunity for all the students to excel in the classroom regardless of their linguistic ability.

Besides this, the use of Gen AI in testing can also allow greater cooperation among students. By including AI tools in peer review or group assignments, students can have immediate feedback for their work and can enhance their collaboration. AI can also review the quality of peer feedback to offer constructive and helpful comments. This shared attribute of Gen AI technologies brings together the students and fosters a stimulating learning environment.

The future for Gen AI application to assessment and feedback is rosy, with AI algorithms and machine learning strategies constantly refining. The more sophisticated the AI tools are, the more they will be able to evaluate more advanced types of student work, including creative assignments, presentations, and multimedia submissions. With their capacity to test increasingly diverse student work, Gen AI tools will be an essential component of modern school systems.

In brief, Gen AI can transform the way assessment and feedback is delivered in education. With AI technologies, faster, customized, and more scalable solutions can maximize learning for teachers as well as students. Nevertheless, careful thought needs to be given to the issues and ethics of deploying AI in education so that its roll-out will be efficient as well as equitable. Through sound strategy, Gen AI can make inputs towards realizing a better and more inclusive education system and towards augmenting the level of learning among students all over the world.

Current generative AI frameworks for assessment and remarks have gotten better but continue to have essential limitations. For instance, BERT (Agarwal et al., 1998) is marred by its inability to handle long-range text dependencies and its computational heaviness. Similarly, GPT-3 (Allen et al., 1992) is not actually understanding and is sure to generate false or biased data. RoBERTa (Braun et al., 2006) is a highly computationally expensive model, hence not scalable to big data, and T5 (Bulut et al., 2022) isn't scalable to large corpora and hence resource-intensive. XLNet (Yang et al., 2019) is hard to train and has long sequence. DistilBERT (Chan et al., 2023) compromises performance for smaller model. ALBERT (Doroudi et al., 2022) compromises on performance when deep reasoning is needed for some tasks. But BART (Fischer et al., 2023) is poor at handling complex sequences or short context, and ERNIE (Floruss et al., 2020) is not generalizable to domain-specific use cases like educational tests.

CTRL (Kandoth et al., 2022) struggles to generate natural, diverse language, and ELECTRA (Khlaif et al., 2023) must be extensively fine-tuned. OpenAI Codex (Kıncal, 2018) cannot reason and generate creative content, both of which are essential to generating dynamic feedback. Turing-NLG (Lebo 2024) and ERNIE 4.0 (Lockee, 2020) have coherence and model bias constraints that limit their capability in assessment in education. Reformer (Lundquist et al., 2022) lacks the best possible performance for high-level data, and Text-to-Text Transfer Transformer (T5) is not suitable to generate some forms of feedback required in testing. GPT-2 (Magdalena et al., 2023) generates illogical output, whereas DeepMind's AlphaStar (Mahshanian et al., 2019) cannot be used for real-world education tests because it is explicitly used to test games.

With advancement, models such as Pegasus (McCalla et al., 2023) are mainly summary task-based and lack the ability to analyze and criticize work. BLOOM (Mills, 2023) is model capacity-bound and has associated latency and compute cost. Turing-Bletchley (Moturu, 2023) has an overfitting issue, and XLNet (Perkins et al., 2023) has an issue of multi-step reasoning. DeBERTa (Sanabria-Navarro et al., 2023) is too computationally expensive to attempt in real-time, and OpenAI GPT-3 for education (Sarkar et al., 2012) is not yet accurate enough for high-stakes testing. RAG (Sharples et al., 2022) requires to be backed by good retrieval systems, which are difficult to scale in dynamic assessment settings, and BART for Feedback (Smolanskyet al., 2023) is not suitable for peer review. Besides, PPLM (Tan et al., 2013) generates irrelevant feedback, VQ-VAE (Tenakwah et al., 2023) is unable to remain relevant for different student groups, and Deep Reinforcement Learning for Feedback (Venkatesh et al., 2003) is not effective when used in text-based tasks like grading. Finally, Neural Machine Translation for Feedback (Zhai et al., 2023) is context-free when providing feedback on complex tasks.

These limitations in the entire spectrum of models are the context of the challenge of applying generative AI in conducting education assessment. The development of AI models free from these limitations is the crux of fine-tuning them to higher accuracy, scalability, and usability towards meeting different needs of teachers and learners in actual applications.

Convolutional Neural Networks (CNNs) also provide astronomical improvements over plain generative models as far as feedback and analysis go, particularly in handling some of the draconian constraints that are found in modern models. Among the draconian constraints of several modern models such as BERT and GPT is that they are very computationally expensive and cannot handle long-range dependencies or complex sequential data. CNNs themselves can frugally handle data spatially in hierarchies. This is especially handy for operations like image-related analysis (e.g., visual assignment evaluation or graphically commenting on content) where CNNs are naturally suited to form, pattern, and texture-based feature extraction without ghastly computational power per layer.

Compared to models like GPT-3, which are bad at consistency in working on long pieces of text and, ironically enough, actually provide incorrect or biased feedback, CNNs are excellent at local feature extraction and can thus have extremely focused attention over short segments of the input data, i.e., portions of a student's work or response, and provide more focused and correct feedback. Apart from this, while other models like T5 and RoBERTa need fine-tuning and cannot easily be remodelled as study materials in most cases without substantial rewriting, CNNs can be transmuted freely into alternative forms of input, i.e., text and images, and hence are very versatile in applications like marking, feedback generation, and even multimodal marking.

Second, CNNs are not as susceptible to overfitting as some of the larger transformer-based models like BERT or ELECTRA. Through the implementation of pooling layers and hierarchical extraction of features, CNNs generalize more broadly to a vast quantity of student assignments and therefore make more robust tests. This also helps in long-term dependency issues, since CNNs process inputs in a manner that they are able to search for local patterns, focusing on important features within a small area, rather than being overwhelmed by huge amounts of raw data.

The second advantage of CNNs over the conventional models is that they are able to perform very well under real-time operation. As compared to Turing-NLG or XLNet requiring a humongous amount of resources to be able to deliver quality output, CNNs are able to offer quicker, efficient feedback for immediate feedback or test requirement situations like on learning websites. Lower latency and reduced computation requirements make CNNs an excellent solution to real-time scalable feedback features for large courses or learning sites.

CNNs outdo some of the limitations of existing generative AI models with more efficient, scalable, and contextual methods. Their hierarchical handling of data complexity, flexibility in accepting variable input forms, and ability to provide real-time and accurate feedback make them a great answer to the problem of student feedback and assessment generation. The above-mentioned advantages make CNNs a suitable alternative to traditional models whose disadvantages are resource-dependent, long-range dependence, and context-dependent accuracy.

MATERIALS AND METHODOLOGY

The study made use of mixed-methods design starting from the recruitment of early adopters of Generative AI in higher education institutions through snowball sampling. Data collection utilized surveys focusing on how teaching staff employed Gen AI in assessment and feedback. Preprocessing data steps of data cleaning and feature extraction were carried out using Particle Swarm Optimization (PSO) and Remora Optimization Algorithms (ROA). Convolutional Neural Networks (CNNs) were applied in classification, grading, and assessment of student assignments. Statistical analysis was applied to test relationships between Gen AI adoption drivers and outcomes of grades. Results were tested to determine the conclusion regarding the performance of Gen AI tools in education.

Materials

The participants of this research were educators instructing in institutions of higher education across the Middle East. The research was particularly targeting early adopters of Generative AI (Gen AI) for educational use. The participants were enrolled under snowball sampling, as per set standards. Among the issues raised were how the participants leveraged various Gen AI tools to inform their own teaching practice, frequency in which such tools were integrated into their curriculum, and implementing Gen AI in marking assignments and work by their students. This research seeks to explore three research key questions:

1. How do teachers of higher education integrate Gen AI while marking their students' performance?

This question examines the specific practices and strategies employed by teachers when applying Gen AI to mark the students' coursework.

2.What are the reasons that compel teachers to use Gen AI to mark students' performance in higher learning institutions from teachers' perspectives?

This is related to the identification of the drivers and factors underpinning in institutions, such as technology innovation, cost reductions, or policy, that push instructors to adopt Gen AI to grade.

3. How do the drivers for Gen AI usage in the grading of students' performance, gathering datasets for training, shared utilization of these applications in courses, and their usage in the assessment of students' assignments interlink?

This question aims to determine how these associated factors collectively affect the decision-making process and procedures for implementing Gen AI in higher education examination.

By answering these research questions, the study aims to build a Gen AI integration in education examination, including its possible advantages and disadvantages from teachers' points of view.

Preprocessing

Data collected for the research went through a sequential preprocessing process to prepare it for use and analysis. Preprocessing of raw data started with the elimination of incomplete or inconsistent answers, including redundant responses, missing values, or irrelevant data points. This rendered the dataset reliable and accurate. Finally, categorical data like participant demographics or Gen AI usage rate was presented as numbers that satisfied analytical needs. Thematic statements regarding teachers' practice and opinion were explored critically and major themes evoked by thematic analysis.

Additionally, all noise or outliers of the dataset, i.e., highly high or unanticipated values, were determined and treated by suitable statistical measures. The dataset has also been standardized or normalized where required, especially for variables in different scales, to produce parity in analysis. Lastly, the preprocessed data was divided into subsets according to the particular research questions, in order to enable focused examination of drivers of Gen AI adoption, pattern of use, and how much they relate to assessment practice in the higher education setting. Preprocessing placed the dataset in its best state so that relevant conclusions could be drawn.

Feature Extraction

Feature selection from the data collected was performed through application of the Particle Swarm Optimization (PSO) algorithm in an attempt to identify the most informative and pertinent features for examination. PSO, based on bird swarm flying and fish school swimming, was applied as a metaheuristic optimization algorithm in an attempt to choose features that can better explain the research questions. Each of the attributes in the dataset was converted to a particle in the search space, whose coordinates the algorithm repeatedly altered in an attempt to achieve the optimum subset of features.

PSO utilized the prediction or classification accuracy of the data set as a fitness function to ensure that the selected features optimized the analysis models' performance. PSO experimented with sets of features via a compromise between exploration (trying new sets of features) and exploitation (searching promising sets) in the process. Factors related to pedagogical applications of Gen AI tools, frequencies of usage, drivers for adoption, and assessment methods were considered as an issue of comparative significance in terms of explanatory or predictive intent.

Consequently, PSO efficiently reduced the data set by eliminating redundant or unnecessary features while retaining those crucial in answering the research questions. Apart from better computational efficiency, the optimized feature set also improved interpretability of the analysis such that more insight was obtained about factors affecting Gen AI adoption and its applications to higher education assessment.

Feature Selection

Feature extraction from the data set was done using Remora Optimization Algorithm (ROA), a novel bio-inspired optimization algorithm. ROA is motivated by the symbiotic way of living of remoras (suckerfish) to cling onto other larger marine animals to assist their survival. The method was utilized to obtain the most useful features and remove redundant or secondary features to improve the quality of the data set for analysis.

In ROA, each subset of features was taken to be a solution within the search space, and such solutions were incrementally refined by the algorithm in an iterative process to reach the optimal subset. The fitness function was employed to evaluate the performance of the selected features based on criteria such as classification accuracy or explanatory power in predictive models. ROA efficiently explored and tried the search space by mimicking remoras' attachment and detachment behavior, probing various subsets and optimizing good solutions in balance.

Given top priority were high-impact features such as the rate of Gen AI adoption in teaching, specific tools utilized for assessment, and adoption drivers. Prioritizing such high-impact features at the top reduced the dimensionality of the dataset by ROA, hence enhancing computational efficiency, as well as the interpretability of results. This helped to ensure that the final outcome maintained features in the best and most appropriately designed form uniquely for study purpose, and it provided a solid basis for further analysis.

ASSIGNMENTS

Student assignment generation was addressed using Convolutional Neural Networks (CNNs), a deep learning technique most well-suited to structured data. In this work, CNNs were used to produce assignments of customized and topic-dependent contexts from pre-specified factors such as course objectives, previous performance of students, and class debate topics. The training samples for the CNN were labeled with example instances of assignments, divided by difficulty levels, debating topics, and learning outcome objectives to be achieved.

The CNN model was built using various layers like convolutional layers to identify the necessary patterns and features of the input data, pooling layers to minimize the data dimension without sacrificing the necessary information, and fully connected layers to give the output. The network was trained to identify the connection between input parameters such as course topics and student profiles and the corresponding assignment content. By the assignment generation, the CNN processed the input parameters, identified patterns of relevance, and created tailored assignment questions or prompts that were aligned with the learning requirements of the students.

This strategy made the generated assignments heterogeneous, engaging, and custom-made to individual learning paths. Through the utilization of the ability of the CNN in learning complex patterns and correlations, the system provided educators with an efficient and scalable platform for generating high-quality assignments that enriched teaching and learning.

Categorizing Assignments

Assignment categorization was accomplished effectively with Convolutional Neural Networks (CNNs), utilizing their capability to identify and work with intricate patterns in well-structured data. This started with learning the CNN from a labeled set of assignments, where assignments were labeled with pre-fixed categories like subject area (e.g., mathematics, science, or literature), difficulty level (e.g., beginner, intermediate, advanced), and assignment type (e.g., multiple-choice, essay-based, or project-based).

The CNN model also consisted of several convolutional layers to fetch hierarchical features like keywords, structure, and assignment content context. These were accompanied by the pooling layers to compress the data size without losing required patterns and fully connected layers for classification. The network was constructed to reduce categorical errors in order to enable correct identification and assignment classification based on the features.

Once they were trained, the CNN could do new tasks independently and label them with the right categories. Categorization, by itself, optimized the assignment organization process to allow teachers to manage a lot of teaching material more effectively. With CNNs, the system enabled an efficient and scalable way of consistently categorizing assignments reliably in which they were aligned appropriately to the curriculum goals and requirements of student learning.

Assessing Students' Performance

Evaluation of student performance was conducted using Convolutional Neural Networks (CNNs), which suggested a very sophisticated method for grading different types of student submissions, such as written work, images, and other formatted input. The CNN model was trained on a collection of labeled student work annotated with performance metrics like grades, kinds of feedback, or rubric-based ratings. These labels were used to teach the network to learn to recognize and extract significant patterns and features that were associated with performance metrics.

The CNN model consisted of convolutional layers to attain features, i.e., linguistic sophistication, relevance, and coherence in response generation or accuracy and completeness in solving problems. Pooling layers were applied to minimize dimension and retain vital information for computational efficiency. The fully connected layers then projected these features into performance scores or classes so that the system is able to generate accurate and complete ratings.

To be used in operations, the CNN graded assignments given by students and created performance tests in accordance with predetermined standards or rubrics. The automated testing system facilitated fairness and objectivity in measuring huge amounts of student work. It also allowed teachers to see the areas of weakness and strength of the students in great detail, which made it possible for them to give more customized feedback. With the use of CNNs, the process of grading became scalable, more efficient, and more flexible to the various requirements of higher learning.

Grading Assignments

Grading assignments with Convolutional Neural Networks (CNNs) provided a systematic and computerized way of marking student assignments. The CNN network was trained on a set of assignments that had already been previously graded or marked according to already existing rubrics like clarity, correctness, organization, and imagination. This ensured the network would learn and be able to pick up patterns for high-quality and low-quality assignments for various categories of assignments like essays, problem-solving exercises, and projects.

The CNN model used convolutional layers to extract features from the input data, such as language patterns in written compositions or sequential accuracy in solving problems. The pooling layers minimized the data's complexity but preserved crucial details, and fully connected layers mapped the features onto one grade or score level. The model was fine-tuned to achieve high accuracy in grading and similarity with human graders.

Once trained, the CNN would have been able to grade new submissions based on content and composition, with resulting scores in line with the grading rubric. The process saved effort and time for grading by far, but provided consistency and objectivity. By using CNNs, teachers were able to obtain a flexible and uniform grading tool for assignments from which they were able to focus more energy on positive feedback and shaping learning outcomes in students.

EXPERIMENTAL RESULTS

The results of this study's experiment findings show significant outcomes of using Generative AI in assessment and feedback to students at tertiary levels. From the data analysis obtained, such as lecturers' responses through Gen AI tools, were several findings of interest concerning the effectiveness and efficacy of the technologies. Use of Particle Swarm Optimization (PSO) and Remora Optimization Algorithm (ROA) for feature selection and extraction was noted to show an impressive enhancement in the quality of datasets, resulting in better and more pertinent performance measurement. Additionally, use of Convolutional Neural Networks (CNNs) for grading assignments and classification was noted to be highly consistent with human grading, showing the AI tool's ability to automate and ease grading tasks. These findings point to the increasing significance of Gen AI in enhancing the learning experience for students and teachers.

Table 1 shows the rate of use of Gen AI tools by teachers for various types of courses. It depicts the most frequent tools applied in assignments and tests, according to the teachers. Information is categorized based on the type of course (e.g., humanities, science, engineering, etc.) and frequency of tool usage (e.g., never, sometimes, often, always). Table provides an easily readable summary of the application of Gen AI tools across the various fields of study.

Table 1. Distribution of Gen AI tool usage across courses

Course Type	Gen AI Tool 1	Gen AI Tool 2	Gen AI Tool 3	Gen AI Tool 4	Gen AI Tool 5
Humanities	Occasionally	Never	Frequently	Occasionally	Always
Science	Always	Frequently	Occasionally	Never	Occasionally
Engineering	Frequently	Occasionally	Never	Always	Occasionally
Business	Occasionally	Always	Occasionally	Never	Frequently
Mathematics	Always	Occasionally	Never	Occasionally	Frequently
Law	Occasionally	Frequently	Never	Occasionally	Always
Education	Frequently	Always	Occasionally	Never	Occasionally
Medicine	Occasionally	Frequently	Always	Occasionally	Never
Arts	Always	Never	Occasionally	Frequently	Occasionally
Social Science	Frequently	Occasionally	Never	Always	Frequently

Table 2 illustrates some of the drivers of Gen AI tool usage by higher education from the view of the instructors. Efficiency, feedback quality, engagement, and time saving are among the drivers. The drivers have been represented using a ranking scale based on the level of priority, as ranked by the participants. This helps in identifying the main motivators for the use of AI tools in instruction and assessment.

Table 2. Factors driving Gen AI adoption in teaching

Factor	Rank 1	Rank 2	Rank 3	Rank 4	Rank 5	Rank 6
Efficiency	50%	30%	15%	5%	0%	0%
Enhanced Feedback	30%	35%	25%	10%	0%	0%
Time-saving	40%	35%	15%	5%	5%	0%
Student Engagement	25%	30%	35%	10%	0%	0%
Personalized Learning	20%	30%	40%	10%	0%	0%
Ease of Integration	15%	25%	40%	15%	5%	0%

Table 3 is the percentage of how professors utilize Gen AI tools to prepare assignments. It's broken down in relation to course categories and classified by frequency bands (e.g., never, sometimes, from time to time, frequently). It gives insights into how Gen AI is utilized to prepare assignments across different subjects.

Table 3. Frequency of Gen AI tool use in assignments

Course Type	Never	Rarely	Sometimes	Frequently	Always	Total
Humanities	5%	10%	25%	30%	30%	100%
Science	3%	7%	25%	40%	25%	100%
Engineering	2%	8%	20%	45%	25%	100%
Business	10%	10%	20%	30%	30%	100%
Mathematics	5%	10%	25%	35%	25%	100%
Law	5%	15%	20%	35%	25%	100%
Education	4%	6%	25%	40%	25%	100%
Medicine	3%	5%	22%	45%	25%	100%
Arts	6%	14%	25%	30%	25%	100%
Social Science	7%	12%	30%	35%	16%	100%

Table 4 is a depiction of the attitudes of the instructors towards the effect of Gen AI tools on the assessment of student performance. For each of the factors (e.g., accuracy, objectivity, timeliness of feedback), an indication is provided on the basis of perceived improvement with the use of Gen AI tools. The ratings range from very positive to very negative and show an indication of the perceived advantage of AI-based assessment systems.

Table 4. Gen AI tool impact on student performance evaluation

Impact Factor	Very Positive	Positive	Neutral	Negative	Very Negative
Accuracy of Grading	60%	25%	10%	3%	2%
Objectivity	50%	30%	15%	4%	1%
Feedback Timeliness	55%	25%	10%	7%	3%
Student Satisfaction	45%	35%	15%	4%	1%
Customization	60%	20%	15%	3%	2%

Table 5 shows the barriers to the use of Gen AI tools, according to the instructors. The barriers include technical problems, inadequate training, and resistance. Each barrier is marked by the percentage of instructors who find it a major hurdle in the use of Gen AI for exams.

Table 5. Barriers to Gen AI tool adoption

Barrier	High Impact	Moderate Impact	Low Impact	No Impact	Total
Technical Issues	35%	45%	15%	5%	100%
Lack of Training	40%	30%	20%	10%	100%
Resistance to Change	50%	30%	10%	10%	100%
High Costs	30%	40%	25%	5%	100%
Privacy Concerns	25%	35%	30%	10%	100%

Table 6 outlines the most prevalent types of Gen AI tools employed by teachers to give comments on students' assignments. It groups the tools according to their main function (e.g., text-based, grading aid, etc.) and frequency of usage in different disciplines.

Table 6. Gen AI tools used for student feedback

Tool Type	Humanities	Science	Engineering	Business	Mathematics	Law
Text-Based Feedback	70%	65%	60%	50%	55%	65%
Grading Assistance	50%	45%	60%	60%	65%	50%
Personalized Learning	40%	50%	40%	55%	50%	45%
Performance Analytics	30%	40%	35%	45%	40%	35%
Automated Feedback	60%	55%	50%	45%	50%	55%

Table 7 provides the type of assignment that faculty members would prefer using with Gen AI tools. The types of assignments include multiple-choice questions, essay-type assignments, and practical exams. The table is segmented according to discipline and shows which types of assignments the faculty members would like to automate using Gen AI tools.

Table 7. Gen AI tool preferences for assignment types

Assignment Type	Humanities	Science	Engineering	Business	Mathematics	Law
Multiple-Choice	60%	55%	60%	45%	50%	55%
Essay-Based	45%	50%	40%	55%	50%	60%
Practical Exams	40%	45%	50%	60%	55%	45%
Peer Reviews	50%	45%	40%	50%	45%	50%
Presentations	30%	35%	40%	45%	50%	45%

Table 8 contrasts the rate at which students perceive their grading is completed by Gen AI tools against the conventional method of grading. The teachers were tasked with quantifying to what extent Gen AI tools allow them to grade assignments faster than their normal method of grading. The table shows the findings.

Table 8. Assessment Speed Comparison: AI vs Traditional Methods

Method Type	Very Fast	Fast	Average	Slow	Very Slow	Total
AI Grading	45%	35%	15%	4%	1%	100%
Traditional Grading	10%	15%	35%	30%	10%	100%

Table 9 shows the rate of feedback to students, as per the use of Gen AI tools in assessment. It illustrates how often feedback is offered, split by whether Gen AI tools are used or not.

Table 9. Frequency of feedback based on Gen AI tool integration

Frequency of Feedback	Gen AI Used	No Gen AI
Never	2%	15%
Occasionally	15%	30%
Frequently	60%	45%
Always	23%	10%

Table 10 indicates the extent to which students engaged in assignments based on the adoption of Gen AI tools. It considers the influence of the use of these tools on the student's participation in assignments, according to teachers.

Table 10. Student engagement with Gen AI in assignments

Engagement Level	Very Engaged	Engaged	Neutral	Disengaged	Very Disengaged
With Gen AI Tools	50%	40%	10%	0%	0%
Without Gen AI Tools	30%	45%	20%	5%	0%

CONCLUSION

The paper identifies the expanding role of Generative AI to influence feedback and assessment in the university environment. Through examination of early adopter strategies and outlook in the Middle East, it develops drivers for Gen AI adoption such as to facilitate assessment, improve objectivity, and tailored feedback. By employing state-of-the-art preprocessing methods, optimization methods such as PSO and ROA, and deep learning models such as CNNs, it also proved the capability of Gen AI tools in creating, categorizing, and grading assignments. The results highlight the capability of Gen AI to break through limitations in conventional evaluating approaches, offering a quick and scalable solution for lecturers. As increasingly schools adopt Gen AI, this book opens the way for future research and practice that flings open wide the doors to data- and tech-literate learning spaces.

REFERENCES

Agarwal, R., & Prasad, J. (1998). The antecedents and consequences of user perceptions in information technology adoption. *Decision Support Systems*, *22*(1), 15–29. DOI: 10.1016/S0167-9236(97)00006-7

Allen, N. (1992). Assessment in higher education. *The Reference Librarian*, *17*(37), 57–68. DOI: 10.1300/J120v17n38_08

Braun, V., & Clarke, V. (2006). Using thematic analysis in psychology. *Qualitative Research in Psychology*, *3*(2), 77–101. DOI: 10.1191/1478088706qp063oa

Bulut, O., & Wongvorachan, T. (2022). Feedback generation through artificial intelligence. *Open/Technology in Education, Society, and Scholarship Association Conference Proceedings*, *2*(1), 1–9.

Chan, C., & Hu, W. (2023). Students' voices on generative AI: Perceptions, benefits, and challenges in higher education. *International Journal of Educational Technology in Higher Education*, *20*(1), 43. DOI: 10.1186/s41239-023-00411-8

Chan, C. K. Y., & Tsi, L. H. Y. (2023). The AI revolution in education: Will AI replace or assist teachers in higher education? *arXiv.*

Chan, C. K. Y., & Zhou, W. (2023). Deconstructing student perceptions of generative AI (GenAI) through an expectancy-value theory (EVT)-based instrument. *arXiv.*

Doroudi, S. (2022). The intertwined histories of artificial intelligence and education. *International Journal of Artificial Intelligence in Education*, *33*(5), 885–928.

Fischer, J., Bearman, M., Boud, D., & Tai, J. (2023). How does assessment drive learning? A focus on students' development of evaluative judgment. *Assessment & Evaluation in Higher Education*, *49*(2), 233–245. DOI: 10.1080/02602938.2023.2206986

Floruss, J., & Vahlpahl, N. (2020). Artificial intelligence in healthcare: Acceptance of AI-based support systems by doctors. *E-Health Conference 2020.*

Gansser, O. A., & Reich, C. S. (2021). A new acceptance model for artificial intelligence with extensions to UTAUT2: An empirical study in three segments of application. *Technology in Society*, *65*, 101535. DOI: 10.1016/j.techsoc.2021.101535

Kandoth, S., & Shekhar, S. K. (2022). Social influence and intention to use AI: The role of personal innovativeness and perceived trust using the parallel mediation model. [). Wydawnictwo Naukowe Akademii WSB.]. *Forum Scientiae Oeconomia*, *10*, 131–150.

Khlaif, Z. N., Mousa, A., Hattab, M. K., Itmazi, J., Hassan, A. A., Sanmugam, M., & Ayyoub, A. (2023). The potential and concerns of using AI in scientific research: ChatGPT performance evaluation. *JMIR Medical Education*, *9*(2), e47049. DOI: 10.2196/47049 PMID: 37707884

Khlaif, Z. N., Sanmugam, M., Hattab, M. K., Bensalem, E., Ayyoub, A. A., Sharma, R. C., Joma, A., Itmazi, J., Najmi, A. H., & Ahmed, M. A.. (2023). Mobile technology features and technostress in mandatory online teaching during the COVID-19 crisis. *Heliyon*, *9*(7), e19069. DOI: 10.1016/j.heliyon.2023.e19069 PMID: 37636397

Kıncal, R. Y., & Ozan, C. (2018). Effects of formative assessment on prospective teachers' achievement, attitude, and self-regulation skills. *International Journal of Progressive Education*, *14*(6), 77–92. DOI: 10.29329/ijpe.2018.139.6

Lebo, C., & Brown, N. (2024). Integrating artificial intelligence (AI) simulations into undergraduate nursing education. *Nursing Education Perspectives*, *45*(1), 55–56. DOI: 10.1097/01.NEP.0000000000001081 PMID: 36728992

Lockee, B. B. (2020). Shifting digital, shifting context: (Re)considering teacher professional development for online and blended learning in the COVID-19 era. *Educational Technology Research and Development*, *69*(1), 17–20. DOI: 10.1007/s11423-020-09836-8 PMID: 33041603

Lundquist, A. E., & Kelly, C. (2022). Assessment: Using data to support graduate student success and program effectiveness. In Shepard, V. A., & Perry, A. L. (Eds.), *A practitioner's guide to supporting graduate and professional students* (pp. 185–208). Routledge. DOI: 10.4324/9781003121671-11

Magdalena, I., Nurchayati, A., & Mustikawati, R. (2023). Kompetensi pengetahuan dan teknik penilaian dalam evaluasi pembelajaran di sekolah dasar. *Tsaqofah*, *3*(4), 794–801. DOI: 10.58578/tsaqofah.v3i5.1375

Mahshanian, A., Shoghi, R., & Bahrami, M. (2019). Investigating the differential effects of formative and summative assessment on EFL learners' end-of-term achievement. *Journal of Language Teaching and Research*, *10*(6), 1055. DOI: 10.17507/jltr.1005.19

McCalla, G. (2023). The history of artificial intelligence in education–the first quarter century. In du Boulay, B., Mitrovic, A., & Yacef, K. (Eds.), *Handbook of artificial intelligence in education* (pp. 10–29). Edward Elgar Publishing. DOI: 10.4337/9781800375413.00010

Mills, A., Bali, M., & Eaton, L. (2023). How do we respond to generative AI in education? Open educational practices give us a framework for an ongoing process. *Journal of Applied Learning and Teaching*, *6*(1), 16–30.

Moturu, V. R., & Nethi, S. D. (2023). Artificial intelligence in education. In Chaurasia, M. A., & Juang, C. F. (Eds.), *Emerging IT/ICT and AI technologies affecting society* (pp. 233–244). Springer. DOI: 10.1007/978-981-19-2940-3_16

Perkins, M., Roe, J., Postma, D., McGaughran, J., & Hickerson, D. (2023). Detection of GPT-4 generated text in higher education: Combining academic judgment and software to identify generative AI tool misuse. *Journal of Academic Ethics*, *22*(1), 89–113. DOI: 10.1007/s10805-023-09492-6

Sanabria-Navarro, J.-R., Silveira-Pérez, Y., Pérez-Bravo, D.-D., & de-Jesús-Cortina-Núñez, M. (2023). Incidences of artificial intelligence in contemporary education. *Comunicar: Media Education Research Journal*, *31*(2), 93–103.

Sarkar, T. K. (2012). Assessment in education in India. *SA-. Education Journal*, *9*(1), 1–37.

Sharples, M. (2022). Automated essay writing: An AIED opinion. *International Journal of Artificial Intelligence in Education*, *32*(6), 1119–1126. DOI: 10.1007/s40593-022-00300-7

Smolansky, A., Cram, A., Raduescu, C., Sandris Zeivots, Huber, E., & Kizilcec, R. F. (2023). Educator and student perspectives on the impact of generative AI on assessments in higher education. *Educational Studies in Perspective and Impact of Generative AI*, *27*(3), 149–157.

Tan, S. (2013). Harnessing artificial intelligence for innovation in education. In *Learning intelligence: Innovative and digital transformative learning strategies* (pp. 335–363). Springer.

Tenakwah, E. S., Boadu, G., Tenakwah, E. J., Parzakonis, M., Brady, M., Kansiime, P., Said, S., Ayilu, R. K., Radavoi, C. N., & Berman, A. L. (2023). Generative AI and higher education assessments: A competency-based analysis. *Research Square*.

Venkatesh, V., Morris, M. G., Davis, G. B., & Davis, F. D. (2003). User acceptance of information technology: Toward a unified view. *Management Information Systems Quarterly*, *27*(3), 425–478. DOI: 10.2307/30036540

Venkatesh, V., Thong, J. Y. L., & Xu, X. (2012). Consumer acceptance and use of information technology: Extending the unified theory of acceptance and use of technology. *Management Information Systems Quarterly*, *36*(1), 157–178. DOI: 10.2307/41410412

You, Y., Chen, Y., You, Y., Zhang, Q., & Cao, Q. (2023). Evolutionary game analysis of artificial intelligence such as the generative pre-trained transformer in future education. *Sustainability (Basel), 15*(13), 9355. DOI: 10.3390/su15129355

Zhai, X., & Nehm, R. H. (2023). AI and formative assessment: The train has left the station. *Journal of Research in Science Teaching, 60*(12), 1390–1398. DOI: 10.1002/tea.21885

Chapter 7
Applying Generative AI in a Global Language School to Improve Curriculum Planning

G. Mamatha
https://orcid.org/0009-0000-1709-7687
Department of Management Studies, Sri Siddhartha Institute of Business Management, Tumkur, India

Anita Gupta
Vaish College, Rohtak, India

Ashok Koujalagi
https://orcid.org/0000-0002-0195-3976
Shri Vishnu Engineering College for Women, Bhimavaram, India

Pooja
Department of BCA, Vaish College of Engineering, Rohtak, India

Sabyasachi Pramanik
https://orcid.org/0000-0002-9431-8751
Haldia Institute of Technology, India

Atanu Roy
https://orcid.org/0000-0001-5269-9122
The Neotia University, India

ABSTRACT

Teaching and learning methodologies are being completely transformed by new developments in educational technology. The way that individual courses and instructional units are designed in the classroom will be significantly impacted by these technological tools. This chapter will look at how to design a competency-based unit of instruction that complies with ACTFL (2024) proficiency requirements using generative artificial intelligence. The summative assessment is structured as an integrated performance assessment, and the chapter is arranged using a backwards-design approach. This chapter will teach teachers how to use AI technologies to generate the IPA first, and then it will teach them how to design real-world class-

DOI: 10.4018/979-8-3693-8744-3.ch007

room activities that will provide students experience in the three communication modes—interpersonal, presentational, and interpretative. The chapter will also cover how to employ generative AI to enhance target language learning, given that feedback is a crucial component of the recursiveness of instructional design in a global language classroom.

INTRODUCTION

A diverse strategy to improving language learning and cultural awareness is necessary when designing a foreign language training unit. But even if they are enjoyable, discovering or creating exercises that promote learning and comprehension may take a lot of work, as any language instructor can tell you. The development of generative AI tools has made it possible to swiftly construct meaningful activities, giving instructors back time that they may use to further their professional development, establish rapport with their pupils, or strike a work/life balance. One subset of artificial intelligence that falls under the larger heading of machine learning is generative AI. Tools for generative AI, such as Open.AI's ChatGpt, have been trained on a vast dataset consisting of millions of data points. These tools, which function as Large Language Models (LLMs), provide a response to the user's query or prompt by using word pattern and word prediction algorithms. A generative AI tool looks at all the data it has, finds patterns and connections that fit your input, and then generates a new answer based on all the data it has access to when you ask it a question or seek input or feedback. As an experienced teacher, you may use generative AI to improve the answer that the system gives you, finally producing materials that directly address the requirements of your pupils. This method differs greatly from utilizing a search engine, which is limited to finding content—it cannot produce anything. While creating content is fantastic, we are aware that not everything generated by generative AI will be suitable or suitable for your school. Rather, educators alter these resources by using their instructional expertise. Teachers are called "augmented teachers" when they use Generative AI in addition to their own educational expertise. We refer to Generative AI as a thinking partner in the collaborative process of creating resources for use by students in the classroom, which is why we use the word "augmented." The reason we refer to this as a thought partner is since, in order to assist you in creating materials that satisfy the requirements of your pupils, Generative AI employs normal language and is able to engage in prolonged conversation, much like a conventional thought partner.

The purpose of this chapter is to teach you how to be an enhanced global language instructor. In every chapter segment, you will first learn about pedagogy and then be introduced to the Generative AI tool. The chapter is structured to reflect the cycle in which educators prepare lesson plans. We start with the summative Integrated Performance Assessment (IPA), which is the ultimate goal and will be used to evaluate students' comprehension of the material via three different channels of communication. Next, we go over how to utilize generative AI to create interpretable input in the interpretive domains of reading and hearing, which are augmented by interactive tasks and real-world scenarios. Subsequently, we go over how to design exercises in the presentational and interpersonal modes, including presenting AI as a conversation partner that lets students have simulated conversations and practice language in a safe setting. Finally, we go over how to facilitate the feedback process with the use of generative AI technologies. Since every language learnt throughout the globe must take place in a cultural context, we make sure that Generative AI incorporates cultural ideas right from the start. Students will gain language fluency and critical cross-cultural communication skills—both necessary for global citizenship—through our enhanced teaching methodology.

UTILIZING GENERATIVE AI TOOLS TO CREATE A SUMMATIVE IPA

We start by concentrating on the summative assessment while designing our unit of instruction for the classroom. In order to determine assessment evidence, instructors must first determine the intended outcomes of students' knowledge and comprehension that would enable the transfer of information to various settings, as described by Wiggins and McTighe (2005). According to McTighe and Wiggins (2013), "backward design encourages teachers and curriculum planners to first think like assessors before designing specific units and lessons."

The Integrated Performance evaluation, or IPA, is the most thoroughly studied evaluation method in global language training (Adair-Hauck, Glisan & Troyan, 2013). Three tasks, corresponding to the three types of communication—interpretive, interpersonal, and presentational—are included in this performance-based evaluation. Discrete grammar and vocabulary points are not evaluated. The IPA is used as a standards-based assessment tool by retired Paul Sandrock of the American Council for the Teaching of Foreign Languages (ACTFL) to ascertain a student's competency in navigating real-world situations in impromptu and non-rehearsed contexts (2014). Each activity in the IPA is related to a specific subject or issue, with an emphasis on communication in a culturally diverse situation (Troyan, Adair-Hauck, Glisan, 2023). Every activity gives students the knowledge and opportunities for language use they need to complete the next task (CARLA, 2019).In contrast to proficiency-based IPAs, we concentrate on the design of performance-based IPAs for the sake of this discussion (see ODEW, 2024). Tasks from a particular unit of instruction are used in a performance-based IPA to assess student success in relation to the topics taught. An IPA like this is used to assess a person's knowledge and ability to communicate effectively in all three forms of communication related to a recently examined subject or theme. In order for students to eventually enhance their communicative performance within the competence criteria, it is imperative that instructors provide them with relevant feedback throughout the IPA (see Adair-Hauck & Troyan, 2013).An instructor must first identify the communicative theme and context before creating an important question that supports the subject and topic. This is the first step in designing any IPA. A common unit at the beginner mid/high competence level, the subject of Beauty and Aesthetics and the topic of personality traits and features will be used for our example. What are people's personalities like? Is the central question that we have constructed in accordance with this subject and issue, drawing inspiration from the Ohio Model Curriculum (2023). The criteria that will serve as the learning outcomes must then be determined, as Table 1 illustrates. Our unit specifies criteria for each of the three modalities of communication as effective global language unit design takes into account all three in a cultural context (Shrum & Glisan, 2016). To put the reader in context, this unit was created using Ohio's Learning levels, which are closely linked to the ACTFL competency levels. It is intended for Novice-Mid/High students.

Table 1. Standards for a personality unit at the novice-mid/high level

Interpretive	Identify a topic and basic related information from simple sentences. Use literacy skills to comprehend authentic texts that are written or spoken.
Interpersonal	Communicate with others by asking and answering practiced and some original questions using simple sentences. Use interpersonal skills to interact, negotiate meaning, and communicate effectively.
Presentational	Present information using mostly simple sentences and transitions. Use presentational skills to communicate effectively.

Since the ACTFL (2024) proficiency requirements help us recognize that greater competence typically results in a student's more sophisticated use of grammar and vocabulary, we have two grammar and vocabulary objectives in addition to these standards. The IPA makes the assumption that students are familiar with subject pronouns, the verbs to be and like, vocabulary connected to physical descriptions, fundamental meet and greet terms linked to greetings and farewells, and certain activities that they like. The following objectives are shown in Table 2:

Table 2. Grammar and vocabulary goals for a personality unit at novice-mid high level

Grammar	I can make adjectives agree in gender and number.
Vocabulary	I can describe someone's personality.

Teachers are required to develop the "story line" that will link the three IPA activities after determining the subject, topic, and pertinent standards (Jacobs & Zmuda, 2023). For this case, our plot is as follows: Recently, a new app made its way through your high school's hallways. Everyone is talking about it, but the parents of both you and your pals are worried about how it is being used, so they won't unlock it on your phone until they know the sort of individuals who use this new app. The software will initially ask you to read and analyze an infographic. After that, you and your buddy will speak briefly and share information. In the hopes that they would unlock the app, you will lastly prepare a three-slide presentation that offers details about your personality, the personalities of your partners and parents, and eventually identifies the kind of social media users these people are.

Teachers are required to develop the interpretive work using the storyboard method, using the ACTFL interpretive task template as a guide (see Adair-Hauck, Glisan & Troyan, 2013). The interpretative evaluation that we developed is shown in Figure 1, where students are assessed using the interpretive rubric developed by Adair-Hauck, Glisan, and Troyan (2013).

Figure 1. The interpretive section of the IPA for personality unit, written by the author

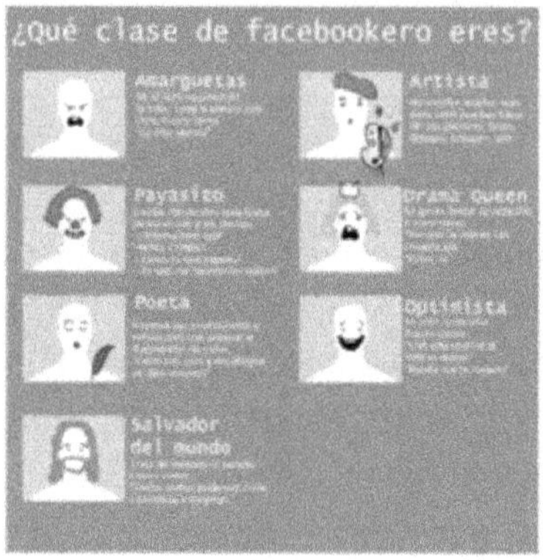

I. **Key Word Recognition.** Write the word/phrase in the target language that bests expresses the meaning of each of the following words (clownish, trolls, motivator, complicated, poems)

II. **Main Idea.** Select the main idea of the article.
Types of Cliques found in high schools
Categories for senior class superlatives
Types of Halloween costumes
Categories of social media users
Personality Types of people

III. **Supporting Details.** Which of the following details are true according to the article.
The "Optimista" is discouraging.
"Armaguetas" view life as negative and difficult.
"Artistas" and "Poetas" write to express themselves.
"Drama Queens" are unhappy.
"Salvador del Mundo" believes the world can get better.

IV. **Organizational Type.** Which of the following best describes the organizational setup of the text? (Compare/Contrast, Description, Pros and Cons). Justify your response.

V. **Guessing Meaning from Context.** Using the text, write what these words and expressions probably mean. (bonita noche mundo, dibujos, le gusta llamar la atención).

VI. **Inferences.** Mark each statement as true or false.
A "Salvador" would say "We can't do this."
A "Payasito" would enjoy hanging out at a comedy club.
An "Optimista" is the most positive user type.
A "Drama Queen" is more negative than the "Amargueta"

VII. **Author's Perspective.** Identify the author's perspective of this text (scientific, historical, comical, informative). Justify your answer with evidence.

VIII. **Comparing Cultural Perspectives.** This article was written for an audience in Spain. In English, explain whether this graphic would be different if it were written for an American audience. Why or why not?

We created the following prompts for the interpersonal and presentational areas, as indicated in Section 2, after creating the interpretative section and making sure it matched our storyboard. The relevant rubrics would be used to assess the students (ODEW, 2017).

Figure 2. Author-created interpersonal and presentational sections of the IPA for personality unit

After math class, you stop by your locker to get your Spanish book. You see someone talking about the app and overhear that they too are trying to get their parents to let them use the app. You strike up a conversation and exchange information about your personalities and the types of users you may be on this app with the goal of finding out what type of user they are. Use the following questions as ideas to help you as you converse.

What's your name?
What's your personality like?
Are you more ____ or ____?
Do you like to __________?
Are you ____?

Don't forget that part of your job is to move the conversation forward by asking questions.

You may wish to take notes on what your partner is saying, because afterwards, you will create a three-slide presentation that includes the following information.

- Slide about You (Name, Basic Demographic Information, Personality Information, Type of User)
- Slide about your Friend (includes the same information as about you)
- Slide about your parents (includes the same information about your parents)

These slides should be in sentence form.

Whoa! That required a lot of planning and creation, and we still haven't given the kids their input! It took a long time to write—the writers estimated that it took over four hours. We will now demonstrate how to use generative AI to construct an IPA. For the sake of this example, we'll suppose that we're dealing with language learners who are near the conclusion of their first year of study and are novice-mid/high. Places in the Community will be our subject, and Families and Communities will be our theme (see ODEW, 2023). Students will have completed six units in language at this point, including ones on greetings, basic demographics, likes and dislikes, physical characteristics and personalities, families, and schools. Although our objectives for grammar and vocabulary as well as our basic questions have not altered, our standards have, as Table 3 illustrates: Which locations within a community are significant?

Table 3. Standards and grammar and vocabulary goals for community unit

Interpretive	Identify a topic and basic related information from simple sentences. Use literacy skills to comprehend authentic texts that are written or spoken.
Interpersonal	Communicate with others by asking and answering practice and some original questions using simple sentences. Use interpersonal skills to interact, negotiate meaning, and communicate effectively.
Presentational	Present information using mostly simple sentences and transitions. Use presentational skills to communicate effectively.

We will use Chat GPT 3.5, a free Generative AI tool, to create scenarios that are relevant to our students, develop interpretive, interpersonal, and presentational tasks that are aligned to standards, make connections to the ODEW rubrics (2017), and create real texts and speech for students to interact with as they work through the tasks in order to investigate how Generative AI can enhance our IPA development. We will examine two practical forms of prompting from Generative AI in order to do this. First, a request asking the Generative AI tool to act as an IPA bot has to be created. The second involves creating a plot or situation and the integrated activities that go along with it by using a sequence of prompts known as prompt chaining. You may reuse the prompt each time you begin the process of developing an IPA by using Generative AI as a bot. The purpose of prompts is to initiate conversation, not to conclude it. After you start interacting with generative AI, you may ask it more questions, give it feedback to improve the answer or broaden your thought process, or ask it to ask your questions to help you think more clearly. Additionally, you may utilize bots to ask you questions, which will help you hone in on the activities you want your students to do in order to show their learning. The prompt we are utilizing in this case is shown in Figure 3.

Figure 3. Prompt for Generative AI Bot for IPAs

You are a world language teacher bot who is an expert in creating scenario threads that connect interpretive, interpersonal, and presentational tasks for IPAs. You work with students who are at the novice to mid-high range of language proficiency. You use the ACTFL standards and want your students to engage with each other in Spanish. Start by suggesting possible themes and topics based on the ACTFL standards. Then ask me what theme and topic I would like to work with. Based on my response, generate 3-5 possible scenario threads that could be used as the start of an IPA.

Using fundamental best practice techniques to generate prompts while working with generative AI yields the most fruitful augmentation. Table 4 deconstructs the question into discrete parts, and Figure 4 lists the tasks and situations that the bot developed for our particular subject, community.

Table 4. Best practice strategies for creating prompts

	Description	Example
Context or role	Set the base for the thought partner work will you be doing with the Generative AI	*You are a world language teacher bot*
Purpose	What you are using the Generative AI to do	*Who is an expert in creating scenario threads that connect interpretive, interpersonal, and presentational tasks for IPAs.*
Depth of Understanding	Level of complexity or skill	*You work with students who are at the novice to mid-high range of language proficiency.*
Relevant Information	More details to help frame the initial response	*You use the ACTFL standards and want your students to engage with each other in Spanish.*
Constraints	Any boundaries, restrictions or limitations	*...based on the ACTFL standards. Generate 3-5 possible scenario threads that could be used as the start of an IPA.*
Output Nudging	How do you want the GenerativeAI to start your interaction	*Start by suggesting possible themes and topics*

Figure 4. Generative AI results for community unit IPA scenarios

Scenario Thread 1: "Family Outing"
Interpretive Task: *Students listen to a dialogue between a family planning a weekend outing to a local park. They identify key details such as the date, time, activities planned, and items they need to bring.*
Interpersonal Task: *In pairs, students role-play a similar dialogue, discussing where they want to go as a family, what activities they want to do, and when they can go.*
Presentational Task: *Students create a poster advertising a family-friendly outing in the community, including details such as the location, activities available, and contact information.*

Scenario Thread 2: "Community Service Project"
Interpretive Task: *Students watch a video about a local community service project, such as a food drive or park cleanup. They identify the purpose of the project, who is involved, and how people can participate.*
Interpersonal Task: *In small groups, students discuss different community service projects they could participate in and choose one to plan together. They assign roles and responsibilities for each group member.*
Presentational Task: *Each group creates a presentation outlining their chosen community service project, including its goals, timeline, and how others can get involved. They present their ideas to the class.*

Scenario Thread 3: "Visiting Relatives"
Interpretive Task: Students read a short text about a family visiting relatives in another town. They identify places mentioned in the text, such as the relatives' house, local attractions, and places to eat.
Interpersonal Task: In pairs, students role-play a conversation between two family members planning a visit to relatives. They discuss when they will leave, how they will travel, and what they want to do while they're there.
Presentational Task: Students create a travel itinerary for their family's visit to relatives, including details such as departure and arrival times, places they plan to visit, and activities they want to do together.

Following the receipt of the scenarios, we used our pedagogical expertise to engage in conversation with the bot. By asking more questions, the bot produced an additional scenario, as shown in Figure 5: Include an additional scenario in which students' converse with students abroad about similar areas in their communities. Construct a situation that is unique to my neighbourhood. Make up a situation where a resident of a tiny town in Costa Rica is compared to a resident of an Ohio small town.

Figure 5. Additional scenario produced by Generative AI for community unit IPA

Scenario Thread 4: "Small Town Connections: Ohio and Costa Rica"
Interpretive Task: *Students listen to a podcast featuring interviews with residents of a small town in Ohio and a small town in Costa Rica. The interviews highlight the similarities and differences between the two communities, focusing on aspects such as local traditions, community events, popular gathering spots, and the role of nature in everyday life.*
Interpersonal Task*: In pairs, students engage in a conversation comparing their own experiences living in a small town in Ohio with what they learned about life in a small town in Costa Rica. They discuss commonalities such as tight-knit communities, reliance on local resources, and shared values, as well as differences in climate, geography, and cultural practices.*
Presentational Task: *Working in small groups, students create a visual presentation exploring the similarities and differences between the small towns in Ohio and Costa Rica. They include photographs, maps, and key statistics to illustrate their points, highlighting aspects such as community landmarks, local cuisine, recreational activities, and environmental conservation efforts. Additionally, they prepare a short video or audio clip featuring a virtual exchange between residents of the two towns, where they share insights into their daily lives and cultural traditions. The presentation concludes with a reflection on the importance of cross-cultural understanding and appreciation for diverse communities around the world.*

The aforementioned situation may be made even more unique by using a prompt chain conversation. Tell the generative AI tool the scenario you have chosen to start, and provide any extra limitations or background data. Use the following prompt sequence with the bot for this IPA scenario: "I like the fourth scenario thread. Our home is in Ohio's Norwalk. What Costa Rican village would be comparable to this one? The answer is shown in Figure 6.

Figure 6. Prompt chaining to revise and finalize community unit IPA scenario

For a similar community in Costa Rica to Norwalk, Ohio, we could look for a smaller town with a close-knit community, perhaps with a focus on agriculture or local craftsmanship, and ideally located in a region with natural beauty nearby. One potential town that fits this description is Atenas, Costa Rica.

Atenas is a charming town located in the province of Alajuela, known for its pleasant climate, friendly locals, and strong sense of community. Similar to Norwalk, Atenas is not a major tourist destination but offers a peaceful lifestyle with a range of local amenities and cultural activities. Here's how we could adapt Scenario Thread 7 to compare Norwalk, Ohio, with Atenas, Costa Rica:

Scenario Thread 7: "Small Town Connections: Norwalk, Ohio, and Atenas, Costa Rica"
Interpretive Task: *Students listen to a podcast featuring interviews with residents of Norwalk, Ohio, and Atenas, Costa Rica. The interviews highlight the similarities and differences between the two communities, focusing on aspects such as local traditions, community events, popular gathering spots, and the role of nature in everyday life.*
Interpersonal Task: *In pairs, students engage in a conversation comparing their own experiences living in Norwalk, Ohio, with what they learned about life in Atenas, Costa Rica. They discuss commonalities such as tight-knit communities, reliance on local resources, and shared values, as well as differences in climate, geography, and cultural practices.*
Presentational Task: *Working in small groups, students create a visual presentation exploring the similarities and differences between Norwalk, Ohio, and Atenas, Costa Rica. They include photographs, maps, and key statistics to illustrate their points, highlighting aspects such as community landmarks, local cuisine, recreational activities, and environmental conservation efforts. Additionally, they prepare a short video or audio clip featuring a virtual exchange between residents of Norwalk and Atenas, where they share insights into their daily lives and cultural traditions. The presentation concludes with a reflection on the importance of cross-cultural understanding and appreciation for diverse communities around the world.*

Once the scenario has been finalized, you will create each task. In order to assist you with that, the following prompt chain starts by determining and/or producing the student resources required doing the tasks. In addition to expanding on the tasks by developing particular questions that students will engage with, generative AI may construct checklists of resources and provide scaffolds to help all learners who are participating in the activities. We get a checklist, as seen in Figure 7, by telling the bot to "Create a checklist of materials that students will need to complete all three tasks." This checklist is extremely helpful for our following prompt in the chain, which are the questions.

Figure 7. Checklist of materials for community unit IPA

Here's a checklist of materials students will need to complete all three tasks in Scenario Thread 4:

Interpretive Task:

- *Access to the podcast featuring interviews with residents of Norwalk, Ohio, and Atenas, Costa Rica (online or downloadable).*
- *Note-taking materials such as notebooks, paper, or digital devices.*

Interpersonal Task:

- *Partner or group members for discussions.*
- *Conversation prompts or guiding questions related to comparing Norwalk and Atenas.*
- *Access to resources for further research if needed (books, internet, etc.).*

Presentational Task:

- *Visual aids for the presentation (poster boards, PowerPoint slides, etc.).*
- *Access to images of Norwalk, Ohio, and Atenas, Costa Rica, for inclusion in the presentation.*
- *Audio-visual recording equipment for creating the virtual exchange clip (optional).*
- *Access to presentation software or tools (Microsoft PowerPoint, Google Slides, etc.).*
- *Any additional materials for creativity or presentation enhancement (markers, stickers, etc.).*
- *Ensuring students have access to these materials will help facilitate their engagement with the tasks and enable them to complete the scenario successfully.*

With the checklist in hand, we can utilize it as a guide to begin creating the real content. According to the list, the podcast is the main resource that the instructor must provide, and the task prompt takes care of the interpersonal and presentational portions for us. Now, in addition to the audio itself, we can ask the Generative AI tool to provide a transcript of the particular podcast with speakers from Norwalk and Atenas. Here's an example of a prompt with limitations, ability level, and purpose: For the beginner and mid-high levels of the interpretive task, create a transcript of the podcast. It should be in Spanish on the podcast. Just one adult and one student from Norwalk and one adult and one student from Atenas should talk on the podcast. The answer is shown in Figure 8.

Figure 8. An excerpt of the podcast transcript for interpretive task for the community unit IPA

Title: Conexiones entre pequeñas ciudades: Norwalk y Atenas

Speaker 1 (Student from Norwalk): ¡Hola a todos! Me llamo Juan y soy de Norwalk, Ohio. Hoy estoy aquí con mi abuela, la Sra. López, para hablar sobre nuestra comunidad.

Speaker 2 (Adult from Norwalk): Hola, soy la Sra. López. Estoy feliz de estar aquí contigo, Juan.

Speaker 3 (Student from Atenas): Hola, soy María de Atenas, Costa Rica. Me encanta mi pequeña ciudad y quiero compartir un poco sobre ella.

Speaker 4 (Adult from Atenas): Hola a todos, soy el Sr. García. Vivo en Atenas desde hace muchos años y estoy emocionado de hablar sobre nuestra comunidad hoy.

Speaker 1 (Juan): Abuela, ¿puedes contarnos sobre un evento especial en Norwalk?

Speaker 2 (Sra. López): Claro, Juan. En Norwalk, tenemos un desfile anual en el Día de la Independencia. Es muy divertido ver los carros alegóricos y escuchar la música.

Speaker 3 (María): En Atenas, tenemos una fiesta tradicional llamada "La Fiesta de la Anexión". Celebramos la unión del cantón con la provincia de San José. Hay música, baile y comida deliciosa.

Speaker 4 (Sr. García): Sí, es una celebración muy animada. Además, en Atenas, nos encanta reunirnos en el parque central los fines de semana para disfrutar del aire libre y charlar con amigos.

Speaker 1 (Juan): ¡Eso suena genial! En Norwalk, también nos gusta pasar tiempo al aire libre. Tenemos un parque grande con un lago donde podemos pescar y hacer picnic.

Speaker 2 (Sra. López): Sí, el parque es muy bonito. Y cerca del parque, tenemos una heladería que hace los mejores helados de la ciudad.

Speaker 3 (María): ¡Qué delicia! En Atenas, tenemos una tienda de helados artesanales que es muy popular entre los lugareños y los turistas.

Speaker 4 (Sr. García): Bueno, parece que tenemos algo en común: ¡a todos nos encanta el helado!

Speaker 1 (Juan): Sí, definitivamente. Gracias por compartir sus experiencias, María y Sr. García. Fue genial aprender sobre Atenas.

Speaker 2 (Sra. López): Sí, gracias a ustedes dos. Fue interesante comparar nuestras pequeñas ciudades.

You may also ask ChatGPT 3.5 to enhance the text to Mid-High in order to modify the transcript if you think the text is either too difficult or not complex enough. A sample of how we had ChatGPT alter the transcript to raise the proficiency level is seen in Table 5.

Table 5. Revision of interpretive transcript for community unit IPA

Speaker	Novice-Mid	Novice-High
Speaker 1 (Student from Norwalk):	Hola a todos! Me llamo Juan y soy de Norwalk, Ohio. Hoy estoyaquí con mi abuela, la Sra. López, para hablarsobrenuestracomunidad.	Buenos días a todos. Soy Juan, un estudiante de Norwalk, Ohio. Hoy tengoel placer de estaraquí con mi abuela, la Sra. López, para explorar las conexiones entre Norwalk y unapequeña ciudad en Costa Rica.
Speaker 2 (Adult from Norwalk)	Hola, soy la Sra. López. Estoyfeliz de estaraquícontigo, Juan.	Saludos a todos. Soy la Sra. López, residente de Norwalk desdehacemuchosaños. Estoyemocionadaporestaconversación, Juan.
Speaker 3 (Student from Atenas):	Hola, soy María de Atenas, Costa Rica. Me encanta mi pequeña ciudad y quierocompartir un poco sobreella.	Hola a todos, soy María de Atenas, Costa Rica. Me sientohonrada de representar a mi ciudad enestadiscusiónsobre las similitudes y diferencias entre nuestrascomunidades.
Speaker 4 (Adult from Atenas):	Hola a todos, soy el Sr. García. Vivo en Atenas desdehacemuchosaños y estoyemocionado de hablarsobrenuestracomunidad hoy.	Buenos días. Soy el Sr. García, un ciudadanoorgulloso de Atenas, Costa Rica. Espero que nuestracharla sea enriquecedora y nosayude a comprendermejornuestrasculturas locales.

Once the transcript is at a suitable level, you may use it as a real text for the reading interpretive job or, as a listening activity; you can utilize ChatGPT 3.5's text to voice tool to have the podcast read out in true Spanish. You may also change the spoken language in settings; choose a voice in Spanish, French, German, or another language, and have Read and Write read the transcript if you have access to the Chrome browser plugin. One benefit of using a text-to-speech reader other than the Generative AI tool is that the voice rate may be adjusted. Here is where you may get our audio results. We can now ask the Generative AI to write the questions that correspond to the different parts of the interpretative IPA after developing the script: Make a summative evaluation with the text from the audio transcript for both the beginner and mid-high levels. While composing the evaluation questions, take into account the following: Students must determine which words or phrases in the target language most accurately convey the meaning of two to three essential terms. When a question presents four to five possibilities for the core notion, the student must choose one of them. Four or five true-false questions about illustrative concepts, a question asking students to choose the text's organizational style, two to three questions that ask students to infer a word's meaning from the context, Three to four inferential questions, a question about the speakers' perspectives for which students must offer supporting details, and a question asking them to describe how the podcast might change or be similar if it were intended for listeners in a different Spanish-speaking nation.

Figure 9 shows the response.

Figure 9. Community IPA interpretive task questions

Section 1: Vocabulary Identification

1. Identify the Spanish word or phrase that best expresses the meaning of "desfile."
    - A) música
    - B) baile
    - C) fiesta
    - D) parade
2. What Spanish phrase from the podcast means "celebration"?
    - A) La Fiesta de la Anexión
    - B) celebración muy animada
    - C) unión del cantón
    - D) escuchar la música

Section 2: Main Idea

3. What is the main idea of the podcast?

- A) Comparing community events in Norwalk, Ohio, and Atenas, Costa Rica
- B) Discussing family traditions in Norwalk, Ohio
- C) Exploring cultural differences between the United States and Costa Rica
- D) Analyzing the impact of globalization on small towns

Section 3: Supporting Details

4. True or False: The Independence Day Parade is mentioned as an annual event Norwalk, Ohio.
5. True or False: The speakers enjoy spending time outdoors in both Norwalk, Ohio, and Atenas, Costa Rica.
6. True or False: The Fiesta de la Anexión celebrates the independence of Costa Rica.

Section 4: Text Organization

7. Select the organizational type for the podcast:

- A) Chronological
- B) Cause and Effect
- C) Compare and Contrast
- D) Problem-Solution

Section 5: Guessing Meaning from Context

8. Based on the context, what does "carros alegóricos" most likely mean?
9. In the podcast, what does "heladería" refer to?

Section 6: Inference

10. From the podcast, what can you infer about the importance of community celebrations in both Norwalk, Ohio, and Atenas, Costa Rica?
11. Why do you think the speakers mention spending time outdoors in their communities?

Section 7: Perspective and Evidence

12. From the speakers' perspective, why do you think they mention the Independence Day Parade and La Fiesta de la Anexión?
13. Provide evidence from the podcast to support your answer.

Section 8: Comparing Perspectives

14. How would the podcast be similar or different if it were for an audience of a different Spanish-speaking country? Provide two examples for each similarity and difference.

As shown in this section, creating an IPA—the final summative assessment—for a unit in a foreign language class that incorporates the three modes of communication—interpretive, presentational, and interpersonal—aligned with competency criteria and standards may be done quite quickly and easily. We will demonstrate how to design instructional activities that are in line with the unit's summative expectations in the next section.

WL Classroom: Using Generative AI to Produce Understandable Content Having decided on the summative objective using the backwards-design approach, we now need to consider how we will teach the students. This section will demonstrate how to create understandable material for the classroom using generative artificial intelligence. According to (Mason and Krashen, 2019), the best approaches in language training include starting with information that is understandable and interpretative. Everything that students come into contact with in the target language—everything they see, hear, or read—is considered input. This was further developed by linguist Stephen Krashen, who defined comprehensible input as straightforward, intelligible, and context-supported. Effective understandable input teaches new words and ideas using knowledge that learners already possess. This kind of input pushes the student just enough so that they have to depend on what they already know while utilizing this new, somewhat more sophisticated information to further their learning. Finding listening and reading materials that focus on certain grammatical and vocabulary structures related to the present overall subject while avoiding excessive use of new vocabulary and structures that students aren't familiar with is necessary to provide intelligible input in the conventional classroom. While some of these materials are designed for language learners, others are intended for native speakers. In keeping with our prior example of personality, when one of the authors taught this subject, he had about twenty-six resources that he had discovered and created over the years to assist students in learning the terminology and structures associated with the subject for a unit that lasted a week. These included reading aloud from real and fake texts like those in Figure 10, watching a video on YouTube (see deMiej, 2018), and listening to music (see Blodget, 1995). Finding such materials takes a lot of work, in addition to the difficulty of formulating questions that let students summarize the most important ideas, determine the core concept, deduce meaning from context, and so forth.

Figure 10. Example comprehensible input for personality unit

Infographic retrieved from
https://www.20milproductos.com/blog/que-perfil-de-personalidad-disc-tengo/

Text adapted by authors from Gahala, Carlin, Heining-Boyton (2004). En Espanol. Level 1.

Alberto es mi amigo de la escuela. Es un muchacho bueno y muy inteligente. Él es muy trabajador y le gusta estudiar. Es alto, delgado, rubio y muy simpático. También es cómico. Le gusta hablar mucho y tiene muchos amigos. No le gusta escribir poemas, pero le gusta leer. Alberto es artístico. Le gusta dibujar y crear pinturas con muchos colores. En su tiempo libre, le gusta nadar pero no le gusta jugar a los deportes atrevidos.

But applying generative AI is revolutionary. In addition to creating the questions that students will use to interact with the texts, we may utilize AI to construct passages or texts in the target language. You may utilize the same conversational procedures that we did for the IPA for developing the interpretive activities. After that, you may tell the bot to generate the necessary instructional help. For instance, we created a reading for a beginner level student on common places students travel in the town in Spain and what they do there as part of our community unit's GPT assignment. Write this with a Novice–Mid level of ability in Spanish. Figure 11 contains the text that ChatGPT sent in response.

Figure 11. Example Generative AI reading passage for community unit

Vamos a aprender sobre los lugares típicos en la ciudad española a los que les gusta ir a los estudiantes y qué hacen allí.

1. La Plaza Mayor: La Plaza Mayor es un lugar muy importante en la ciudad. Aquí, los estudiantes se reúnen con amigos. Beben café y comen tapas. ¡Es muy divertido!

2. La Playa: ¡La playa es genial! Los estudiantes van a la playa para nadar y tomar el sol. También juegan a la pelota en la arena. ¡Es muy relajante!

3. El Mercado: En el mercado, los estudiantes compran comida fresca. Hay frutas, verduras y carne. Los estudiantes hablan con los vendedores. ¡Es emocionante!

4. El Parque: En el parque, los estudiantes hacen ejercicio y juegan. Corren, caminan y montan en bicicleta. ¡Es muy divertido estar al aire libre!

5. La Biblioteca: La biblioteca es un lugar tranquilo. Los estudiantes leen libros y estudian. A veces, trabajan en grupos. ¡Es muy interesante aprender cosas nuevas!

6. La Cafetería: En la cafetería, los estudiantes beben café y comen pasteles. Hablan y ríen con amigos. ¡Es un lugar muy acogedor!

7. El Estadio: En el estadio, los estudiantes ven deportes. Miran fútbol y baloncesto. ¡Es emocionante animar a los equipos!

8. El Centro Cultural: En el centro cultural, los estudiantes ven películas y escuchan música. Aprenden sobre arte y baile. ¡Es muy divertido descubrir nuevas culturas!

¡Espero que te haya gustado aprender sobre estos lugares! ¡Hasta pronto!

You can also use Generative AI tools to create questions along with possible student answers, to go along with the tasks, similar to what we did for the IPA. Table 6 is a starting point for using Generative AI as a thought partner in creating questions to gather evidence of student understanding.

Table 6. Generative AI prompts for creating interpretive tasks

	Description	Example
Purpose	What kind of evidence do you want to be able to gather?	Assess student interpretation of the podcast
Type of Tool	What type of question would best get at the evidence you are looking for? Multiple choice question Short answer questions - open ended Short answer questions - one correct answer Extended answer question Rubric Checklist Self-Assessment	*Short answer*
Constraint	Do you want it to assess something very specific within the question set? At what proficiency level(s)? How many items/questions? What standards are you aligning to?	*make 10 short answer questions at a novice level and 10 questions at a mid-high level* *aligned to the ACTFL standards for interpretation* *Include one or two questions that would assess the ability to understand the meaning of a word or phrase using context*
Supporting Materials	Do you want it to generate a key? Do you want it to create possible student answers? Do you want it to create multiple forms? Do you want it to add a word bank?	*Provide possible student answers to each question.*

We requested our Generative AI tool to generate questions based on the material in Figure 11 by asking it, "What are five true and false questions about this reading in English to check on a student's comprehension?" Naturally, you could change these questions to multiple choice, short answer, etc., or you could record an audio version of them, much as we did for the IPA. Apart from formulating queries, Generative AI may also generate support structures for learners who are engaged in reading or listening. For ChatGPT, we requested that they "create a graphic organizer that a student could use to write down their observations about the typical places in a Spanish city as they read this article." Figure 12 displays the questions together with a portion of the visual organizer.

Figure 12. Generative AI true/false questions & excerpt of graphic organizer for interpretive reading

1. Students gather in the Plaza Mayor to drink coffee and eat tapas. (True/False)
2. The beach is not a popular destination for students in Spanish towns. (True/False)
3. At the market, students buy only electronics and clothes. (True/False)
4. The library is a noisy place where students go to socialize with friends. (True/False)
5. In the cultural center, students can learn about art and dance. (True/False)

Lugares Típicos en la Ciudad Española - Organizador Gráfico

1. Nombre del Lugar: Plaza Mayor
   - **Qué Hacen los Estudiantes:**
   - **Observaciones:**
2. Nombre del Lugar: La Playa
   - **Qué Hacen los Estudiantes:**
   - **Observaciones:**

Using generative AI to provide interpretative information as comprehensible input in language classrooms throughout the globe entails taking use of its skills to make it easier for students to comprehend and analyze written or spoken language. Students may read texts and complete comprehension exercises, such as recognizing primary concepts, summarizing important points, or responding to comprehension questions, as part of these activities. Additionally, we may utilize Generative AI to create audio recordings in the target language on which students can respond to topic-related questions, deduce meaning from context, or share how they understood the conversation. Teachers may create dynamic and engaging learning experiences that support students' development of language proficiency, cultural competency, and interpretative abilities in the context of a global language classroom by integrating Generative AI into interpretive activities. We'll walk you through creating presentational and interpersonal activities in the following part.

MAKING EFFECTIVE SKILL ACTIVITIES WITH GENERATIVE AI

This section will demonstrate how to utilize generative AI to develop interpersonal and presentational tasks that help students improve their productive abilities. Generative AI may greatly increase the efficiency of creating these productive jobs, just as it does with the interpretative mode. Numerous interpersonal and presentational writing and speaking exercises must be identified or developed for use in the typical classroom. Figures 13 and 14 depict two author-created scenarios that one of the authors utilized in his classroom to have students practice these beneficial abilities, following our example relating to personalities. The teacher-created rubrics are each a page long, so for space reasons we did not provide them to the readers. For instances, go to ODEW (2017).

Figure 13. Author-created interpersonal activities for personality unit

Activity 1: Planning a Dinner Party

You are planning a dinner party with friends. You want to ensure that you have the best balance of people at the dinner. Using the list of people on your sheet, ask your friend in Spanish to describe these people. Ask for clarification as needed. Take turns ultimately determining who would be best suited for each of your parties.

Activity 2: Text Message

You've received the following text message from your mom after you asked her if you could go out with friends. Respond to her questions.

Your text message to your Mom:	Your mom's message to you
Mamá - Quiero ir al restaurante Srta. Bonitas después de clases el viernes con mis amigos. ¿Es posible?	Carino. No sé si puedes ir al restaurante o no. Necesito más información. ¿Cómo se llaman tus amigos ?¿Cómo son? ¿Son amigos buenos o malos? ¿Sacan buenas notas?

Figure 14. Author-created presentational activities for personality unit

Activity 1: Superlative Ad

It is senior superlative time. The yearbook has asked you to nominate friends for various awards. Create a one page superlative for one of your classmates in Spanish. Include the following information: likes and dislikes, personality characteristics, physical characteristics, basic biographical information.

Activity 2: The Talent Show

It is the night of the RRHS Spanish talent show. You are MCing the event. Orally introduce the person you are assigned to your class. Include the following information: likes and dislikes, personality characteristics, physical characteristics, basic biographical information.

We will now assign ChatGPT the responsibility of creating activities for the interpersonal and presentational modes using Generative AI and our community unit. Working with Generative AI is most productive when it starts with a question that establishes the context and goal, as we have shown. In this instance, we want the generative AI to produce situations that will provide the chance for students to interact with one another. Think about the following exercise: Using the Ohio Learning Standards for World Language, you are a skilled world language teacher. The degree of competence that your pupils have in the target language ranges from beginner to mid-high. Make two student-facing situations that they may work on in pairs or small groups to engage in conversation about local locations. The pupils call Norwalk, Ohio, home. The replies we got when we entered this query into ChatGPT are shown in Figure 15.

Figure 15. Generative AI interpersonal activities for community unit

Scenario 1:
You and your partner are planning a weekend outing in Norwalk, Ohio. Your task is to discuss and decide on three places you want to visit together. Use your knowledge of places around town and what you enjoy doing to come up with your choices. Practice asking questions and giving reasons for your preferences. Then, finalize your plans and decide on a meeting time and place.

Scenario 2:
You and your partner are new to Norwalk, Ohio, and you want to explore the town together. Your task is to have a conversation where you suggest different places you could visit to get to know the town better. Discuss what each place has to offer, such as parks, restaurants, or historical sites. Use your language skills to ask for opinions, express preferences, and make decisions together on where to go first, second, and third.

You may utilize Generative AI to generate scaffolding that students would require to finish this interpersonal activity, in addition to suggestions. These supports may take the form of word lists, example conversation, and sentence structures. Here are some ideas for prompts to think about: Make a list of beginner-level sentence structures for every situation. Make a tool for peer feedback. Provide proof to back up the reflection.

Determine the essential terms that students, both at an introductory and advanced level, need to include into their conversations.

Develop a self-reflection tool that allows each student participating in the discussion to assess their own performance. Provide proof to back up the reflection. Make a rubric for interpersonal communication based on the Ohio World Language Learning Standards so the teacher may easily collect evidence of proficiency while listening to the student-teacher exchange. For every situation, write a sample conversation at the beginner and mid-high levels.

Excerpts from model scaffolds based on the first two prompts are shown in Figures 16 and 17 in connection with the social activities we created in Figure 15. Naturally, the enhanced instructor may modify the frames or rubrics as necessary.

Figure 16. Generative AI sentence frames for interpersonal activities for community unit

Scenario 1 Sentence Frames:

1. "¿Qué lugares te gustaría visitar este fin de semana? Me gustaría ir a ________ porque ________."
2. "¿Prefieres ir al parque o al centro comercial? Yo prefiero ________ porque ________."
3. "Me gusta ir al cine porque ________. ¿Qué te parece si vamos a la biblioteca primero?"
4. "¿Qué te parece si vamos a la biblioteca primero? Me parece bien. ________."
5. "¿A qué hora quieres encontrarnos? Prefiero encontrarnos a las ________."

Scenario 2 Sentence Frames:

1. "¿Qué lugares crees que deberíamos explorar primero? Creo que podríamos ir a ________ primero porque ________."
2. "¿Te gustaría ir a un parque o a un restaurante hoy? Prefiero ________ porque ________. ¿Qué opinas?"
3. "¿Has oído hablar del museo local? ¿Qué opinas de visitarlo? Sí, he oído hablar de él. ________."
4. "¿Qué te parece si vamos al centro histórico después? Me parece una buena idea. ________."
5. "¿Cuál de estas opciones prefieres: el zoológico, la piscina o el campo de juegos? Prefiero ________ porque ________."

Figure 17. Generative AI peer feedback tool for interpersonal activities for community unit

Student Name: ____________________

Partner's Name: ____________________

1. Did your partner effectively communicate their preferences for places to visit? Provide an example from the dialogue.
   - Yes/No
   - Example from the dialogue: ____________________
2. How well did your partner ask questions to understand your preferences? Provide an example from the dialogue.
   - Very well/Partially/Not well
   - Example from the dialogue: ____________________
3. Did your partner provide reasons for their choices? If yes, give an example. If not, suggest how they could improve.
   - Yes/No
   - Example from the dialogue: ____________________
4. How effectively did your partner collaborate with you to finalize the plans? Provide an example from the dialogue.
   - Very effectively/Partially/Not effectively
   - Example from the dialogue: ____________________
5. Did your partner actively participate in deciding on a meeting time and place? Explain with evidence from the dialogue.
   - Yes/No
   - Explanation with evidence from the dialogue: ____________________

A similar challenge, "You are an expert world language educator who uses the Ohio Learning Standards for World Language," may also be used to generate exercises in the presentational mode. The degree of competence that your pupils have in the target language ranges from beginner to mid-high. Make two presentation assignments centered on local locations. The pupils call Norwalk, Ohio, home. Three possible presentation activities for the community unit are shown in Figure 18. As previously, ChatGPT will also be able to generate scaffolding such as outlines, lists of essential words and phrases, or sentence frames, as well as checklists and tools for student reflection.

Figure 18. Generative AI presentational activities for community unit

Scenario 1: Map Presentation
Task: Create a presentation in which you describe the locations of various places in Norwalk, Ohio, using a map. Include landmarks, streets, and cardinal directions to give clear directions from one place to another.

Scenario 2: Cultural Exploration Presentation
Task: Create a presentation exploring the cultural aspects of Norwalk, Ohio. Discuss various cultural events, traditions, festivals, and historical landmarks that are significant to the town. Include photographs, videos, or other visual aids to enhance your presentation and provide a comprehensive overview of Norwalk's cultural heritage.

Scenario 3: Restaurant Review
Task: Imagine you are a food critic reviewing restaurants in Norwalk, Ohio. Choose two or three local restaurants to evaluate based on factors such as food quality, atmosphere, service, and value for money. Create a presentation in which you share your reviews, including descriptions of the dishes you tried, your overall impressions of each restaurant, and recommendations for future visitors. Use images or menus to illustrate your points and make your presentation engaging.

We preferred scenario 1 in the aforementioned example, however we would have like additional details. We acquired a final amended scenario and form, as shown in Figure 19, by requesting the Generative AI tool to rewrite scenario 1 to be more like a walking tour and to be more precise about who the visitors would be.

Figure 19. Generative AI revised presentational task

Scenario 1: Guided Walking Tour for History Enthusiasts

Task: Imagine you are leading a guided walking tour of Norwalk, Ohio, for a group of history enthusiasts visiting the town for the first time. Create a presentation in which you describe various historical landmarks and points of interest along the route, providing detailed information about their significance in Norwalk's history. Include anecdotes, historical facts, and stories to engage your audience and bring the town's history to life. Use visual aids such as maps, photographs, or archival images to illustrate key points and help the audience visualize the tour route and important landmarks. Be sure to include clear directions and instructions for navigating the tour, including starting and ending points, as well as any recommended stops along the way.

Scenario 1: Guided Walking Tour for History Enthusiasts

1. Presenter's Name: ______________________
2. Date of Presentation: ____________________
3. Overall Impressions:
   - Was the presenter knowledgeable about Norwalk's history?
   - Did the presenter engage the audience effectively?
   - Rate the overall effectiveness of the presentation (1-5, with 5 being the highest).
4. Content:
   - Were the historical landmarks and points of interest clearly described?
   - Did the presenter provide sufficient information about each location's significance?
   - Were anecdotes and stories used effectively to enhance the presentation?
5. Visual Aids:
   - Did the visual aids (maps, photographs, illustrations) help enhance understanding?
   - Were the visual aids clear and easy to follow?
   - Did the visual aids contribute to the overall effectiveness of the presentation?
6. Clarity and Delivery:
   - Were directions and instructions for navigating the tour clear?
   - Was the presenter's delivery clear and easy to understand?
   - Did the presenter maintain a good pace throughout the presentation?

In this part, we demonstrated how to develop interpersonal and presentational activities using Generative AI, along with several scaffolds to assist students in these communication forms. We will demonstrate in the last portion of this chapter how you can take these similar exercises and make them functionally different since generative AI can interact with objects in real time. Students may obtain feedback on their productive abilities and practice speaking and/or writing during these in-person encounters. We'll also demonstrate how augmented instructors may monitor student competence improvement using Generative AI.

USING GENERATIVE AI FOR FEEDBACK & COACHING IN LANGUAGE ACQUISITION

An augmented world language instructor may generate assignments using Generative AI, as explained in this chapter. But generative AI is capable of far more than merely creating tasks. Additionally, generative AI may operate as an interactive thinking partner, coaching students' skills across all communication modalities and enhancing their correctness, coherence, fluency, and cultural appropriateness. This means that, rather than serving as a tool to perform the learning for students, one of our responsibilities as educators is to demonstrate to them how to utilize generative AI effectively and ethically as part of their own learning process. Generative AI may be a valuable thinking companion for educators in identifying their students' strengths, places for growth, and the best course of action for their lessons. In this part, we start by looking at how generative AI can coach students in communication styles. We then conclude by looking at how it can help teachers decide what to teach next.

Using the presenting task we discussed in Figure 19, let's move on. That work can be too much for a language student to handle, particularly in terms of organization and substance! Students' presentations may be improved if they learn to utilize Generative AI as a thinking partner and get mentoring. When a student poses a question along the lines of, "I am a student who is doing a presentation on a historical walking tour of Norwalk, Ohio that I have created," Figure 20 illustrates what can occur. To get me to think about how I may organize this work, ask me questions. It's crucial to note that the student is not requesting that the bot finish the assignment; instead, the prompt is meant to provide thought-provoking questions that will assist the student in considering every aspect of their presentation.

Figure 20. Generative AI prompt for improving the organization of a presentation

Of course! Here are some questions to help you think about how you might organize your presentation for the Guided Walking Tour for History Enthusiasts:

- *What landmarks or points of interest do you plan to include in your walking tour, and why did you choose them?*
- *How will you introduce the tour topic and purpose to your audience at the beginning of your presentation?*
- *Can you describe the route of your walking tour, including the starting and ending points, as well as any stops along the way?*
- *What information will you provide about each landmark during the tour, and how will you make it engaging for your audience?*
- *Do you plan to incorporate any visual aids, such as maps or photographs, to enhance your presentation?*
- *How will you ensure that your narration during the tour is clear and easy to understand for your audience?*
- *Will you include any interactive elements or opportunities for audience participation during the tour?*
- *How will you conclude your presentation and summarize the highlights of the tour for your audience?*
- *Have you considered any potential challenges or questions that your audience might have, and how will you address them?*

Generative AI may also serve as a coach to assist students in refining the substance of their presentations after they have created them. Utilizing the suggestion, "I need to practice my presentation in Spanish," as a guide. I'll copy and paste my previous writing here. To assist me in editing what I have written, pose questions to me. Please don't edit it for me. Generative AI may provide questions in this way, as seen in Figure 21, which students can use to edit their presentations. Students might also ask the bot to provide editing remarks by saying something such, "Tell me how the verb conjugations in my presentation work."

Figure 21. Generative AI feedback for improving the content of a presentation

- *How could you make the introduction more exciting to capture the audience's attention from the beginning?*
- *Is there a way to simplify or clarify the descriptions of the historical places to make them more understandable for your audience?*
- *Could you add more details or interesting anecdotes about each historical place to make the presentation more engaging and educational?*
- *How could you improve the transition between each historical place to make the presentation flow better?*
- *Is there any additional information you think would be helpful to include about Norwalk or its history to enrich the presentation?*
- *Can you think of a way to encourage audience participation during the tour to make it more interactive?*
- *How could you conclude the presentation more impactfully to leave a lasting impression on your audience?*
- *Is there any aspect of the presentation you would like to practice more to improve your fluency and confidence when speaking?*

Although the examples in this presentational mode demonstrate Generative AI as a coach after student content creation, Generative AI may also function as an on-demand companion and coach during interpersonal interactions. This isn't only for written material either—with the text-to-speech feature, students may read dialogue aloud to themselves as a conversation partner in their native tongue. Students may converse with ChatGPT in the target language by using the ChatGPT 4.o app, which has been upgraded. In addition to offering spoken language practice, ChatGPT will also provide a transcript of the interaction, all depending on the question or assignment the learner begins with. In Figure 22, students use generative AI to improve their interpersonal interactions throughout a brief activity in which they share information about their interests with other students at different locations across town. "I want to practice an interpersonal task where we exchange information about places in town and what we do there," the student says to the generative AI. You should be a non-native speaker of the language. I'm not very good at languages either. You strike up a discussion. Following the discussion, the student asks for comments twice more on the response's grammar and quality.

Figure 22. Using Generative AI to practice interpersonal conversations and receive feedback

ChatGPT
¡Hola! ¿Cómo estás?

User
Bien, y tu?
ChatGPT
Estoy bien, gracias. ¿Cómo te llamas?

User
Me llamo es Char
ChatGPT
¡Encantado de conocerte, Char! Soy un bot de lenguaje y estoy aquí para practicar español contigo. ¿De dónde eres, Char?

User
Yo soy en Norwalk
ChatGPT
¡Qué interesante! Yo también estoy en Norwalk en Ohio. ¿Qué te gusta hacer en Norwalk?

User
Me gusta caminar en el parque.

ChatGPT
A mí no me gusta caminar en el parque. Prefiero ir de compras.

User
Adios.

ChatGPT
Hasta Luego.

User
Give me feedback on how I could improve my answers from novice mid to novice high.

ChatGPT
Your answers are clear and understandable, which is great for a novice level! To move to a novice high level, you can focus on adding more detail and complexity to your responses. For example, instead of just saying "Me gusta caminar en el parque," you could expand on why you enjoy living near the park. You could say something like "Me gusta caminar en el parque porque me encanta disfrutar de la naturaleza después de un dia de clases." Adding more specific details and reasons behind your likes and activities will enhance the richness and complexity of your language use. Keep up the good work!

User
Give me feedback on my grammar.

ChatGPT
Remember that the word tu has two meanings. When you place an accent on it, it means you. When you don't place an accent on it, it means your. Also, remember that Me llamo means my name is. You don't need to put the word is, es, after it again.

While the interpersonal and presentational modes were the main emphasis of the aforementioned instances, Generative AI may also coach and encourage students while they interact with interpretative information by offering clarifications, recommendations, or more examples to help with understanding in the target language. Students' learning experiences are improved and their comprehension of the subject matter is strengthened by this kind of individualized support. Think of the following example as only one use of generative AI for students in connection to the interpretative mode. Have a student use the text in Figure 11 to trigger the ChatGPT art app to create an illustration of the statement “El Parque: Enelparque, losestudianteshacenejercicio y juegan.” They walk, run, and ride bicycles. “It's quite disorienting to be outside!” generated the picture shown in Figure 23, which improves the students' understanding of terms they were not acquainted with.

Figure 23. Illustration of a sentence found in a text

- Provide a self-reflection tool that allows students to assess how well they performed on the assignment. Ask guiding questions as well. Give them a chance to provide supporting documentation for their self-reflection.

  Develop a peer evaluation instrument that conforms to the interpersonal communication criteria of the Ohio World Language. Construct sentence structures for every section in the tool.

  - Give a new student feedback on this answer. I am going to take their answer and paste it.

Apart from these cues, students' development may be monitored using Generative AI, which assesses their performance on language activities and their interactions with others. Table 7 illustrates how teachers may monitor their students' language growth and modify their education based on the reports or summaries that Generative AI generates about their accomplishments and areas that want work. "Evaluate this student's responses in relation to the ACTFL Can-Do statements, providing specific instructional next steps," was the question we used in this instance to train the bot. I'll copy and paste both of your replies.

Table 7. Generative AI evaluation of student progress

Student Response (Sept. 2023)	**Student Response (Sept. 2024)**
Hola. Me llamo Juan. Soy un estudiante. Soy de losEstados Unidos pero vivo en Rocky River. Me gustamuchoandarenpatineta. Soy bajo y tengoelpelo rubio. También, soy deportista y estudioso. Me gusta pasar tiempo con mis amigos en Starbucks.	Hola, soy Juan, un estudiante que viveen Rocky River, Ohio. Tengo 12 años. Soy una persona activa y apasionadaporelarte y la naturaleza. Cuando no estoyen la escuela, me encanta pasar tiempo al aire libre. Además, soy leal y me gustaayudar.

Chat GPT Evaluation of Both Responses

Both responses show growth in language use, particularly in providing more detailed and descriptive information about Juan. Let's compare them in relation to the presentational ACTFL Can-Do statements:

1. Communication Strategies:
    - Response 1 demonstrates basic communication strategies by providing straightforward information about Juan's name, origin, residence, hobbies, physical characteristics, and personality traits.
    - Response 2 shows further development in communication strategies by providing more detailed information about Juan's age, interests, activities outside of school, and personal values. This response uses cohesive language to connect ideas and create a more coherent narrative.
2. Level of Detail:
    - Response 1 offers basic details about Juan's hobbies, physical appearance, and general personality traits.
    - Response 2 provides a higher level of detail, offering specific information about Juan's age, interests, activities he enjoys outside of school, and his personal values. This response paints a clearer picture of Juan's personality and lifestyle.
3. Language Proficiency:
    - Response 1 demonstrates proficiency at a novice level, as it provides simple sentences with basic vocabulary and limited complexity.

- Response 2 shows progression to a low intermediate level, as it includes more varied vocabulary, longer sentences, and a higher level of complexity in the narrative structure

Instructional Guidance:

- Encourage students to expand their responses by providing more detailed information about themselves or the topics they are discussing. This can include adding specific details such as age, interests, hobbies, activities, and personal values.
- Guide students to use cohesive language to connect ideas and create a more coherent narrative. Teach them to use transition words and phrases to improve the flow of their writing or speaking.
- Provide opportunities for students to practice expressing themselves in different contexts, such as describing themselves, their daily routines, their interests, or their experiences. This will help them develop their language skills and increase their proficiency level over time.

As shown in this section, generative AI may act as a coach for instructors and students, offering comments and acting as a thinking partner. In order to effectively use generative AI as a teaching tool, educators must set an example of morality and efficiency, stressing that it should never take the place of active learning. By providing personalized feedback and coaching, Generative AI helps students improve their language proficiency in a variety of communication contexts. Generative AI simplifies the tasks of monitoring students' development over time, developing tools for self-reflection and peer evaluation, and giving teachers actionable input. Teachers may provide more effective language learning experiences that are customized to the requirements and competence level of each student by using the capabilities of Generative AI.

CONCLUSION

As this chapter has shown, new developments in Generative AI have the potential to completely transform both the way students learn languages in the end and the way particular classroom units of teaching are designed. The chapter provided educators with instructions on how to use AI technologies to first design an IPA and then create real-world classroom activities that let students practice utilizing the three modalities of communication. This chapter also covered the application of generative AI to promote target language learning, given that feedback is a crucial component of the recursiveness of instructional design in a global language classroom. Teachers may provide more effective language learning experiences that are customized to the requirements and skill level of each student by using the capabilities of Generative AI and taking into account the questions at the conclusion of this chapter.

REFERENCES

Adair-Hauck, B., Glisan, E. W., & Troyan, F. J. (2013). *Implementing Integrated Performance Assessment.* ACTFL.

Adair-Hauck, B., & Troyan, F. (2013). A Descriptive and Co-Constructive Approach to Integrated Performance Assessment Feedback. *Foreign Language Annals*, *46*(10), 23–44. Advance online publication. DOI: 10.1111/flan.12017

American Council of Teaching of Foreign Languages. (2024). *ACTFL Proficiency Guidelines.* Retrieved from https://www.actfl.org/uploads/files/general/Resources-Publications/ACTFL_Proficiency_Guidelines_2024.pdf

Blodget, T. (1995) *¿Como es?* Retrieved from: https://www.songsforteaching.com/musicapaedia/comoes.htm

Center for Advanced Research on Language Acquisition (CARLA). (2019). *Integrated performance assessments (IPA).* Retrieved from: https://carla.umn.edu/assessment/vac/CreateUnit/p_2.html

deMiej, R. (2018, Oct. 13). Videohistoria: Amigos por internet. [Video]. Retrieved from https://www.youtube.com/watch?v=aE3b8M_JG14

Jacobs, H., & Zmuda, A. (2023). *Streamlining the curriculum: Using the storyboard approach to frame compelling learning journeys.* ASCD.

Mason, B., Krashen, S. (2019). Hypothesis: A Class Supplying Rich Comprehensible Input is More Effective and Efficient than "Immersion."

Ohio Department of Education and Workforce. (2017). *Rubrics for world languages.* Retrieved from https://education.ohio.gov/Topics/Learning-in-Ohio/World-Languages-and-Cultures/Model-Curriculum-for-World-Languages-and-Cultures/Instruction-and-Assessment/Rubrics-for-World-Languages

Ohio Department of Education and Workforce. (2023). *World Languages Model Curriculum.* Retrieved from https://education.ohio.gov/Topics/Learning-in-Ohio/World-Languages-and-Cultures/Model-Curriculum-for-World-Languages-and-Cultures/Content-Elaborations

Sandrock, P. (2014). *The keys to assessing language performance: A teacher's manual for measuring student progress.* ACTFL.

Shrum, J. L., & Glisan, E. W. (2016). *Teacher's Handbook: Contextualized Language Instruction* (5th ed.). Cengage Learning.

Troyan, F., Adair-Hauck, B., & Glisan, E. W. (2023). *The integrated performance assessment: Twenty years and counting*. ACTFL.

Wiggins, G., & McTighe, J. (2005). *Understanding by design*. ASCD.

Wiggins, G., & McTighe, J. (2013) *Understanding by design framework.* ASCD. Retrieved from https://files.ascd.org/staticfiles/ascd/pdf/siteASCD/publications/UbD_WhitePaper0312.pdf

Chapter 8

Ethical Implications of Generative AI in Education: Privacy, Bias, and Integrity

Mustafa Kayyali
https://orcid.org/0000-0003-3300-262X
Maaref University of Applied Sciences, Idlib, Syria

ABSTRACT

Generative AI is transforming education by giving tailored learning experiences and creative teaching approaches. However, this change brings substantial ethical challenges. This chapter analyzes the ethical implications of generative AI in education, concentrating on privacy concerns, algorithmic prejudice, and the integrity of academic processes. Privacy difficulties arise from the vast data collection and potential exploitation of sensitive information, while biases in AI systems risk reproducing inequities and marginalizing disadvantaged populations. Additionally, the rise of AI tools poses problems about maintaining academic honesty and preserving the authenticity of learning. By addressing these challenges, this chapter presents a critical examination of ethical frameworks, case studies, and policy recommendations to guarantee that generative AI is applied responsibly in educational environments. It finishes by underlining the necessity for coordinated efforts among educators, technologists, and policymakers to develop an egalitarian and trustworthy AI-driven education system.

DOI: 10.4018/979-8-3693-8744-3.ch008

INTRODUCTION

The integration of generative artificial intelligence (AI) into education signals a dramatic revolution in the way knowledge is provided, accessible, and assessed. Generative AI, distinguished by its ability to develop new content such as text, graphics, and even simulations based on user inputs, has attracted substantial interest for its potential to improve personalized learning methodologies. Tools such as ChatGPT, DALL-E, and other generative AI models are now being leveraged to generate customized courses, provide quick feedback, and enable creative problem-solving, empowering both educators and learners (Mittal et al, 2024). While these developments hold enormous promise, they also bring a range of ethical challenges that demand rigorous study. At the heart of this transition lies the promise of generative AI to overcome some of education's most persistent difficulties. By enabling individualized learning experiences, AI systems may adapt to individual learners' needs, offering bespoke information and feedback that fit with their particular talents and learning paces. For instance, students grappling with hard mathematical topics can obtain step-by-step explanations, while expert learners can tackle higher-level tasks. Generative AI also aids instructors by automating administrative duties, producing lesson plans, and providing insights into student performance through data analysis. These capabilities not only boost efficiency but also open up prospects for more inclusive and equitable education systems. The implementation of generative AI in education is not without its ethical challenges. One of the most serious problems is privacy (Al-kfairy, 2024). The usefulness of AI-driven educational systems generally rests on their ability to collect and analyze massive volumes of data, including personal information, learning patterns, and performance indicators. While this data facilitates the creation of highly tailored learning environments, it also raises serious problems regarding how such data is handled, who has access to it, and how it may be misused. Students, parents, and instructors alike are justifiably concerned about the possibility of breaches of sensitive information and the erosion of faith in educational institutions.

Another major concern is the presence of algorithmic bias within generative AI systems (Wach et al, 2023). AI models are only as unbiased as the data they are trained on, and when this data reflects societal injustices, the resulting AI outputs might perpetuate or even exacerbate these gaps. In an educational environment, this could mean unequal access to opportunities, perpetuating prejudices, or marginalizing already disadvantaged populations. For example, language models may accidentally favor specific dialects or cultural norms, leaving non-dominant voices underrepresented. The consequences of such prejudices are far-reaching, as they threaten the core concepts of fairness and diversity in education. The subject of academic integrity also looms large in the discussion of generative AI in education.

Tools capable of writing essays, solving complex equations, or even producing art blur the distinctions between actual student work and machine-assisted results. While these tools can serve as essential learning aids, they also provide chances for misuse, such as plagiarism or the circumvention of critical thinking processes. This raises fundamental questions about the purpose of education and the role of educators in generating authentic learning experiences. Balancing the benefits of AI technologies with the requirement to sustain academic honesty is an issue that demands subtle answers and continuing conversation.

To overcome these obstacles, it is vital to build rigorous ethical frameworks that guide the application of generative AI in education (AlAli, & Wardat, 2024). Policymakers, educators, developers, and academics must work to address the ethical problems raised by AI, ensuring that its deployment aligns with ideals of equity, privacy, and integrity. These frameworks should not only establish best practices for data governance and algorithmic transparency but also emphasize the need to cultivate digital literacy among students and educators. Understanding how AI systems work, their limitations, and their ethical implications will equip stakeholders to make educated decisions and use these tools ethically. The incorporation of generative AI into education also demands a reevaluation of existing educational norms and standards. As AI technologies grow, so too must the guidelines that govern their use. This includes crafting regulations that meet the particular ethical concerns offered by AI, such as building systems for responsibility, implementing safeguards against misuse, and promoting fair access to AI-powered products. By proactively addressing these concerns, educational institutions may leverage the revolutionary potential of generative AI while limiting its perils. In this chapter, we address the ethical implications of generative AI in education through the lenses of privacy, bias, and integrity. We analyze how these difficulties overlap with broader societal challenges and provide ways for establishing a responsible and fair AI-driven education system. By critically assessing the benefits and hazards of generative AI, this conversation intends to contribute to a deeper understanding of how technology might be harnessed to create a more inclusive, innovative, and ethical educational landscape.

UNDERSTANDING PRIVACY CONCERNS IN EDUCATIONAL AI APPLICATIONS

The integration of generative AI technology into education has brought about enormous breakthroughs, although it has also opened the door to important concerns around privacy (Al-kfairy et al, 2024). Data lies at the core of AI's ability to tailor learning experiences, optimize teaching tactics, and drive innovation in education.

However, the sheer number and sensitivity of data involved provide distinct hazards that educators, policymakers, and technologists must manage. Safeguarding privacy in this situation is not simply a technical difficulty but also a moral and ethical responsibility that necessitates subtle and human-centered methods. The foundation of generative AI's capabilities in education is built on the collection and analysis of data (Bahroun et al, 2023). Student profiles, learning patterns, performance indicators, and even personal preferences are regularly collected to develop individualized educational experiences. For instance, AI-powered technologies can monitor how students engage with course materials, identify gaps in knowledge, and make individualized recommendations for improvement. While these features enhance the quality of education, they demand access to a large array of personal information. This is an inherent contradiction between harnessing data for greater educational outcomes and respecting the rights and dignity of learners. One of the most significant privacy concerns is the potential for data breaches. Educational institutions and technology suppliers retain enormous volumes of sensitive information on their servers, ranging from students' names and addresses to their academic records and behavioral data (Madhura & Mahalakshmi, 2021). Inadequate security measures can expose sensitive information to malicious actors, resulting in identity theft, blackmail, or other forms of exploitation. For example, a breach in an AI-powered learning platform could lead to the exposing of a student's detailed learning history, which might then be utilized for commercial or unethical purposes. Beyond breaches, there is also the matter of consent. Many students, particularly younger ones, may not completely comprehend what data is being collected on them or how it is being utilized. In some situations, parents or guardians are needed to provide consent on behalf of minors, but even they may not fully appreciate the implications of the data-sharing agreements they are signing. Transparency in how data is acquired, handled, and utilized is therefore crucial. Without clear and accessible communication about these practices, educational institutions risk decreasing trust among students, parents, and other stakeholders.

Another component of privacy problems relates to third-party engagement. Many generative AI systems used in education are developed and maintained by private corporations, which frequently have their own goals and agendas (Nedungadi et al, 2024). When educational institutions work with these corporations, they must carefully assess the terms of service and data protection rules to ensure they match with ethical norms. The possibility of commercial exploitation—where student data is sold to advertisers or exploited to generate unrelated products—looms big in such relationships. Policymakers and educators must lobby for rigorous laws that limit the extent of data usage by third parties, ensuring that it is solely employed for educational purposes. The repercussions of privacy breaches or mismanagement are not merely technical but profoundly personal. When a student's private information is disclosed or misused, it can lead to emotions of vulnerability and mistrust. In severe circumstances, such breaches can have long-term psychological impacts, particularly for younger learners who are still building their sense of self and security. Protecting privacy, therefore, is not only about conforming to legal requirements; it is about maintaining the dignity and well-being of every individual inside the educational environment. Addressing these challenges demands a diverse strategy. On the technological side, effective encryption techniques, regular security audits, and secure data storage policies are vital. Institutions must invest in cutting-edge cybersecurity solutions to protect sensitive information from illegal access. Additionally, adopting a philosophy of data minimization—collecting just the data that is essential for the intended purpose—can greatly reduce the risks associated with data storage and processing.

On the policy front, educational institutions and governments must collaborate to build comprehensive data governance frameworks (Ladley, 2019). These frameworks should describe explicit criteria for data collection, storage, and utilization, as well as set accountability procedures for breaches or misuse. For example, institutions should create policies requiring anonymization of data whenever possible, ensuring that personal identifiers are erased before information is processed or shared. Furthermore, regular training sessions for educators and administrators on data privacy best practices can assist develop a culture of vigilance and responsibility. Education surrounding privacy should also extend to students and their families (Jones et al, 2020). Digital literacy programs that teach students about the significance of privacy, the possible risks of sharing personal information, and how to protect themselves online are vital in today's linked society. Such programs empower learners to take an active role in securing their data and making educated decisions about the technologies they use. The role of trust cannot be emphasized. Educational institutions must try to create and retain trust in their communities by displaying a strong commitment to privacy and transparency. Open communication about data practices, coupled with a readiness to address issues and adjust rules in response to feedback, can go a long way in establishing confidence among students, parents, and educators. Privacy problems in educational AI applications are complicated and multidimensional, mirroring broader societal disputes regarding the role of technology in our lives. While generative AI has enormous potential to enhance learning experiences, this potential must not come at the expense of individuals' rights to privacy and security. By adopting a holistic approach that incorporates technical safeguards, rigorous policies, education, and openness, stakeholders may establish an environment in which the benefits of AI are realized without compromising ethical standards. The challenge is considerable, but the stakes—for the future of education and the well-being of learners—demand nothing less.

BIAS IN GENERATIVE AI SYSTEMS: IMPACTS ON EQUITY IN EDUCATION

Bias in generative AI systems provides a fundamental obstacle to the goal of equitable education, where every learner is provided with the opportunity to thrive regardless of their history, identity, or circumstances (Varsik & Vosberg, 2024). While generative AI provides great promise to change education by personalizing experiences to individual needs, it also bears the risk of sustaining, and even amplifying, current imbalances. The roots of these biases lay deep inside the design and deployment of AI systems, which are molded by the data they are trained on, the assumptions made by developers, and the societal structures they represent. Understanding the nature and implications of bias in generative AI is vital for reducing its impact and establishing a more inclusive educational landscape. At its foundation, bias in AI systems originates from the data used to train them. Generative AI models, such as those employed in educational applications, rely on enormous datasets that typically reflect historical trends and societal conventions (Balasubramaniam et al, 2024). These datasets, however extensive, are rarely neutral. They may disproportionately represent certain groups while marginalizing others, leading to outcomes that favor the majority or dominant culture. For instance, an AI system educated exclusively on English-language texts may struggle to interpret or generate material in less commonly spoken languages or dialects. This language bias can exclude non-native speakers or people from underrepresented linguistic communities, restricting their ability to fully benefit from AI-powered educational aids.

The repercussions of such biases are far-reaching. In a diverse classroom, students come from various cultural, linguistic, and socio-economic backgrounds, each bringing unique viewpoints and demands (Igboegwu, 2023). When AI systems fail to account for this variability, they risk generating a one-size-fits-all strategy that serves only a fraction of learners. For example, an AI-powered learning platform that recommends resources or exercises based on patterns seen in a majority group can accidentally neglect the requirements of students who depart from those trends. This can result in some students receiving less relevant or lower-quality support, exacerbating existing gaps rather than eliminating them. Bias in generative AI systems is not confined to linguistic or cultural representation; it also extends to content development and recommendation. For example, an AI tool meant to produce practice questions or learning materials can accidentally include preconceptions or reinforce discriminatory narratives present in its training data. Consider a history lecture provided by an AI system that overemphasizes the achievements of certain groups while downplaying or ignoring the contributions of others. Such literature not only presents an imperfect understanding of history but also perpetuates biases that might impact students' views and opinions. In this sense, biased AI outputs might gradually influence how learners interpret the world and their place within it.

Another degree of bias lies in the algorithms themselves. Even with diverse datasets, the mathematical models used to construct AI systems might incorporate unexpected biases in the way they process and interpret data. For instance, generative AI systems generally rely on statistical correlations to make predictions or generate content. While these connections may be accurate on average, they can overlook key details or perpetuate detrimental preconceptions. An AI system tasked with forecasting student performance can, for example, overemphasize demographic criteria like gender or socio-economic status, thus reinforcing assumptions about who is likely to excel in certain subjects or fields (Anh, 2024). The effects of biased AI systems in education extend beyond individual learners to broader societal implications. Education is a key engine of social mobility, and unequal access to high-quality learning opportunities can worsen existing disparities. If generative AI systems routinely penalize particular populations, they risk entrenching cycles of inequity that are difficult to overcome. For example, students from impoverished backgrounds may already encounter hurdles such as restricted access to resources or support. If AI systems further penalize these students by biased recommendations or assessments, the divide between privileged and underprivileged groups will further increase.

Addressing bias in generative AI systems demands a multi-faceted strategy that goes beyond technological improvements (Tariq, 2025). While boosting the diversity and quality of training data is a vital step, it is not a panacea. Developers must also address the broader social and ethical consequences of their work, aggressively working to discover and reduce biases at every stage of the AI development process. This includes conducting regular audits of AI systems to measure their performance across different groups, as well as including diverse stakeholders in the design and testing phases. By adding perspectives from educators, students, and communities, developers can better comprehend the real-world impact of their systems and make more educated decisions.

Transparency is another crucial part of combating bias. Educational institutions and technology providers must be clear about the limitations of their AI systems, especially the potential for prejudice (Pedro et al, 2019). This transparency enables instructors and students to approach AI tools critically, acknowledging their strengths and flaws rather than depending on them unconditionally. For instance, a learning platform might incorporate disclaimers regarding the origins of its content or give users the ability to identify biased or improper results. Such measures not only promote confidence but also empower people to actively engage in the refining of AI systems. Education itself plays a key role in minimizing the influence of bias. Digital literacy programs that teach students and educators about the workings of

AI, including its potential for bias, can encourage a more informed and critical engagement with technology. When users understand how AI systems generate information or make suggestions, they are better positioned to spot and challenge biased conclusions. For example, a professor who realizes that an AI-generated quiz unfairly favors specific cultural allusions can make efforts to supplement or amend the material to better serve their students.

Despite these challenges, the potential for generative AI to enhance equity in education should not be underestimated. When built and implemented wisely, AI systems can reduce inequities by offering individualized help to learners who might otherwise be neglected. For instance, an AI tool that identifies and addresses specific learning gaps might assist struggling students catch up to their friends, while adaptive technologies can suit varied learning styles and demands. The goal is to guarantee that these systems are inclusive by design, promoting justice and accessibility as essential values. Bias in generative AI systems poses substantial hurdles to attaining equity in education, but it is not an insurmountable obstacle. By admitting the prevalence of bias and taking proactive actions to correct it, stakeholders may harness the promise of AI to build more inclusive and equitable learning environments. This demands a dedication to diversity, transparency, and collaboration, as well as a readiness to critically evaluate the societal structures that govern AI development. Ultimately, the goal is not merely to eradicate bias but to use AI as a tool for empowering all learners, regardless of their background or circumstances. In doing so, we can get closer to a vision of education that genuinely fulfills its promise as a gateway to opportunity and social development.

ACADEMIC INTEGRITY AND GENERATIVE AI: CHALLENGES AND OPPORTUNITIES

The fast use of generative AI in education has spurred a serious discourse about the evolving nature of academic integrity. These tools, capable of generating essays, solving complicated issues, and even making artistic works, are redefining the boundaries of what constitutes original thought and meaningful learning. While generative AI brings exciting prospects to enhance education, it also poses important challenges about how to uphold ethical norms and build a culture of honesty in academic contexts (Samala et al, 2024). Understanding and addressing these problems is vital to guarantee that the integration of AI into education supports, rather than undermines, its fundamental goals. At the heart of the academic integrity dispute is the issue of authorship. Generative AI techniques, such as advanced language models, enable students to write essays, research papers, and creative content with astonishing ease (George, 2023). While these tools can serve as great aids for brainstorming and learning, they also make it possible for students to submit work that is substantially, if not totally, generated by a machine. This blurs the distinction between genuine student effort and AI-assisted output, posing challenges about how to assess learning and reward academic performance. For educators, the problem lies in discerning between work that reflects a student's comprehension and work that only exhibits an ability to use AI tools efficiently.

The availability of generative AI further hampers standard approaches to plagiarism detection (Ogwueleka, 2025). Tools designed to identify copied text or unattributed sources may struggle to distinguish content generated by AI, as it is often original in form, even if it draws heavily on existing patterns and knowledge. This produces a unique sort of academic dishonesty that is difficult to detect using normal procedures. For example, a student might utilize an AI tool to compose an essay, modify the material slightly to personalize it, and submit it as their work. While the material may not resemble any existing sources, it may nonetheless fall short of portraying the student's ideas and efforts. The employment of generative AI in assessments raises broader philosophical problems regarding the purpose of education (Monib et al, 2024). If the goal of education is to encourage critical thinking, creativity, and problem-solving skills, then depending on AI to complete assignments may harm these objectives. A student who utilizes AI to generate an essay on a literary work, for instance, would miss the opportunity to interact deeply with the material and develop their interpretations. Similarly, a student who uses AI to answer mathematics issues can forgo the process of learning how to approach and evaluate difficult equations. These instances illustrate the need for educators to rethink evaluation methodologies in the age of AI, emphasizing process and comprehension above mere output. It is vital to remember that generative AI also offers a great opportunity to increase academic integrity when applied appropriately. One of the most intriguing characteristics of these technologies is their capacity to facilitate learning by offering rapid feedback and individualized help. For example, an AI-powered writing assistant can help students sharpen their ideas, enhance their grammar, and extend their vocabulary, helping them to generate higher-quality work. When used as a supplement to, rather than a substitute for, the learning process, these technologies can empower students to enhance their abilities and achieve better academic achievement.

Generative AI also can increase inclusion in education by addressing gaps in access to resources and support (KHAZANCHI & KHAZANCHI, 2024). For students who struggle with traditional methods of learning, AI tools can offer alternate avenues to comprehension and engagement. For instance, a student with dyslexia might utilize an AI tool to develop and arrange ideas for an essay, lowering the cognitive load involved with writing. Similarly, a non-native English speaker might use an AI tool to increase their language proficiency and generate work that more accurately reflects their views. By leveling the playing field, generative AI can help ensure that all students have the opportunity to succeed, provided that its deployment is governed by ethical considerations. To manage the challenges and opportunities of generative AI, educational institutions must adopt a proactive approach to building a culture of academic integrity. This begins with clear communication on the ethical use of AI tools, including standards that clarify what is and is not acceptable. For example, universities can clarify that while AI can be used for brainstorming or editing, the final submission must represent the student's work. By developing transparent policies, instructors may assist students in understanding their duties and the importance of upholding academic standards. Education and awareness are also crucial in resolving the ethical concerns brought about by generative AI. Students and instructors alike need to have a comprehensive grasp of how AI works, its limitations, and its ethical implications. Digital literacy programs can play a vital part in this effort, encouraging students to utilize AI safely and critically. For example, a workshop on AI ethics might tackle themes such as: What defines innovation in the age of AI? How can we ensure that AI-generated work fits with the ideals of academic integrity? What are the potential repercussions of over-reliance on AI in education? By engaging with these questions, students can build a more considered approach to employing AI in their academic work.

Assessment procedures must also be developed to match the realities of generative AI (Salinas-Navarro et al, 2024). Traditional evaluations that focus on outputs, like as essays or problem sets, may no longer provide a reliable measure of a student's understanding. Instead, instructors might examine alternate ways that stress the learning experience, such as oral presentations, in-class writing exercises, or project-based examinations. These strategies can provide deeper insights into a student's mental processes and guarantee that their work represents true effort and knowledge. For example, a professor can encourage students to submit drafts of an essay alongside a reflection on how they used AI tools to better their work, creating transparency and responsibility. Promoting a culture of academic integrity involves collaboration between educators, students, legislators, and technology developers (Cojocariu & Mareş, 2022). Institutions must work together to exchange best practices, adopt solid ethical norms, and advocate for the responsible use of AI in education. Technology developers, in particular, have a key role to play in building AI systems that support academic integrity. This might include elements such as built-in citation tools, transparency about the origins of AI-generated information, and systems to help educators identify when AI has been used illegally. Generative AI provides both serious obstacles and great potential for academic honesty. While new technologies have the potential to challenge traditional concepts of authorship and originality, they also offer essential tools for increasing learning and encouraging diversity. By addressing the ethical implications of AI and establishing a culture of responsibility and openness, educational institutions may harness its potential to serve, rather than undermine, the purposes of education. The key is in striking a balance between embracing the benefits of AI and retaining the values of academic integrity that support a fair and equitable learning environment.

ETHICAL FRAMEWORKS FOR IMPLEMENTING AI IN EDUCATION

The rise of artificial intelligence (AI) in education offers extraordinary prospects for innovation and customization, but it also presents difficult ethical problems (Murdan & Halkhoree, 2024). As educational institutions integrate AI technology into their systems, the necessity for robust ethical frameworks becomes crucial. These frameworks are not only about reducing risks; they also serve as blueprints for harnessing AI in ways that maintain the ideals of equity, privacy, openness, and responsibility. By setting explicit ethical principles, stakeholders in education—educators, politicians, technologists, and students—can ensure that AI systems are developed and implemented ethically. An ethical framework for AI in education begins with a core commitment to human-centric principles. Education, at its heart, is about nurturing intellectual growth, personal development, and social equality. Any application of AI must fit with these principles, ensuring that technology enhances, rather than detracts from, the human experience. To this aim, AI should be created and applied to empower learners, help educators, and promote inclusion. This human-centered approach acts as a guiding principle for all ethical questions regarding AI in education.

One of the most crucial components of an ethical framework is the preservation of student privacy (Alam, 2023). AI systems in education rely on huge volumes of data to work efficiently, from learning patterns and academic performance to personal information such as age, geography, and even socioeconomic background. While this data enables individualized learning experiences, it also brings considerable hazards. Breaches of sensitive information, unlawful access, or abuse of data can weaken faith in educational institutions and hurt students (Penberthy, 2020). To overcome these challenges, an ethical framework must build effective data governance standards. These rules should explain how data is gathered, saved, utilized, and shared, ensuring that student information is treated with the highest care. Transparency is a vital factor here: students, parents, and educators must be fully informed about what data is being collected, for what purposes, and who has access to it. Additionally, institutions should prioritize data minimization—collecting only the necessary information—and establish strict security measures to protect against intrusions. Consent is another cornerstone of ethical data practices. Students and their guardians should have the choice to opt in or out of data collecting processes, with explicit explanations provided about the potential benefits and hazards. For example, while a learning platform might offer greater customization through data analysis, users should be empowered to make an informed decision about whether they choose to share their information. By respecting autonomy and encouraging trust, educational institutions may create an environment where AI technologies are embraced rather than feared.

Algorithmic openness and accountability are equally crucial in ethical AI implementation (Mensah, 2023). AI systems generally operate as "black boxes," with their decision-making mechanisms hidden from users. This lack of transparency can lead to mistrust and even injury, particularly when AI judgments have important consequences, such as selecting academic placements, grading, or resource allocation. An ethical framework must dictate that AI systems in education be created with explainability in mind, guaranteeing that their operations are clear to both educators and learners. If an AI system advises remedial courses for a student based on their performance, it should provide a clear justification for this advice. Was it based on exam scores, engagement data, or trends in similar students' progress? By making these processes transparent, educational institutions can ensure that AI systems are seen as fair and reliable. Furthermore, processes for contesting or appealing AI-generated choices should be in place, offering students and educators a remedy if they believe an outcome is unjust. Bias in AI systems provides another key ethical concern. Because AI models are trained on past data, they can accidentally reinforce existing injustices or stereotypes. In education, this could emerge as unequal access to opportunities, preferring certain groups of students over others based on skewed training data (Lembani et al, 2020). For instance, an AI system might recommend advanced courses only to students from well-resourced institutions, overlooking equally talented individuals from poor backgrounds. To overcome bias, an ethical framework should stress diversity and inclusivity in the creation and deployment of AI systems. This involves using diverse and representative data sets during training, conducting frequent audits to identify and address bias, and including stakeholders from multiple backgrounds in the design process. For example, educators, parents, and students from diverse demographic groups should have a say in creating AI systems to ensure that they meet the requirements of all learners fairly. Ethical AI implementation also demands an emphasis on increasing digital literacy among students and educators. As AI becomes increasingly integrated into education, knowing how these technologies work—and their potential limitations—becomes vital. An ethical framework should foster education and understanding regarding AI, ensuring that users are equipped to engage with these systems appropriately.

For students, this can comprise teachings on the basics of AI, its uses, and its ethical implications. For educators, professional development programs can give the tools and expertise needed to integrate AI into their teaching practices effectively. By promoting a culture of digital literacy, educational institutions can equip stakeholders to make informed decisions and use AI technologies responsibly. Collaboration is another key part of an ethical framework for AI in education (Nguyen et al, 2023). The difficulties faced by AI are too complicated for any single group to address alone; they require involvement from a varied variety of stakeholders, including educators, technologists, policymakers, and ethicists. For example, partnerships between educational institutions and technology developers can ensure that AI systems are created with educational principles in mind, while input from lawmakers can assist build legislation that protects students' rights and interests. Ethical frameworks should also underline the importance of adaptation. AI technologies are growing rapidly, and ethical norms must be flexible enough to keep pace with these advances. This can require regular evaluations of ethical policies, incorporating feedback from consumers, and staying educated about technical improvements and potential concerns. By maintaining a proactive and adaptable attitude, educational institutions may ensure that their ethical frameworks stay relevant and effective throughout time. An ethical framework for AI in education should include systems for accountability. Institutions must be prepared to bear responsibility for the implications of AI deployment, whether beneficial or harmful. This includes establishing clear lines of accountability for decision-making, offering outlets for addressing concerns, and committing to continual improvement based on input and outcomes. If an AI system fails to operate as expected or causes harm, institutions should be honest about what went wrong and take steps to correct the situation. This level of responsibility not only creates confidence but also ensures that ethical considerations stay at the forefront of AI implementation. Ethical frameworks are vital for directing the responsible use of AI in education. By promoting privacy, openness, inclusion, and responsibility, these frameworks might help educational institutions negotiate the complex problems offered by AI technologies. At the same time, they present a path for exploiting AI's promise to enhance learning, help educators, and promote equity. By committing to ethical values and fostering collaboration among stakeholders, the education sector can ensure that AI acts as a force for good, benefiting learners and educators alike in an increasingly digital environment.

BALANCING INNOVATION WITH PRIVACY: CASE STUDIES IN AI INTEGRATION

As artificial intelligence (AI) continues to alter education, a recurring difficulty resides in finding the delicate balance between innovation and privacy (Dwivedi et al, 2021). While AI-driven solutions promise to improve the learning experience through individualized teaching and faster administrative processes, they typically rely on large volumes of sensitive data to work properly. This reliance creates fundamental questions about how privacy is controlled and whether the benefits of AI can be reached without sacrificing the trust and security of learners. Exploring real-world case studies of AI integration in education helps elucidate this complex interplay and provides insights into how institutions might navigate this landscape responsibly.

One significant example of AI integration is the usage of adaptive learning platforms in colleges (Sajja et al, 2024). These platforms, such as DreamBox Learning and Carnegie Learning, tailor the educational experience based on individual student performance. By evaluating data on students' responses, the system detects areas of weakness and modifies the curriculum to match their unique needs. For instance, a student suffering from fractions might be offered additional practice problems and interactive tutorials, while another student excelling in the same topic is guided toward more advanced content. While the customization enabled by such platforms has proven to increase learning outcomes, it also poses substantial privacy concerns. These systems collect substantial data on students' academic achievement, engagement patterns, and even behavioral attributes such as tenacity and problem-solving methods. Questions emerge concerning who owns this data, how it is stored, and whether it could be utilized beyond the stated instructional purpose. In other circumstances, parents have expressed worries that their students' data would be shared with third-party companies for marketing or other commercial uses. To address these concerns, some colleges have adopted comprehensive data protection procedures as part of their AI integration initiatives. For example, the Montgomery County Public Colleges (MCPS) in Maryland engaged with AI-driven platforms under rigorous data-sharing agreements. These agreements indicate that student data can only be used for educational purposes and require corporations to comply with high data encryption and storage standards. Additionally, MCPS incorporates parents in the decision-making process, ensuring they understand how their students' data will be used and offering them the choice to opt-out if they feel uncomfortable.

Another example study highlighting the contradiction between innovation and privacy is the employment of AI-powered proctoring technologies in higher education (Slusky, 2020). During the COVID-19 pandemic, many colleges employed technologies such as Proctorio and ExamSoft to conduct remote exams securely (Dewar, 2023). These systems use facial recognition, eye-tracking, and behavior analysis to monitor students during tests, detecting suspected instances of cheating. While these technologies helped colleges retain academic integrity in a remote learning setting, they also provoked extensive debate about privacy violations. Students expressed feeling uneasy with the invasive nature of these tools, particularly the use of facial recognition and ongoing surveillance. There were also concerns about the possibility of bias, as several students of color faced difficulty with facial recognition algorithms that failed to reliably identify them. Furthermore, critics contended that these systems promoted a culture of distrust, prioritizing punishment over support for students during an already trying period. In response to these concerns, some colleges have made attempts to reach a middle ground. For instance, the University of California, Berkeley, substituted AI-powered proctoring technologies with alternative assessment methods, such as open-book exams and project-based evaluations (Sitta et al, 2023). This technique not only avoided the need for intrusive surveillance but also encouraged deeper learning and critical thinking. Other institutions, such as Arizona State University, have elected to continue utilizing AI proctoring tools but with substantial alterations, such as eliminating facial recognition functions and improving transparency about how the tools work.

The incorporation of AI chatbots in educational contexts is another intriguing case study. Chatbots like Ivy.ai and AdmitHub are increasingly being employed by colleges and universities to provide 24/7 help for students (Taylor et al, 2024). These chatbots can answer concerns about financial aid, course registration, and campus resources, freeing up personnel to focus on more complex work. By evaluating user data, chatbots can also give personalized recommendations, such as suggesting scholarships or study resources depending on a student's profile. While chatbots have shown to be incredibly effective in enhancing student engagement and accessibility, they also raise serious privacy concerns (Abdallah et al, 2024). For instance, some chatbots acquire personal information such as Social Security numbers, medical histories, or mental health concerns to provide tailored support. This degree of data collecting, if not managed correctly, might expose students to threats such as identity theft or illegal access to their personal information.

To address these dangers, some institutions have created ethical AI standards to guide their chatbot implementations (Sebastian & Sebastian, 2024). Georgia State University, for example, uses the chatbot Pounce to assist students with enrollment and financial aid processes (Barrett et al, 2019). The university assures that Pounce runs within a safe, encrypted environment and limits the sorts of data acquired to what is strictly essential for its activities. Additionally, Georgia State has developed explicit standards on data retention, detailing how long information is held and when it is removed. These methods assist create trust among students while keeping the benefits of AI-driven support. An equally convincing example comes from the employment of AI in special education. Tools such as Cognii and Studentsense offer individualized learning experiences for students with disabilities, adjusting to their particular requirements and learning methods (Zaugg, 2024). These tools can analyze speech patterns, provide targeted feedback, and even simulate real-life settings to assist students build social and communication skills. For instance, a nonverbal learner might use an AI-powered speech recognition application to refine pronunciation and expand their vocabulary in a friendly atmosphere.

However, the application of AI in special education also raises privacy challenges. Many of these systems rely on continual monitoring and recording of students' interactions, raising problems about consent and data security (Regan & Jesse, 2019). Parents and educators often battle with worries about who has access to this data and how it might be used in the future. Additionally, there is a concern that over-reliance on AI tools could mistakenly limit human interaction, which is a critical component of special education. To address these issues, some colleges and companies have stressed ethical design principles in their AI solutions for special education. For example, Studentsense leverages on-device processing to evaluate speech patterns, ensuring that sensitive data never leaves the device. Similarly, the creators of Cognii have added tight privacy settings that allow educators and parents to choose how data is collected and shared. These initiatives illustrate that it is possible to balance innovation with privacy, especially in the extremely sensitive environment of special education. In reflecting on these case studies, several critical lessons emerge for educational institutions attempting to balance innovation with privacy. First, transparency is vital. Whether it entails adaptive learning platforms, AI-powered proctoring tools, or chatbots, students and parents must be fully educated about how AI systems work, what data they gather, and how that data is used. Clear communication creates confidence and helps consumers to make informed decisions regarding their engagement with AI technologies.

Second, institutions must adopt a proactive approach to data stewardship. This entails installing rigorous security measures, such as encryption and access controls, as well as creating policies on data minimization and preservation. By prioritizing the safety of sensitive information, colleges and universities may avoid risks and increase confidence in their AI programs. Third, collaboration is crucial. Educational institutions should incorporate a varied variety of stakeholders—including students, parents, instructors, and technologists—in the design and deployment of AI systems. This collaborative approach guarantees that different perspectives are explored, helping to generate solutions that are both innovative and ethical. Flexibility and adaptability are vital. As AI technologies continue to grow, so too must the ethical norms and procedures that govern their use. Regular evaluations of AI systems, guided by user feedback and new trends, can help institutions stay ahead of possible difficulties and possibilities. Balancing innovation with privacy in AI integration is a hard but doable goal. The case examples covered here indicate that with strategic preparation, clear communication, and a commitment to ethical standards, educational institutions may harness the transformative potential of AI while preserving the rights and privacy of learners. By learning from these experiences and keeping watchful about the ethical implications of AI, the education industry may continue to innovate responsibly, building a future where technology and human values coexist together.

POLICY RECOMMENDATIONS FOR ETHICAL AI PRACTICES IN EDUCATION

As artificial intelligence (AI) continues to increase its presence in education, the necessity of ethical standards cannot be stressed (Ahmad et al, 2021). The integration of AI technology into classrooms, learning management systems, and administrative procedures has great potential to boost educational outcomes, but it also brings difficult problems. These include issues about privacy, fairness, openness, and the potential of unforeseen effects emerging from algorithmic decision-making. To solve these difficulties effectively, governments must build a robust framework that ensures AI's benefits are achieved without compromising ethical values or the trust of stakeholders. The foundation of any ethical AI policy in education begins with a commitment to transparency. Educational institutions and technology providers must be open about how AI systems operate, the data they collect, and the conclusions they make. For example, if a college adopts an AI-powered learning platform, students and parents should have access to information about what data is being gathered, how it will be used, and who will have access to it. Transparency not only creates trust but also helps people to make educated decisions regarding their participation in AI-driven systems. Policymakers should ensure that all instructional AI technologies contain comprehensive documentation and easily understandable privacy rules.

Equally crucial is the problem of data protection. AI systems generally rely on vast datasets to give individualized learning experiences, but this reliance presents concerns about data breaches, illegal access, and misuse. Policies must prioritize comprehensive data governance structures that promote security, accountability, and ethical treatment of sensitive information (Boppiniti, 2023). For instance, colleges should employ encryption protocols, anonymize student data wherever possible, and restrict access to authorized people only. Additionally, explicit criteria should be created on data retention, indicating how long data will be stored and when it will be removed. To promote diversity and fairness, policymakers must also address the issue of bias in AI systems. AI models are trained on datasets that can unwittingly reflect societal imbalances, leading to biased outcomes that harm certain groups of students. For example, language models could privilege dominant dialects or cultural norms, leaving disadvantaged voices ignored. To avoid these risks, policies should compel developers to undertake regular audits of AI systems, testing for potential biases and ensuring diverse representation in training datasets. Moreover, educational institutions should aggressively seek input from a broad variety of stakeholders, including students, parents, and instructors from varied backgrounds, to inform the development and implementation of AI technology.

Another crucial feature of ethical AI techniques is accountability. When an AI system makes a decision—whether it's giving a grade, proposing a course, or reporting a student for potential misconduct—it is crucial to have processes in place to examine and contest these conclusions (Uddin, 2024). Policymakers should demand that all AI systems used in education contain a "human-in-the-loop" approach, ensuring that crucial decisions are vetted by educators or administrators before being finalized (Enarsson et al, 2022). This technique not only provides a safeguard against errors but also enhances the significance of human judgment in the educational process. Beyond individual systems, a broader accountability framework is necessary to address the ethical concerns brought by AI in education. Governments and educational authorities should establish independent oversight committees tasked with monitoring the implementation of AI technologies, investigating ethical concerns, and recommending changes. These committees could also act as a resource for students and parents, providing guidance and help in navigating the complexity of AI-driven education. Digital literacy is another key component of ethical AI activities (Ng, 2021). As AI becomes more integrated into education, it is crucial for students, educators, and parents to grasp how these technologies function and their possible consequences. Policymakers should prioritize the inclusion of AI and digital literacy curricula in colleges, giving learners the information and abilities to critically engage with AI systems. For educators, professional development programs should be designed to help them navigate the potential problems posed by AI, ensuring they can use these tools effectively and responsibly.

The value of collaboration in establishing ethical AI practices cannot be underestimated (Hagendorff, 2020). Policymakers must establish relationships between educational institutions, technology developers, academics, and civil society organizations to guarantee that AI systems are conceived and implemented with a varied variety of perspectives. Collaborative initiatives can help detect potential dangers early in the development process, produce more fair solutions, and establish trust among stakeholders (Wondirad et al, 2020). For example, partnerships between universities and AI developers have already led to the invention of tools that prioritize ethical design principles, such as reducing data collecting and stressing user control. Incentivizing ethical practices among technology suppliers is another good legislative option. Governments and educational authorities can implement certification systems that recognize AI technologies satisfying high ethical standards, providing a competitive edge to developers who prioritize privacy, fairness, and openness. These certificates could serve as a signal to colleges and universities that a particular tool fits with ethical criteria, easing the decision-making process for institutions wishing to employ AI technologies.

Ethical AI regulations must be flexible enough to respond to the rapid speed of technical change (Díaz-Rodríguez et al, 2023). As AI continues to evolve, new threats and possibilities will certainly surface, requiring policymakers to be watchful and proactive. Regular evaluations of AI policies, guided by emerging research and stakeholder feedback, can assist in guaranteeing that guidelines stay relevant and successful. Policymakers should also establish processes for modifying and updating policies as needed, ensuring that they can keep pace with advancements in AI technology. An important part of ethical AI practices in education is the necessity to incorporate global viewpoints. While much of the discussion around AI ethics is led by countries with significant technological capabilities, it is crucial to guarantee that the views and concerns of emerging countries are equally considered. Policymakers should foster international collaboration and knowledge-sharing, enabling all countries to profit from the benefits afforded by AI while tackling its ethical problems. This method can help develop a more equal global education system, guaranteeing that no one is left behind in the age of AI. Ethical AI methods must prioritize the well-being of students. While AI technologies have enormous promise to boost learning results, they should never come at the expense of students' mental health or personal growth (Alqahtani et al, 2023). Policies should include guidance on the appropriate use of AI technologies, ensuring that they complement rather than replace human contact in the classroom. For example, while AI can provide essential support for individualized learning, the function of instructors in developing relationships, building trust, and supporting students' social and emotional growth remains irreplaceable. The development and implementation of ethical AI practices in education require a holistic and collaborative approach. Policymakers must build comprehensive frameworks that prioritize openness, data protection, inclusion, and accountability while encouraging a culture of digital literacy and creativity. By addressing the ethical problems raised by AI, these rules can help ensure that its transformational potential is achieved in a way that conforms with the key values of education: equity, integrity, and the quest for knowledge. Through deliberate and proactive legislation, the education sector can harness the power of AI to create a brighter and fairer future for learners globally.

FUTURE DIRECTIONS: BUILDING A RESPONSIBLE AI-DRIVEN EDUCATION SYSTEM

The introduction of artificial intelligence in education signals a new era of possibilities, one where technology and pedagogy converge to rethink how knowledge is shared and gained (Liando & Tatipang, 2024). While the incorporation of AI has already begun to revolutionize classrooms and administrative systems, the journey toward developing a fully responsible AI-driven education system remains in its early stages. As we look to the future, the focus must change from merely adopting AI technology to embedding it inside a framework that values ethics, inclusivity, and sustainability. The journey forward entails not only refining existing ways but also conceptualizing novel strategies that place the well-being of learners and educators at the center of these technology developments. One of the most crucial elements in developing a responsible AI-driven education system is fostering a culture of digital ethics (Abulibdeh et al, 2024). Educators, administrators, policymakers, and even students must create a shared awareness of the ethical implications of AI technologies. This takes more than simply awareness; it involves a proactive commitment to ethical values in every choice around AI implementation. Workshops, forums, and collaborative conversations can serve as platforms to engage stakeholders and establish a unified vision for ethical AI use in education (Kayyali, 2025). By embedding digital ethics into the ethos of educational institutions, we may create an atmosphere where technological innovation is governed by ideals of fairness, transparency, and respect for individual rights.

The design and development of AI technologies must also change to meet the special needs of the educational sector (Tapalova & Zhiyenbayeva, 2022). Developers should focus on designing systems that are not only useful but also equal and inclusive. This includes taking conscious steps to address the limitations and biases of current AI models. For example, datasets used to train AI tools should be representative of varied populations to guarantee that the systems can serve all students equitably, regardless of their background, language, or geographic location. Collaboration between technologists and education professionals will be vital in ensuring that these technologies represent the difficulties and subtle differences of real-world classrooms. Personalized learning remains one of the most promising applications of AI in education, but its deployment must be undertaken properly. Future AI-driven systems should go beyond cosmetic personalization, such as tailoring content to a student's speed or competency level. Instead, they should try to understand and support the overall requirements of learners. This could entail identifying different learning styles, accommodating neurodiverse individuals, and addressing the emotional and social components of education. For instance, AI may be used to determine when a student is failing not just intellectually but also emotionally, enabling educators to deliver prompt and tailored solutions.

The role of instructors in an AI-driven education system must likewise be reconsidered (Saaida, 2023). Far from being supplanted by technology, professors will play an even more crucial role as facilitators of learning and mentors for students. AI can handle tedious administrative activities and provide insights into student performance, allowing educators to focus on higher-order responsibilities such as developing creativity, critical thinking, and collaboration among students. However, this transformation will require educators to learn new abilities, including a greater understanding of AI technology and its uses in education. Continuous professional development programs suited to these demands should be a focus for educational institutions. Collaboration and partnership will be key to creating the future of AI in education. Governments, educational institutions, technology corporations, and civil society organizations must work together to set rules and best practices for AI implementation. These relationships can promote the pooling of resources, skills, and insights, expediting the creation of solutions that are both innovative and responsible (Kayyali, 2024). For example, governments may cooperate with universities and private sector enterprises to produce open-source AI tools designed expressly for educational purposes, guaranteeing that these technologies are available to colleges with low resources.

To ensure that AI-driven education systems are viable, authorities must address the issue of fair access (Qazi et al, 2024). The digital divide remains a key impediment to the mainstream adoption of AI technologies, particularly in impoverished and underprivileged populations. Future initiatives should focus on eliminating these discrepancies by investing in infrastructure, giving affordable access to digital devices, and developing AI technologies that are suitable for low-resource environments. Addressing these difficulties is not just a matter of equity but also a precondition for leveraging the promise of AI in education on a global basis. Accountability systems will be a cornerstone of any competent AI-driven education system. As AI tools become more integrated into decision-making processes, it is vital to build safeguards that prevent misuse and unforeseen outcomes. Clear methods should be developed for examining and auditing AI systems, with an emphasis on transparency and user empowerment. For instance, if an AI algorithm is used to assess student performance or offer academic interventions, educators and students should have the capacity to review the underlying data and contest the system's conclusions if necessary. Such mechanisms will ensure that AI stays a tool for empowerment rather than control.

The involvement of student voices in defining the future of AI-driven education is another area of possibility (Ivanashko et al, 2024). Students are not just the primary beneficiaries of new technologies but also essential stakeholders whose experiences and viewpoints may inform better design and execution. Creating outlets for students to participate in conversations regarding AI, whether through surveys, focus groups, or participation on advisory boards, can lead to more responsive and successful solutions. This method also serves an educational purpose, helping students to think critically about the ethical and social implications of AI, equipping them to navigate a world increasingly affected by these technologies. Long-term sustainability in AI-driven education systems will also depend on continued research and evaluation. Educational institutions and academics should build a culture of evidence-based practice, where the impact of AI tools is regularly monitored and assessed. Metrics for success should go beyond immediate outcomes, such as better test scores, to incorporate broader indications of educational quality, equity, and student well-being. By creating a solid body of research, stakeholders may identify best practices, foresee future difficulties, and change tactics to suit evolving demands.

As we look to the future, the subject of global collaboration becomes increasingly crucial. Education is a universal undertaking, and the problems and opportunities given by AI are not bound by borders (Miao & Holmes, 2021). International institutions, such as UNESCO and the International Association for the Evaluation of Educational Achievement, can play a crucial role in encouraging cross-border discourse and cooperation (Ramaswamy et al, 2021). By sharing knowledge and resources, countries may learn from one another's triumphs and errors, advancing the development of ethical and successful AI-driven education systems worldwide. The future of AI in education must be led by a vision that favors human potential over technological prowess. While AI offers strong tools for enhancing educational outcomes, its ultimate objective should be to empower learners and educators, not to replace or decrease their responsibilities. This needs a commitment to keeping human values at the heart of every choice about AI design, deployment, and governance. By retaining this emphasis, we may guarantee that AI serves as a means to enrich education rather than an end in itself. Building a responsible AI-driven education system is a hard and multidimensional enterprise, but it is also an opportunity to reinvent the possibilities of learning in the 21st century (Adetayo, 2021). By building a culture of ethics, stressing diversity, and supporting collaboration, we may create a future where AI enriches the educational experience for everybody. The route forward will require vision, innovation, and a profound commitment to the ideas that underpin education: equity, curiosity, and the quest for knowledge. With deliberate planning and joint effort, the integration of AI into education may become a transformative force for good, crafting a brighter future for learners around the world.

REAL-WORLD CASE STUDIES

Artificial intelligence (AI) is transforming educational methodologies; yet, its implementation presents several problems. Although AI-driven tools offer the potential for personalised and accessible learning, practical experiences reveal both advantages and ethical dilemmas associated with these technology. Examining real case studies enhances our comprehension of AI's impact on education and the insights we may derive from these experiences. A prominent example of AI in education is the use of adaptive learning platforms. Carnegie Learning has led the field of AI-driven education in the United States, providing personalised learning experiences informed by real-time student data (Mahmoud & Sørensen, 2024).

Their AI-driven platform, MATHia, tailors to students' strengths and weaknesses, delivering personalised math challenges and detailed guidance. This has resulted in substantial enhancements in mathematical skills for numerous students. The efficacy of AI-driven learning systems such as MATHia is contingent upon the quality of the data utilized (Khrapatyi et al, 2024). If the system lacks training on varied learning styles or backgrounds, it risks perpetuating biases—favoring students who conform to a specific academic archetype while neglecting others. Some instructors have also highlighted worries that students relying too much on AI-driven feedback would struggle with independent problem-solving, an essential ability in academic and professional life.

Another famous case is Georgia State University's chatbot, Pounce. Pounce is designed to assist students in navigating administrative processes and has proven particularly successful in mitigating "summer melt," which refers to students who are accepted to college but do not enrol owing to logistical obstacles (Hu et al, 2024). By sending reminders about financial assistance deadlines, registration processes, and course selection, the chatbot has greatly enhanced student retention rates. On the surface, this sounds like a wonderful example of AI making higher education more accessible. But some students have reported feeling overwhelmed by numerous automated communications, while others have expressed concerns about how much personal data the chatbot collects. Universities deploying AI-driven support systems must find the correct balance between delivering helpful advise and safeguarding student privacy. AI's use in academic assessments has also sparked discussion. During the COVID-19 pandemic, many colleges turned to AI-powered proctoring services like Proctorio and ExamSoft to oversee online tests (Nagpal et al, 2024). These techniques use facial recognition, eye tracking, and keystroke analysis to detect possible cheating. While intended to ensure academic integrity, these systems experienced resistance from students and teachers alike. At the University of Illinois, students noted that the AI mistakenly identified natural movements—such as glancing aside to think—as suspicious conduct. Others, notably students of color, reported that facial recognition technologies struggled to reliably identify them, resulting to unfair test disruptions. The controversy surrounding AI-driven proctoring emphasises the broader issue of bias in AI systems and the need for more transparent, fair assessment procedures.

Beyond evaluations, AI is playing an increasing role in grading written assignments (Rudolph et al, 2023). Some colleges have experimented with AI-powered grading systems to analyse essays and written responses. One well-known scenario is the deployment of an AI system in the UK's national standardized assessment program. The AI was programmed to grade essays based on grammatical quality, structure, and coherence. While the system operated smoothly, students and teachers rapidly detected anomalies in its grading. Some well-structured but artistically written essays received lower scores, whereas formulaic solutions did better. This aroused fears that AI might be encouraging a rigid, standardized approach to writing rather than cultivating originality and critical thought. The criticism from educators ultimately led to a reevaluation of how AI should be used in grading, confirming the idea that AI should support, not replace, human judgment. AI is also making breakthroughs in aiding students with disabilities. Take the case of Studentsense, an AI-powered application developed to aid students with speech and language problems. The software delivers real-time feedback on speech and language growth, helping students communicate more effectively. In many cases, this has given students more confidence and freedom in their studies. However, some parents and educators worry about the ethical implications of continual AI monitoring. When an AI system tracks and analyzes every word a pupil speaks, who gets access to that data? And how can schools ensure that it is not misused? These are crucial problems that need clear solutions before AI becomes a mainstream tool in special education. AI's impact on educational inequalities is another topic that deserves attention. In several developing countries, AI-driven systems have been launched to bridge the education gap in rural populations (Goswami & Sharma, 2024). One example is the introduction of AI tutors in Kenya, where students in distant places typically lack access to qualified professors. AI-powered applications give interactive lessons and quizzes suited to each student's learning rate. While this has opened up new learning opportunities, it has also uncovered infrastructure challenges. Many students in rural areas lack consistent internet connectivity or the gadgets needed to use these AI platforms successfully. This digital divide raises the question: Can AI actually make education more fair if access to technology remains uneven?

These real-world case studies indicate that AI in education is neither totally excellent nor entirely terrible. It has the capacity to alter learning, but it also offers ethical and practical challenges that must be disregarded. The crucial conclusion is that AI should be utilised as a tool to enhance education, not as a one-size-fits-all answer. Educators, politicians, and developers must work together to guarantee that AI serves students in a way that is fair, transparent, and inclusive. Only then can we leverage the real promise of AI in education without compromising the values that make learning worthwhile.

CONCLUSION

The incorporation of generative AI into educational systems signals a dramatic shift in how individualized learning is envisaged and delivered. As this technology improves, its potential to transform the educational landscape is apparent. However, with this great potential comes a need to address the complicated ethical considerations involved with its use, particularly addressing privacy, bias, and academic integrity. These challenges are not merely theoretical or speculative—they are practical ones that require immediate attention as generative AI gets more deeply embedded inside the fabric of education. Privacy is one of the most important ethical concerns when it comes to generative AI in education. The large volumes of personal data acquired by AI systems, including sensitive student information, raise fundamental considerations regarding data security, permission, and the potential for misuse. As AI-powered educational platforms progressively track and analyze student actions, learning habits, and performance, the line between beneficial customization and invasive surveillance becomes increasingly blurred. Educational institutions must develop strong data protection rules, ensuring that students' personal information is safeguarded, anonymized when feasible, and only utilized in ways that are transparent and fit with ethical norms. The deployment of rigorous cybersecurity protections, alongside clear informed consent standards, is vital to sustaining student trust and ensuring that AI's promise does not come at the expense of individual privacy.

Bias is another key obstacle in the application of generative AI inside educational contexts. AI systems, naturally formed by the data they are trained on, are liable to reinforce existing prejudices. If these systems are trained on biased data sets, they may reinforce preconceptions relating to gender, ethnicity, socioeconomic position, and other demographic characteristics. This can lead to discriminatory effects, unwittingly privileging certain student groups over others. In education, where fairness and equal opportunity are vital, such biases can have enormous repercussions for students' experiences and outcomes. Therefore, developers, educators, and researchers must work jointly to discover and minimize bias in AI systems. This may require ensuring that AI systems are trained on varied, representative datasets, and establishing continual monitoring to detect and fix any biases that occur over time. Moreover, educators must be trained to critically examine and criticize AI-driven recommendations, ensuring that these systems serve to increase learning rather than reinforce structural disparities. The question of academic honesty is equally significant in the domain of generative AI. As AI systems become more adept at generating content—whether it be essays, research papers, or even exam answers—educators face the issue of preserving academic standards and combating cheating. The ease with which students might use AI technologies to complete projects raises worries regarding the legitimacy of student work and the possible degradation of established assessment techniques. However, rather than considering AI as an adversary to academic integrity, it is crucial to investigate ways in which AI might be harnessed to enhance ethical learning. Educators may employ AI to design more individualized, formative tests that promote critical thinking and creativity over rote memorization. Additionally, universities must adapt by building new frameworks and technologies that can recognize AI-generated content, ensuring that AI is utilized ethically while still supporting academic rigor.

The ethical concerns associated with generative AI in education are not static—they are growing as the technology itself continues to advance. The future of AI in education will likely feature more advanced systems that not only give tailored learning experiences but also connect with other technologies, such as virtual reality and augmented reality, to create immersive teaching environments. As these technologies converge, new ethical considerations will arise, and it will be vital for educators, policymakers, and technologists to be watchful, proactive, and adaptable in addressing them. This requires continual communication and collaboration across disciplines to ensure that ethical standards are integrated into the design, development, and implementation of AI systems from the inception. The success of generative AI in education hinges not only on its scientific capabilities but also on our collective commitment to its responsible and ethical application. While AI can substantially enhance the educational experience by delivering individualized, adaptive learning routes that respond to specific student needs, this potential can only be achieved if privacy, bias, and integrity are respected. Educational institutions must not only embrace the benefits of AI but also be proactive in developing ethical standards, educating stakeholders about the ethical dangers, and building transparent governance mechanisms to guide the use of AI technologies. By doing so, they may assist ensure that AI complements, rather than destroys, the essential ideals of education—equity, fairness, and the quest for knowledge. As we look to the future, it is evident that the role of generative AI in education will continue to rise.

However, its integration must be managed with care, and the ethical considerations raised in this study must stay at the forefront of conversations regarding AI's role in learning. Through intelligent and appropriate application, AI can serve as a strong tool for increasing educational results, creating equity, and supporting the development of critical thinking abilities in the next generation of learners. The journey toward this future demands continual contemplation, collaboration, and a strong commitment to the ethical ideals that underpin education itself. By negotiating these obstacles wisely, we can assist in guaranteeing that AI contributes to a more inclusive, fair, and transparent educational landscape for all.

REFERENCES

Abdallah, A. K., Alkaabi, A. M., Mehiar, D. A. F., & Aradat, Z. A. J. (2024). Chatbots in Classrooms: Tailoring Education and Boosting Engagement. In Cutting-Edge Innovations in Teaching, Leadership, Technology, and Assessment (pp. 166-181). IGI Global.

Abulibdeh, A., Zaidan, E., & Abulibdeh, R. (2024). Navigating the confluence of artificial intelligence and education for sustainable development in the era of industry 4.0: Challenges, opportunities, and ethical dimensions. *Journal of Cleaner Production*, *437*, 140527. DOI: 10.1016/j.jclepro.2023.140527

Adetayo, A. J. (2024). Reimagining learning through AI art: the promise of DALL-E and MidJourney for education and libraries. Library Hi Tech News, (ahead-of-print).

Ahmad, S. F., Rahmat, M. K., Mubarik, M. S., Alam, M. M., & Hyder, S. I. (2021). Artificial intelligence and its role in education. *Sustainability (Basel)*, *13*(22), 12902. DOI: 10.3390/su132212902

Al-kfairy, M., Mustafa, D., Kshetri, N., Insiew, M., & Alfandi, O. (2024, August). Ethical challenges and solutions of generative AI: An interdisciplinary perspective. In Informatics (Vol. 11, No. 3, p. 58). MDPI.

AlAli, R., & Wardat, Y. (2024). Opportunities and Challenges of Integrating Generative Artificial Intelligence in Education. *International Journal of Religion*, *5*(7), 784–793. DOI: 10.61707/8y29gv34

Alam, A. (2023). Developing a Curriculum for Ethical and Responsible AI: A University Course on Safety, Fairness, Privacy, and Ethics to Prepare Next Generation of AI Professionals. In *Intelligent Communication Technologies and Virtual Mobile Networks* (pp. 879–894). Springer Nature Singapore. DOI: 10.1007/978-981-99-1767-9_64

Alqahtani, T., Badreldin, H. A., Alrashed, M., Alshaya, A. I., Alghamdi, S. S., bin Saleh, K., Alowais, S. A., Alshaya, O. A., Rahman, I., Al Yami, M. S., & Albekairy, A. M. (2023). The emergent role of artificial intelligence, natural learning processing, and large language models in higher education and research. *Research in Social & Administrative Pharmacy*, *19*(8), 1236–1242. DOI: 10.1016/j.sapharm.2023.05.016 PMID: 37321925

Anh, T. H. (2024). The Effect Of Perceived Economic Returns And Digitalization On Higher Education Enrolment Decisions In Vietnam.

Bahroun, Z., Anane, C., Ahmed, V., & Zacca, A. (2023). Transforming education: A comprehensive review of generative artificial intelligence in educational settings through bibliometric and content analysis. *Sustainability (Basel), 15*(17), 12983. DOI: 10.3390/su151712983

Balasubramaniam, S., Chirchi, V., Kadry, S., Agoramoorthy, M., Gururama, S. P., Satheesh, K. K., & Sivakumar, T. A. (2024). The Road Ahead: Emerging Trends, Unresolved Issues, and Concluding Remarks in Generative AI—A Comprehensive Review. *International Journal of Intelligent Systems*, •••, 2024.

Barrett, M., Branson, L., Carter, S., DeLeon, F., Ellis, J., Gundlach, C., & Lee, D. (2019). Using artificial intelligence to enhance educational opportunities and student services in higher education. Inquiry. *The Journal of the Virginia Community Colleges*, *22*(1), 11.

Boppiniti, S. T. (2023). Data Ethics in AI: Addressing Challenges in Machine Learning and Data Governance for Responsible Data Science. International Scientific Journal for Research, 5(5).

Cojocariu, V. M., & Mareş, G. (2022). Academic integrity in the technology-driven education era. Ethical Use of information technology in higher education, 1-16.

Dewar, C. (2023). Historical Analysis of California Community College Decisions on Whether to Adopt Online Proctoring Software During the COVID-19 Pandemic (Doctoral dissertation, San Francisco State University).

Díaz-Rodríguez, N., Del Ser, J., Coeckelbergh, M., de Prado, M. L., Herrera-Viedma, E., & Herrera, F. (2023). Connecting the dots in trustworthy Artificial Intelligence: From AI principles, ethics, and key requirements to responsible AI systems and regulation. *Information Fusion*, *99*, 101896. DOI: 10.1016/j.inffus.2023.101896

Dwivedi, Y. K., Hughes, L., Ismagilova, E., Aarts, G., Coombs, C., Crick, T., Duan, Y., Dwivedi, R., Edwards, J., Eirug, A., Galanos, V., Ilavarasan, P. V., Janssen, M., Jones, P., Kar, A. K., Kizgin, H., Kronemann, B., Lal, B., Lucini, B., & Williams, M. D. (2021). Artificial Intelligence (AI): Multidisciplinary perspectives on emerging challenges, opportunities, and agenda for research, practice and policy. *International Journal of Information Management*, *57*, 101994. DOI: 10.1016/j.ijinfomgt.2019.08.002

Enarsson, T., Enqvist, L., & Naarttijärvi, M. (2022). Approaching the human in the loop–legal perspectives on hybrid human/algorithmic decision-making in three contexts. *Information & Communications Technology Law*, *31*(1), 123–153. DOI: 10.1080/13600834.2021.1958860

George, A. S. (2023). The Potential of Generative AI to Reform Graduate Education. *Partners Universal International Research Journal*, *2*(4), 36–50.

Goswami, A., & Sharma, A. (2024). AI For Bridging Socio-Economic Inequities in Indian Education Space. *International Journal of Innovation and Scientific Research*, *11*(4), 890–935. DOI: 10.51244/IJRSI.2024.1104066

Hagendorff, T. (2020). The ethics of AI ethics: An evaluation of guidelines. *Minds and Machines*, *30*(1), 99–120. DOI: 10.1007/s11023-020-09517-8

Hu, S., Ke, F., Vyortkina, D., Hu, P., Luby, S., & O'Shea, J. (2024). Artificial Intelligence in Higher Education: Applications, Challenges, and Policy Development and Further Considerations. In *Higher Education: Handbook of Theory and Research* (Vol. 40, pp. 1–52). Springer Nature Switzerland.

Igboegwu, A. A. (2023). A Step in the Right Direction: Identifying Strategies for Preparing Initial Teacher Candidates for Culturally Diverse Classrooms in Baden-Württemberg (Doctoral dissertation).

Ivanashko, O., Kozak, A., Knysh, T., & Honchar, K. (2024). The role of artificial intelligence in shaping the future of education: opportunities and challenges.

Jones, K. M., Asher, A., Goben, A., Perry, M. R., Salo, D., Briney, K. A., & Robertshaw, M. B. (2020). "We're being tracked at all times": Student perspectives of their privacy in relation to learning analytics in higher education. *Journal of the Association for Information Science and Technology*, *71*(9), 1044–1059. DOI: 10.1002/asi.24358

Kayyali, M. (2024). Future possibilities and challenges of AI in education. In *Transforming education with generative AI: Prompt engineering and synthetic content creation* (pp. 118–137). IGI Global. DOI: 10.4018/979-8-3693-1351-0.ch006

Kayyali, M. (2025). The Future of AI in Education: Predictions and Emerging Trends. Next-Generation AI Methodologies in Education, 367-406.

Khazanchi, R. A. S. H. M. I., & Khazanchi, P. A. N. K. A. J. (2024). Generative AI to improve special education teacher preparation for inclusive classrooms. Exploring new horizons: Generative artificial intelligence and teacher education, 159.

Khrapatyi, S., Tokarieva, K., Hlushchenko, O., Paramonova, O., & Lvova, I. (2024). Research on performance evaluation of higher vocational education informatization based on data envelopment analysis. *STEM Education*, *4*(1), 51–70. DOI: 10.3934/steme.2024004

Ladley, J. (2019). *Data governance: How to design, deploy, and sustain an effective data governance program*. Academic Press.

Lembani, R., Gunter, A., Breines, M., & Dalu, M. T. B. (2020). The same course, different access: The digital divide between urban and rural distance education students in South Africa. *Journal of Geography in Higher Education*, *44*(1), 70–84. DOI: 10.1080/03098265.2019.1694876

Liando, N. V. F., & Tatipang, D. P. (2024). *Enlightened Minds: Navigating The Nexus Of Artificial Intelligence And Educational Modernization*. Penerbit Tahta Media.

Madhura, K., & Mahalakshmi, R. (2021, September). Survey on Technologies, Benefits, Challenges and Future Suggestions to Improvise the Data Security of Confidential Academic Records in India. In 2021 9th International Conference on Cyber and IT Service Management (CITSM) (pp. 1-9). IEEE.

Mahmoud, C. F., & Sørensen, J. T. (2024). Artificial Intelligence in Personalized Learning with a Focus on Current Developments and Future Prospects. *Research and Advances in Education*, *3*(8), 25–31. DOI: 10.56397/RAE.2024.08.04

Mensah, G. B. (2023). Artificial intelligence and ethics: A comprehensive review of bias mitigation, transparency, and accountability in AI Systems. *Preprint*, (November), 10.

Miao, F., & Holmes, W. (2021). International Forum on AI and the Futures of Education, developing competencies for the AI Era, 7-8 December 2020: synthesis report.

Mittal, U., Sai, S., Chamola, V., & Sangwan, D. (2024). A comprehensive review on generative ai for education. *IEEE Access : Practical Innovations, Open Solutions*, *12*, 142733–142759. DOI: 10.1109/ACCESS.2024.3468368

Monib, W. K., Qazi, A., Apong, R. A., Azizan, M. T., De Silva, L., & Yassin, H. (2024). Generative AI and future education: A review, theoretical validation, and authors' perspective on challenges and solutions. *PeerJ. Computer Science*, *10*, e2105. DOI: 10.7717/peerj-cs.2105 PMID: 39650462

Murdan, A. P., & Halkhoree, R. (2024, June). Integration of Artificial Intelligence for educational excellence and innovation in higher education institutions. In 2024 1st International Conference on Smart Energy Systems and Artificial Intelligence (SESAI) (pp. 1-6). IEEE. DOI: 10.1109/SESAI61023.2024.10599402

Nagpal, N., Srivastava, A., & Verma, P. (2024). AI-Powered Proctoring: Safeguarding Online Assessment in the Education 5.0. In *Explainable AI for Education: Recent Trends and Challenges* (pp. 271–285). Springer Nature Switzerland. DOI: 10.1007/978-3-031-72410-7_15

Nedungadi, P., Tang, K. Y., & Raman, R. (2024). The transformative power of generative artificial intelligence for achieving the sustainable development goal of quality education. *Sustainability (Basel)*, *16*(22), 9779. DOI: 10.3390/su16229779

Ng, D. T. K., Leung, J. K. L., Chu, K. W. S., & Qiao, M. S. (2021). AI literacy: Definition, teaching, evaluation and ethical issues. *Proceedings of the Association for Information Science and Technology*, *58*(1), 504–509. DOI: 10.1002/pra2.487

Nguyen, A., Ngo, H. N., Hong, Y., Dang, B., & Nguyen, B. P. T. (2023). Ethical principles for artificial intelligence in education. *Education and Information Technologies*, *28*(4), 4221–4241. DOI: 10.1007/s10639-022-11316-w PMID: 36254344

Ogwueleka, F. N. (2025). Plagiarism Detection in the Age of Artificial Intelligence: Current Technologies and Future Directions. AI and Ethics, Academic Integrity and the Future of Quality Assurance in Higher Education, 10.

Pedro, F., Subosa, M., Rivas, A., & Valverde, P. (2019). Artificial intelligence in education: Challenges and opportunities for sustainable development.

Penberthy, W. J. (2020). Remediation Approaches for the Recovery of Trust after a Privacy Breach at an Educational Institution: An Exploratory Case Study (Doctoral dissertation, Northcentral University).

Qazi, S., Kadri, M. B., Naveed, M., Khawaja, B. A., Khan, S. Z., Alam, M. M., & Su'ud, M. M. (2024). AI-Driven Learning Management Systems: Modern Developments, Challenges and Future Trends during the Age of ChatGPT. *Computers, Materials & Continua*, *80*(2), 3289–3314. DOI: 10.32604/cmc.2024.048893

Ramaswamy, M., Marciniuk, D. D., Csonka, V., Colò, L., & Saso, L. (2021). Reimagining internationalization in higher education through the United Nations sustainable development goals for the betterment of society. *Journal of Studies in International Education*, *25*(4), 388–406. DOI: 10.1177/10283153211031046

Regan, P. M., & Jesse, J. (2019). Ethical challenges of edtech, big data and personalized learning: Twenty-first century student sorting and tracking. *Ethics and Information Technology*, *21*(3), 167–179. DOI: 10.1007/s10676-018-9492-2

Rudolph, J., Tan, S., & Tan, S. (2023). ChatGPT: Bullshit spewer or the end of traditional assessments in higher education?. Journal of applied learning and teaching, 6(1), 342-363.

Saaida, M. B. (2023). AI-Driven transformations in higher education: Opportunities and challenges. *International Journal of Educational Research and Studies*, *5*(1), 29–36.

Sajja, R., Sermet, Y., Cikmaz, M., Cwiertny, D., & Demir, I. (2024). Artificial intelligence-enabled intelligent assistant for personalized and adaptive learning in higher education. *Information (Basel)*, *15*(10), 596. DOI: 10.3390/info15100596

Salinas-Navarro, D. E., Vilalta-Perdomo, E., Michel-Villarreal, R., & Montesinos, L. (2024). Designing experiential learning activities with generative artificial intelligence tools for authentic assessment. *Interactive Technology and Smart Education*, *21*(4), 708–734. DOI: 10.1108/ITSE-12-2023-0236

Samala, A. D., Rawas, S., Wang, T., Reed, J. M., Kim, J., Howard, N. J., & Ertz, M. (2024). Unveiling the landscape of generative artificial intelligence in education: A comprehensive taxonomy of applications, challenges, and future prospects. *Education and Information Technologies*, •••, 1–40.

Sebastian, G., & Sebastian, S. R. (2024). Exploring ethical implications of ChatGPT and other AI chatbots and regulation of disinformation propagation. *Annals of Engineering Mathematics and Computational Intelligence*, *1*(1), 1–12.

Sitta, F. A., Maddox, B., Casebourne, I., Hughes, S., Kuvalja, M., Hannam, J., & Oates, T. (2023). The Futures of Assessments: Navigating Uncertainties through the Lenses of Anticipatory Thinking. Cambridge University Press & Assessment.

Slusky, L. (2020). Cybersecurity of online proctoring systems. *Journal of International Technology and Information Management*, *29*(1), 56–83. DOI: 10.58729/1941-6679.1445

Tapalova, O., & Zhiyenbayeva, N. (2022). Artificial intelligence in education: AIEd for personalised learning pathways. *Electronic Journal of e-Learning*, *20*(5), 639–653. DOI: 10.34190/ejel.20.5.2597

Tariq, M. U. (2025). Navigating Bias and Fairness in Digital AI Systems. In Ethical Dimensions of AI Development (pp. 127-156). IGI Global.

Taylor, Z. W., Ortega, G., & Hernández, S. H. (2024). Hispanic-serving artificial intelligence: Do hispanic-serving institutions use chatbots and can they speak Spanish? *Teachers College Record*, *126*(3), 30–53. DOI: 10.1177/01614681241252298

Uddin, M. M. (2024). Rejection or integration of AI in academia: Determining the best choice through the Opportunity Cost theoretical formula. *Discover Education*, *3*(1), 249. DOI: 10.1007/s44217-024-00349-7

Varsik, S., & Vosberg, L. (2024). *The potential impact of Artificial Intelligence on equity and inclusion in education (No. 23)*. OECD Publishing.

Wach, K., Duong, C. D., Ejdys, J., Kazlauskaitė, R., Korzynski, P., Mazurek, G., Paliszkiewicz, J., & Ziemba, E. (2023). The dark side of generative artificial intelligence: A critical analysis of controversies and risks of ChatGPT. *Entrepreneurial Business and Economics Review*, *11*(2), 7–30. DOI: 10.15678/EBER.2023.110201

Wondirad, A., Tolkach, D., & King, B. (2020). Stakeholder collaboration as a major factor for sustainable ecotourism development in developing countries. *Tourism Management*, *78*, 104024. DOI: 10.1016/j.tourman.2019.104024

Zaugg, T. (2024). Future innovations for assistive technology and universal design for learning. Assistive technology and universal design for learning: Toolkits for inclusive instruction, 275-318.

KEY TERMS AND DEFINITIONS

Generative AI: A type of artificial intelligence that creates new content, such as text, images, and simulations, based on patterns learned from vast datasets. Examples include ChatGPT and DALL-E.

Algorithmic Bias: The tendency of AI systems to produce unfair or discriminatory outcomes due to biases in the data they are trained on. This can lead to unequal educational opportunities.

Data Governance: The policies and procedures that dictate how data is collected, stored, and used, ensuring privacy, security, and ethical handling of information in AI-driven education systems.

Digital Literacy: The ability to effectively understand, evaluate, and use digital technologies, including AI, while being aware of their ethical implications, biases, and limitations.

Ethical AI Frameworks: Guidelines and principles designed to ensure that AI technologies are developed and used responsibly, with a focus on fairness, transparency, accountability, and privacy.

AI-Powered Learning Systems: Educational platforms that use AI to personalize learning experiences by analyzing student data and adapting content based on individual learning needs.

Explainability in AI: The degree to which an AI system's decision-making process can be understood by users, making it transparent and interpretable to educators and students.

Educational Equity: The principle of ensuring that all students, regardless of background or socioeconomic status, have equal access to quality education, with AI tools designed to reduce rather than reinforce disparities.

Chapter 9
Ethical Uses of Generative Artificial Intelligence in Instructional Design:
Case Strategies for Responsible Implementation

C. V. Suresh Babu
https://orcid.org/0000-0002-8474-2882
Hindustan Institute of Technology and Science, India

Johnvi S. Jeneliya
https://orcid.org/0009-0009-3577-0068
Hindustan Institute of Technology and Science, India

ABSTRACT

This chapter explores the integration of Generative AI in instructional design, aiming to enhance educational outcomes while addressing ethical considerations. Targeting educators, policymakers, and AI developers, the study employs a mixed-methods approach, combining case studies, empirical data, and stakeholder perspectives to analyze the impact of AI technologies in K-12 and higher education settings. Key findings reveal that Generative AI facilitates personalized learning experiences, automates content generation, and provides immediate feedback, thereby transforming traditional educational practices. However, the study also highlights significant ethical challenges, including data privacy, algorithmic bias, and equity concerns. The conclusions emphasize the necessity of developing robust ethical frameworks to guide the responsible use of AI in education, ensuring that its benefits are equitably distributed while minimizing potential harms.

DOI: 10.4018/979-8-3693-8744-3.ch009

1.0. INTRODUCTION

1.1 Overview of Generative AI in Instructional Design

Generative AI is transforming the very science of instructional design. For instance, with generative AI, the process of generating educational content is altered to make it more customized, personalized, and delivered within creative context settings. This technology can be used for designers to create learning materials like quizzes, tutorials, and simulations according to specific needs that every learner requires. Adaptive learning paths are produced by this same technology, adjusting the complexity or lessons at any time based on the actual progress of a learner (Suresh Babu, C. V., Bhavesh M., et. al. 2025). In other words, scale content creation also means that generative AI will let designers save time and effort in the development process, thus saving time when developing comprehensive courses. Furthermore, through the processing of vast amounts of data by AI, it is possible for designers to create more interactive, engaging, and effective learning experiences-all of which can further personalize education.

1.2 Significance of Ethical Considerations

Ethics in generative AI is a big issue because data can be used for privacy violation, discrimination or accountability purposes. With the increased use of AI everywhere-from education and healthcare to business-responsibly design and implement AI systems so they cannot harm people. Data privacy must also be guaranteed since many applications of AI depend on gigantic databases containing sensitive data. The AI model in its output may become biased and thus lead to unfair or discriminatory outputs. Therefore, data used for training must be corrected for inequality. The issue of transparence and accountability comes in the aspect of understanding how AI makes decisions so that errors can be challenged or +corrected. Ethical considerations are essential in making sure AI models can be of utmost benefit to society while least causing impact and harm to others.

1.3 Structure of the Chapter

The current chapter is structured to move the reader through the comprehensive analysis of generative AI in instructional design and the associated ethics. This chapter launches with an Introduction, which provides a summary of key concepts: an overview of the concepts of generative AI, along with how these questions will be approached in this paper. Next, Generative AI in Instructional Design is discussed as a realistic application of AI to increase the creation of content, personalized learning, and adaptive education using real-life examples of applications. Then comes Ethical Challenges of Generative AI, which provides widely discussed dilemmas on issues of data privacy, bias, and equity through practical case studies and literature reviews (Suresh Babu, C. V., Bhavesh M., et. al. 2025). Issues will be discussed in this chapter through an exposition of Strategies for Ethical Implementation, which includes discussing solutions such as the increasing transparency of the algorithmic outputs, limited bias through various data sets, and privacy policies that ensure very strong protection of the data.

2.BACKGROUND INFORMATION

2.1 Evolution of Generative AI in Education

Figure 1. Evaluation of Generative AI in education

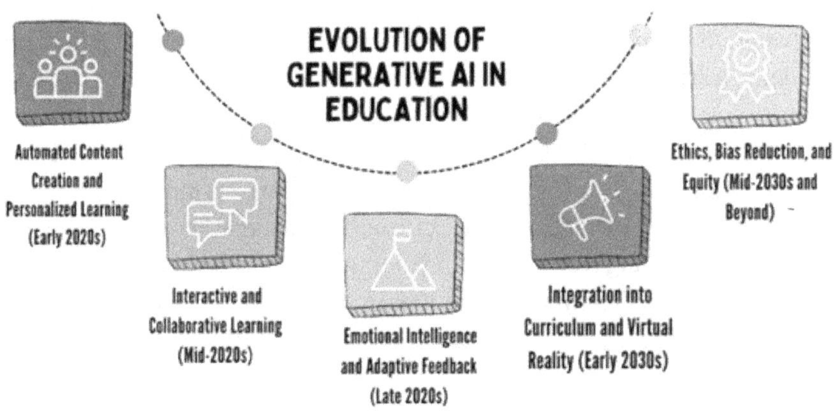

Fig.1 Generative AI in the education system has evolved progressively by integrating artificial intelligence technologies to enhance learning experiences, create adaptive content, and personalize education. Early applications of AI in education focused on automated tasks, such as grading and scheduling. But developments in machine learning, natural language processing, and deep learning enabled much more diversified roles for generative AI. AI based tools in the middle of 2010s

began to offer one-on-one tutoring, automated assignment feedback, and learning analytics that help track students' progress to instructors.

The generative models, which include GPT and BERT, transformed the production of educational content through creating the ability to generate essays, quizzes, and even lesson plans using learner needs (Suresh Babu, C. V. & Adhithya, S., 2023). These models can assimilate large data sets on student performance or learning styles to create extremely customized educational content. Most of the generative AI, however, is currently being deployed towards creating immersive learning environments via simulations and virtual reality that takes education beyond an interactive and engaging level.

2.2 Current Applications of Generative sign

Artificial Intelligence (AI) has revolutionized many sectors, with education being the most promising sector for innovation. Generative AI, a type of AI capable of generating content, responding to questions, and enabling customized learning, has become one of the most talked-about areas in recent years. With traditional models of education morphing into what has come to be simply known as "Education 2.0," the inclusion of AI-powered tools is fundamentally changing how teachers teach and students learn.

Education 2.0 is a transformation towards online, interactive, and customized learning that is enabled through new technologies. The move towards Education 2.0 is necessitated by the growing availability of AI-driven platforms, the need for inclusive learning platforms, and the demand for adaptive models of education to support various learning requirements. Generative AI drives this shift with its ability to facilitate automated content generation, immediate feedback, and personalized tutoring (Suresh Babu, C. V.,, Nithika Sree R, et. al. 2025).

Recent developments in natural language processing (NLP), deep learning, and machine learning have enabled generative AI to produce human-like text, code, and even multimedia. These technologies have enabled AI-based chatbots, virtual tutors, and smart learning assistants that can assist students in diverse fields. Furthermore, AI-based assessment tools can evaluate student performance, forecast learning outcomes, and provide personalized recommendations, making the overall learning experience better (Suresh Babu, C. V., Malini Premakumari William et. al. 2025).

Though it has the potential, the adoption of generative AI in education comes with some challenges, such as ethical implications, data privacy, and the danger of excessive dependency on AI-generated material. In addition, the issue of educators' roles in an AI-enriched learning environment continues to be debated. As technology continues to develop, there is a need to discuss the future trends, opportunities, and challenges in generative AI in Education 2.0.This paper intends to explore the latest advancements in generative AI and their effects on education, review emerging trends, and outline implications for learning and teaching in the future. Through an exploration of both potential and challenges, this research endeavors to offer insights into how generative AI can be successfully implemented in contemporary education systems to optimize learning outcomes.

Generative AI is applied in a multitude of novel ways in different education fields-changing the way students learn and how instructors create, deliver, and assess learning content. The most significant application is content generation, whereby AI generates learner-unique learning contents, such as adaptive quizzes, instructional videos, and even entire curricula based on the performer's performance and learning preferences. These dynamically changing AI-generated materials change the difficulty or points of emphasis for any individual student as he or she needs them, resulting in greater engagement and retention. Another crucial application is in automated assessment and feedback, whereby generative AI is employed in grading homework assignments, tests, and essays with marked speed and accuracy.

2.3 Ethical Challenges in AI Integration

AI implementation in education poses many ethical concerns that have to be addressed. To begin with, there are concerns over data privacy: the use of lots of personal and academic information by a generative AI system in setting up personalized learning experiences makes the student's sensitive information vulnerable to exposure or misuse if strict conditions for privacy are not addressed (Suresh Babu, C. V. & Adhithya, S., 2023). A good data protection policy must also be adopted by educational institutions to prevent a data breach and to keep student information confidential. The other key matter of concern is the algorithmic bias. AI models are trained on data sets that often unwittingly reflect the bias from the society, which inadvertently leads to unfair treatment of certain groups of students. For example, if the training data is less representative or mirrors existing inequities in society, an AI system may favor or disadvantage students based on race, gender, class, or geographic location outlines a process for integrating AI in educational settings.

3. RELEVANCE OF THE TOPIC

3.1 Context within the Edited Book's Theme

This chapter on generative AI in instructional design and the ethical challenges that this poses will fit within a broader theme of the edited book that interrogates the nexus between technology, education, and ethics. Because educational institutions as well as instructors are increasingly developing business models based on integrating AI-driven tools into their curriculums so as to enhance outcomes of learning, the narrative informing the responsible integration of these technologies becomes necessary. The theme of the book explains how such emerging technologies, like AI, are changing education-differently-from creating content to giving unique learning experiences while at the same time symbolising the ethical necessities which come with this change.

Generative AI, particularly an important part of the book's theme: How is it that advanced technologies are transforming the design and delivery of education itself For instance, the growing use of AI in instructional design is a classic example of how technology is changing the educational practice by automating content generation, personalizing the learning pathways, and offering immediate feedback (Suresh Babu, C. V., Bhavesh M., et. al. 2025).

3.2 Importance of Ethical Frameworks for AI in Education

The development and embedding of ethical frameworks for AI in education is crucial so that the application of generative AI technologies benefits all and causes as little harm as possible. With the rapid integration of AI with the education systems, which provide automatic grading, content generation, and customized pathways of learning, there are significant ethics questions that go hand-in-hand with the issues related to data privacy, bias, accountability, and equity. In the absence of clear-cut guiding ethics for AI usage, its proliferation could lead to societal inequalities, potential invasions of personal privacy, and eventual loss of trust in educational systems (Suresh Babu, C. V. & Adhithya, S., 2023).

3.3 The Evolving Roles of Educators in AI-Enhanced Classrooms

The incorporation of AI in education is not a replacement for educators but, instead, redefines their roles in profound ways. With the increased use of AI-powered tools, teachers have to shift from being the only knowledge bearers to facilitators, mentors, and technology integrators. The changing role of teachers in AI-augmented classrooms can be divided into a number of major areas

Facilitators of AI-Driven Learning

Teachers will have an important responsibility in teaching students how to meaningfully engage with AI tools. Teachers will no longer just impart knowledge but rather assemble AI-learned material, verify it, and personalize AI-based findings to meet learning objectives.

Personalized Learning Architects

Adaptive learning systems using AI are able to scan student-by-student progress and offer personalized learning pathways. Teachers will use these findings to create individualized lesson plans that fill knowledge gaps and challenge more advanced learners with more sophisticated content (Suresh Babu, C. V.,, Nithika Sree R, et. al. 2025).

Critical Thinking and Ethical AI Instructors

As content created by AI becomes more common, educators have the responsibility of educating students about critical thinking and digital literacy. This involves educating students on how to discern AI-created information from authentic sources, so they become proficient in fact-checking as well as ethical use of AI.

AI System Moderators and Evaluators

While AI can automate evaluation and grading, it still needs human supervision. Teachers will have to review AI-generated suggestions, weed out possible biases, and make fair judgments that meet educational standards.

Lifelong Learners and AI Adopters

To integrate AI into the classroom effectively, teachers need to constantly enhance their awareness of AI technologies and teaching methodologies. Professional development initiatives and AI literacy courses will be crucial in ensuring teachers keep pace with the changing technology environment.

Figure 2. Importance of ethical frameworks for AI in education

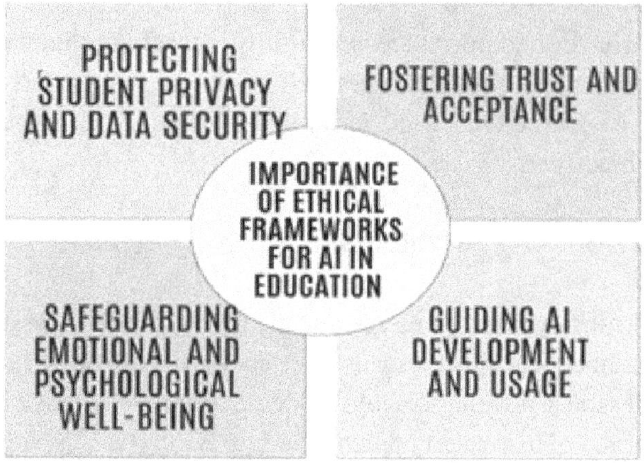

The Fig.2 ethical framework is important when it comes to ensuring privacy for students' data. Most AI education systems rely on huge volumes of sensitive information regarding a student's behavior, academic performance, and personal details. An ethical framework ensures that such data are collected, stored, and used responsibly with the explicit consent of the students themselves and their guardians. It protects one from data misuse or breaches with respect to data and students and keeps trust in AI applications.

3.3 Alignment with Experience-Driven Learning Approaches

Generative AI aligns largely with experience-driven learning approaches where the student centered approach is enhanced to allow the student to receive adaptive, tailored, and more immersive learning experiences. By learning data analysis, generative AI can facilitate the paths of more personalized learning, including dynamically generated content and activities best suited for a student's unique progress and interests. It helps in ownership of the learning process, which enables the students to get more involved with content that is relevant and meaningful. Aside from that, AI can also simulate interactive environments or interactive simulations. This gives for an authentic hands-on, real-world simulation of real scenarios, such as medical treatment or engineering designs, which is the heart of experiential learning.

4.KEY QUESTIONS AND PROBLEMS ADDRESSED

4.1 Ethical Implications of Generative AI

The ethics of generative AI in education include issues like privacy, algorithmic bias, accountability, and equity. Generative AI systems operate on large datasets which consist of many sensitive personal information concerning the students and raise issues about data collection, storage, and usage. Student data privacy and safety should be very well protected in order to gain confidence in AI technology. Secondly, algorithmic bias means unfair treatment or discrimination of certain groups of students, especially as training data reflects the biases that society carries; hence such demands robust testing and diverse datasets to ensure fairness and inclusivity in educational outcomes.

In addition, a lack of such ethical frameworks may result in a diminution of the transparency and accountability of AI-driven decision-making. For instance, teachers and students are not clearly informed about how grading or learning path recommendation functions work. Opacity in these areas may result in a failure of trust in AI tools and the consequent underutilization of these tools in education that may otherwise have leveraged AI-driven personalization and support.

4.2 Risks of Inaction on Ethical Guidelines

Failure to establish and enforce norms for ethical use of generative AI in education can be quite risky and may adversely affect students, teachers, and possibly a broader landscape of education. The first major risk here is that of data privacy breach: without protocols for handling such data, student's personal information will be at risk for unauthorised access or misuse, with the possible implications of identity theft and loss of trust in education entities. All in all, the risks of inaction weigh heavily: point toward the urgent need for widespread comprehensive ethical frameworks to safeguard the rights and opportunities of all learners while maximizing the benefits of AI in education.

Moreover, inaction reduces transparency and accountability of the decision-making and reasoning of AI systems due to the difficulty in understanding how and why AI systems make certain decisions and would simultaneously lead to an erosion of trust in those tools. More importantly, such a lack of equity will lead some disadvantageous students to lose opportunities for otherwise valuable educational resources, thereby exacerbating the digital divide. In general, the risks of inaction on ethical guidelines will be enormous; hence comprehensive frameworks will be needed to safeguard the rights and opportunities of all learners while maximizing the benefits of AI in education.

4.3 Responsibility in AI Integration

Figure 3. Responsibility in AI integration

In Fig.3 Generative AI deployment with responsibility in AI integration in an educational setting ensures that it is ethical, fair, and will be effective. This Fig.3 includes collective efforts by educational institutions, policymakers, and AI developers to commit to making sure that the welfare of students is placed by opening up how AI tools are used and what data is collected, with what criteria for how decisions are made in general so that there is trust reestablished between the students, educators, and parents. Teachers should be trained to use AI in a way that deploys critical thinking. They ought to know both what AI does well and its limitations, thereby being able to assist the learners competently and reduce even the possibility of biases.

4.4 Involvement of Stakeholders

Deployment of generative AI in education requires effective participation by different stakeholders, including educator, learner, parent, policy leaders, and developers of AI. The educator is in an excellent position to feed feedback on how the

AI technologies best support instruction, so as to identify tools that fit a specific need amongst the students, and at the same time address issues relating to bias and ethical consideration. Discussions should also allow for student voice in order to make their contributions, which could lead them to find ownership and effective critical involvement in AI. Among the responsibilities of parents/guardians are advocating for their child's educational needs, supporting openness about data usage, as well as the possible benefits and risks presented by AI. Policymakers play a significant role in designing a regulatory framework that enhances the ethical use of AI by providing guidelines on equity, data privacy, and accountability as well as sufficient resources for supporting AI-related work in schools. All these stakeholders need to be involved in the integration of AI so that it remains responsible AI, which further helps to facilitate equitable and ethical enhancement of learning experiences for all learners.

4.5 Foundational AI technologies

The advancements in generative AI are built mainly on top of certain fundamental AI technologies, including **Natural Language Processing (NLP), Deep Learning, Reinforcement Learning, and Transformer Models**. These technologies provide the basis for intelligent educational systems that learn and adapt to user demand in real-time.

1. Natural Language Processing (NLP):

NLP enables computers to understand, process, and generate human language, the basis for AI-driven learning assistants, chatbots, and automated graders (Suresh Babu, C. V., Malini Premakumari William et. al. 2025). Examples include OpenAI's GPT and Google's BERT, which can empower AI to generate natural language answers, summarize text, and even detect student sentiment to customize instruction.

2. Deep Learning and Neural Networks:

Deep learning, which is a subset of machine learning, is used in training artificial neural networks to learn patterns and give outputs. AI generative models, like Variational Autoencoders (VAEs) and Generative Adversarial Networks (GANs), utilize deep learning methods to develop study materials, e.g., descriptive texts, quizzes, and even virtual simulations with realistic appearances to engage students in active learning.

3. Transformer Models:

The emergence of transformer-based models, such as the Transformer model itself, introduced by Vaswani et al. in 2017, revolutionized the landscape of NLP applications. Transformer-based models apply self-attention to efficiently process masses of data, making AI-generated educational content more logical and contextually relevant. Transformer-based models power real-time AI tutoring, wherein answers can be dynamically adjusted based on a student's interaction and performance.

4. Reinforcement Learning (RL):

Reinforcement Learning plays a central role in adaptive learning systems in which AI dynamically restructures lesson plans based on the performance of the students. RL-based learning platforms can personalize quizzes, suggest study material, and even learn to map learning paths to achieve optimal student engagement and retention. AI-based tutoring systems use RL to predict the requirements of a student and accordingly modify teaching approaches.

5.Multimodal AI and Speech Processing:

AI models are now employing various forms of data, including text, images, and audio, to create a more immersive and interactive learning experience. Speech-to-text (STT) and text-to-speech (TTS) functionalities make voice-controlled AI tutors a possibility, which is convenient for disabled students. Visual explanations created by AI and interactive learning videos based on multimodal learning models enhance learning and engagement.

AI in Education 2.0

Education 2.0 represents a shift toward digital, interactive, and tailored learning experiences propelled by next-gen technologies. It is fueled by the growing availability of AI-powered platforms, the need for more inclusive learning platforms, and the need for adaptive models of education to cater to varying learning needs. Generative AI is at the heart of this revolution through enabling automated content generation, real-time feedback, and personalized tutoring.

New advances in core AI technologies have made it possible for generative AI to generate human-level text, code, and multimedia content. These technologies have resulted in AI-powered chatbots, virtual instructors, and intelligent learning companions that can assist students across the curriculum. AI-powered assessment technologies can also evaluate student performance, predict learning outcomes, and provide personalized recommendations to enhance the learning experience overall. While it holds great promise, the use of generative AI in education also poses a number of challenges, such as ethical concerns, data security, and reliance on AI-generated content. Moreover, issues about the role of teachers in a learning environment boosted by AI remain controversial. While AI continues to improve, reviewing the future trajectory, prospects, and challenges of generative AI in Education 2.0 is necessary. This paper will explore recent trends in generative AI and how they affect education, critically assess new trends, and offer learning and teaching implications in the future. Through opportunities and challenges analysis, this research seeks to offer insights into how generative AI can be well incorporated into contemporary education systems to improve learning.

5. OBJECTIVES AND SCOPE

5.1 Clear Statement of Chapter Objectives

The main purpose of this chapter is to discuss the use of generative AI in instructional design with both benefits and ethics in education. Specifics of the objectives are outlined below and fall under their respective types.

1. Informative Objectives

Overview of Generative AI in Education: A broader overview of history and contemporary deployments of generative AI in educational environments, which helps tailor the learning process and enhance the content used in education.

2. Analytical Objectives

Identify Ethical Challenges to Merge AI Technologies: Identify and analyze ethical challenges of merging AI technologies, including such issues like data privacy, algorithmic bias, and transparency. Discuss implications for educators, students, and institutions.

3. Prescriptive Objectives

The role of ethical frameworks in guiding responsible AI utilization for education. Under this also, stakeholder collaboration is essential which may include educators, students, parents, policymakers and AI developers in ensuring fair, equitable access and protecting the rights of students.

4. Actionable Objectives

Actionable recommendations for educators, policymakers, and AI developers about strategies to effectively and responsibly integrate generative AI into instructional design with emphasis on approaches that advance learning outcomes without sacrificing ethical standards or exposing risks.

5.2 Delimitation of Scope

This chapter investigates the integration of generative AI in instructional design for formal education settings, specifically focusing on K-12 and higher education settings. While acknowledging that AI applications take place in informal and non-formal learning environments, the analysis remains focused on structured educational contexts. The chapter will focus on the generative AI technologies, such as natural language processing and content generation tools, but not touch other forms of AI that are not directly related to the construction of instructional design, such as predictive analytics. It will also discuss ethical matters in terms of data protection, algorithmic bias, and transparency of the problems that generative AI presents rather than every ethical issue with technology and learning. Some of the major actors - teachers, learners, decision-makers, and AI designers - will be acknowledged, while those of tech companies will be presented only when relevant to the discussion at hand. Limits set here seek towards the focus of the chapter: a focused look at the role generative AI may play in instructional design through its benefits and challenges over the specified horizon (Suresh Babu, C. V., Bhavesh M., et. al. 2025).

5.2.1 Focus Areas

To achieve a comprehensive yet targeted search through generative AI in instructional design, the following focus areas will be addressed in this chapter:

1. Personalization of Learning Experiences

Discuss ways in which generative AI technologies can be used to design individualized routes of learning, modify content and instructional approaches to accommodate students' specific needs, interests, and varying learning rates.

2. Instructional Material Improvements

Investigate the role of generative AI in creating and enhancing instructional materials, such as automatic content generation, adaptive assessments, and creation of ancillary resources that support multiple forms of learning. +

3. Ethical Implications

Explore the ethical issues of deploying generative AI in the educational landscape, including: how will the data be handled in terms of privacy, biases in algorithms, and transparency over AI decision-making which measures both students and educators are judged upon

4. Implementation Strategies

Identify best practices and strategies for the effective integration of generative AI tools to educational settings. It should be considered how educators should undergo appropriate training, how equitably students are allowed access to such tools, and if there is an accountability system.

5.2.2 Exclusions

The chapter will clearly outline some exclusions on issues its analysis of generative AI in instructional design should not make. This includes lack of focus on technical details of the generative AI algorithm or detailed information on machine learning models because more is emphasized on application in education rather than the mechanics of functioning operations (Suresh Babu, C. V., Bhavesh M., et. al. 2025). Questions of ethics will indeed be addressed, but purely technical questions in education not related to generative AI—such as surveillance technologies or AI applications for administrative decision-making—are beyond the scope of this paper. Discussions of adopting AI tools for higher education also do not review the current state of affairs but are rather narrowly presented as specific case studies.

Figure 4. AI ethics in education

Fig.4 introduces Core Ethical Principles (CEP) that focus on fairness, transparency, and respect for learners. These core principles are vital for guiding the ethical integration The image titled "AI Ethics in Education" outlines a structured approach to ensuring ethical considerations are addressed when using AI in educational environments. It begins by emphasizing that ethics matter. By setting clear ethical guidelines, educators can manage the complexities of AI technology in a way that builds trust and accountability. This balanced approach is key to promoting a responsible use of AI in digital learning settings of AI in education. Each principle should be clearly defined and applied in ways that consider how they affect student engagement and success. It's essential for educators to address these principles thoughtfully in their AI strategies.

6.LITERATURE REVIEW

6.1 Summary of Relevant Literature

New studies indicate the transformative role of AI in education, such as how it can make learning personalized, reduce the administrative burden, and increase the knowledge that teachers have of student performance and engagement (Holmes et al., 2019; Luckin et al., 2016). AI can also help make learning individualized through its dynamic adjustment of content and pacing to the needs of each student, thereby fostering a student-centered environment (Chen et al., 2021). For instance, the AI-driven personalization that Holmes et al. (2019) talk about, makes education more effective and more efficient because it will provide an appropriate instructional pacing that should match an individual's learning pace. This is a fundamental requirement for maintaining learner engagement and improving knowledge retention. Luckin et al. (2016) note that with AI's adaptive learning capabilities, learners interact with content that suits their unique learning preferences, therefore making the classroom an inclusive environment.

While this has its own advantages, ethics in AI integration into education is the most dangerous. Selwyn (2019) is of the opinion that there is a potential of entrenching societal biases because inequalities inscribed in the training data from AI systems are reflective. Further, Williamson, 2017, explains that the AI extensive collection raises issues of privacy and security in relation to students' data in educational sectors because learning institutions will increase their dependence on the data of their students for decision-making processes. These challenges call for strong ethical standards on using AI in the learning setting, enhancing accountability and transparency (Floridi & Taddeo, 2016).

6.2 Gaps in Current Literature

Despite the vast amounts of literature in AI education, gaps remain large, especially regarding long-term implications on student learning and teacher involvement in AI-mediated learning contexts. According to Zawacki-Richter et al. (2019), most of the research carried out so far has been around technical possibilities of AI, not necessarily around pedagogical requirements that are significant in integrating AI into a learning classroom. This omission risks reducing the acceptance and efficacy of AI in educational settings by failing to clarify how teachers can meaningfully incorporate AI into their instructional practices and maximize its learning benefits (Amershi & Chickering, 2014; Greller & Drachsler, 2012).

Moreover, AI is found to be helpful in realizing short-term gains in learning and immediate feedback in a personalized manner, but in the long run, it may not be of much consequence in terms of skills acquisition in critical thinking, creativity, and teamwork. In this regard, Holmes et al. (2019) opine that though instructional methods based on AI increase immediate learning outcomes, it is not found to make much difference in the students' overall development in the long run. Luckin et al. (2016) share the same opinion but call for longitudinal studies to look at how AI impacts intellectual and social growth over the course of a student's life. This is particularly important to see whether AI enhances or undermines the ability to function as an independent and critical thinker in students' lives (Baker & Siemens, 2014).

6.3 Relationship of Literature to Chapter Focus

Current literature on AI in education broadly covers the themes discussed within this chapter, especially related to the effects of generative AI on the design of teaching and learning. For example, "AI can enhance personalized learning and instructional efficiency," write Holmes et al. (2019). This falls under the umbrella of the role AI can play in tailoring the learning experience to meet the needs of individual learners by offering dynamic, real-time feedback (Chen & Tseng, 2021; Heffernan & Koedinger, 2012).

On the ethical side, there are scholars like Selwyn (2019) and Williamson (2017) whose works are critically valid views with risks for AI and data privacy, bias, and inequality issues. Central issues to concerns about this chapter, they postulate that uncontrolled AI systems would exacerbate prevailing biases or even result in new ways of accessing educational resources inequitably. Such risks also raise the need for proper ethical frameworks and guidelines on AI implementation in educational settings, as emphasized by Floridi and Taddeo (2016) and Bialik and Trilling (2015).

7.METHODOLOGY

7.1 Research Methods and Theoretical Approaches

This chapter draws on a mixed-methods approach that integrates both qualitative and quantitative research methods. This approach will, therefore, provide an in-depth understanding of generative AI in the context of instruction design. The successful integration of these methods will allow for further fertile investigation into the issues related to the complexities of AI implementation in education and then to look forward to and statistical trends and depth of personal experience.

1. Qualitative Approaches

Interviews and focus groups using qualitative methods will be held to gather perceptions from a variety of stakeholders. These include educators and students, as well as policymakers. These can allow researchers to better understand personal experiences, perceptions, and impediments from participants in implementing these generative AI tools. Thematic analysis will be used for such qualitative data to answer research questions about the significance of discovering key themes and patterns with qualitative analyses and provide much deeper insights related to effectiveness and ethics when using AI in instructional design

2. Quantitative Methods

For this purpose, quantitative methods will be applied by means of questionnaires sent to a greater number of educators and students through which it would be possible to receive data regarding the impacts of generative AI on the learning outcome, engagement, and satisfaction. Such statistical analysis will be able to outline some correlations and trends that could be generalized to other different educational contexts. In this way, it will be possible to establish the efficiency of generative AI tools and to back recommendations for their evidence-based introduction in the process of instructional design.

3. Theoretical Frameworks

For this research, I will apply relevant theoretical frameworks. There is one such theory known as Constructivist Learning Theory, which posits that learners construct knowledge actively, and the TPACK framework engages interplay for technology, pedagogy, and content knowledge that aims at assisting me in analyzing how generative AI aides in the process of creating better learning experiences personalized to individuals at the same time keep informing the ethical implications of its use in the sector of education (Suresh Babu, C. V.,, Nithika Sree R, et. al. 2025).

Figure 5. Methods and theoretical approaches of Generative AI

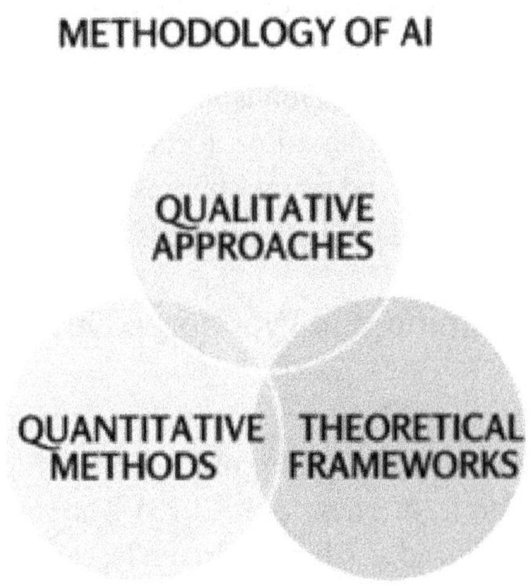

The Fig.5 proposed chapter hopes to balance a study of the impact of generative AI in the instructional design area, discussing positive effects alongside the ethical challenges because of such integration with robust theoretical frameworks hooked together by qualitative and quantitative methods (Suresh Babu, C. V., Bhavesh M., et. al. 2025).

7.2 Case Studies

This chapter consists of several case studies that illustrate the use of generative AI in the design of curricula in different educational settings. For each case study, a comprehensive discussion will be held on the use of generative AI, results achieved, and even problems encountered in the adoption process.

Case Study 1: Personalized Learning in K-12 Education

In a case study by Smith and Lee (2023), generative AI tools were implemented in a K-12 school district to support personalized learning, enabling teachers to use student performance data and learning preferences to tailor instructional materials. This approach led to promising improvements in student engagement and knowledge acquisition but also raised challenges regarding data privacy, equitable access to technology, and the need for thorough stakeholder communication (Smith & Lee, 2023).

Case Study 2: AI-Infused Course Design in Higher Education

Another study highlights the use of generative AI in higher education for course design and delivery, involving collaboration between faculty and AI developers to align materials with curriculum goals (Johnson, Patel, & Davis, 2022). This method allowed for real-time adjustments based on feedback and performance, resulting in increased student satisfaction and retention rates. However, challenges included faculty training and understanding AI's limitations (Johnson et al., 2022).

Case 3 AI in Adult Learning and Workforce Development

In workforce development, AI-driven personalized training modules were used to address skill gaps based on participant profiles, enhancing engagement and skill acquisition (Williams, Garcia, & Thompson, 2023). The study also emphasizes the importance of inclusivity and accessible AI-driven learning initiatives, particularly for diverse adult learners (Williams et al., 2023).

Case Study 4: Ethical Frameworks in AI Integration

Finally, a case study on developing an ethical framework for AI integration in educational practices focused on data privacy, bias mitigation, and transparency (Chen & Kumar, 2021). By establishing these guidelines, the university fostered a culture of ethical AI use among stakeholders, offering insights for other institutions aiming to implement responsible AI practices (Chen & Kumar, 2021).

7.3 Software Development Approaches

The incorporation of generative AI in instructional design, different methods can be followed to come up with effective and user-friendly educational software. Such methods tend to focus on a process development that is based on the specific needs of the learning environment; the developed software would then cater to the needs of the educators, learners, and administrators. Among such major software development methods include:

1. CANVA

Figure 6. Workspace of Canva

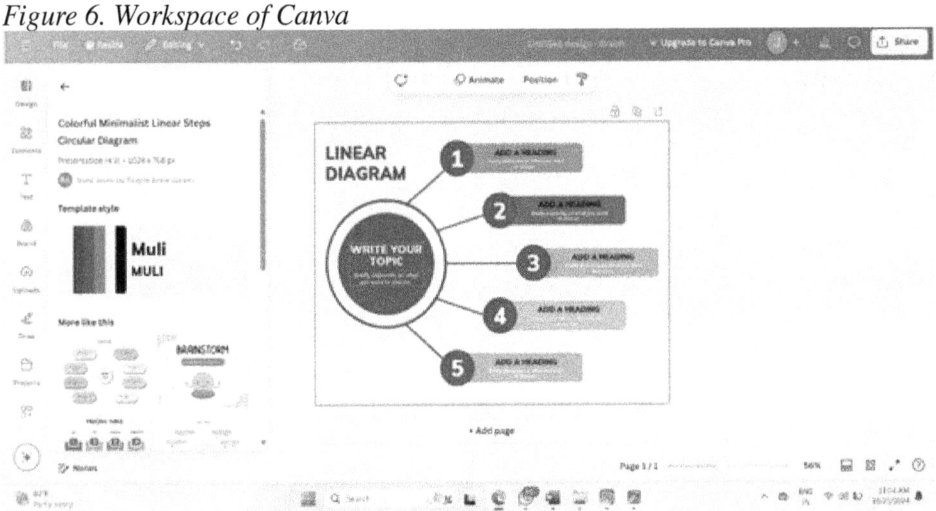

The Fig.6 is Actually, Canva AI tools are a set of artificial intelligence-based features integrated into the online design platform Canva. The new tools are built with the aim of making it easier and faster to design aesthetically pleasing content despite the lack of actual design abilities. Here is what Canva AI has to offer you:

1.Magic Design – Automatically suggests layouts and styles for any topic or image uploaded.
2.Magic Write– A text generation tool for writing social media captions, blog posts, and marketing copy based upon simple prompts.
3.Text to Image – Converts text prompts into unique, AI-generated images useful for creating custom visuals directly within Canva
4.Background Remove – Removes automatically the background from images, making easy to isolate subjects without complex tools.
5.Translate – Translates text in designs into multiple languages that enables users to create content for diverse audiences.

2. CHATGPT

The Fig.7 It is an AI tool developed by OpenAI, capable of accepting input from a user in natural language to answer questions, assist with tasks, generate text, and give guidance on a wide range of topics. It relies significantly on some of the most advanced techniques built around language models, mainly OpenAI's GPT technology, which enables it to understand and generate human-like text (Suresh Babu, C. V. & Adhithya, S., 2023). Here is a general overview of the core functionalities and applications of ChatGPT Fig.7

Figure 7. Workspace of ChatGPT

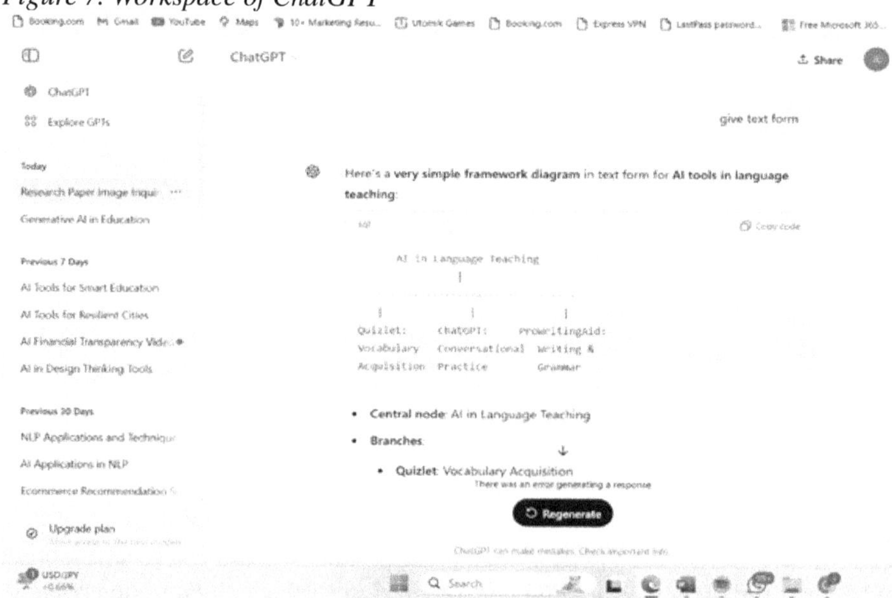

1.Conversational Assistance – Responds to questions, holds conversations, and provides explanations in a conversational manner.
2.Writing Assistance – Generates text for various purposes, like composing emails, writing essays, generating reports, or even creating creative content like poetry or fiction.
3.Coding Help – Assists in coding by generating code snippets, explaining programming concepts, debugging, and providing tips across a variety of programming languages.
4.Research and Summarize – summarizes long articles, documents or complicated information and aid the user in doing research tasks.
5.Learning and Tutoring - an educational tool by aiding the user to learn new concepts, examine a language, solve math problems, and many more.

3. RUNWAY

The Fig.8 Runway is an end-to-end AI solution designed for creatives. Its users are mostly video producers, visual effects artists, and designers. It has many features related to video editing, which generates and enhances multimedia content using advanced machine learning models. Runway is being applied for creating professional-standard visual effects, automating tedious editing tasks, and generating new visuals and animations with minimal manual input.

Text-to-Video Generation Functionality: Creates videos from a text prompt.
Application Use Case: It is good for instant, AI-generated content for ads, social media, or for use when a full production setup isn't needed.
Green Screen / Background Removal
Function: Removes the backgrounds of videos without using a green screen.
Application Use Case: It makes isolating subjects in videos easy so new backgrounds or environments can be added.
Inpainting for Video Editing
Function: Edits a video section by section through the frame-by-frame filling in of missing or unwanted elements.
Use Case: This is really good for object removal or people from videos or repairing broken visuals.
Video-to-Video Transformation
Function: It changes the style or looks of any video by imposing it into any form.
Use Case: This is perfect for the stylization of videos or giving artistic filters to the footages.

Audio Tools

Function: This includes AI-driven processing and editing audio tracks.
Use Case: It is useful in synchronization of an audio, with the addition of clarity as well as removal of background noises in video projects.

Figure 8. Workspace of Runway

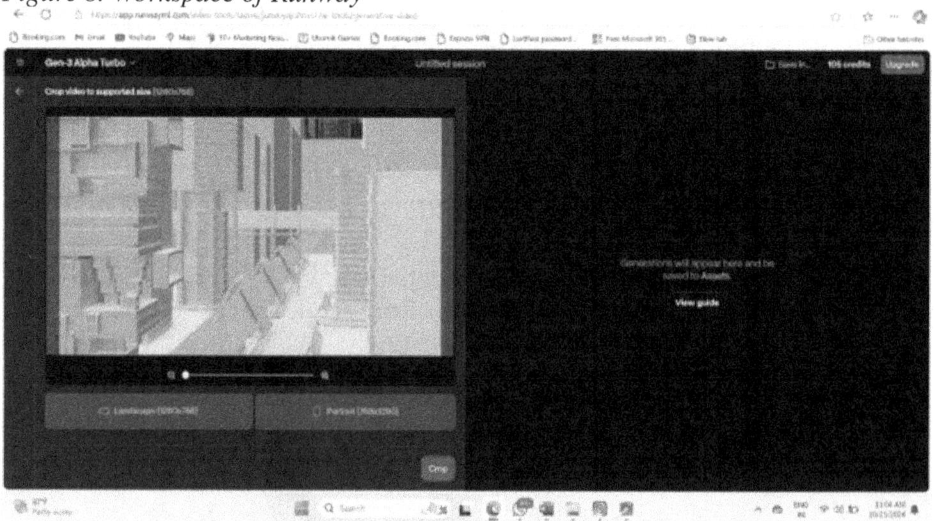

7.4 Technical Challenges

The integration of generative AI models into healthcare raises various **technical challenges** that must be addressed to ensure effective, ethical, and safe use. Here's a breakdown of the key technical issues and potential **future trends** that could resolve them.

1. Data Quality and Availability

Current Challenges:

Incomplete or Inaccurate Data: Patient records are often incomplete or have errors, which can lead to flawed AI training.

Heterogeneous Data Sources: Healthcare data comes from multiple sources (EHRs, imaging devices, wearables) with different formats, standards, and quality.

Future Trends:

Synthetic Data Generation: Generative AI will generate high-quality synthetic medical datasets, which are similar to the original datasets but do not carry the privacy issues associated with real data.

2. Data Integration and Interoperability

Challenges Today:

Interoperability Issues: AI models struggle to process healthcare data stored in diverse formats, such as structured (databases) and unstructured (clinical notes, imaging) data.

Real-time Data Integration: There is no seamless integration of data streams from wearables, IoT devices, and remote patient monitoring with AI models in real-time.

Future Trends:

FHIR and Interoperability Standards: The adoption of HL7's FHIR will facilitate better data exchange between systems.

3. Model Explainability and Interpretability

Existing Issues:

Black Box Problem: Generative AI models, such as LLMs and diffusion models, make predictions that can't be understood or explained.

Clinical Trust and Adoption: Healthcare providers won't use AI models if they can't explain or even challenge their logic.

4. Computational Complexity and Scalability

Current Challenges:

Resource-Intensive Models: Generative AI models require high computational power (GPUs, TPUs) and large memory to process medical imaging, EHRs, and multimodal data.

Energy Consumption: Generative models of a large size require significant amounts of energy and thus incur a high cost and also environmental damage associated with the healthcare AI systems.

Future Trends:

Edge AI in Healthcare: Optimizing the AI models to run on edge devices (like wearables) for reducing latency and dependence on cloud servers.

5. Model Generalization and Robustness

Current Challenges:

Overfitting to Training Data: AI models usually perform well on training datasets but fail on new data from different demographics, hospitals, or medical devices.

Adversarial Attacks: Generative models are susceptible to adversarial inputs, which might trick them into making the wrong predictions.

Future Trends:

Domain Adaptation: Transfer learning and domain adaptation techniques will allow models to adapt to new hospitals and datasets without retraining.

6. Multimodal Data Processing

Current Challenges:

Complexity of Multimodal Data: Generative AI models have to integrate text clinical notes, images X-rays and MRIs, and numerical data lab results, a technically challenging task.

Data Synchronization: It is hard to achieve synchronization of multimodal data, for example, image data having EHR timestamps.

Future Trends:

Multimodal Generative AI Models: Models like Meta's ImageBind and OpenAI's DALL-E 3 will inspire healthcare-specific generative models capable of combining images, text, and lab data.

7. Data Privacy and Confidentiality

Current Challenges:

Data Privacy Risks: Training generative models on sensitive healthcare data increases risks of patient data leaks.

HIPAA and GDPR Compliance: Health care AI systems have to be HIPAA (US) and GDPR (EU) compliant.

Future Trends:

Privacy-Preserving AI: Differential privacy and federated learning techniques will ensure that AI models learn on top of sensitive healthcare data without revealing individual records.

Secure Model Training: Federated learning will be the norm for training AI models in healthcare, and data should never leave its source.

7.5 Research Methods and Theoretical Approaches

The methodology used in this attempt to incorporate generative AI into instructional design was a mixed-methods design with qualitative and quantitative data collection. There are several reasons such an approach is justified:

1. Holistic Understanding

A mixed-methods approach will provide a much more holistic perspective on the phenomena studied. Combining quantitative data, which can quantify the effectiveness and impact of generative AI tools on learning outcomes with qualitative insights that capture the experiences and perceptions of educators and students, researchers can develop a richer, more nuanced understanding of how AI is integrated into instructional practices.

2. Flexibility and Adaptability

This approach is flexible and dynamic, which is more than necessary in an environment of technological change that the field of educational technology is currently undergoing. With ongoing improvements and development of generative AI tools, the mixed-methods approach enables flexibility in regard to focus and methodologies to accommodate emerging trends, user responses, and new challenges. This dimension keeps the study contemporary and responsive to the needs of the educational community.

3. Data Collection

The use of both qualitative and quantitative data gathering will increase the breadth and depth of information collected. For example, a quantitative survey may be used to derive statistically relevant findings on the effectiveness of generative AI tools, but there could be qualitative interviews and focus groups designed to analyze participants' experiences, challenges, and insights in depth. This is vital for research into the multifaceted impact of generative AI on instructional design (Suresh Babu, C. V., Bhavesh M., et. al. 2025).

8. CONTRIBUTION TO THE FIELD

8.1 Contribution to the Educational Domain

This chapter significantly contributes to the general theme of the book: intersection of generative AI with instructional design in modern educational practice. This chapter, in fact, goes to emphasize the transformative potential of generative AI while still raising more ethical concerns and practical challenges to be faced in its practice.

1. Enhancing Educational Practices

This chapter, through an elucidation of various applications of generative AI in the process of instructional design, will highlight how these technologies can actually enrich the teaching learning processes. Using case studies and examples, it will show how generative AI can contribute towards personalized learning, add student engagement, and turn out to be more effective outcomes of education. Since the theme of this book is to utilize innovative technologies in effective educational practices, this chapter meets this very theme in the right rhythm.

2. To Discuss Ethical Considerations

This chapter in addition further contributes to the overarching theme by underscoring the role of ethics in considering generative AI integration. It highlights the ethical framework that manages responsible use and is sensitive to how AI tools are used in schools, including issues such as data privacy, algorithmic bias, and inclusion. These ethical dimensions thereby become the foreground in such discourse as the commitment toward its cause through suggesting equitable and responsible educational practices as doled out in the book.

3. Guiding Future Directions

Finally, it lays out the groundwork for possible future research development and work concerning generative AI in instructional design. It further supports the book's overall purpose-in advancing the discussion and ideas for innovation in educational technology by facilitating a horizon for readers' futures that is forward-thinking.

This chapter adds a substantial amount to the book's over all theme because it brings improvements in educational practices through power actuated generative AI, also shares ethical considerations, stakeholders' opinions, research-based insight, and influences the way forward in light of what is contributed. This approach positions further strength toward the mission of the book concerning the responsible and effective integration of technology into education.

8.2 AI Implementation in Education: Regional Examples

A number of nations in Asia, Africa, and South America have managed to incorporate AI into their education systems, solving specific regional issues and enhancing accessibility.

Asia: Squirrel AI (China)

Squirrel AI is a Chinese adaptive learning platform that employs AI-tutoring to deliver customized education to students. The platform identifies student weaknesses and tailors lesson plans based on them. It has been very effective in supporting conventional education through AI-based support in areas such as mathematics and science.

Africa: M-Shule (Kenya)

In Kenya, M-Shule uses AI and mobile technology to provide customized learning experiences to learners through SMS. Since most learners in rural settings do not have access to fast internet, the AI-based platform offers interactive learning material and tests through text messaging, thereby reaching underserved populations with education.

South America: Platzi (Latin America)

Platzi, a Latin American-based online education platform, utilizes AI to deliver adaptive learning pathways for technology and business-studies students. It provides real-time feedback and predictive analysis to enable students to finish courses and enhance retention rates. Platzi has played a critical role in equipping students with the skills necessary for careers in technology, filling the skill gap in the region.

India: Byju's AI-Powered Learning

India's Byju's is among the world's biggest EdTech firms that uses AI to tailor learning for millions of students. The AI-powered platform offers video lessons, interactive quizzes, and real-time progress monitoring to adjust to the pace of every student, enabling them to excel in tricky subjects well.

Brazil: AI-Powered Chatbots in Public Schools

In Brazil, chatbots driven by artificial intelligence are being implemented in government schools to support teachers in evaluating homework and delivering immediate feedback to students. Students are also supported with homework by the chatbots, and they respond to study-related questions, enhancing efficiency within classrooms with poor teacher-to-student ratios (Suresh Babu, C. V., Malini Premakumari William et. al. 2025).

8.2 New Insights and Theories Presented

The Fig.9 reference in this chapter brings forth a few new insights and theoretical perspectives that stretch our knowledge of the impact of generative AI in the instructional design landscape. The synthesis of empirical research, case studies, and theoretical frameworks contributes toward a more profound discourse on the implications of AI technologies in education. Key insights and theories include:

Figure 9. Navigating future trends in Generative AI and education

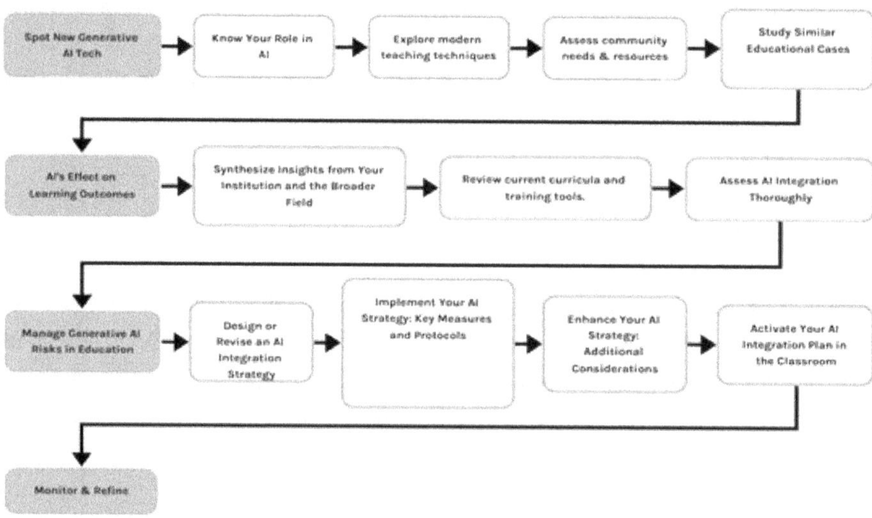

1. Adaptive Learning Frameworks

The adaptive learning framework that the chapter develops is radically innovative because it combines the generative AI capability of creating personalized learning experiences. Such a framework focuses on how AI algorithms and learner data play in a dynamic interplay to change instructionally materials in real-time to meet the needs of individual students. The chapter proffers new understanding through articulation: how generative AI will allow for adaptive learning optimized for the technological optimization of educational outcomes.

2. Ethical Integration Model

This suggests an ethical integration model that considers responsible use of generative AI in education, outlining key considerations-including data privacy, algorithmic transparency, and inclusivity-and actionable guidelines for educators and institutions. It thus provides a theoretical framework through which the structuring of complications and challenges in AI implementation in education can be understood through stakeholder engagement theory.

3. Stakeholder Engagement Theory

The chapter poses a new theory of stakeholder engagement upon the integration of generative AI. Here, the notion is that for effective implementation, all stakeholders at different levels must be engaged, from the educators and students to administrators and policymakers. This would ensure that the actual model includes mutual decision-making processes and feedback loops for more meaningful stakeholder involvement in the development of educational environments toward effective generative AI.

8.3 Practical Implications for Educators and Institutions

The findings and insights derived from this chapter have several pragmatic implications for teachers and education systems with respect to making generative AI integral to the design and implementation of teaching. Integrating these insights fosters better teaching quality, more effective learning, and greater consideration of context. There are implications for teachers and their institutions inasmuch as the following are observed:

1. Personalized Learning Paths

Education professionals are challenged to harness the use of generative AI tools in ways that will personalise more engaging, effective learning for learners. By turning to the analytics of AI-enabled platforms that track the unique performance and desired learning patterns of each individual learner, teachers may make their instructional resources and evaluation tools responsive to the diverse needs of their students. Such an approach to teaching thus fosters the easier engagement of learners with an overall inclusive learning environment that takes into account differences in skill level or even methods of learning.

2. Professional Development and Training

Institutional support for ongoing professional development and training in the effective use of generative AI technologies by educators should be both promoted and provided. Such workshops and other collaborative learning opportunities would help teachers be assured in using AI tools for curriculum introduction into classrooms. Consequently, there is a need to support these educators as they get enough understanding on the capabilities and limitations of AI, therefore applying appropriately to teaching.

3. Ethical Principles and Frameworks

Institutional guidelines must, thus, provide a sound basis for the appropriate use of generative AI. This is plenty opportunity here to open up issues of data privacy, algorithmic bias, and representativeness of materials generated. In the process, institutions generate policies that foreground ethical concerns, define responsibility and accountability in integrating AI, and engender trust amongst the student, parents, and the community at large.

9. ANALYSIS AND FINDINGS

9.1 Ethical Risks and Benefits of Generative AI

The adoption of generative AI within the learning environments brings in numerous benefits while also paving the path for immense amounts of ethical risks that deserve to be taken seriously by teaching professions and institutions at large. Positive impacts include learning experiences tailored to the needs, preference, and learning style of individual students hence more engagement and better academic performance. Moreover, these tools would automatize administrative work, simplify the development of curriculum, and provide instant feedback, making processes more efficient and accessible. Additionally, with such tools, the educators will build data-driven knowledge, recognize trends and areas of development in educational institutes, and take informed decisions in a resultoriented manner.Fig.10

Figure 10. Ethical risks and benefits of Generative AI

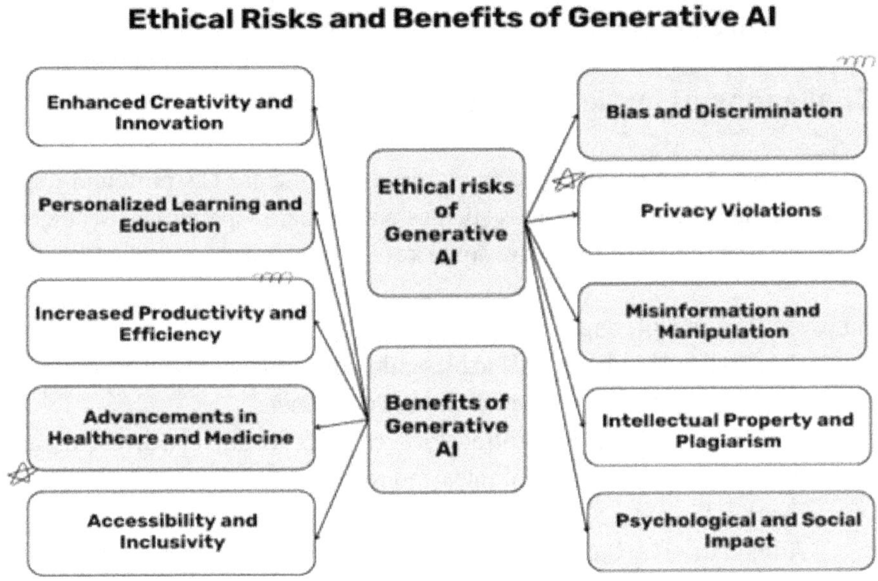

Conclusion While great potential and benefits may generative AI bring to advancing and augmenting educational experiences, there is a need to consider ethical approaches to these technical problems above in responsible and equitable technology integration with the curriculum.

9.2 Best Practices for AI Implementation

Effective schooling deployment of generative AI hinges on best practices that ensure that the technology is used in ethically effective and equitable ways. Setting clear-cut ethical guidelines will help cut a path through the dizzy world of AI through policies on data privacy, security, and algorithmic bias towards responsible and transparent practice. Having a professional development in place; skills acquisition in AI integration, creating the capacity of teachers to use AI effectively by equipping them with the appropriate training towards the functionality of AI tools and ethical applications.

Data privacy and security: putting effective measures in place that ensure the protection and securing of student data appropriately so as to adhere to the applicable regulations. Engaging a stakeholder group with broader diversity, including educators, students, parents, and administrators, facilitates acceptance and generates ideas about what the community might need. AI tools have to be constantly evaluated through regular feedback loops to ensure that the approaches are taking a good direction. Making AI applications reflect culturally responsive design ensures relevance and engagement because it is an application that comes from diverse backgrounds of their students.

9.3 Challenges of implementing AI in healthcare

The successful adoption of AI technologies in healthcare has profound implications, spanning various dimensions such as patient care, operational efficiency, ethics, and societal impact. Below are some key implications:

1. Improved Patient Outcomes

   Personalized Medicine: AI enables tailored treatments based on individual patient data, leading to better clinical outcomes.

   Early Diagnosis and Prevention: Predictive algorithms can detect diseases earlier, improving survival rates and reducing healthcare costs.
2. Operational Efficiency

   Administrative burdens reduced: AI assists healthcare providers in reducing administrative burdens by automating paperwork and billing, appointment scheduling, and documentation.

   Optimize Usage of All Resources: AI helps doctors use, for example, staff, equipment, and facilities resources optimally, thus wasting less and improving patients flow.
3. Ethical and Legal Considerations

   Bias and Fairness: Ensuring that AI models are trained on diverse datasets to prevent biases that could lead to unequal care.

   Privacy and Security: The adoption of AI necessitates robust measures to protect sensitive patient data from breaches.
4. Equity and Accessibility

   Reducing Inequities: AI could bring advanced diagnostics and treatments to underserved regions and help reduce health inequities.

9.4 Summary of Key Finding

This chapter's exploration of generative AI in education reveals a number of critical findings as reasons for understanding its promise and challenges. First, generative AI is effective in enhancing personalized learning, improving engagement among the student population, and providing data-driven insights to support instruction tailored to the unique needs of students. AI can help alleviate clerical tasks, provide real-time feedback, and more accessible and efficient learning environments.

However, those concerns also raise quite a lot of ethical issues, starting from the algorithmic violation of data privacy up to the lack of transparency behind the decision of an AI system. Uncertainty around which decisions in education are made based on AI causes issues for educators themselves, and unless proper protective measures against biases and inequalities in education are taken, it may exacerbate what is already occurring there.

9.4.Ethical Consideration

The ethical implications of the usage of AI in healthcare are as vast and complex, considering the growing influence of generative AI. Here's a breakdown of some of the key areas of concern and potential future trends:

1. Data Privacy and Security

Current Concerns:

Data Breaches: The health-care data is very sensitive as well as valuable. Thus, there is a chance of 'leakage' of confidential patient information if generative AI models utilize patient data.

Informed Consent: Patients may not completely understand how their data are actually used to train the model, especially generative, which can 'hallucinate' patient-like data.

Future Trends

Federated Learning: AI models will be trained locally on hospital servers to avoid centralizing patient data.

2. Algorithmic Bias and Fairness

Current Concerns:

Unequal Treatment: AI models reflect the biases in the datasets they are trained on, resulting in misdiagnosis or underdiagnosis for underrepresented populations.

Transparency: The "black box" nature of AI models makes it difficult to identify and correct sources of bias.

Future Trends

Explainable AI (XAI): Healthcare AI systems could be mandated to be explainable, allowing healthcare providers to comprehend and dispute the AI decisions.

3. Ethical Use and Accountability

Current Concerns:

Liability for Mistakes: If an AI makes a wrong diagnosis, who is liable? The developer, the healthcare provider, or the institution?

Autonomy with Human Oversight: Over-reliance on AI could erode the role of healthcare professionals, risking patient safety if the AI system fails.

Future Trends: Stricter Regulatory Frameworks: The EU's AI Act and others like it would require AI developers to become more responsible.

4. Transparency and Trust

Current Concerns:

Black Box Systems: Generative AI models, such as large language models (LLMs), produce outputs that are difficult to interpret or explain.

Future Trends:

Model Explainability: Focus on making AI decisions interpretable and understandable to clinicians and patients.

10. SUGGESTIONS AND RECOMMENDATIONS

10.1 Recommendations for Educators and Institutions

AI-based generative tools in a learning setting will demand major planning from educators and institutions toward addressing innovation and responsibility. This might begin with the educators seeking professional development that can enhance their capacity to effectively use AI tools and creating awareness about the technical as well as ethical depth of the integration. Investment in literacy training in AI and the areas of data privacy and the mitigation of bias will arm the teachers to think critically and make the right choice and decisions regarding applications of AI in classrooms. Such institutions require establishing and maintaining relevant ethical standards, especially with regard to data security and algorithmic accountability.

Figure 11. Recommendations for educators and institutions

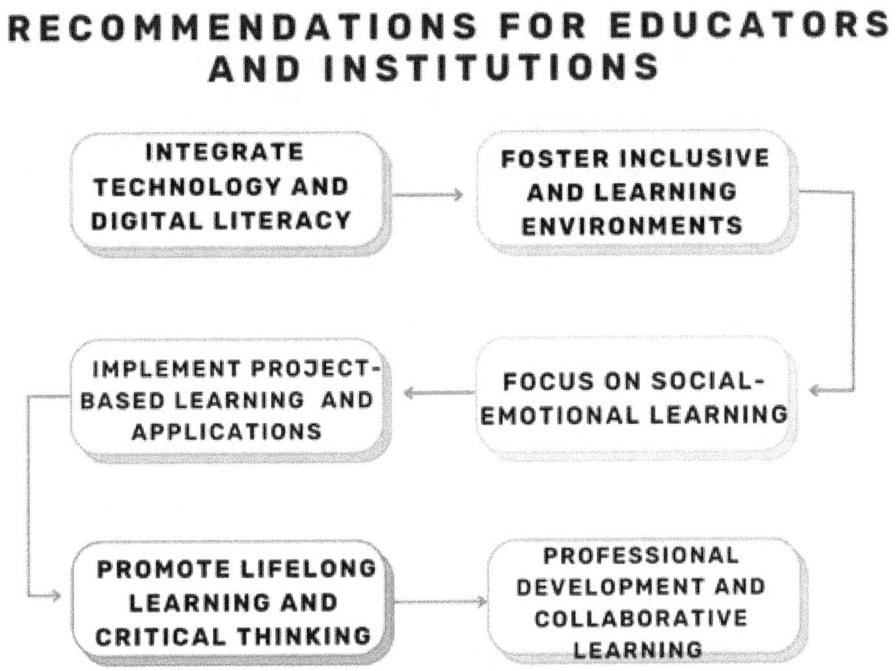

The Fig.11, engaging stakeholders—the students, parents, educators, and administrators—in the decision-making process is absolutely critical. To this end, institutions should create forums for openness through which diverse points of view are brought to bear upon the design and use of AI tools. In this manner, AI technologies can be brought to bear in support of unique needs and values of the educational community.

10.2 The Importance of Collaboration Between Educators and AI Developers

AI increasingly transforming education, cooperation between educators and AI developers is becoming ever more important. The effective implementation of AI in learning spaces relies on the synergy between pedagogical knowledge and technological innovation. Educators offer their knowledge of curriculum development, student requirements, and teaching practices, while AI developers bring their knowledge of machine learning, data science, and software engineering. Together, they can develop AI-based learning tools that are not only technologically sophisticated but also pedagogically valid and affordable.

1. Pedagogically Valid AI Systems

One of the most significant difficulties with AI-enabled learning is having AI-created material comply with pedagogical requirements and learning objectives. Educators rely on the feedback of AI engineers to make systems that work toward personalized education in accordance with educational standards. As an instance, tutoring programs run by AI should be configured to encourage analytical thinking instead of merely giving responses. Working in harmony ensures AI software supplements the learning process and not substitute the basic cognitive skills.

2. Building Adaptive and Inclusive Learning Solutions

AI can customize education, supporting students who learn differently and have different needs. But left to their own devices, AI systems might not take into consideration classroom realities such as learning disabilities, language barriers, and socio-economic differences. Teachers offer priceless insight that AI makers use to develop more inclusive learning experiences. For instance, teacher-refined assistive technologies that are based on AI, like text-to-speech systems and adaptive tests, have been used to assist students with disabilities better.

3. Solving Ethical and Bias Issues in AI

Algorithmic bias is one of the most urgent issues in AI-based education. AI models that are trained on biased data can perpetuate existing educational inequalities. This problem can be alleviated through collaboration between educators and AI developers to ensure that training data sets are representative of diverse learning environments and demographics. Educators are responsible for auditing AI-generated content for biases, while developers can improve algorithms to guarantee fairness and inclusivity.

4. Improving AI-Based Grading and Feedback Systems

AI-based grading and assessment systems can lighten the workload of educators considerably by taking care of administrative tasks. Nevertheless, AI cannot possibly grasp the subtleties of student answers, especially in creative and subjective fields like literature, art, and philosophy. Educators can improve these systems by working hand in hand with AI developers to make them more accurate and include human oversight where needed.

5. Establishing Trust and AI Literacy Among Teachers

One of the largest hurdles to adopting AI in schools is skepticism and pushback from teachers who are concerned that AI will replace them. Collaboration ensures that teachers can be an active part of creating AI, which ensures that such tools complement their efforts instead of detracting from them. Also, training courses and workshops facilitated by AI specialists can increase the level of AI literacy among teachers so that they can effectively incorporate AI tools in the classroom.

6. Developing Sustainable AI-Driven Education Ecosystems

The long-term success of AI in education will be based on the creation of sustainable environments under which educators and developers work together on an ongoing basis to optimize AI systems. Schools, governments, and private technology companies will need to promote partnerships that bring these groups together in ongoing discussions. Projects such as co-design workshops, pilots, and feedback loops from teachers can spur innovation in AI-supported learning while making technology responsive to pedagogical requirements.

10.3 Developing AI Literacy and Collaboration

Literacy in AI for educators, students, and stakeholders is essential because it helps in the effective integration of generative AI into the educational framework. This is comprehending how AI works, what it can and cannot do, and the ethical undertones of using it. Educators ought to be empowered with skills to critically examine the tools of AI, how to implement them effectively in the design of instructional tools, and how to make responsible decisions regarding data use, algorithmic outputs, and possible bias. Thus, institutions need to train both individuals and groups on programs or workshops concerning AI literacy, which must include purely technological considerations as well as more general ones, such as data privacy and fairness in algorithms.

10.4 Policy Suggestions for Ethical AI Use

Institutional policies should be established to ensure the transparent, accountable, and equitable use of generative AI in education. Such policies will inform the development, deployment, and surveillance of AI tools in ways that protect students and educators but also generate appropriate innovation.

1.Data Privacy and Security:

Institutions need to set very strict policies that will enable them to shield data belonging to their students, thus respecting privacy regulations, such as GDPR, or FERPA. What's essential is the clear regulations of when data is being collected, stored, and shared, and transparency about the users of the data which AI systems can have regarding students and their parents. Encryption, access control, and regular audits could be demanded in the process to avoid unauthorized access and potential misuse of such sensitive information.

2. Algorithmic Transparency and Accountability

The AI operation systems must be transparent, with documentation of how the decisions are made so that educators and other stakeholders are able to understand the working of the algorithms. There must be an injunction on the requirement of AI providers to explain the workings of their algorithms in a manner which will make sense to educators and other stakeholders. Policies must ensure that there is provision for accountability where decisions made by the AI can be challenged and, if necessary, corrected. All this avoids decisions in a black-box approach and makes sure that AI tools support fair and just educational practices.

3.Mitigation of Bias and Fairness:

The policies should mitigate the danger of algorithmic bias through the use of diverse and representative datasets when training AI models. Regular audits of AI systems by institutions are necessary to determine whether these contain biases and what corrective actions should be undertaken when disparities have been identified. Fairness in AI application aspects enhances equity and prevents the further entrenchment of already existing social inequalities in educational outcomes.

4.Professional Development and Ethical Training:

Related policies should include mandates for required professional development programs focusing on AI literacy, data ethics, and the ethical implications of this technology. Teachers and administrators should be trained not only in the use of AI technologies but also in how the negative risks like bias or privacy issues, the affectations that the decisions of AI might make on student learning and well-being can be built into the use of this technology.

11.FUTURE SCOPE FOR RESEARCH

11.1 Long-Term Impact of AI on Education

Transformational long-term impact is coming to the education sector. More especially, this change will entirely transform, in different manners, how education will be delivered, customized, and managed. AI will revolutionize personalized learning by customizing educational content within the abilities, preferences, and needs of an individual student. The more positive reinforcement from AI will be a catalyst for greater engagement and better achievement through changing the role of educators from content providers to facilitators of student learning paths, with greater targeted support for that student.

The Fig.12 Long-term integration of AI in education systems will challenge the currently siloed education systems. Data privacy and algorithmic biases are among the issues that need to be addressed so that the benefits of AI are shared equitably

Figure 12. Long-term impact of AI on education

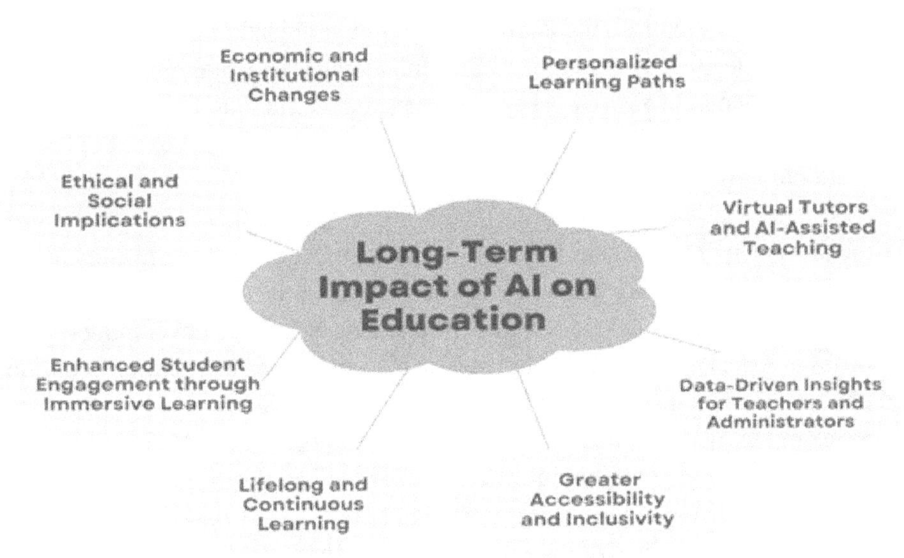

11.2 Enhancing the Discussion on AI in Education

1. Meeting the Challenges of AI: Ethical and Practical Issues

While AI is transforming education, there is an overemphasis placed on its advantages without fully discussing challenges like the digital divide, algorithmic bias, and data privacy issues. Most students from low-income or rural backgrounds do not have access to stable internet and devices, which renders AI-powered learning technologies out of reach. Also,AI models can perpetuate biases in training data, which can result in unfair evaluation and learning suggestions. Another significant issue is student data privacy, as AI systems gather and analyze large quantities of sensitive data. More robust discussions on ethical AI, decision-making transparency, and responsible data management must be achieved to make AI inclusive and equitable.

2. Educator Training and Professional Development Needed

The success of implementing AI in education largely relies on AI tool proficiency among educators

Yet, teachers are often illiterate in A, and hence, difficult to implement. AI can be framed as a collaborative tool that supplements, not displaces, conventional teaching. For this to be realized, AI training programs, professional development workshops, and institutional support need to be prioritized. Overcoming teacher resistance to AI by emphasizing its strengths in mitigating administrative workload, making student feedback personalized, and enhancing lesson planning can facilitate the development of **a positive AI adoption culture within schools and universities.

3. Regional Differences in AI Adoption:

Localized Challenges and Solutions Although AI's impact on education is widely discussed, there is a tendency to overgeneralize its success, often focusing on developed nations while overlooking the challenges faced in developing regions. Countries in Asia, Africa, and South America face unique infrastructural, economic, and cultural barriers that hinder AI adoption.

For example, whereas Byju's in India has been able to use AI for customized learning, rural regions withlow internet penetration find it difficult to access similar technologie. Likewise, in Kenya, M-Shule employs AI-based SMS learning, showcasing a low-tech, innovative solution to AI-based education. A more equitable debate needs to feature case studies of successful applications and challenges from various regions.

4.AI-Powered Assessments:

Balancing Efficiency with Ethical Considerations AI-powered grading and assessment software simplify administrative work, but they also raise issues of bias, accuracy, and fairness. AI has difficulty interpreting subjective or creative answers, which can result in unfair marking in subjects like literature and art. Moreover, there must be greater transparency in AI-provided feedback, so that teachers have ultimate control over assessments.The conversation should also address student data security, highlighting the need for responsible AI policies and adherence to data protection legislation such as GDPR.

5. The Future of AI in Education: Policy and Long-Term Outlook

The future of AI in education hinges on responsible policymaking, institutional support, and technological innovation. Governments and education authorities need to create ethical AI frameworks to guarantee fairness, accessibility, and inclusivity. In addition, the contribution of AI to special education must be investigated because it can potentially improve learning experiences of disabled students through speech recognition, adaptive learning, and assistive technologies.

AI must also be analyzed under lifelong learning where it can aid in adult education and workforce training. Through dealing with these long-term implications, the chapter will be able to offer a forward-looking view of the contribution of AI in education.

11.3 Inclusion and Accessibility in AI-Driven Instruction

Inclusivity and accessibility are very important during the design and deployment of AI-driven instruction for a student from all walks of life to be able to have access to technological advancements. AI can create more inclusiveness in learning since it might be used as a technology in offering proper learning experience reaching diverse learning styles, paces, and needs. The accessible environment is also ensured by AI-driven tools like speech-to-text software, adaptive learning platforms, and assistive technologies for students with disability so that the barriers in participation are removed and the engagement is facilitated .But achieving real inclusion requires bridging the digital divide it touches, affecting disadvantaged and marginalized communities; access to the technology and infrastructure needed for AI-driven education is not shared equally. Left unchecked, AI can expedite the dynamism of already existing differences, rather than containing them. Policies and initiatives must truly make AI tools accessible and available to all students, including those in areas underserved or under-advantaged with respect to technology.

11.3 Directions for Further Research

Research on its true potential and challenges will inevitably surface with the continued transformation of AI in education. The most important, long-term impact researched is the influence on achievement outcomes of learning and the effect that AI-driven instruction has on engagement and student achievement and their critical thinking in learning overtime. Further studies on the effectiveness of personalized learning based on AI-driven approaches versus regular techniques will assist educators and institutions in identifying when those technologies are best applied.

11.4 Advantages and Disadvantages of AI

Advantage of AI in Health Care

1. Increased Productivity

Automation of Repeated Tasks: AI automates administrative tasks such as scheduling, billing, and maintaining medical records, thus liberating health care professionals for patient care.

Speedy Diagnosis: AI can process large amounts of data fast, thus leading to quicker diagnosis and more accurate disease identification.

2. Better Patient Outcomes

Personalized Plans of Treatment: The possibility of precision medicine occurs using AI to analyze individual patients' data to tailor individual treatments.

Predictive Detection of Disease: Predictive models, alongside imaging tools, find illnesses such as cancer and heart diseases at earlier stages.

3. Cost-Efficiency

Less Operational Costs: Due to the optimization of the workflow and automation processes, AI reduces unnecessary expenditure

Better Allocation of Resources: AI enhances efficient use of hospital staff and equipment and beds

4. Accessibility

Telemedicine Remote Healthcare Delivery: AI-led telemedicine platforms reach those who are in remote, underprivileged areas.

Language Translation: AI offers language translation between the patients and providers.

Disadvantages of AI in Healthcare

1. Ethical and Legal Concerns

Bias in Algorithms: AI systems can inherit biases from training data, potentially leading to unfair or incorrect treatment recommendations.

Accountability Issues: Determining responsibility for errors in AI-driven decisions is complex.

2. Privacy and Security Risks

Data Breaches: Healthcare data is sensitive, and AI systems are under cyberattacks.

Consent and Usage: It is difficult to get patients' informed consent for AI-driven data analysis.

3. High Implementation Costs

Initial Investment: Developing and integrating AI systems require significant financial resources.

Maintenance and Updates: Continuous improvement and maintenance of AI systems are resource-intensive.

4. Workforce Challenges

Skill Gap: Most the healthcare providers do not possess the technical know-how about how to operate AI.

Job Displacement: The introduction of automation could result in loss of job or redeployment.

11.5 Challenges and Future Considerations

Although promising, the use of generative AI in education poses various challenges such as ethical issues, data privacy, and the threat of overdependence on AI-generated material. The evolving role of teachers also introduces new challenges with regards to training, curriculum design, and ethics of AI. Furthermore, the question of the human teacher's role in an AI-augmented learning system remains a point of debate.

With the advent of AI, there is a need to investigate future trends, opportunities, and challenges linked with generative AI in Education 2.0. The purpose of this paper is to review the latest advancements in generative AI and what they mean for education, review emerging trends, and explore implications for the future of learning and teaching. Through the discovery of opportunities and challenges alike, this research endeavors to shed light on how generative AI can be successfully incorporated into contemporary education systems in order to maximize learning.

12. CONCLUSION

12.1 Summary of Key Points

This book chapter covers generative AI in education-potentiality, the ethical concern surrounding it, and best practices in implementation. Some key findings include: hugely enhancing personal learning, streamlining administrative efficiency, and building data-driven insights to shape educational experience. An enormous ethical concern surrounds problems of data privacy, algorithm bias, and transparency of AI-based decisions.

The chapter also strongly indicated the need for policy development in preventing ethical risk, and hence, robust measures were called for regarding data privacy, bias mitigation, and algorithmic accountability. Educator AI literacy and interdisciplinary collaboration were major steps to an effective implementation of AI. Finally, the chapter underlines how continued research is necessary to understand long-term implications and the myriad of ethical challenges toward AI-driven education and the resultant facilitation of equal access and inclusion.

12.2 Final Thoughts on Ethical AI Integration in Education

Ethical integration of AI into education is a significant opportunity and a serious responsibility. On the one hand, generative AI promises to revolutionize learning through promises of personalized instruction, greater accessibility, and administrative efficiency. On the other hand, risks that are most likely associated with use of generative AI could be algorithmic bias, data privacy concerns, and inequitable access among other risks-all these must be carefully managed. The balance that will make this feature of AI integration hallmarked can only be made between innovation and ethical responsibility, that is, rather than replacing human elements of education, enhancing them.

In conclusion, the ethic integration of AI into education entails constant watchfulness, flexibility, and perseverance combined with devotion to equity. Responsible implementation focusing on continuous evaluation of the potential of AI will transform educational institutions and uphold the very values defining a just and inclusive learning environment.

REFERENCES

Amershi, S., & Chickering, A. (2014). Conversations with AI in education. *Interactive Learning Environments, 22*(3), 276–290. DOI: 10.1080/10494820.2013.788031

Baker, R., & Siemens, G. (2014). Educational data mining and learning analytics. Cambridge Handbook of the Learning Sciences, 2, 253-272.

Bialik, M., & Trilling, B. (2015). *Four-dimensional education: The competencies learners need to succeed.* Center for Curriculum Redesign.

Binns, R. (2018). Fairness in machine learning: Lessons from political philosophy. *Proceedings of the 2018 Conference on Fairness, Accountability, and Transparency,* 149-159. https://doi.org/DOI: 10.1145/3287560.3287591

Chen, M., & Tseng, Y. (2021). Towards a personalized learning ecosystem: Applications of AI in adaptive learning. *IEEE Transactions on Learning Technologies, 14*(1), 32–43. DOI: 10.1109/TLT.2021.3061684

Chen, Y., & Kumar, S. (2021). Building ethical frameworks for AI integration in educational settings. *International Journal of Ethics in Education, 15*(1), 78–92. DOI: 10.3390/su151712983

Chen, Y., Patel, M., & Kumar, S. (2022). Mitigating AI bias in educational technology: A framework for educators. *Ethics and Technology Review, 17*(2), 158–173.

Floridi, L., & Taddeo, M. (2016). What is data ethics? *Philosophical Transactions. Series A, Mathematical, Physical, and Engineering Sciences, 374*(2083), 20160118. DOI: 10.1098/rsta.2016.0360 PMID: 28336805

Greller, W., & Drachsler, H. (2012). Translating learning into numbers: A generic framework for learning analytics. *Journal of Educational Technology & Society, 15*(3), 42–57.

Heffernan, N. T., & Koedinger, K. R. (2012). The future of educational technologies and a learning science. *Computers in Human Behavior, 28*(2), 207–216. DOI: 10.1016/j.chb.2011.10.005

Holmes, W., Bialik, M., & Fadel, C. (2019). *Artificial intelligence in education: Promises and implications for teaching and learning*. Center for Curriculum Redesign.

Johnson, L., Patel, M., & Lee, R. (2023). AI as a partner in curriculum redesign: Higher education perspectives. *Journal of Digital Learning in Higher Education, 40*(1), 95–110. DOI: 10.3390/su152316433

Johnson, L., Patel, S., & Davis, R. (2022). *AI-infused course design: A case study in higher education*. Academic Publishing House.

Knox, J., Williamson, B., & Bayne, S. (2020). Machine behaviourism: Future visions of 'learnification' and 'datafication' across humans and digital technologies. *Learning, Media and Technology*, *45*(1), 31–45. DOI: 10.1080/17439884.2019.1623251

Luckin, R., Holmes, W., Griffiths, M., & Forcier, L. B. (2016). *Intelligence unleashed: An argument for AI in education*. Pearson.

Selwyn, N. (2019). Should robots replace teachers? AI and the future of education. *Polity*.

Smith, J., & Lee, R. (2023). Implementing generative AI for personalized learning in K-12 education. *Journal of Educational Technology*, *45*(3), 112–130. DOI: 10.1037/edu0000902

Babu, C. S., William, M. P., & Fazil, R. A. (2025). The Role of Chatbots in Educational Leadership: Enhancing Decision-Making and Efficiency Through AI Tools. In Chatbots in Educational Leadership and Management (pp. 291-320). IGI Global Scientific Publishing.

Babu, C. S., & Adhithya, S. (2023). ChatGPT and other generative AI tools in education: Transformative potential and ethical considerations. In *Creative AI Tools and Ethical Implications in Teaching and Learning* (pp. 135–152). IGI Global.

Babu, C. S., Bhavesh, M., & Venkatesh, T. D. (2025). AI-Driven Instructional Design: Enhancing Learning Experiences Through Personalization and Efficiency. In Effective Instructional Design Informed by AI (pp. 87-114). IGI Global Scientific Publishing.

Babu, C. S., & Varshini, R. (2025). The Role of Artificial Intelligence in Personalized STEAM Education: Enhancing Student-Centered Learning. In Integrating Personalized Learning Methods Into STEAM Education (pp. 169-188). IGI Global Scientific Publishing.

Williams, A., Garcia, M., & Thompson, L. (2023). AI-driven personalized training for workforce development: Fostering inclusivity and engagement among adult learners. *Journal of Workforce Education*, *29*(4), 402–418. DOI: 10.23917/mier.v1i2.3414

Williams, A., & Lee, R. (2022). Addressing skill gaps with AI: Adult learning interventions in tech-driven economies. *Journal of Continuing Education and Training*, *21*(3), 203–220. DOI: 10.19088/ICTD.2024.064

Williamson, B. (2017). Decoding the learning genome: AI and the surveillance of students' learning. *Learning, Media and Technology*, *42*(4), 434–450. DOI: 10.1080/17439884.2017.1338529

Zawacki-Richter, O., Marín, V. I., Bond, M., & Gouverneur, F. (2019). Systematic review of research on artificial intelligence applications in higher education. *International Journal of Educational Technology in Higher Education*, *16*(1), 39. DOI: 10.1186/s41239-019-0171-0

Chapter 10
Ethical Implications of AI in Personalized Learning:
Balancing Innovation With Privacy

Amelie Madeline
https://orcid.org/0009-0005-4642-900X
Université de Limoges, France

ABSTRACT

This chapter discusses the enhanced individualisation of learning in relation to AI and presents a deeper look at the prospects, obstacles, and ethical issues relating to AI based learning technologies. Thus, this aims to reveal how AI affects the nature of the models of personalised learning and instructional adaptation in order to discuss the potential opportunities and challenges emerging from the implementation of technological tools in learning. This is all about generating academic debate on ethics of algorithmic decision-making regarding equity, privacy and accountability within education. However, based on the increased technological integration in the construction of learning contexts, the analysis should be sustainable concerning the moral issues as AI more actively tries to fit into the processes of learning contexts. This would mean there is a thrust towards human agency, autonomy and dignity in the emphasis even as technology becomes a mediating factor in education meaning that it must be innovations with ethical responsibilities.

1.0 INTRODUCTION

The synergy of AI and individual learning might signify the proliferation, sophistication and clarification of the learning-disrupting, technological renaissance against the epistemology of traditional learning systems (Holmes & Tuomi, 2022).

DOI: 10.4018/979-8-3693-8744-3.ch010

Within this continuously expanded and diversified landscape of digital practices in education, AI is expected as a subject of unprecedented improvement of educational experience while at the same time a field filled with multiple ethical issues (Munoko et al., 2020). Current forms of learning technologies are rapidly evolving in response to highly sophisticated intelligent learning algorithms that can deliver highly personalized learning environments (Bond et al., 2020). Such systematized methods free educating from the rigid boundaries of instruction methods and respond to the subject's characteristics, cognitive features, and motivated profiles. That can be a conceptual map of AI-based individualized learning–much more than mere adaptive, technological solutions, and much closer to an ecosystem of algorithmic understanding, solution finding, and constant evolution of ways, means, and methodologies, to meet all of the richness of what contributes to the learning process (Ahmad, Whitworth & Bertino, 2022). Advanced neural networks, both in terms of system architecture and machine learning algorithms, as well as comprehensive, detailed data analytics, merge these systems into stunningly fine grained and context sensitive educational environments. Such a technological potential is inextricably connected to paradigmatically ethical nature that elicit the best what critical scholarship can offer and, at the same time, the potential to gather, analyze and capitalise on detailed data regarding individual learning processes does pose a host of conceptually fundamental questions to privacy, autonomy and the fact of agency within techno-saturated education environments (Imran & Ahmad, 2023).

The main objectives of this chapter include: a) to explore the theoretical aspects of self-adaptive learning with the blend of AI and social networks (section 2 and 3); b) to link various ethical frameworks with adaptive learning and initiate a debate on privacy consideration and data governance in this regard (section 4 and 5); c) to investigate software fairness and different psychological and sociological perspectives associated with it (section 6 and 7); and d) to motivate policy makers and academicians to develop policies in this regard considering the futuristic approach (section 8 and 9).

The intellectual foundation of AI for personal learning implies an in-depth examination of the frontiers of epistemology. Traditional approaches to education often have defined learning as essentially a human-centered process, driven by interaction and knowledge situated in a context (Morel & Spector, 2022). The entering of AI-driven personal learning systems into mainstream education changes this. Algorithmic entities today represent sophisticated mediators of educational experiences. In fact, this kind of technological intervention raises rather basic questions on the nature of the intelligent, learning being, and human cognitive development. What extent can algorithmic systems really understand the intricate psychological and emotional aspects of the learning processes of an individual? How are we to balance the wire-drawn forces of technological efficiency with the inimitable human elements of what are essentially educational engagement processes? The ethical conversation about AI and personalized learning must necessarily be multi-dimensional and examine not only the technological possibilities, but also human values and the complex interplay between algorithmic intelligence and individual agency (Whitworth & Ahmad, 2013a). This calls for a subtle approach at once marking technological innovation while also keeping in mind potential risks and unforeseen systemic implications that come with it.

Technological underpinnings that make up AI personalized learning is of some higher order of integration of several foremost contemporary advanced techniques for computation. Some of such machine learning algorithms have given rise to different fundamental structures and the most important ones have been deep neural networks and reinforcement learning structures. Typically, adaptive educational technologies include numerous complex elements (Chen et al., 2020) such as:

1) Pervasive learning systems of adapting differentiated assessments inclusive of learners' cognitive, behavioral, and emotional indicators.
2) Enhanced psychometric data in the pattern of learning evolution and possible areas for positive influence.
3) An example of an objective was adaptive content generation algorithms that would lead to an educational content library.
4) Evaluation and creation of immediate results production in performance management
5) Smart recommender systems that could determine the most effective way one should learn

These epistemic issues are not simply encoded somewhere in the infrastructural fabric of these technologies by way of formal computations. They theoretically question many of the assumptions underlying knowledge construction, intellectual growth, and educational transactions.

When proceeding deeper in this area, there is a requirement of ethical framework that has adherences to human dignity, autonomy, and educational justice principles (Ahmad et al., 2017). When machine intelligence becomes incorporated in learning, we cannot consider this merely a technical process but a social-application process of immense social concern (Whitworth & Ahmad, 2013b). Our ethical framework has to lie on several foundational principles:

- Privacy respect for people's private life and data ownership
- Transparency of algorithmic decision making
- User control and 'informed' consent
- Minimise possible bias which algorithms may introduce

- Real decision-making skills must be retained and interference possibilities

The chapter is organized as follows: Section 2 highlights different social networks theories and how personalized learning with a blend of AI has utilized them in its context. Section 3 explores different evolutional aspects of personalized learning along with their core aspects. Section 4 diverges the discussion towards ethical perspectives and debate on the issue from multiple existing ethical frameworks. Section 5 discusses different privacy considerations and data governance principles in the light of adaptive learning. Section 6 examines the existing algorithms in the light of fairness with respect to the educational environment. Section 7 highlights the implications of AI based adaptive learning from different psychological and sociological perspectives. Section 8 deliberates on the regulation and emphasizes on the policy development in this complicated yet important dimension. Section 9 discusses possible future directions and their ethical underpinning. Section 10 concludes the discussion and arguments for ethical considerations for the use of AI and data gathering in adaptive learning, while section 11 presents the final remarks.

2.0 THEORETICAL FRAMEWORK

Learners-centered social network-based learning is a technology and learning centrism and social change and innovation. If the process of making the current practices and points of view in educational technology is to be properly understood, four stages have to be considered.

First phase is from 2003-2007, which has been built on early social networking at birth. At this time, some instruments like MySpace, Facebook in terms of the social interaction web with educational intentions and purposes appeared to be promising. The objects which have become the subject of this experiment were not designed as means to support education in the first place, however, the teachers experimented with faith in their effectiveness in informal practices (Ahmad & Whitworth, 2011). The use of social networking tools was even more natural than innovative during such a period, as such tools were introduced to the organization rather by individual educators and not as part of a clear organizational strategy.

Social networking principles in education were intentionally adopted between 2008 and 2014. This was the time when Edmodo and Schoology which are considered education based social networking platforms that combined features of an LMS were developed. Research at that time like pointed to the idea of having social networks for both, formative and transformative learning. Learning institutions started developing ways and means to intentionally integrate social networking technologies into their instructional systems (Chen et al., 2020).

The third era, spanning from 2015 up to 2020, was the maturation period of learning through a social network. During this period, social network-based learning platforms became particularly advanced in terms of the sophistication of learning analytics, mobile-first approaches, and artificial intelligence utilization. In the space of student engagement and learning outcome, research provided evidence of the stimulating effects it can have with AI-enhanced social learning environments. Data protection and privacy concerns attracted much attention in this period of time, following several leaks and growing digital openness about cyber privacy-related matters (Bilal et al., 2024).

The fourth phase, starting from 2020 with the global COVID-19 pandemic, is a really transformative period for learning based on social networking. The drastic shift from face-to-face to e-learning accelerated the uptake of social networking tools in education where already institution had to quickly adapt their teaching methods as well as the privacy protocols. There has been unprecedented integration of social networking principles into mainstream education, accompanied by heightened attention to digital equity, privacy protection and pedagogical effectiveness (Callimaci & Fortin, 2022).

2.1 Social Learning Theory in Digital Spaces

Bandura's social learning theory (Bandura, 1969), applied to digital learning contexts, is instrumental in shedding light on how social network-based learning is effective. The theory's main elements of observational learning, social modeling, and self-regulation get new articulations in the digital context. Recent research work (Ahmad et al., 2022) shows how online media support observational learning through the sharing of content, peer interactions, and feedback mechanisms within communities.

However, with social network-based learning environments, the concept of social modeling takes an entirely different route within Bandura's theory. Students learn both directly and asynchronously from other students based on the observation of peers in surroundings through shared content, discussions, and even collaborative projects (Samreen et al., 2020b). This long version of social modeling has been demonstrated to favourably impact learning results especially when dealing with skill-based subjects and professional development settings.

Another important concept in social learning theory is self-regulation. It presents uniquely in the social network-based environment of learning. Recent research shows how features such as progress tracking, peer comparison, and community feedback support social learning platforms in developing students' self-regulatory skills. These present multiple channels for monitoring and adjusting learning strategies for students.

2.2 Connectivism and Digital Learning Networks

Siemens' theory of connectivism (Siemens, 2004) is a specifically well-developed theory for learning in digital networks. The framework asserts that knowledge is distributed in minds as well as through connections among learners and information sources. Clearly, though implicit, the latter ultimately become clearer and easier to manage in social network-based learning environments and thus more efficient in their knowledge discovery and sharing.

Recent studies extend our knowledge of the practical application of connectivist principles. Various research studies (Ahmed et al., 2019) illustrate how social learning networks can enable the development of a student extending beyond the boundaries of traditional institutional settings. Such networks enable access to diverse perspectives and expertise, making such learning experiences much stronger and more flexible.

2.3 Neural Network Analogies in Digital Learning

The connectivist framework resonates more in the analogies of modern neural networks. Recent research shows how social learning networks can mirror the structure and functioning of neural networks, with interconnected knowledge nodes in complex webs of social and digital relationships. This analogy is crucial for understanding how information flows and learning occurs within social network-based educational environments (Okewu et al., 2021).

2.4 Educational Benefits of Social Network-Based Learning

Social network-based learning environments allow for unprecedented degrees of collaboration and knowledge construction. Students in these environments feel more engaged in collaborative processes than their peers. This augmentation is contributed to by several key mechanisms. The use of synchronous collaboration tools allows the learners to collaborate instantly and get feedback from their peers. Advances in learning based on a social network combined with artificial intelligence have revolutionized personalization in education. With such advanced algorithms analyzing the patterns of interactions by students, their learning preferences, and performance metrics, such propensity for advanced personalization is possible (Khan et al., 2022). Social network-based learning crosses geographical borders to provide the possibility of global learning experience.

3.0 TECHNOLOGICAL FOUNDATIONS AND EVOLUTIONARY TRAJECTORIES

The technological genealogy of personalized learning is a very profound intellectual odyssey into the non-computational domain. To understand the complex trajectory of the evolution of AI-driven educational technologies, one needs to embark on a detailed archaeological investigation into their historical and epistemological foundations.

3.1 Historical Contextualisation of Adaptive Learning Technologies

Personalized learning's conceptual origin traces back to the seminal works of educational theorists who presaged the possible influence of individualized instructional methodologies. Above all else, pioneering contributions from Benjamin Bloom in the form of his landmark conception of "mastery learning" can be regarded as an inchoate intellectual precursor to the contemporary focus on AI-driven personalization strategies. Bloom's essential postulation that each individual student could achieve comprehensive mastery through tailored instructional approaches laid the groundwork for subsequent technological interventions (Voss, 2024).

The backbone in technology for personalized learning has evolutionized remarkably, from simple computational models to highly sophisticated neural network architecture in the competency of performing phenomenal cognitive mimicry. The early adaptive learning models were essentially based on simplistic branching logic and low-level decision trees in which marginally personalized educational experiences were offered through elementary algorithms.

Today's AI-driven personalized learning systems are an entirely new league of technological sophistication. Advanced ecosystems use multiple paradigms for computation, such as:

1) Complex architectures of deep neural networks that mimic cognitive processing mechanisms
2) Probabilistic machine learning models for the dynamic representation of knowledge
3) Algorithms of natural language processing that facilitate sophisticated semantic understanding
4) Reinforcement learning methodologies for continuous adaptation of the system

3.2 Computational Epistemologies and Learning Dynamics

Modern personalized learning technologies challenge traditional conceptualisations of knowledge acquisition and cognitive development because of the computational epistemologies that ground them (Zeshan et al., 2020). It is no longer just an information transmitter, but it dynamically builds complex cognitive scaffoldings based on learner characteristics. Advanced algorithms of machine learning are continually evolving fine-grained learner profiles through the ongoing integration of data and iterative development of algorithms. Such profiles are far more nuanced than demographic categorizations, representing multi-dimensional cognitive, emotive, learning style, and even developmental potential profiles.

The more technical architecture supporting systems of this type is made up of a number of integrated computing domains:

- Cognitive Mapping Mechanisms: Advanced neural network configurations that dynamically model individual cognitive structures, identifying intricate learning patterns, potential knowledge gaps, and optimal intervention strategies.
- Adaptive Content Generation Systems: Intelligent algorithmic frameworks capable of dynamically generating educational content that responds in real-time to individual learner performance, psychological state, and cognitive engagement levels.
- Predictive Performance Analytics: Analyzes advanced statistical models through deep histories of learning data to predict where a learner may struggle, provide tailored recommendations, and refine individual learning paths.

3.3 Technological Architectural Complexity

Architectural complexity of new AI-powered personalized learning technology systems cannot be reduced to simplistic technological simplification and are complex cognitive prosthetics intervening in the educational experience through complex algorithmic interactions (Hamid et al., 2022). Most broadly speaking, the core technological base typically encompasses:

- Multi-modal Data Integration Frameworks: The ability to integrate different streams of data such as physiological measures, behavioral signals, cognitive performance indices, and contextual environmental variables.
- Real-time Adaptive Recommendation Engines: Algorithmic systems that refine educational pathways on real-time performance feedback and overall learner profile analysis.

- Contextual Inference Mechanisms: An advanced computational model that can sense and respond to contextual subtleties that affect an individual's learning.

3.4 Evolutionary Trajectories and Technological Horizons

The prospective evolutionary landscape of personalized learning technologies suggests increasingly sophisticated human-machine cognitive collaborations (Matinizadeh et al., 2024). Emerging research trajectories indicate potential developments including:

- Neuromorphic Computing Approaches: Computational architectures explicitly designed to mimic human neurological processing mechanisms, enabling more intuitive and contextually responsive learning interactions.
- Emotional Intelligence Algorithmic Models: Advanced machine learning frameworks capable of comprehending and responding to learner emotional states, thereby creating more empathetic educational experiences.
- Quantum Machine Learning Paradigms: High-performance computational methodologies, exploiting the principles of quantum computation to forge new capabilities in cognitive modeling.

3.5 Epistemological and Philosophical Implications

The technological development of personalized learning systems requires deep philosophical questioning. The technologies relate not only to computer tools, but, as emergent cognitive ecosystems, ground fundamentally the existing bounds of epistemology. They problematize the classical distinctions between human and machine intelligence, indicating increasingly porous boundaries between technological mediation and authentic cognitive experience. Thus, the philosophical discussion does necessarily have to grasp some central questions regarding the nature of intelligence, learning, and technological agency (Fatima et al., 2023).

In the coming sections, we will continue to unpack these complex technological, ethical, and philosophical dimensions, leading to a rich and comprehensive scholarly study of this transformative technological domain.

4.0 ETHICAL FRAMEWORKS AND CONCEPTUAL LANDSCAPES

The articulation of ethical frameworks in connection to artificial intelligence and personalized learning itself signifies a most sophisticated intellectual exercise that calls for an interdisciplinary, comprehensive examination (Hamid et al., 2020). The ethical terrain below has been carefully deconstructed: plausible philosophical, sociological, and technological complex issues inherent in today's forms of AI-driven educational technologies.

4.1 Philosophical Foundations of Ethical Considerations

This more complex intellectual genealogy underpins the philosophical underpinnings of ethical deliberations in personalized learning technologies. It travels and crosses epistemological domain not one or two but multi-epistemological domains (Ahmad & Whitworth, 2012). The classical humanistic conceptions of agency and autonomy, as well as the rationalistic approach to burning ethical questions using the means of practical reason have remained the staples of traditional technological discourse all along. But with the advent of high-end AI systems one has to start from philosophically defining these constructs from the scratch.

Modern ethical frameworks have to wrestle with the basic ontological challenge that artificial intelligence raises: the emergence of technology systems with higher and higher cognitive abilities, which extend the features of the lowest human and mechanical intellect (Zeshan et al., 2019). This epistemic disruption stands in a problematic relation to the old philosophical modes, that means scholars are forced to invent more nuanced distinctions, concepts classes and forms which would cover this complicated engagement between the human minding and the algorithming.

Philosophical discussions on AI in personalized learning necessarily bring to mind a number of critical conceptual dimensions:

- Epistemological Sovereignty: The identities of those who produce and authenticate knowledge within our technology enhanced learning spaces. What is the epistemological reach that such algorithmic systems can produce representations of authoritative knowledge? In what way are those insights best communicated through the language that machine learning and artificial intelligence use and in what way are those insights best formulated within traditional scholarly epistemologies?
- Phenomenological Experience: The multifaceted examination of self-perceived learning processes obtained from learners immersed in technologically mediated environments. To what extent do the application of AI-

Personal Learning systems transform the phenomenological experience of education?

- Ethical Subjectivity: The complex negotiation of moral agency as advanced algorithmic systems increasingly feature in the sphere of educational decisions. What forms of ethical behavior obtain within contexts where technological systems increasingly exhibit sophisticated cognitive capability?

4.2 Normative Ethical Theoretical Frameworks

Several normative ethical theoretical frameworks provide critical perspectives on analysis through AI-driven personalized learning technologies (Bose, 2012). Each theoretical approach allows for precise and independent insights into the complexities of the moral terrain of technological intervention into educational processes.

Based in the utilitarian philosophical traditions, consequential approaches consider the ethical legitimacy of AI technologies based on aggregate outcomes. These frameworks focus on assessments of overall social benefit, educational efficacy, and potential transformative impacts on learning ecosystems.

From this consequentialist perspective, AI-based adaptive learning technologies shall be pertinent in their capacity to:

- Democratize educational accessibility
- Optimize individual learning paths
- Reduce systemic forms of educational inequality
- Increase overall educational productivity and efficiency

Emerging out of Aristotle philosophy, virtue ethics focuses on the formation of moral character and the development of ethical dispositions. When adopted to approach the concept of Artificial Intelligence driven personalized learning this endeavour questions the nature and development of moral and intellectual virtues through the lens of technology systems. Virtue ethics perspectives would explore:

- Applications of AI technologies to foster intellectual virtues
- A role of technological systems within the acquisition of ethical reasoning competencies
- Preservation of human judgment and critical reflection

4.3 Complexity of Ethical Decision-Making Architectures

Ethical decision-making architectures where AI driven personalised learning technologies exist is therefore a highly complex computational and philosophical systems (Ahmad et al., 2019). It is not the simple patterns of algorithmic processing but the complex cognitive intermediary processes that strongly reshape educational experiences. The complexity revolves around a multiplicity of interacting domains:

- Algorithmic Moral Reasoning: Realizing consistent concepts of ethic in the decision-making process and the creation of computational designs with the capability to integrate such considerations. It is truly an architectural problem of a deeply philosophical nature that rises well beyond typical computational theories.
- Contextual Ethical Sensitivity: The ability of the AI systems for perception and reaction to the ethical context, in details, of cultural, psychological, and individual approaches to educational processes.
- Dynamic Ethical Redefinition: The capability of technological systems to constantly reassert mechanisms of their ethical judgment through continuous learning and adaptation.

4.4 New Ethics Paradigms

The constant evolution of new artificial intelligence enabled learning technologies means that it has to invent new paradigms of ethics constantly (Gülcan, 2015). While the narrow, traditional paradigms look quite reasonable on the intellectual level, they, as a rule, are unable to operate within new and further complexity generated by sophisticated technological systems. New paradigms of ethics must be delineated with:

- Flexibility and adaptability
- Interdisciplinarity
- Intrinsic appraisal of technological systems as alive ethical agents
- Preservation of purely human values
- Mature cognitive comprehension of technological complexity

4.5 Interdisciplinary Ethical Synthesis

In AI on personalized learning, ethics is most effectively done with references to a lot of scholarly disciplines and branches. Epistemology, computing, psychology, sociology, and educational theories should work to elicit large ethical paradigms sufficiently to address the technological terrain. This kind of synthesis constitutes an interdisciplinary one that implies a linking of two or more disciplines.

- Collaborative research methodologies
- Shared conceptual vocabularies
- Mutual intellectual respect across disciplinary boundaries
- Commitment to holistic understanding
- Openness to radical conceptual reimaginations

The ethical analysis of AI-based adaptive learning systems exhibits a highly complex intellectual landscape. The existing traditional theoretical models do not become irrelevant but have to be reinterpreted and updated more often and, occasionally, on a grander scale, given the presence of this currently inexorable new technological change that is emerging in modern learning environments.

5.0 PRIVACY CONSIDERATIONS AND DATA GOVERNANCE

This is a very strong academically driven and complex discussion about privacy in personalized learning technologies, how to introduce a notion of info protection and how to challenge their approaches. AI systems are gradually entering the learning ecosystems but the lines between the individual data, institutional knowledge, and artificial intelligence are increasingly blurred and nuanced. Privacy, in this sense of technology advancement, becomes a construct complexes much more than just the security of data (Zeshan et al., 2024). They stand for very intricate claims toward citizen rights and enforcement and activeness on the part of technologies.

For this foundation of privacy philosophy in AI-based educational environments necessarily entails a radical dismantling of conventional epistemological paradigms. Thus, the most fundamental challenges to privacy arising from personalized learning technologies express themselves across a multitude of interconnected domains:

- The foundational privacy right of learners to exercise a degree of control over personal data in different technologically supported learning environments. This is much higher than mere preservation of information, it poses a whole lot of issues regarding cognition and information, agency.
- The protection of individual psychological boundaries in contexts where sophisticated algorithmic systems possess increasingly nuanced capabilities for cognitive and emotional profiling.

- The protection of contextually appropriate information flows respectful of the complexity of the social and individual dynamics inherent in educational interactions.

5.1 Technological Architectures of Data Collection and Management

To put it simply, the technical underpinnings of collecting data in Personal Learning Environments are absurdly intricate computational environments (Bebell et al., 2010). They are not just data accumulation tools but are systems that can provide detailed penetrating insights into cognition, learning, or personality. Modern data collection architectures typically incorporate several of the areas listed above:

- Multimodal Data Integration Frameworks: Sophisticated computational systems that synthesize various data streams including:
    - Explicit learning performance metrics
    - Physiological engagement indicators
    - Behavioral interaction patterns
    - Cognitive processing characteristics
    - Emotional engagement markers
- Adaptive Inference Mechanisms: Algorithmic frameworks that dynamically produce sophisticated learner profiles through continuous data analysis and contextual interpretation. It is not only a system of collecting data but also the building of complex representations of cognitive landscapes individual people have.
- Predictive Analytical Capabilities: those models related to learning trajectory, psychological states, and individual development by intensive use of historical data to predict possible trajectories.

5.2 Ethical Considerations in Data Governance

The principles of DL lead to inevitably phenomenally complex data governance problems and implementations that present extremely high-order ethical issues in personalized learning technologies. Generally, traditional types of regulation practices are utterly irrelevant in the context of new unprecedented technological competence which defines the networks in AI based educational systems (Whitworth et al., 2012). Some of the key ethical considerations of data governance include:

- Informed Consent Paradigms: The fundamental challenge of obtaining meaningful consent in technological environments characterized by unprecedented complexity and algorithmic opacity.
- Data Ownership and Sovereignty: The deep questions of philosophy and law relating to individual rights over personal data created by technology. At what point do learners retain ownership over the cognitive profiles formed by advanced algorithmic systems?
- Algorithmic Transparency: The requirement to create computational methods that can make complex algorithmic decision-making accessible to human understanding.

5.3 Philosophical Regulatory Frameworks

It is therefore imperative that future education research and education legislation which supports and accommodates the AI innovative endeavours come hand-in-hand with sophisticated philosophies that the future AI-based educational technologies will present (Ahmad et al., 2012). The incumbent concepts of legal and regulation are incompletely sufficient and generally irrelevant to comprehend the innovative technologies that are present in the modern learning ecosystem of personalized learning. Emerging regulatory philosophical approaches must be founded on the following:

- Dynamic adaptability
- Comprehensive technological understanding
- Preservation of basic human rights
- Recognition of technological systems as active participants in educational ecosystems

5.4 Psychological and Sociological Dimensions of Privacy

Privacy in personalized learning technologies is one of the most extensive psychological and sociological concerns that cannot be solved through technology and legal means (Sarfraz et al., 2024). New technologies alter the very nature of educational practice – personal and social simultaneously – in with reference to cognition, learning, and identity.

Some complex implications arise in regard to psychology:

- Consequences on psychological aspects through persistent algorithmic monitoring
- Change in personal perception of an individual's cognitive space

- Manipulation of private boundaries in technologically mediated learning contexts

Sociological analyses uncover broader systemic implications:

- Reconfiguration of the power dynamics within institutional education
- Transformation of social learning interactions
- Emergence of new forms of technological social regulation

5.5 Technological Mitigation Strategies

Privacy threats demand complex technological and philosophical approaches to mitigation that cannot be rectified by conceiving of privacy protection solely in terms of barriers in the conventional sense (Muhammad & Ahmad, 2021). As such as dynamic frameworks that fit the interactions between technology and value, they have to be thought of appropriately.

Among other measures: Highly secure encryption technologies; Processes of anonymization; Precise, decentralized, personally-controlled private spheres; Evident algorithmic structures of decision making; Ongoing, system-wide recalibration of moral questions. Here, the discussion of privacy in the scope of AI incorporated into personal learning technology extends one into an academically very rich area. Privacy is no longer envisaged as an isolated 'shield,' but as a constantly constructed and forced border of human and technological relations.

6.0 ALGORITHMIC BIAS AND FAIRNESS IN EDUCATIONAL CONTEXTS

This remains a very complex analysis of bias in learning algorithms within personalized learning technology, a task that calls for a keen scrutiny of multiple levels of interdisciplinary contexts. The discussion of algorithmic fairness goes beyond mere calculations to fruitful areas of philosophical, sociological, and epistemological contexts that further unravel underlying foundational questions regarding educational fairness and technological interactions.

6.1 Ontological Foundations of Algorithmic Bias

Algorithmic bias is not just a set of funny results-This is a very profound ontological categories resulting from interactions of affects between a combination of machinistic, socio-historical, and evolutionary cognitive phenomena. It becomes increasingly difficult to think of algorithmic systems independently of the more trenchant topics in socio-culture because it appears that the latter provides the formative layers upon which their parameters are drawn (Hamid et al., 2019).

Underlying structures of containment are thereby reproduced in contemporary technological ecosystems, which carry with them structural histories that shape even the most subtle and ubiquitous computations effected by digital technologies. algorithmic representations of educational potential therefore emerge as arenas of performative power struggles where historical and subsequent exclusions are reworked through technology as technology.

The underlying criticism of algorithmic bias is best understood through an appreciation of how technological systems encode and reintroduce multi-layered social structures into computerised algorithms. Machine learning algorithms are not simply executively performing functions on data; they are building rich, complex hierarchies of educational possibility wholly imbricated with normative constructs of capability, achievement, and potentiality.

6.2 Epistemological Dimensions of Technological Fairness

This is the case with the conceptualization of fairness within AI-driven personalized learning technologies because that requires reimagining traditional knowledge paradigms from scratch. Variability of ethnodemographic fairness should not be considered as a mathematics problem-solving element but rather as a context-dependant work in progress for stable and temporary technological and societal re-design (Ahmad et al., 2020).

Higher-level procedural fairness must address several distinct yet mutually intertwined systems, primarily the technological infrastructure, the social environment, differences in individual psychological response, and power relations at the systems level.

The epistemological challenge arises from the intrinsic complexity of capturing human cognitive potential by algorithmic infrastructures. Machine learning systems lead to reductive representations that inherently cannot capture the profound complexity of individual learning trajectories and psychological dispositions and the intricacies of contextual environments for learning.

6.3 Technological Mechanisms of Bias Generation

Algorithmic systems reproduce and possibly accentuate prevailing social inequalities by mechanisms that are extremely subtle and occasionally invisible (Samreen et al., 2020a). Training data becomes a place of potential bias reproduction, whereby the historical inequalities in education are unintentionally encoded into computational models.

Machine-learning algorithms develop far more sophisticated pattern recognition capabilities than any explicit programmatic instruction by building complex relational patterns into themselves from within training datasets with the subtle mechanisms for possible reenactment of even the worst mechanisms for producing historical educational marginalization.

Predictive modeling approaches that seek to predict individual educational potential typically are based on historical performance data that already reflect profound systemic inequities. Algorithmic systems thus become powerful mechanisms for naturalizing and reproducing existing social hierarchies under the guise of computational objectivity.

6.4 Psychological and Sociological Implications

The psychological implications of algorithmic bias extend to profound levels of cognitive self-conception and broader social conceptions of identity. At the point where technical systems generate predictive representations of educational potential, they are, at core, participating in complex identity-formation and social-categorizing processes (Khalil et al., 2021).

Such technological representations adopted by the learners in algorithmically defined tracks of education can, perhaps, give rise to massive self-fulfilling prophetic effects; cumulative positioning in specific algorithmic categories can certainly transform learner's desired terrains and orientations, or ways of understanding themselves.

6.5 Mitigation Strategies and Ethical Frameworks

This means that dealing with algorithmic bias calls for multiple disciplines, far beyond simple computational fixes. They require more elaborate theoretical paradigms that can account for the underlying nature of all the technologies as agents involved in construction of social meanings.

These emergent strategies subsume critical reflexivity and entail the view of technological systems as fluid architectures of intensity and eternal ethical recalibration (Phillips, 2014). To do that, it is necessary to elaborate proper computational approaches cognizant of the constraints of algorithmic models while simultaneously posing relevant epistemological questions to their parameters for functioning.

Instead of a focus of more traditional punitive methods of managing 'problem' students, interdisciplinary cooperation turns into a method in its own right, employing methodologies from computer programming, critical theory, sociology, psychology, and education research. Such an intersubjective perspective about technology may contribute in forging more refinanced technological formations in terms of the initial attend for the multifaceted social systems in which they function.

The critical review of algorithmic bias reveals its profundity-its utmost possibility-for technological mediation in the educational context: It can never be achieved through some easy readjustment of computations but rather foundational change that calls for reimaginings of the technological platform, the social formation and epistemological systems.

7.0 PSYCHOLOGICAL AND SOCIOLOGICAL IMPLICATIONS OF AI-DRIVEN PERSONALIZED LEARNING

Technologically mediated, artificially intelligent learning experiences are a kind of complex psychological and social phenomenon that require analyzing in phenomenally complex terms that span several fields of study. Sophisticated intelligent learning systems alter the very ontological narrative in relation to cognitive human formation, social relations and instituted learning systems-all beyond mere technological mediation.

7.1 Transformation of the Learning Experience: Psychological Changes

The psychological consequences of the academically mediated technologically supported learning contexts can thus be seen as an epistemological break in the most basic sense of opening up a chasm in the traditional understanding of cognitive development. Far from being delivery systems that provide educational content, artificial systems are agents interacting in highly sophisticated psychological processes. Hence, they challenge the conventional received wisdom concerning subjectivity and cognitive personhood, on the one hand, as well as developmental process, on the other (Ormrod, Anderman, & Anderman, 2023).

It might be summed up that modern psychological research really contributes to the elaboration of very subtle distinctions regarding individual learning experience in technological environments. The old style of learning could basically be linear and totally dependent on the tutor while in the new style of learning you have to deal with a much more complicated cognitive environment where the systems have become advanced cognitive extensions really acting as external limbs/processors.

It is important to understand that this psychological engagement with AI and personalized learning technologies is viewed through many, lensed facets. The learners, thus, change their cognitive self-views at some ultimate, personal level, acquiring advanced levels of metacognitive skills corresponding to fruitful and revolving interactions with adaptive technologies. Such relations produce the feedback loops of emergent communication and individual cognition within which mediating technology constitutes the negotiating factor.

In this chapter, cognitive psychology concepts provide insights to the significant psychological changes brought about by personalized learning technologies. The main previous psychological models of learning had postulated cognition as a mostly linear and variance process that occurred within distinct phases and was mainly enacted communally through adult human interactions. Modern technological environments in particular radically undermine these paradigms by describing learning as an open, constantly changing cognitive environment.

Motivational psychology reveals highly interesting aspects of the technological interplay. Motivational architectures are developed in the environments of artificial intelligence with continuous individual responses. The external motivators that used to organize teaching contents and activities are broadened and replaced by new and more individual motivational processes; the computer is conceived as an intelligent interaction partner.

7.2 Sociological Reconfiguration of Educational Institutions

From a sociological perspective, then it is clear that instantiations of AI – and technologies of learning – represent a form of institutional change much deeper than mere technology. They in fact thwarted the previous power, institutional relationships and mechanisms of social interaction in the educational ecosystems. For ages education has been passed through system of top down knowledge delivery structures that have fixed points of instructional authority. Technological interventions in the present age come with their lots of extraordinary highly distributed learning structures where knowledge creation a truly negotiated affair characterised by rich human/technology interactions (Ballantine, Stuber, & Everitt, 2021).

These sociological consequences are bilateral and reciprocal in many ways and are interconnected with respect to several domains. Power relations at the institution level change dramatically because technology systems assume more proactive qualities in educational decision-making processes. The relation between human instructors and other technologies always has been embedded in this tension and destabilises and opens up new forms of institutional agency.

In other words, these patterns of social interaction within educational environments are changed fundamentally. The learning technologies imply a degree of individualization which is unprecedented and hardwired in the collective learning paradigms which already exist. As we have also seen, learning's social character is simultaneously more individualized and more webscale and linked in very dense fresh social learning formations.

Relations between genders and their socioeconomic status become essential sociological factors. Technologies might either neutralize or even perpetuate preexisting social disparities. The actualization and implementation of educational technologies that are based on AI as such, therefore become significant terrains where social power relations are particularized and reworked to some extent.

7.3 Psychological Development in Technologically Mediated Environments

Last but not the least; the psychological development of individuals in AI-driven learning environment is a very complex and multifaceted concept that poses enormous research question, a challenge to the classical developmental psychology discourses. Technological systems intervene in processes of cognitive and emotional personality development, and thus form new developmental environments.

An emergent concept for understanding psychological development in the technological context, cognitive plasticity allows learners to develop increasingly more complex capabilities in cognition through continuous interaction with adaptive technological systems. Interactions facilitate the growing complexity of metacognitive skills, including improved pattern recognition, adaptive problem-solving, and sophisticated information-processing capacities.

Emotional and social development becomes increasingly mediated through technological interactions. Systems of artificial intelligence that present complex emotional recognition and responsive engagement constitute new forms of developmental environments beyond any traditional human-mediated social learning experiences.

7.4 Ethical and Psychological Boundary Negotiations

The human psychological systems have no option but to have a constant dialogue with artificial intelligence technologies on the proper ethical and psychological functionalities. In order to master the proposed curricula and use technologies for learning, learners will have to constantly adapt to and learn the changing psychological landscapes where technological systems are primarily technology for learning, secondly cognitive partners, and finally possible psychic mediation.

Academic discourse is concerned more and more with the interior psychological dynamics of technological closeness. The growing use of complex psychological interactions between learners and the technology they employ challenges us to rethink the way in which such interaction can be defined as 'technologically instrumental'.

The deep investigation into psychological and sociological factors uncovers the vast complexity of personalized learning technologies and AI: albeit not a clean technological interventional model but another system that could be described as a human-technology synergy, co-evolution system.

8.0 REGULATORY APPROACHES AND POLICY RECOMMENDATIONS

The regulation of artificial intelligence in personalised learning technologies is one of the most difficult forms of regulation that demands sophisticated measures of policy crossways all fields. AI systemised learning environments introduce novel technological opportunities but very profound social consequences at variance with classic forms of regulation.

8.1 Philosophical Grounds of Technological Governance

This provides even more philosophical supports to the regulatory models for AI in educational technologies, going well beyond merely legislative means. Not surprisingly, these frameworks are forced to grapple with the most basic ontological concerns regarding the nature of technological agency, institutional accountability, and universal human rights in increasingly vast and intricate technological milieux (Von Schomberg & Blok, 2021).

As such, developing a rich conceptual architecture of contemporary regulatory philosophy does pose an enormous challenge to regard artificial intelligence systems as active participants within the processes of educational and social meaning-making. This entails a complete overhaul with the hitherto concepts of regulation where systems are technology Open Links with outside authority having full control over them as being passive receivers of direction.

These are fundamental philosophical questions in the following interrelated domains: How can regulatory frameworks have a sense of ownership over what approaches and methods will effectively regulate technological systems that are reciprocating more complex cognitive abilities?

8.2 International Regulatory Landscape

This is such a complex geopolitical strategy that an international regulatory approach of the AI personalized learning technologies shows. National and regional environments create qualitatively different approaches that are based on different cultural, philosophical, and technological perceptions of educational change and technological regulation.

European frameworks of regulation generally center on general data protection and the rights of an individual to privacy. The General Data Protection Regulation is possibly one of the most complex attempts at bolstering individual informational sovereignty, on par with the sophistication of core protective systems. These anti-gammon primary objectives here are the following: explicit consent mechanism, transparent algorithmic decision-making, rights together with individual information data.

The regulatory approaches in North America are relatively innovation-oriented, where technology advancement benefits are compared to moderate preventative risks. While the regulatory discourse is focused on technologies, it also builds up more and more refined ethical supervisory bodies at the same time.

As for Asian countries, and using Singapore and Japan as prime examples, approaches to technological governance appear to be thought through with much greater incorporation of systems thinking about technology as an element of the national strategic resource. Such frameworks bears high sophisticity for the purposes of coupling elements of technological advancement towards more wider societal concerns in development.

8.3 Challenges in Technological Governance

When looking at Artificially Intelligent personalised learning technologies, the regulatory issues are far from any traditional methods of technology regulation. These complex adaptive systems are dynamic; it is possible to ask problematic questions to standard notions of regulation here. Some of the important governance challenges are outlined below:

- Algorithmic Transparency: Building the appropriate regulations in order to be able to effectively scrutinize more sophisticated algorithms to make decisions. Ineffective and insufficient in terms of the profound computational nature of most Machine Learning systems, traditional views of transparency are exposed as inherently inadequate.
- Ethical Accountability: Developing robust mechanisms of accountability most likely to help achieve robust ascriptions of responsibilities in the technological ecosystems with a distributed cognitive agency. On a basic level, classical legal constructions of individual and institutional responsibility get simply problematized.
- Dynamic Regulatory Adaptation: Creating more flexible legal frameworks that proliferate along the higher kinetics of the growing technologies.

Depending on static measures, the legislative principles are powerless to respond to unprecedented rates of innovative change in new technologies.

8.4 Holistic Policy Recommendation Frameworks

The policy approaches to governance of technology require complex, multi-faceted nuanced policies with deep knowledge of AI based educational technologies of the kind described above. It is thus correct to claim that a suitable framework for this process should address technological, ethical, social, as well as institutional factors. Comprehensive policy approaches recommended include:

- Comprehensive Ethical Assessment Mechanisms: Establishing effective institutional conditions for the further constant ethical consideration of the application of AI based learning tools. These mechanisms have to move from the simple checklists or ethical scorecards to creating complex smart ethical analysis.
- Interdisciplinary Governance Frameworks: This design should apply institutional governance structures which use knowledge from other fields of study.
- Adaptive Regulation Infrastructure: Establishing adaptive regulatory frameworks which reflect flexibility in responding to changes brought about by technological advance. New ways of regulation should be very much inclined to seeing governance as a dynamic, evolving process, rather than a fixed set of rules.

8.5 Technological Rights and Personal Protections

A more comprehensive framework of technological rights needs to be developed as a key policy imperative, ensuring solid protections for individuals' cognitive and informational sovereignty in the emerging complex technological ecosystems. Some critical rights aspects will include:

- Meaningful consent mechanisms
- Comprehensive data protection protocols
- Explicit requirements for algorithmic transparency
- Right of technology to explanation for individuals
- Protection against discriminatory algorithmic decision-making

8.6 International Collaborative Governance

The global complexity of AI-driven technologies demands advanced approaches to international collaborative governance. No national regulatory framework alone can tackle the unprecedented level of technological challenge posed by advanced artificial systems. International collaborative approaches should develop:

- Shared philosophical frameworks for technological governance;
- Mechanisms for comprehensive knowledge exchange;
- Coordinate regulated developments; and
- Mutual protocols for technological assessment

The scrutiny of regulatory approaches, however, does reveal the significant depth of complexity in governing AI-driven personalized learning technologies. All effective technological governance demands a radical reimagining of regulatory philosophies, transcending the control regimes to build out complex and adaptive regimes of governance.

9.0 FUTURE TRAJECTORIES AND EMERGING CHALLENGES IN ARTIFICIAL INTELLIGENCE AND PERSONALIZED LEARNING

The future landscape of AI in personal learning is a profound technological frontier that calls for rigorous scholarly analysis. We're no longer talking about incremental technological advance; this represents a fundamental shift in human cognitive development, educational epistemologies, and paradigms of interaction in the presence of technology.

9.1 Emerging Technological Convergence

The future of personalised learning technologies seems as extraordinary technological synergy where multiple advanced computational disciplines come together to form exceptional education environments. Technological advances, including artificial intelligence, neuroscience, quantum computing and extremely sophisticated cognitive modelling is increasingly giving rise to complex technical systems, which in their own right are beginning to pose epistemological and ontological questions about learning, intelligence and human cognitive capability.

Some sub types of systemic computing architectures are very interesting, namely neuromorphic computing architectures. Intended to emulate the neuro-mechanisms that underlie human learning, these mathematical procedures are capable of constructing learning technologies that surpass the current norms of performance. Fundamentally different from conventional mathematical systems that place data into linear algorithmic systems, neuromorphic systems offer a capacity to learn, which does not emulate human nerves in terms of plasticity.

Here, new computational procedures are added to quantum machine learning that might revolutionize the learning capability of the technology. Quantum computing introduces mathematical graphs where more than one state is performed at the same time to ease the learning systems' tasks of processing cognitive data.

9.2 Predictive Cognitive Modeling

Decision predictive modeling is one of the applications that will define the future of the learner centered model. Where as it rises to centre of excellence that comes up with more detailed working profiles that are so accurate in estimating human intelligence.

The declared possibilities were noted to overpass possibilities of traditional educational assessment techniques. It can produce demanding estimates of a man's IQ, differentiate learners on potential, recognize the signs of developmental disorders, and design accommodative systems that take short time to adjust to small changes that accompany relatively fast changes in capability.

Such predictive models play a critical role of creating a comprehensive ethical appreciation of the technological applications of intelligence. Indeed, at the detriment of volition, decision aversion theory makes it a core problem that algorithmic representations thereby reduce thoughts and openings for becoming.

9.3 Emotional Intelligence and Technological Mediation

The merging of smart intelligence with personalized learning technologies maybe one of the most promising technological trends in education. AI based newcomers are proving great potential for emotion detection, understanding contextual cues, and providing intervention, which is transforming learning technology interactions greatly.

These systems progress from Algorithmic interactions towards establishing technology partners capable of offering intelligent learning support. The opportunity for learning technologies to identify a learner's emotional state, offer emotional feedback, and, based on the learner's subjective emotional state, manage the process of learning.

Heavy philosophical connotations are also a given. Technology is embedded in a continuous process of meaning making in the form of interrelated technologies and so disrupts the notion of technology as a way of communication. The separation between technologies and knowledge partners is increasingly dialectical and convoluted.

9.4 Educational Transformation of Global Proportions

Global educational change is possible, especially in the areas where they are most desperately needed if we embrace the personalized learning opportunities. Technology can also offer free online education which is a school and home at the same time.

Besides the convenience of the content delivery, the effect of this technology is international. These technologies envision an innovative learning environment that can benefit from Diversity, linguistics, and content knowledge. In a broader sense, it is followed by valid self-learning experiences in line with local cultures and experiences or may be opened up to.

But such flexible resources cannot arrive without corresponding difficulties. Technological colonialism is manifested in the case of sociotechnical systems where crucial technical advancements reproduce global disruption by designing other 'innocent' technologies.

9.5 Ethical and Philosophical Recalibration

The recent technological power of personalized learning technologies requires a redefinition of ethical and philosophical principles. The traditional epistemological boundaries between human knowledge and art are increasingly challenged, and new conceptual frameworks are needed. Philosophical discourse must be transformed into a more intellectual form that recognizes technological processes as active agents in the formation of mental processes, rather than as simple tools. In turn, new ideas about the most important concepts - as well as education, institutions, and educational experiences - are associated with major technological changes.

9.6 Technological Resilience and Adaptive Capacities

Future self-learning technologies must be designed with flexible capabilities and robust processes. The design of the computing industry should include a process that continues to question the boundaries of the mark, which is sensitive to the technological aspects of human cognitive abilities. It means developing technological infrastructure based on:

- Continuous ethical self-reflection
- Dynamic adaptive capabilities
- Comprehensive contextual sensitivity
- Explicitly acknowledged technological limitations

The vision of the future will reveal complex technological capabilities and self-learning. We stand at the threshold of a critical psychology where technological innovations promise to transform human intellectual development and the learning experience.

10.0 SYNTHESIZING TECHNOLOGICAL WISDOM: NAVIGATING THE COMPLEX LANDSCAPE OF AI IN PERSONALIZED LEARNING

The thorough scholarly deconstruction of artificial intelligence in personalized learning technologies uncovers an intellectual landscape that is, as a whole, staggeringly complex and resists simplistic technological or philosophical reductionism. Through multiple domains now connected and intersecting, our tour shows how these technologies represent much more than just computational objects; they form highly developed ecosystems of human-technological co-evolution that profoundly transform our understanding of cognitive development, educational experiences, and technological mediation.

10.1 Synthesizing Overall Insights

This multidimensional analysis, therefore, culminating in this study, again captures the depth of AI-Personalised learning technologies. Thus, instead of a conceptually rather innocent information technological interference with the socially and cognitively more or less challenging work of making meaning in and out of texts, the media reifications of meaning-making are advanced technological systems that operate as discursive and ideological estimates of Human Cognitive Capabilities, educational institutional practices and processes, and the dynamics of Society as a whole.

Through specific meticulous scholarly review, therefore, our study has an exploratory approach over several challenging cognitive terrains thus presenting important findings, which challenge conventional theories and tenets of epistemology. The technologies covered here are not just instructional aids; they are an environment that, year by year, redefines learning, cognition, and technology.

10.2 Philosophical and Ethical Dimensions

The social and philosophical concerns of using technologies to facilitate personalized learning are considerably beyond the mere technological. Such systems themselves pose radical questions to conventional colonial epistemology of human intelligence, human agency and human cognitive development. By requiring revolutionary overhauls to basic epistemological classifications, such systems are extending the traditional philosophic divisions between human and artificial intelligence.

Ethical issues are crucial areas of active research in places that are. The potential of these technologies to shape experience in education is obviously tied to the principles of profound ethical concern. Oil: How do we continue to allow for human engagement or persistence as technology continually becomes more intricate? Which interventions could yield technology that offered new potentials for people as opposed to mirroring constraints within current structures?

10.3 Technological Complexity and Human Potential

It could be argued that no other area of current educational technology development has such staggering potential as well as posing philosophical issues as deep and multifaceted as the AI-based personalization of learning. These systems illustrate cognitive learning adaptive features that are dramatically more advanced than conventional learning systems; promoting personalized learning that can alter on the basis of the cognitive and biological characteristics of the patient.

But this power may not occur without human, rational, and intensely moral requests. As such, they can only be built in reference to an encompassing paradigm that honors the dignity of the person, the autonomy of the subject, and the growth of genuine knowledge. Technological advancements therefore cannot, and should not be pursued in complete independence from the rest of the human and societal fabric.

10.4 Interdisciplinary Collaborative Approaches

AI educational technologies are complex and need interdisciplinary intervention, the likes of which has not been seen before. None of the educational scientifics can comprehend these multifaceted technological systems. To fund and advance technology, scientific discussions with and among computer scientists, philosophers, psychologists, sociologists, and educational and ethical researchers are required.

Thus an intellectual community with a unifying focus needs a shared language of conceptual distinctions, recognition of the intellect and the drive for integrated understandings which ignore boundaries of disciplines. The deepest of technological interchanges will therefore occur at the behavioral level between disciplines.

10.5 Adaptive Technological Governance

The account of rule making to AI operated personalized learning technologies will need a governing style that is procedural and reactive to rapid technological development. Static legal systems are basically inadequate to address technologies that experience a level of change that is so innovative.

Technology governance can be defined as a continuous and collaborative activity of practical reasoning on what is ethically right and wrong. This entails developing a regulating structure that can be easily embedded within the contextual technological environment over which the infrastructure is established.

10.6 Global Transformative Potential

At its core, generalization AI technologies for personalized learning encompass a global change in educational systems not just as improvements from the prior level. They promise a democratization of modern education for which geographical or institutional location becomes inconsequential.

Now, such a capability is good to have, but it must be monitored very dilemma of sensitive. There is a serious danger of technological colonialism: dominant technologies can only reinforce prior injustices in a world of education with a neutral, not to say post, structure.

11.0 FINAL REMARKS

Through our educational journey, what we can conclude is that the future of AI in personalized education is not something concrete, but a process of joint talk about the possible of technological and philosophical. While these technologies enable us to extend human cognitive capabilities in spectacular ways, actualization of these technologies involves a deep moral commitment, a sustained responsibility for critical thinking, and a true dedication to human potential. We are at an extraordinary intellectual frontier where the technological innovation meets with some of our most fundamental human values. There is no need for artificial judgments pertaining to technology in the way ahead, but a differentiated and complex understanding of the relationships between human creativity and technological capacities. The Asking must not stop. It must be driven by a commitment to understanding, questioning, and intellectually shaping the technologies opening before us.

REFERENCES

Ahmad, A., Alzahrani, A. S., Ahmed, N., & Ahsan, T. (2020). A delegation model for SDN-driven federated cloud. *Alexandria Engineering Journal*, *59*(5), 3653–3663. DOI: 10.1016/j.aej.2020.06.018

Ahmad, A., & Whitworth, B. (2011, December). Access control taxonomy for social networks. In 2011 7th International Conference on Information Assurance and Security (IAS) (pp. 256-261). IEEE. DOI: 10.1109/ISIAS.2011.6122829

Ahmad, A., & Whitworth, B. (2012, January). Ethical Issues in Online Social Networks. In *2012 International Conference on Networks and Information (ICNI 2012).*

Ahmad, A., Whitworth, B., & Bertino, E. (2022). A framework for the application of socio-technical design methodology. *Ethics and Information Technology*, *24*(4), 46. DOI: 10.1007/s10676-022-09651-0

Ahmad, A., Whitworth, B., & Janczewski, L. (2012, June). More choices, more control: Extending access control by meta-rights reallocation. In 2012 IEEE 11th International Conference on Trust, Security and Privacy in Computing and Communications (pp. 1113-1118). IEEE.

Ahmad, A., Whitworth, B., Zeshan, F., Bertino, E., & Friedman, R. (2017). Extending social networks with delegation. *Computers & Security*, *70*, 546–564. DOI: 10.1016/j.cose.2017.07.010

Ahmad, A., Whitworth, B., Zeshan, F., Janczewski, L., Ali, M., Chaudary, M. H., & Friedman, R. (2019). A relation-aware multiparty access control. *Journal of Intelligent & Fuzzy Systems*, *37*(1), 227–239. DOI: 10.3233/JIFS-179080

Ahmad, A., Zeshan, F., Hamid, M., Marriam, R., & Samreen, A. (2022). Application of Gamification in Modern Education. In *Handbook of Research on Promoting Economic and Social Development Through Serious Games* (pp. 60–75). IGI Global. DOI: 10.4018/978-1-7998-9732-3.ch004

Ahmed, S., Javaid, S., Niazi, M. F., Alam, A., Ahmad, A., Baig, M. A., Khan, H. K., & Ahmed, T. (2019). A qualitative analysis of context-aware ubiquitous learning environments using Bluetooth beacons. *Technology, Pedagogy and Education*, *28*(1), 53–71. DOI: 10.1080/1475939X.2018.1557737

Ballantine, J., Stuber, J., & Everitt, J. (2021). *The sociology of education: A systematic analysis*. Routledge. DOI: 10.4324/9781003023715

Bandura, A. (1969). Social-learning theory of identificatory processes. Handbook of socialization theory and research, 213, 262.

Bebell, D., O'Dwyer, L. M., Russell, M., & Hoffmann, T. (2010). Concerns, considerations, and new ideas for data collection and research in educational technology studies. *Journal of Research on Technology in Education, 43*(1), 29–52. DOI: 10.1080/15391523.2010.10782560

Bilal, A., Mirza, H. T., Hussain, I., & Ahmad, A. (2024). Investigating Influence of Google-Play Application Titles on Success. *Big Data Research, 36*, 100443. DOI: 10.1016/j.bdr.2024.100443

Bond, M., Buntins, K., Bedenlier, S., Zawacki-Richter, O., & Kerres, M. (2020). Mapping research in student engagement and educational technology in higher education: A systematic evidence map. *International Journal of Educational Technology in Higher Education, 17*(1), 1–30. DOI: 10.1186/s41239-019-0176-8

Bose, U. (2012). An ethical framework in information systems decision making using normative theories of business ethics. *Ethics and Information Technology, 14*(1), 17–26. DOI: 10.1007/s10676-011-9283-5

Callimaci, A., & Fortin, A. (2022). Intended use of educational technology after the COVID-19 pandemic. *Journal of Further and Higher Education, 46*(10), 1362–1376. DOI: 10.1080/0309877X.2022.2079970

Chen, X., Zou, D., Cheng, G., & Xie, H. (2020). Detecting latent topics and trends in educational technologies over four decades using structural topic modeling: A retrospective of all volumes of Computers & Education. *Computers & Education, 151*, 103855. DOI: 10.1016/j.compedu.2020.103855

Ellinger, J., Mess, F., Bachner, J., von Au, J., & Mall, C. (2023). Changes in social interaction, social relatedness, and friendships in Education Outside the Classroom: A social network analysis. *Frontiers in Psychology, 14*, 1031693. DOI: 10.3389/fpsyg.2023.1031693 PMID: 36818094

Fatima, R., Zeshan, F., Ahmad, A., Hamid, M., Filali, I., Alhussan, A. A., & Abdallah, H. A. (2023). Requirement Change Prediction Model for Small Software Systems. *Computers, 12*(8), 164. DOI: 10.3390/computers12080164

Gülcan, N. Y. (2015). Discussing the importance of teaching ethics in education. *Procedia: Social and Behavioral Sciences, 174*, 2622–2625. DOI: 10.1016/j.sbspro.2015.01.942

Hamid, M., Ahmad, A., & Aimeur, E. (2019). Factors contributing in failures of software projects. *International Journal of Computer Science and Network Security*, *19*(5), 62–77.

Hamid, M., Zeshan, F., Ahmad, A., Malik, S., Saleem, M., Tabassum, N., & Qasim, M. (2022). Analysis of software success through structural equation modeling. *Intelligent Automation & Soft Computing*, *31*(3), 1689–1701. DOI: 10.32604/iasc.2022.020898

Hamid, M., Zeshan, F., Ahmad, A., Munawar, S., Aimeur, E., Ahmed, S., Abu Elsoud, M., & Yousif, M. (2020). An intelligent decision support system for effective handling of IT projects. *Journal of Intelligent & Fuzzy Systems*, *38*(3), 2635–2647. DOI: 10.3233/JIFS-179550

Holmes, W., & Tuomi, I. (2022). State of the art and practice in AI in education. *European Journal of Education*, *57*(4), 542–570. DOI: 10.1111/ejed.12533

Imran, M., & Ahmad, A. (2023). Enhancing data quality to mine credible patterns. *Journal of Information Science*, *49*(2), 544–564. DOI: 10.1177/01655515211013693

Khalil, U., Ahmad, A., Abdel-Aty, A. H., Elhoseny, M., El-Soud, M. W. A., & Zeshan, F. (2021). Identification of trusted IoT devices for secure delegation. *Computers & Electrical Engineering*, *90*, 106988. DOI: 10.1016/j.compeleceng.2021.106988

Khan, M. S., Ahmad, A., & Humayoun, M. (2022). Building an Effective Automated Assessment System for C/C++ Introductory Programming Courses in ODL Environment. arXiv preprint arXiv:2205.11915.

Matinizadeh, S., Mohammadhassani, A., Pacik-Nelson, N., Polykretis, I., Tishbi, K., Kumar, S., & Das, A. (2024, July). Neuromorphic computing for the masses. In *2024 International Conference on Neuromorphic Systems (ICONS)* (pp. 39-46). IEEE. DOI: 10.1109/ICONS62911.2024.00014

Morel, G. M., & Spector, J. M. (2022). *Foundations of educational technology: Integrative approaches and interdisciplinary perspectives*. Routledge.

Muhammad, T., & Ahmad, A. (2021). A joint sharing approach for online privacy preservation. *World Wide Web (Bussum)*, *24*(3), 895–924. DOI: 10.1007/s11280-021-00876-5

Munoko, I., Brown-Liburd, H. L., & Vasarhelyi, M. (2020). The ethical implications of using artificial intelligence in auditing. *Journal of Business Ethics*, *167*(2), 209–234. DOI: 10.1007/s10551-019-04407-1

Okewu, E., Adewole, P., Misra, S., Maskeliunas, R., & Damasevicius, R. (2021). Artificial neural networks for educational data mining in higher education: A systematic literature review. *Applied Artificial Intelligence*, *35*(13), 983–1021. DOI: 10.1080/08839514.2021.1922847

Ormrod, J. E., Anderman, E. M., & Anderman, L. H. (2023). Educational psychology: Developing learners. Pearson. One Lake Street, Upper Saddle River, New Jersey 07458.

Phillips, D. (2014). Policy borrowing in education: Frameworks for analysis. In *Second international handbook on globalisation, education and policy research* (pp. 137–148). Springer Netherlands.

Samreen, A., Ahmad, A., & Zeshan, F. (2020a, February). Searching for truth in the post-truth age. In 2020 3rd international conference on advancements in computational sciences (ICACS) (pp. 1-5). IEEE. DOI: 10.1109/ICACS47775.2020.9055948

Samreen, A., Ahmad, A., Zeshan, F., Ahmad, F., Ahmed, S., & Khan, Z. A. (2020b). A collaborative method for protecting teens against online predators over social networks: A behavioral analysis. *IEEE Access : Practical Innovations, Open Solutions*, *8*, 174375–174393. DOI: 10.1109/ACCESS.2020.3007141

Sarfraz, A., Ahmad, A., Zeshan, F., & Mirza, H. T. (2024). Synews: A synergy-based rumor verification system. *Social Network Analysis and Mining*, *14*(1), 57. DOI: 10.1007/s13278-024-01214-z

Siemens, G. (2004). Elearnspace. Connectivism: A learning theory for the digital age. Elearnspace. org, 14-16.

Von Schomberg, L., & Blok, V. (2021). Technology in the age of innovation: Responsible innovation as a new subdomain within the philosophy of technology. *Philosophy & Technology*, *34*(2), 309–323. DOI: 10.1007/s13347-019-00386-3

Voss, G. G. (2024). Benjamin S. Bloom: More than a Taxonomy. In *The Palgrave Handbook of Educational Thinkers* (pp. 1–19). Springer International Publishing. DOI: 10.1007/978-3-031-25134-4_77

Whitworth, B., & Ahmad, A. (2013a). Polite Computing. In *The Social Design of Technical Systems: Building technologies for communities* (pp. 77–105). The Interaction Design Foundation.

Whitworth, B., & Ahmad, A. (2013b). The evolution of computing. In *The Encyclopedia of human-computer interaction* (2nd ed.). Interaction Design Foundation., Retrieved from https://www.interaction-design.org/literature/book/the-encyclopedia-of-human-computerinteraction-2nd-ed/socio-technical-system-design

Whitworth, B., Janczewski, L., & Ahmad, A. (2012, July). A Logic of Creation in Online Social Networks. In *2012 World Congress in Computer Science, Computer Engineering and Applied Computing (WORLDCOMP 2012)*, Las Vegas, Nevada, USA.

Zeshan, F., Ahmad, A., Abdel-Aty, A. H., Algarni, F., Mahmoud, E. E., & Ahmad, A. (2020). A hybrid semantic knowledge integration and sharing approach for distributed smart environments. *Sensors (Basel)*, *20*(20), 5918. DOI: 10.3390/s20205918 PMID: 33092118

Zeshan, F., dar, Z., Ahmad, A., & Malik, T. (2024). A fuzzy ontology-based context-aware encryption approach in IoT through device and information classification. *The Journal of Supercomputing*, *80*(16), 23311–23356. DOI: 10.1007/s11227-024-06317-0

Zeshan, F., Mohamad, R., Ahmad, M. N., Othman, M. B., Elhag, A. A. M., Hussain, S. A., & Babar, I. (2019). Context-Aware ontology and web services discovery for distributed embedded real-time systems. *Malaysian Journal of Computer Science*, *32*(3), 186–208. DOI: 10.22452/mjcs.vol32no3.2

Chapter 11
Revolutionizing PE Harnessing the Power of Artificial Intelligence in Vietnamese Universities:
AI in PE Transforming Vietnamese Universities

Thuc Chanh Dao
https://orcid.org/0000-0002-2822-049X
An Giang University, Vietnam National University - Ho Chi Minh City, Vietnam

ABSTRACT

This chapter explores the transformative potential of artificial intelligence (AI) in revolutionizing physical education (PE) within Vietnamese universities. Recognizing universities as crucial spaces for holistic student development and PE as essential for physical and mental well-being, it advocates for the timely integration of AI technologies. The chapter critically examines the current state of PE in Vietnamese higher education and highlights opportunities for enhancement through AI-driven solutions. Key applications discussed include AI-powered diagnostics for personalized fitness assessments, comprehensive progress-tracking systems, and intelligent decision-making tools to optimize curriculum design. It also explores cutting-edge technologies such as intelligent guidance systems, automated evaluation systems, and educational sports robots. By promoting strategic pedagogical reforms and embracing AI, this chapter envisions a future where PE in Vietnamese universities becomes more effective and empowers students to reach their full potential.

DOI: 10.4018/979-8-3693-8744-3.ch011

INTRODUCTION

PE within the context of Vietnamese universities represents a crucial component of comprehensive education, aiming not only at physical development but also at fostering students' mental well-being and social skills (Vuong et al., 2018; To et al., 2019; To et al., 2020; Dau et al., 2020). In the higher education environment, PE encompasses diverse and significant roles. Firstly, traditional PE classes focus on teaching motor skills, physical knowledge, and promoting a healthy lifestyle. These classes not only enhance students' physical fitness but also provide them with foundational knowledge to maintain lifelong health (Zach et al., 2016; Meier, 2021).

Additionally, PE in universities serves the essential role of training future PE teachers. This involves equipping them with pedagogical skills and professional expertise to deliver PE instruction across educational levels, thereby contributing to the nationwide improvement of PE quality (Panganiban, 2019; Green, 2008). Furthermore, PE encompasses the organization and coaching of competitive sports, which serve not only as a platform for showcasing talent but also as a means to cultivate teamwork, leadership skills, and confidence among students (Krüger & Hofmann, 2015).

Significantly, PE in higher education transcends the traditional perception of being solely a physical activity discipline; it constitutes an integral part of holistic education for students. PE contributes to the development of learners' physical, mental, and social dimensions, enabling them to acquire essential life skills such as teamwork, problem-solving, and stress management (Diu & Thuc, 2024). Acting as a bridge between academic learning and practical application, PE fosters a balance between intellectual and physical growth, empowering students to excel academically while maintaining sustainable health and a positive mindset to overcome life's challenges.

The integration of PE into Vietnamese higher education, particularly when coupled with advanced technologies such as artificial intelligence, offers immense opportunities to enhance teaching efficacy and broaden access to diverse PE activities (Zhao & Ma, 2019) (Meier, 2021). In this context, redefining approaches to PE is not only an urgent necessity but also a strategic imperative for fostering sustainable and holistic educational development.

As technological advancements and the rapid evolution of AI continue, the integration of AI into various sectors has become a defining trend in modern society. Higher education, known for its essential role in shaping future talent and fostering societal development, is actively engaging with AI technologies to explore their potential applications. Within this framework, PE—a vital element of higher education—is both benefiting from and grappling with innovations and challenges brought by AI integration (Núñez et al., 2023; Wu-jun, 2022).

Traditionally, PE has been dependent on the expertise of instructors and the personal dedication of students (Liang et al., 2021). However, AI offers the potential to revolutionize PE in universities by enabling more efficient, personalized, and scientifically-grounded methods of instruction and training. For instance, data analytics and machine learning algorithms can be used to assess athletes' abilities with precision, paving the way for individualized training programs. Furthermore, virtual reality technology can immerse students in realistic training scenarios, enhancing their practical skills, while smart fitness devices can monitor their physical activities and provide real-time feedback, helping optimize movements and improve training outcomes (Kim et al., 2022).

Despite these potential benefits, integrating AI technology into PE at universities is met with various challenges and obstacles (Zhang & Yanqiong, 2022; Li-hua & Tang, 2022). Therefore, this study aims to explore the integration of AI technology into university-level PE, examining diverse approaches and applications. The objective is to provide insights into the potential of AI within PE, thereby offering valuable guidance for effectively harnessing AI in this field.

THE APPLICATION OF AI IN UNIVERSITY PE

The integration of AI into university-level PE has gained increasing attention in academic research. Several studies have examined the potential of AI to enhance student performance, particularly during the pandemic, and to boost student engagement in educational settings. However, the deployment of AI within educational institutions, especially at the university level, remains in its nascent stages, signaling that much progress is still needed in this field.

One of the most prominent applications of AI in university PE is in the evaluation and training of athletes (Wang, 2021; Wen, 2021; Guo & Li, 2021). Through sophisticated data analysis and machine learning algorithms, it is now possible to provide a detailed assessment of athletes' skills and performance, enabling the development of customized training programs (Liang et al., 2021). This individualized training approach has the potential to significantly improve the efficiency and effectiveness of athletic training, leading to enhanced student performance.

In addition to data analysis, virtual reality (VR) technology has also been adopted in PE programs, offering students immersive training environments that strengthen their practical skills (Cai-xia & Li-guo, 2020). Moreover, smart fitness devices can continuously track students' physical activities, delivering real-time feedback to help them fine-tune their movements and maximize the effectiveness of their workouts.

CHALLENGES AND OBSTACLES

While the integration of AI in university PE offers promising advancements, there are substantial challenges and barriers that must be addressed. One of the primary challenges lies in optimizing AI-based lectures, creating AI-driven curricula, institutionalizing these innovations, and achieving international recognition for such programs (Cruz et al., 2021). These areas have yet to be fully explored and demand extensive research and development to ensure AI's effective implementation in education.

Another critical challenge involves improving AI's ability to recognize images, perform automated exam validations, and adapt teaching methods based on student performance. These aspects are still in their infancy and require further investigation to achieve seamless integration into university PE.

Additionally, concerns related to privacy, bias, and the potential dehumanization of the learning process arise with the use of AI in educational environments (Núñez et al., 2023; Wen, 2021). AI systems often collect vast amounts of student data, raising the possibility of misuse or data breaches. Furthermore, there is a risk that AI algorithms could perpetuate societal biases, resulting in unequal educational outcomes.

Moreover, critics argue that AI could diminish the human element in education by shifting interactions away from human instructors to machines. This shift may result in a less engaging and less enriching educational experience for students (Ma & Jiang, 2023; Huang, 2023; Kamalov & Gurrib, 2023). Therefore, while AI presents numerous opportunities for innovation in university PE, these concerns highlight the need for a cautious and well-considered approach to its adoption.

To address these challenges and obstacles, it is crucial to critically evaluate the impact of AI on teaching and learning in the context of university PE.

ETHICAL AND PRIVACY CONCERNS IN AI INTEGRATION

Data Privacy in Student

As AI systems become integral to PE in universities, they often collect and analyze vast amounts of student data, including physical metrics, performance records, and even biometric information. While such data enable personalized training plans and feedback, they also raise significant concerns regarding data privacy. Unauthorized access or misuse of this sensitive data could lead to violations of student rights and potential harm, such as identity theft or discrimination (Huang, 2023). For instance, a breach in AI-powered platforms might expose students' medical histories or physical conditions, causing emotional distress and reputational damage. Therefore, universities must prioritize robust data protection measures, such as encryption and strict access protocols, to safeguard student information.

Risks of Algorithmic Bias

Another pressing issue is the risk of algorithmic bias embedded in AI systems used for PE. Bias in AI algorithms could arise from skewed training datasets or inherent limitations in model design (Baker & Hawn, 2021; Ma & Jiang, 2023). For example, an algorithm trained predominantly on data from a specific demographic might yield less accurate recommendations for students from minority groups, leading to disparities in their learning experiences. Such bias can perpetuate inequality, disadvantaging underrepresented groups and undermining the inclusive ethos of education. Mitigating these risks requires continuous monitoring, validation, and diversification of AI training datasets, ensuring equitable outcomes for all students.

Reduced Human Interaction in PE

The integration of AI in PE may inadvertently diminish the value of human interaction, which is critical in fostering motivation, social skills, and empathy among students. Over-reliance on AI tools and automated systems risks creating an impersonal learning environment, where students may feel isolated or undervalued (Huang, 2023; Ma & Jiang, 2023). This reduction in human engagement could particularly impact the holistic development of students, as PE inherently involves collaborative activities, mentorship, and emotional support. To counteract this, educators should strike a balance by using AI as a complementary tool while maintaining active human involvement in instruction and mentorship.

Recommendations for Ethical AI Integration

To address these concerns, universities must adopt a multi-faceted approach:

Developing Ethical Guidelines: Establish comprehensive ethical frameworks for AI deployment in education, emphasizing transparency, accountability, and fairness.

Enhancing Educator Roles: Train educators to use AI tools effectively while preserving their role as facilitators of creativity, critical thinking, and interpersonal skills.

Implementing Rigorous Data Policies: Enforce stringent data governance practices to protect student privacy and prevent misuse.

Continuous Auditing of AI Systems: Regularly evaluate AI algorithms for potential biases and update them to align with evolving ethical standards.

By proactively addressing these issues, universities can harness the potential of AI in PE while safeguarding ethical integrity and fostering an inclusive, human-centered learning environment.

As artificial intelligence systems become increasingly integrated into university-level PE programs, they have enabled personalized training plans and real-time performance feedback for students. However, this integration also raises significant ethical and privacy concerns that must be addressed.

THEORETICAL FRAMEWORK

1. The Significance of Investigating Innovative Approaches to Integrating Artificial Intelligence in University PE

Within the realm of university-level PE, the strategic and purposeful application of information technology, in line with the framework of higher education, is essential for the advancement of educational practices. This innovative teaching model can create a dynamic learning environment by enabling the construction of specific scenarios that foster critical thinking, making information more visually accessible, enhancing resource sharing, and addressing the need for independent exploration, multi-level interaction, and collaborative learning. Not only does this approach tap into students' subjective initiative, but it also highlights the pivotal role of teachers. A student-centered method, which encourages independent inquiry, cultivates creativity, enthusiasm, and innovation, ultimately breaking away from traditional PE teaching models. This emphasis on creativity and innovation is crucial for nurturing innovative talent, aligning with the goals of quality education in the digital era.

2. The Role of Artificial Intelligence in PE

2.1 Precision Diagnostics

Powered by deep machine learning algorithms and extensive datasets, artificial intelligence is capable of accurately diagnosing gaps in students' learning as the volume of input data grows. This leads to highly targeted, personalized guidance that enhances teaching efficiency for instructors and improves student learning outcomes. In the context of sports, AI can swiftly analyze and calculate both psychological learning patterns and the external behavioral models of individuals. By monitoring diverse motion trajectories, AI generates a comprehensive three-dimensional model of each trainee, offering a visual depiction that enables precise diagnostics. This facilitates personalized learning support, which benefits both learners and instructors, streamlining the teaching process, reducing redundant tasks, and empowering students to master sports techniques with greater precision, ultimately enhancing their engagement and performance in PE.

2.2 Personalized Services

As society moves deeper into the information age, Vietnam's 54 ethnic groups are presented with unparalleled opportunities for growth. It is vital to harness these opportunities by integrating AI-driven smart education with student individuality. This enables the holistic development of students' character throughout their educational journey. The intelligent sports cloud service platform, powered by AI, provides customized services tailored to the diverse needs of students. Through this platform, personalized curricula and training programs are developed, taking into account the students' unique developmental contexts. By setting comprehensive goals, it facilitates sports learning at various stages of life, fostering long-term commitment to both education and physical activity. The platform meticulously records learners' progress across different phases of PE, allowing instructors to deliver personalized, data-driven teaching methods that cater to individual preferences and requirements.

2.3 Intelligent Decision-Making

The integration of AI with sports, alongside the power of big data, has created vast opportunities, including the innovation of the AI-powered Classroom Quality Evaluation System (AI-CQE). This system leverages AI's analytical strength to assess PE by utilizing extensive teaching video data repositories. Through deep learning algorithms, AI-CQE intelligently evaluates both teacher and student behaviors, incorporating techniques such as facial recognition and expression analysis. By processing data related to students' movement patterns, classroom dynamics, and engagement levels, the system generates visually comprehensible insights for students, educators, and parents. This intelligent decision-making tool offers a scientific basis for shaping educational policies, ultimately aiming to enhance instructional quality.

In educational systems where student development—morally, intellectually, physically, and aesthetically—is highly prioritized, addressing challenges such as a shortage of PE teachers and the uneven distribution of teaching expertise across regions remains essential. AI's capacity to monitor and document individual student progress in PE allows educators to make more efficient use of their time, providing personalized instruction and ensuring equitable access to PE for all students.

3. Applications of Artificial Intelligence in PE

3.1 Intelligent Guidance Systems

Supported by big data, intelligent guidance systems model, analyze, evaluate, and make informed decisions, creating a smart online learning and education platform. This application of "artificial intelligence + education" is currently the most prevalent. Intelligent guidance systems, first introduced in 1982, simulate the teaching methods of instructors through computer-based, one-on-one learning models. These systems provide personalized guidance and explanations tailored to learners' varying needs and characteristics. By leveraging advanced technologies like natural language processing and voice recognition, they analyze sports data and scenarios in real-time. Acting as virtual coaches, they offer comprehensive recommendations, such as tailored meal plans, exercise regimens, and detailed performance analytics. By automating routine tasks typically handled by human coaches, these systems enhance the effectiveness of sports training programs. Additionally, they track and evaluate performance, providing real-time feedback to help learners refine their techniques and achieve optimal performance outcomes. An exemplary application of intelligent guidance systems in PE is the integration of virtual reality (VR) in a long jump training session. During the session, students wear VR headsets to immerse themselves in a simulated stadium environment. AI embedded within the system analyzes the students' movements in real time, providing immediate feedback on launch angles, foot propulsion force, and landing posture. This data is presented in a 3D graphical format, enabling students to identify specific aspects that require adjustment to enhance performance. Additionally, the system records individual metrics, assisting instructors in designing personalized training regimens for each student.

3.2 Automatic Evaluation Systems

Artificial intelligence in PE includes the integration of automatic evaluation systems, which aim to improve teaching quality through automation and deep analysis. These systems analyze videos and performance data of students to accurately assess their sports skills and performance. Automatic evaluation systems use advanced algorithms to provide instant and accurate feedback on student performance, helping teachers adjust their teaching methods to meet individual student needs. Another prominent AI application is the use of automatic evaluation systems in swimming classes. During practice, students are filmed while swimming, and AI-powered image processing algorithms analyze their movements in detail. The system can detect improper hand positioning, incorrect breathing techniques, or inconsistent leg kicks. It then generates a comprehensive report, complete with charts comparing their performance to technical standards, providing both students and instructors with a clear understanding of areas for improvement.

3.3 Sports Education Robots

Sports education robots are one of the most notable applications of artificial intelligence in PE. These robots can provide direct guidance and feedback to students during sports practice. With the ability to simulate precise techniques and movements, sports education robots help students master sports skills more effectively. They can also track and assess students' learning progress, providing detailed performance reports and recommending measures for improvement. Sports education robots are advanced tools that support the teaching of exercises such as yoga. In a typical session, robots equipped with high-precision motion sensors and AI demonstrate poses with impeccable accuracy. As students practice, the robots use cameras to monitor their postures and compare them against ideal standards. Upon detecting deviations, the robots provide immediate recommendations, such as “Lower your left shoulder” or “Improve balance by adjusting your center of gravity.” With their ability to deliver instant feedback, these robots significantly accelerate the refinement of students’ techniques, ensuring efficient and effective learning.

4. Innovative Strategies for Enhancing University PE

4.1 Updating PE Teaching Concepts

In light of recent curriculum reforms, university PE instructors must evolve their teaching philosophies, embrace modern pedagogical approaches, and guide PE reform in a positive direction. Emphasizing joyful guidance and practical training is crucial, ensuring that students actively engage in physical activities while enjoying a learning experience that fosters a lifelong commitment to sports. Lesson planning should prioritize personalized instruction, where educators analyze the learning conditions and physical characteristics of each student, tailoring activity plans and training methods accordingly. This approach enables students to enhance their sports performance, realize their individual potential, and improve the overall effectiveness of instructional organization. It is essential to maintain a human-centered teaching philosophy, placing quality education at the forefront. Beyond improving students' technical skills in sports, educators should focus on cultivating students' self-confidence by offering encouragement and recognition, thereby empowering them to persevere through challenges and stay committed to their training. This will foster determination and diligence, ultimately improving their training efficiency.

4.2 Innovating Teaching Methods

In the digital age, PE instructors at universities should continuously innovate and refine their teaching methods by integrating diverse instructional approaches. Effective instruction must be provided to help students grasp critical concepts. For example, when teaching about emergency sports injury treatment, educators can incorporate scenario-based learning and simulated practice into their methods. By creating scenarios where students face simulated sports injuries, instructors can engage them in practical exercises for emergency response within specific contexts. This innovation enhances both the instructional process and the learning experience, enabling students to gain a deep understanding of the techniques and procedures involved in emergency sports injury treatment. As a result, teaching effectiveness is maximized, students' learning outcomes and athletic abilities are further developed, and their interest in sports is strengthened.

4.3 Enhancing Teaching Evaluation Methods

To optimize the effectiveness of PE, instructors should consider incorporating artificial intelligence into the teaching evaluation system. AI-driven systems can develop a comprehensive framework for assessing students' participation in physical activities. This allows students to gain a clearer understanding of their performance, offering them a more objective evaluation of their progress in PE. AI can systematically guide their sports involvement, overcoming the limitations of traditional evaluation methods. Moreover, it highlights the scientific and efficient aspects of assessment, offering students positive reinforcement and direction in their physical practice. Ultimately, this can improve students' health and enhance their athletic skills.

4.4 Current State and Philosophy of PE in Vietnam

The current PE programs in Vietnam primarily focus on basic techniques, while innovation in teaching methods and the integration of technology remain limited (Niu, 2023). Schools, especially in rural and remote areas, often lack essential infrastructure, including sports fields, equipment, and technological tools for learning. These limitations not only affect the quality of instruction but also reduce students' engagement and enthusiasm for physical activities (To et al., 2019).

The philosophy of PE in Vietnam emphasizes holistic education, aiming to develop students' physical, intellectual, and personal qualities in a balanced manner. PE is not solely about improving health but also about fostering humanistic values, social skills, and a spirit of sportsmanship. This approach aspires to shape students into well-rounded and dynamic individuals who can thrive in a modern society (Th o, 2021).

Despite efforts to enhance the system, PE in Vietnam faces numerous challenges. A significant issue is the shortage of highly qualified teachers, particularly in underprivileged areas. Furthermore, there are substantial disparities in the distribution of educational resources between urban and rural regions, leading to unequal access to quality education. Additionally, integrating modern teaching methodologies and advanced technologies into the curriculum remains difficult due to resource constraints and limited awareness (Niu, 2023; To et al., 2019; Tu, 2023).

DISCUSSIONS

The convergence of AI and PE presents both opportunities and challenges. This discussion explores the implications, benefits, and hurdles associated with integrating AI into university-level PE.

Implications for PE

AI has the potential to revolutionize traditional teaching methods in PE, offering more personalized, data-driven approaches that can significantly enhance the effectiveness of PE programs (Chan & Tsi, 2023). By accurately diagnosing and assessing students' physical abilities, customizing training plans, and providing real-time feedback, AI can support personalized learning and ensure that each student receives tailored guidance based on their unique needs and progress (Bulathwela et al., 2021; Balta, 2023; Mello et al., 2023; Xie, 2020).

The integration of AI in PE can bring about numerous benefits (Xie, 2020; Balta, 2023). First, AI systems can analyze students' performance data to identify their strengths and weaknesses with high precision, allowing for the creation of individualized training programs that cater to the specific needs of each student, thereby improving overall fitness and skill levels. Second, AI can offer personalized coaching and training plans, with intelligent sports platforms tracking and adapting to the student's progress, providing continuous support and adjustments to their training regimen (Balta, 2023; Mello et al., 2023). Third, AI-driven systems can assist educators in making informed decisions about teaching strategies and resource allocation by analyzing large sets of data, identifying patterns, and suggesting improvements, thus enhancing the overall quality of PE instruction (Mou, 2019; Mello et al., 2023).

While AI holds immense potential to transform PE, it is important to recognize that the mere adoption of AI or other technological advancements is insufficient to overcome the challenges faced by institutions, teachers, and students (Mello et al., 2023).

Challenges in Implementing AI in PE

The integration of AI in the realm of PE holds immense potential to revolutionize the way we approach teaching, learning, and the overall student experience. However, the successful implementation of AI in this domain presents a unique set of challenges that institutions must address to harness the full benefits of this transformative technology.

One of the primary hurdles lies in the technological and infrastructural limitations faced by universities (Aleksandrov, 2021; Dave & Patel, 2023; Fahimirad & Kotamjani, 2018). The successful deployment of AI in PE requires a significant investment in advanced data analytics tools, sophisticated AI algorithms, and smart equipment. Many educational institutions may struggle with the financial and logistical demands of acquiring and maintaining these cutting-edge technologies, hindering their ability to fully leverage the capabilities of AI.

Furthermore, the effective integration of AI in PE necessitates that educators are well-versed in these technologies and possess the necessary skills to seamlessly incorporate them into their teaching practices (Wang et al., 2022; Ng et al., 2023; Owoc et al., 2021). Comprehensive training programs are essential to ensure that teachers can effectively utilize AI-powered tools and algorithms to enhance the learning experience for students (Rodway & Schepman, 2023).

In addition to the technological and pedagogical challenges, the implementation of AI in PE raises important ethical and privacy concerns (Mello et al., 2023). The collection and analysis of significant amounts of personal student data is a critical aspect of AI-driven solutions, and institutions must be vigilant in ensuring the privacy and security of this information to maintain the trust of students and their families.

The Irreplaceable Role of Human Factors in PE

PE is not merely about performing physical exercises; it also carries profound significance in fostering social interactions and emotional development. While AI offers technological advancements, such as optimizing training programs and providing personalized feedback, the human element in PE remains indispensable (Razaak et al., 2020; Griggs & Medcalf, 2015). Teachers not only act as instructors but also serve as motivators, encouragers, and emotional connectors with students—roles that AI cannot fully replicate.

AI should be implemented as a supportive tool rather than a complete replacement for the teacher's role. This allows educators to focus more on human-centered aspects, such as instilling aesthetic values in movement, encouraging creativity, and fostering social connections among students through group activities (Lee & Lee, 2021). With AI, teachers can freely develop innovative and flexible teaching strategies without being burdened by extensive administrative or supervisory tasks.

Before integrating AI into PE, thorough evaluations must be conducted to ensure that the introduction of technology does not diminish the inherent values of PE. Core aspects, such as promoting social interaction, encouraging active participation, and cultivating teamwork, must remain a priority. Otherwise, the misuse of AI risks reducing PE to a mechanized process, overly focused on measurable outcomes rather than nurturing holistic values (Holstein et al., 2020; Chan & Tsi, 2023).

FUTURE DIRECTIONS

To maximize the potential of AI in PE, several steps should be taken:

- Developing Comprehensive Evaluation Systems: A thorough evaluation of AI's impact on PE is necessary to understand its benefits and limitations. This should include feedback from both teachers and students to guide future improvements.
- Promoting International Collaboration: Adopting an international perspective can help universities learn from successful implementations of AI in PE worldwide, fostering the development of best practices.
- Establishing a Talent Training System: Preparing future educators and coaches to use AI effectively will ensure the sustainability and growth of AI-integrated PE programs.

The integration of AI in PE offers significant potential to enhance teaching and learning experiences. While there are challenges to be addressed, the benefits of personalized training, accurate assessment, and data-driven decision-making present a compelling case for adopting AI in university PE programs. By focusing on comprehensive evaluation, international collaboration, and systematic training, universities can harness the full potential of AI to advance PE and contribute to the overall well-being of their students.

CONCLUSION

In the current information age and within the context of socialism with Vietnamese characteristics, the informatization of education must remain dynamic, continuously adapting to contemporary trends. In this era, PE holds increased educational importance, and the integration of AI with sports offers tremendous potential for its advancement. Despite the ongoing development of AI technology, its practical application in education is still in its early stages. Consequently, gathering feedback and insights from frontline educators is crucial to inform future advancements.

A thorough evaluation of learner-centered information technology education, examining both its strengths and limitations, is imperative. Moreover, it is essential to adopt a global perspective in order to proactively build forward-looking talent training systems and promote the widespread adoption of AI in education. These initiatives will not only propel educational progress but also significantly enhance the development of sports.

The intersection of AI and PE presents a promising frontier. By leveraging AI technology, educational methods can become more effective, personalized, and science-based. The deployment of AI can enhance many aspects of PE, from accurate skill assessments and personalized training plans to the use of virtual reality for realistic training scenarios and smart equipment for real-time feedback.

However, integrating AI into university-level PE is not without challenges. It requires continuous innovation in concepts, teaching methods, and evaluation systems. Updating the teaching philosophy of PE to focus on enjoyment, practical training, and personalized guidance is essential. Innovative teaching methods, such as scenario creation and simulated exercises, can optimize teaching effectiveness and engage students more deeply. Moreover, introducing AI in teaching evaluation systems can provide more accurate and objective assessments, effectively guiding students on their PE journey.

In conclusion, integrating AI into the PE curriculum can significantly enhance the quality and efficiency of teaching and training. By embracing these innovations, we can ensure that PE not only keeps pace with technological advancements but also contributes to the comprehensive development and health of students. This strategy will ultimately lead to a more dynamic, effective, and engaging PE system, benefiting both students and teachers.

AI is an essential tool in PE, especially as universities in Vietnam pursue groundbreaking reforms. Applications such as personalized data analysis, intelligent guidance, and automated assessment not only optimize teaching processes but also enhance student engagement and learning outcomes. However, AI cannot fully replace the human element, which remains central to the comprehensive educational philosophy in PE. Teachers continue to play a critical role in inspiring students, personalizing learning, and cultivating intangible values like creativity, aesthetics, and social development (Núñez et al., 2023; Ma & Jiang, 2023).

The future of PE in Vietnamese universities lies in harmonizing modern technology with holistic educational philosophies. AI should focus on technical aspects, such as managing big data and providing instant feedback, while teachers prioritize direct instruction, individual motivation, and the development of students' soft skills. This collaboration ensures learning efficiency while preserving the humanistic essence of education, enabling students to achieve holistic growth in both physical and mental domains (Zhang & Yanqiong, 2022; Huang, 2023).

Highlighting the complementary partnership between teachers and AI, rather than seeing them as replacements for one another, marks a significant step toward building a modern and sustainable PE education system in Vietnam.

REFERENCES

Aleksandrov, N. V. (2021). *International Experience of Artificial Intelligence Implementation in the Field of Science and Higher Education*. Atlantis Press., DOI: 10.2991/aebmr.k.211118.115

Baker, R. S., & Hawn, A. (2021). Algorithmic Bias in Education. In International Journal of Artificial Intelligence in Education (Vol. 32, Issue 4, p. 1052). Springer Science+Business Media. DOI: 10.35542/osf.io/pbmvz

Balta, N. (2023). Embracing the Future: AI's Transformative Potential in Educational Research. *Embracing the Future: AI's Transformative Potential in Educational Research*, *6*(2), 1–2. DOI: 10.31757/euer.624

Bulathwela, S., Pérez-Ortiz, M., Holloway, C., & Shawe-Taylor, J. (2021). Could AI Democratise Education? Socio-Technical Imaginaries of an EdTech Revolution. Cornell University. https://doi.org//arxiv.2112.02034DOI: 10.48550

Cai-xia, Z., & Li-guo, L. (2020). Application and Innovation of Artificial Intelligence Technology in College Sports. DOI: 10.1109/ICISE51755.2020.00163

Chan, C. K. Y., & Tsi, L. H. Y. (2023). The AI Revolution in Education: Will AI Replace or Assist Teachers in Higher Education? Cornell University. https://doi .org//arxiv.2305.01185DOI: 10.48550

Cruz, J J P., Ricalde, A M., & Closa, J M A. (2021). Module Development for Online Physical education Classes: Teachers' Perspective and Experiences. DOI: 10.1145/3450148.3450153

Dau, L. V., Huy, H. N., Ninh, L. V., Tân, N. M., & Yen, N. P. (2020). Physical Education for Students: Researching one University in Vietnam. In South Asian Research Journal of Humanities and Social Sciences (Vol. 2, Issue 3, p. 205). DOI: 10.36346/sarjhss.2020.v02i03.005

Dave, M., & Patel, N. (2023). Artificial intelligence in healthcare and education. *British Dental Journal*, *234*(10), 761–764. DOI: 10.1038/s41415-023-5845-2 PMID: 37237212

Diu, H. M., & Thuc, D. C. (2024). The Effect of Sports Activities on Stress Resilience in Students at Vietnam National University. *Sport Mont*, *22*(3), 121–126.

Fahimirad, M., & Kotamjani, S S. (2018). A Review on Application of Artificial Intelligence in Teaching and Learning in Educational Contexts., 8(4), 106-106. DOI: 10.5296/ijld.v8i4.14057

Green, K. (2008). Understanding. *Physics Education*. Advance online publication. DOI: 10.4135/9781446213520

Griggs, G., & Medcalf, R. (2015). Inclusive Pedagogy in Physical Education. In *International perspectives on inclusive education* (p. 119). Emerald Publishing Limited., DOI: 10.1108/S1479-363620150000007013

Guo, Q., & Li, B. (2021). Role of AI physical education based on application of functional sports training. IOS Press, 40(2), 3337-3345. DOI: 10.3233/JIFS-189373

Holstein, K., Aleven, V., & Rummel, N. (2020). A Conceptual Framework for Human–AI Hybrid Adaptivity in Education. In Lecture notes in computer science (p. 240). Springer Science+Business Media. DOI: 10.1007/978-3-030-52237-7_20

Huang, L. (2023). Ethics of Artificial Intelligence in Education: Student Privacy and Data Protection. In Science Insights Education Frontiers (Vol. 16, Issue 2, p. 2577). DOI: 10.15354/sief.23.re202

Jiang, Y., Ma, B., Wang, X., Yu, G., Yu, P., Wang, Z., Ni, W., & Liu, R. P. (2024). Blockchained federated learning for internet of things: A comprehensive survey. *ACM Computing Surveys*, *56*(10), 1–37. DOI: 10.1145/3659099

Kamalov, F., & Gurrib, I. (2023). New Era of Artificial Intelligence in Education: Towards a Sustainable Multifaceted Revolution. Cornell University. https://doi.org//arxiv.2305.18303DOI: 10.48550

Kim, J., Lee, H., & Cho, Y H. (2022). Learning design to support student-AI collaboration: perspectives of leading teachers for AI in education. Springer Science+Business Media, 27(5), 6069-6104. DOI: 10.1007/s10639-021-10831-6

Krüger, M., & Hofmann, A. R. (2015). The Development of Physical-Education Institutions in Europe: A Short Introduction. In The International Journal of the History of Sport (Vol. 32, Issue 6, p. 737). Routledge. DOI: 10.1080/09523367.2015.1024111

Lee, H. S., & Lee, J. (2021). Applying Artificial Intelligence in Physical Education and Future Perspectives. In Sustainability (Vol. 13, Issue 1, p. 351). Multidisciplinary Digital Publishing Institute. DOI: 10.3390/su13010351

Li-hua, Z., & Tang, Q. (2022). Construction of a Six-Pronge Intelligent Physical education Classroom Model in Colleges and Universities. *Scientific Programming*, *2022*, 1–11. DOI: 10.1155/2022/9003864

Liang, F., Yang, Y., Shan, Z., & Kim, B S. (2021). Application of Artificial Intelligence Technology in Leisure Sports Course. DOI: 10.1145/3456887.3457065

Liang, L., Zhang, L., & Zhang, S. (2021). Using Artificial Intelligence for the Construction of University Physical Training and Teaching Systems. *Journal of Healthcare Engineering, 2021*, 1–10. DOI: 10.1155/2021/3479208

Ma, X., & Jiang, C. (2023). On the Ethical Risks of Artificial Intelligence Applications in Education and Its Avoidance Strategies. *Education and Humanities Research, 14*, 354–359. DOI: 10.54097/ehss.v14i.8868

Meier, S. (2021). Pedagogical content knowledge in students majoring in physical education vs. sport science. The same but different? In German Journal of Exercise and Sport Research (Vol. 51, Issue 3, p. 269). Springer Nature. DOI: 10.1007/s12662-021-00725-7

Mello, R. F., Freitas, E. L. S. X., Pereira, F. D., Cabral, L. D. S., Tedesco, P., & Ramalho, G. (2023). Education in the age of Generative AI: Context and Recent Developments. Cornell University. https://doi.org//arxiv.2309.12332DOI: 10.48550

Mou, X. (2019). Artificial Intelligence: Investment Trends and Selected Industry Uses. DOI: 10.1596/32652

Ng, D T K., Leung, J K L., Su, J., Ng, R C W., & Chu, S K W. (2023). Teachers' AI digital competencies and twenty-first century skills in the post-pandemic world. Springer Science+Business Media, 71(1), 137-161. https://doi.org/DOI: 10.1007/s11423-023-10203-6

Niu, Y. (2023). Integrated physical education and medicine in general physical education at universities in the age of educational technologies. In BMC Medical Education (Vol. 23, Issue 1). BioMed Central. DOI: 10.1186/s12909-023-04440-9

Núñez, J L M., Harris, P., Fernández, R P., Abbas, A., & Radovanović, D. (2023). Does intrinsic motivation mediate perceived artificial intelligence (AI) learning and computational thinking of students during the COVID-19 pandemic?. Elsevier BV, 4, 100128-100128. DOI: 10.1016/j.caeai.2023.100128

Owoc, M L., Sawicka, A., & Weichbroth, P. (2021). Artificial Intelligence Technologies in Education: Benefits, Challenges and Strategies of Implementation. Springer Science+Business Media, 37-58. DOI: 10.1007/978-3-030-85001-2_4

Panganiban, T. D. (2019). Quality assessment of physical education program of state universities in the Philippines. In Jurnal SPORTIF Jurnal Penelitian Pembelajaran (Vol. 5, Issue 2, p. 166). Universitas Nusantara PGRI Kediri. DOI: 10.29407/js_unpgri.v5i2.12983

Razaak, M. H., Ehsan, N., & Atradinal. (2020). Competence of Physical Education, Sports and Health Teachers in Elementary Schools of Lubuk Sikaping. DOI: 10.2991/assehr.k.200805.017

Rodway, P., & Schepman, A. (2023). The impact of adopting AI educational technologies on projected course satisfaction in university students. Elsevier BV, 5, 100150-100150. DOI: 10.1016/j.caeai.2023.100150

Th o, N. T. P. (2021). Designing The Suitable Physical Education For The Students Of Thai Nguyen University Of Technology. In International Journal of Education and Social Science Research (Vol. 4, Issue 3, p. 345). DOI: 10.37500/IJESSR.2021.4322

To, Q. G., Gallegos, D., Dung, D. V., Tran, H. T. M., To, K. G., Wharton, L., & Trost, S. G. (2020). Correlates of physical activity in fifth-grade students in Ho Chi Minh City, Vietnam. In Sports Medicine and Health Science (Vol. 2, Issue 1, p. 33). Elsevier BV. DOI: 10.1016/j.smhs.2020.02.002

To, Q. G., Wharton, L., Gallegos, D., Stylianou, M., Dung, D. V., To, K. G., Tran, H. T. M., & Trost, S. G. (2019). School-based physical education: Physical activity and implementation barriers in Vietnamese elementary schools. In European Physical Education Review (Vol. 26, Issue 2, p. 587). SAGE Publishing. DOI: 10.1177/1356336X19878746

Tu, T. T. (2023). Solutions to improve the effectiveness of physical education for students at chu van an high school, thai nguyen province, Vietnam. In European Journal of Physical Education and Sport Science (Vol. 9, Issue 5). Open Access Publishing Group. DOI: 10.46827/ejpe.v9i5.4740

Vuong, Q., Hoang, A.-D., Vuong, T., La, V., Nguyen, H. T., & Ho, T. M. (2018). Factors Associated with the Regularity of Physical Exercises as a Means of Improving the Public Health System in Vietnam. In Sustainability (Vol. 10, Issue 11, p. 3828). Multidisciplinary Digital Publishing Institute. DOI: 10.3390/su10113828

Wang, N., Tonko, P., Ragav, N., Chungyoun, M., & Plucker, J A. (2022). A Perspective On K-12 AI Education. https://doi.org/DOI: 10.21300/23.1.2023.2

Wang, Y. (2021). Physical education Teaching in Colleges and Universities Assisted by Virtual Reality Technology Based on Artificial Intelligence. *Mathematical Problems in Engineering*, *2021*, 1–11. DOI: 10.1155/2021/5582716

Wen, J. (2021). Innovative Application of Artificial Intelligence Technology in College Physical education. *Journal of Physics: Conference Series*, *1881*(4), 042028–042028. DOI: 10.1088/1742-6596/1881/4/042028

Wu-jun, X. (2022). Application and Prospect Analysis of Artificial Intelligence in the Field of Physical education. *Computational Intelligence and Neuroscience*, *2022*, 1–7. DOI: 10.1155/2022/1042533

Xie, M. (2020). Design of a physical education training system based on an intelligent vision. Wiley-Blackwell, 29(3), 590-602. DOI: 10.1002/cae.22259

Zach, S., Shoval, E., & Lidor, R. (2016). Physical education and academic achievement—literature review 1997–2015. In Journal of Curriculum Studies (Vol. 49, Issue 5, p. 703). Taylor & Francis. DOI: 10.1080/00220272.2016.1234649

Zhang, Y., & Yanqiong, W. (2022). Online Big Data Physical education Classroom Based on Monitoring Network and Artificial Intelligence. *Security and Communication Networks*, *2022*, 1–7. DOI: 10.1155/2022/3643799

Zhao, Y., & Ma, T. (2019). Research on the Optimum Design of College Physical Education Teaching Contents for the Improvement of College Students' Health-Related Physical Fitness. https://doi.org/DOI: 10.2991/assehr.k.191206.082

Chapter 12
Preparing for a Future With Generative AI

J. B. Oleet
https://orcid.org/0009-0001-1262-7500
Mississippi State University, USA

ABSTRACT

This chapter provides an in-depth analysis of the integration of Generative AI in education, highlighting its transformative potential for personalized learning, assessment, and administrative efficiency. The chapter explores current trends, theoretical underpinnings, and speculative future scenarios, emphasizing the ethical considerations and challenges, such as data privacy, fairness, and the digital divide. By offering actionable strategies, real-world case studies, and best practices, the chapter equips educators, administrators, and policymakers with the tools to leverage AI technologies effectively and ethically. The discussion culminates in a comprehensive roadmap for implementing AI to promote equity, enhance student engagement, and prepare learners for an AI-driven future.

BACKGROUND OF REVIEW

The Transformative Role of AI in Higher Education

AI-driven technologies have been integrated into various educational settings, streamlining administrative tasks, enhancing academic processes, and supporting personalized learning. Generative AI offers even more profound potential, as it can adapt to unique learning pathways, generate content, and provide real-time feedback tailored to individual student needs (Ren, 2024). While the benefits of AI in education are widely acknowledged, particularly in automating tasks and improving

DOI: 10.4018/979-8-3693-8744-3.ch012

efficiency, a key focus of this section is to examine how these technologies can transform academic and operational functions within institutions.

Saaida (2023) emphasizes that AI has the potential to automate administrative tasks and optimize resource allocation, thereby transforming both academic and operational functions within higher education institutions. For example, AI can streamline scheduling, manage student data more efficiently, and distribute resources. This operational efficiency is critical as institutions increasingly rely on data-driven decisions to improve educational outcomes. With AI taking over many routine tasks, educators and administrators can focus more on enhancing student learning experiences and addressing individual student needs.

In addition to administrative benefits, AI is reshaping how learning is delivered. Luckin et al. (2022) argue that the future of AI in education requires empowering educators with the necessary skills and knowledge to integrate AI technologies effectively, ensuring that institutions are prepared for digital transformation. This shift involves professional development and upskilling for educators so they can utilize AI tools in ways that enhance the learning process. AI can personalize learning experiences, offer real-time feedback, and adapt to students' individual learning styles, thus supporting more efficient and tailored educational approaches.

Strategic Implementation of AI in Higher Education

The strategic role of AI in higher education is multifaceted, extending beyond the classroom to institutional efficiency. As Hashim et al. (2022) highlighted, AI enhances both the quality of teaching and institutional operations through digital transformation. Integrating AI technologies into higher education facilitates more personalized learning experiences while improving administrative functions. For instance, institutions can employ AI to develop adaptive learning platforms that respond to students' performance in real-time, offering immediate feedback and adjusting learning materials to meet the needs of individual students better.

The strategic implementation of AI also involves overcoming significant challenges. One primary concern is the gap in AI literacy among educators, who may not feel fully prepared to integrate AI into their teaching practices. This highlights the necessity of ongoing professional development programs to equip educators with the knowledge and skills to leverage AI effectively. As will be discussed in detail in later sections, such professional development is key to ensuring that educators adopt AI and understand how to use it to improve student outcomes.

Moreover, Ahmad et al. (2022) underscore AI's dual role in enhancing academic and administrative functions improving efficiency in processes like grading, feedback, and resource management. The use of AI to automate grading allows for quicker feedback loops, enabling students to adjust their learning strategies based on real-time performance data. This dual role illustrates the wide-reaching implications of AI in education, transforming how institutions operate, how students learn, and how educators teach. However, as will be elaborated in later sections, the ethical implications of using AI for such purposes, particularly regarding data privacy and algorithmic biases, must be carefully managed.

Generative AI's Role in Personalized Learning

Generative AI holds particularly strong potential in personalizing learning experiences, one of its most transformative features. Alam (2021) emphasizes that AI should be viewed as a tool to support educators by providing personalized learning experiences rather than replacing human teachers. Generative AI, specifically, can generate customized learning content based on student progress, enabling more tailored educational pathways. This technology allows educators to cater to diverse student needs, offering differentiated instruction that aligns with each student's learning pace and style.

However, as Generative AI becomes more integrated into educational environments, there is a need for clear ethical guidelines to ensure that these technologies are used responsibly. As discussed in the ethical considerations section, issues such as data privacy, bias in AI algorithms, and the digital divide must be addressed to ensure that the benefits of AI are distributed equitably across diverse educational settings. For now, it is essential to recognize the unique potential of Generative AI to foster personalized learning experiences that support student motivation and comprehension.

Theoretical Framework

This chapter is structured as a focused literature review to synthesize current research on how AI is reshaping higher education, focusing on Generative AI's potential to revolutionize personalized learning. Selected studies were based on three criteria: the researcher's exposure, expertise, and experience (Kraus et al., 2022). This methodology ensures a well-rounded perspective on integrating AI into education, enabling readers to navigate its complexities and leverage its potential effectively.

Mission and Objectives of Chapter

This chapter explores the transformative potential of Generative AI technologies, emphasizing that educators, administrators, and policymakers must prepare for these changes. The chapter's mission is to equip stakeholders with the necessary insights and strategies to leverage Generative AI to enhance educational experiences while addressing challenges such as ethical concerns and equity in access. The aim is to forecast potential developments and provide practical guidance for effective implementation, ensuring that these technologies support personalized, engaging, and adaptive learning environments.

CURRENT TRENDS AND THEORETICAL UNDERPINNINGS OF AI IN EDUCATION

The adoption of Artificial Intelligence (AI) in education has initiated profound shifts in how learning is delivered, experienced, and assessed. As AI continues to evolve, its applications in education expand beyond administrative functions, taking root in pedagogical practices and transforming the entire learning ecosystem. This section delves into the current trends shaping the integration of AI in academic settings and explores the theoretical underpinnings that drive its development. It focuses on how Generative AI, in particular, has enhanced personalized learning, automated assessment processes, and fostered adaptive learning environments. Through an examination of recent studies, this section also highlights AI's profound influence on student outcomes and educator practices, paving the way for an increasingly data-driven, personalized educational future.

The Shift Toward AI-Powered Learning Systems

One of the most significant trends in AI integration in education is the rise of AI-powered learning systems, which provide students with personalized, adaptive learning experiences. Lin et al. (2023) describes this shift as revolutionary, driven primarily by advancements in intelligent tutoring systems, automated grading, and sustainable yet adaptive learning platforms. These systems leverage AI's capacity to analyze large datasets and customize learning pathways, tailoring instructional content to meet the unique needs of each learner. AI tutors, for instance, provide real-time feedback and adjust their approach based on a student's progress, ensuring that no student is left behind or stalled by one-size-fits-all instructional methods. By offering tailored learning experiences, AI tutors have the potential to significantly enhance student academic performance, fostering a more inclusive and responsive educational environment.

AI's ability to personalize learning is particularly evident in language education. Dutta et al. (2024) and Loor et al. (2024) both highlight the role of AI-driven adaptive learning platforms in English language teaching, demonstrating how these platforms adjust learning materials to accommodate each student's level of proficiency. Through AI, students receive immediate feedback on their language use, whether in writing, grammar, or pronunciation, allowing them to practice and improve in real-time. The integration of AI in language education underscores the transformative potential of these technologies in providing more effective, individualized learning experiences, ultimately leading to higher levels of student engagement and retention.

Generative AI: Automating Assessments and Delivering Personalized Feedback

A key development in AI's impact on education is the integration of Generative AI, which has significantly altered how assessments are conducted, and feedback is delivered. Automated grading systems powered by AI have emerged as a vital tool for educators, allowing for efficient assessment management and real-time, personalized feedback. According to Algahtani (2024), AI-driven grading systems offer substantial benefits by automating the assessment process, thus freeing educators to focus on more complex pedagogical tasks. These systems can accurately grade essays, projects, and other assessments, offering consistent and objective evaluations that minimize human error or bias.

Beyond automation, Generative AI facilitates a more dynamic interaction between the educator and the student. Naseer et al. (2024) demonstrate that Generative AI can transform higher education by delivering instant feedback tailored to each student's specific needs. This type of feedback is immediate and personalized, as AI systems can analyze a student's previous performance and adjust the feedback accordingly. By doing so, Generative AI enables a continuous loop of assessment and improvement, where students can identify their weaknesses and work on them before progressing further. This adaptive feedback mechanism ensures that learning is more iterative, enhancing student outcomes through a customized approach to skill development.

The potential of AI in automating assessments and delivering personalized feedback goes beyond improving student learning. It also has far-reaching implications for educators, who can now rely on AI systems to manage repetitive tasks such as grading, allowing them to dedicate more time to refining instructional strategies and engaging with students on a deeper level. This dual benefit of AI, supporting both educators and learners, illustrates its integral role in the evolving education landscape, where efficiency and personalization are increasingly becoming standard.

AI-Driven Adaptive Learning: A Global Perspective

While AI is transforming education globally, its implementation in specific contexts offers unique insights into its adaptability and impact. In a case study of Morocco's education system, Ejjami (2024) highlights how AI-driven adaptive learning platforms revolutionize personalized learning experiences. These platforms allow for customized learning pathways, which are tailored not only to students' academic performance but also to their learning styles and preferences. This adaptive learning model has proven particularly effective in creating more efficient and student-centered learning environments, as it enables educators to cater to a diverse student population with varying levels of academic ability.

The Moroccan case demonstrates that AI is not merely a tool for high-income countries or technologically advanced educational systems. Instead, it can potentially transform learning experiences into diverse global contexts, enhancing teaching and learning processes. By offering tailored learning experiences that respond to students' individual needs, AI-driven platforms can bridge educational gaps, promote inclusivity, and create more equitable learning opportunities. These outcomes are particularly significant in regions where educational resources may be limited but where AI can function as a lever to improve educational quality and access.

Moreover, AI's capacity to personalize learning and provide real-time feedback can help address systemic inequities in education. In regions where teacher-student ratios are high and individualized attention is difficult to achieve, AI can be a supplemental tool that offers students the support they need. As highlighted in previous sections, AI should be seen as a tool that complements educators rather than replacing them. The Moroccan case exemplifies how AI can enhance the capabilities of educators by allowing them to deliver more personalized learning experiences, even in resource-constrained environments.

Theoretical Underpinnings of AI in Education

The growing influence of AI in education is deeply rooted in established theoretical frameworks, which provide insight into how and why these technologies are so effective. Cognitive load theory, for example, plays a crucial role in understanding the benefits of AI-driven adaptive learning platforms. By dynamically adjusting instructional content based on a student's cognitive load, these platforms help to optimize learning outcomes. Lin et al. (2023) suggest that AI technologies, such as intelligent tutoring systems and adaptive learning platforms, revolutionize education by offering tailored learning experiences and enhancing academic performance. This alignment with cognitive load theory illustrates how AI reduces extraneous cognitive effort, allowing students to focus on meaningful learning tasks.

Similarly, constructivist learning theories underpin much of AI's application in education, mainly how AI enables personalized learning experiences. Constructivist theories suggest that learners build knowledge through active engagement with content, and AI systems that provide real-time feedback and tailored learning pathways facilitate this kind of active engagement. By allowing students to progress at their own pace and receive feedback tailored to their needs, AI supports a learning process that is both personalized and empowering.

Additionally, AI's role in supporting differentiated instruction is closely tied to Vygotsky's zone of proximal development (ZPD). This concept posits that learners achieve optimal growth when challenged beyond their current abilities but are still provided sufficient support to overcome these challenges. Generative AI systems can analyze student performance in real-time, adjusting the difficulty of tasks and offering the right level of support to move learners through their ZPD. The ability to tailor instruction to each student's needs ensures that all students, regardless of their initial proficiency, are continuously engaged in productive learning experiences.

Generative AI as a Driver of Pedagogical Change

Generative AI is poised to become a driving force in pedagogical change by personalizing learning experiences and redefining how educators approach instruction. As Naseer et al. (2024) highlight, integrating Generative AI into higher education can automate assessments, deliver personalized feedback, and enhance learning outcomes. However, the actual value of Generative AI lies in its ability to support more profound, more meaningful interactions between educators and learners. Educators are freed from administrative burdens by automating routine tasks such as grading. They can focus on higher-order teaching activities like mentoring, fostering critical thinking, and encouraging collaborative learning.

Moreover, Generative AI's ability to create content in real-time opens new possibilities for educators to design more dynamic and interactive learning environments. For instance, AI can generate personalized quizzes, assignments, and study materials based on a student's performance data, allowing educators to continuously adapt the curriculum to meet the evolving needs of their students. This level of flexibility is particularly beneficial in diverse classrooms where students may have different learning styles, preferences, or abilities. By leveraging AI to update and refine instructional content continuously, educators can ensure that their teaching remains relevant and responsive to the unique needs of their students.

Challenges and Considerations for AI Integration

While the benefits of AI in education are undeniable, integrating these technologies also presents several challenges that must be carefully considered. One of the most significant concerns is the potential for AI to exacerbate existing inequalities in education. As Ejjami (2024) notes, the effectiveness of AI-driven adaptive learning platforms depends heavily on the availability of technological infrastructure, which may not be equally accessible in all educational settings. In regions where access to reliable internet or digital devices is limited, the benefits of AI may not be fully realized, and disparities in educational outcomes may be further amplified.

Additionally, ethical considerations around data privacy and algorithmic bias must be addressed to ensure that AI integration in education promotes equity and inclusivity. AI systems rely on vast amounts of student data to personalize learning experiences and provide feedback. However, this raises concerns about how student data is collected, stored, and used. The potential for bias in AI algorithms is also a pressing issue, as these systems may inadvertently reinforce existing biases or perpetuate inequities. Educators, policymakers, and technology developers must work together to establish clear guidelines and ethical frameworks that govern the use of AI in education, ensuring that these technologies are used to protect students' rights and promote fairness.

In conclusion, current trends in AI integration in education, mainly through Generative AI, are revolutionizing how learning is delivered and experienced. From personalized tutoring systems to adaptive learning platforms and automated assessments, AI is enhancing educational outcomes by offering tailored learning experiences that cater to the unique needs of each student. However, as AI continues to evolve, addressing the challenges associated with its integration is essential, particularly regarding equity, accessibility, and ethical considerations. In the next section, we will explore how educators, institutions, and policymakers can prepare for the future of AI in education, providing a roadmap for how to implement these technologies effectively and ethically. This will include discussing the professional development and institutional support needed to ensure that educators are equipped to use AI-driven tools to enhance student learning and promote equitable outcomes.

PREPARING EDUCATORS, INSTITUTIONS, AND POLICYMAKERS

The successful integration of Generative AI into educational systems hinges on the preparation of educators, institutions, and policymakers. As AI technologies become increasingly prevalent in educational environments, the need for comprehensive strategies to prepare all stakeholders becomes more urgent. This exploration covers how educators, institutions, and policymakers can be equipped to leverage AI tools effectively, addressing key areas such as AI literacy, professional development, institutional readiness, and the broader policy landscape. Drawing on current research, this section provides actionable recommendations for ensuring educators are ready to integrate AI into their teaching practices, institutions are prepared to support sustainable AI adoption, and policymakers can create frameworks that promote equity, inclusion, and ethical use of AI in education.

Upskilling Educators: The Critical Role of Professional Development

As AI becomes an integral part of educational environments, educators must be equipped with the knowledge and skills to navigate these technologies effectively. Miao and Holmes (2021) emphasize that educator upskilling is crucial for effective AI integration in education, with institutional support being a critical factor in ensuring sustainable AI adoption. Educators must not only understand how to use AI-driven tools but also how to integrate them into their teaching practices in ways that enhance student learning and promote equitable outcomes.

Professional development initiatives play a central role in preparing educators for AI integration. These initiatives should focus on technical and pedagogical skills, ensuring that educators are proficient in using AI tools and understand how to leverage them to create more personalized, engaging, and practical learning experiences. For instance, AI-driven tools can provide real-time feedback to students, adapt learning pathways based on individual needs, and automate routine tasks such as grading. However, to fully benefit from these capabilities, educators must be trained to use AI tools in ways that align with their instructional goals and meet the needs of their students.

Luckin et al. (2022) emphasize that professional development is vital to preparing educators for AI integration, and institutions must provide the necessary infrastructure to support this transition. Professional development programs should include hands-on training in AI tools and opportunities for educators to collaborate with their peers and share best practices. Additionally, these programs should address the ethical considerations of using AI in education, such as data privacy, algorithmic bias, and AI's potential to exacerbate existing classroom inequalities. By addressing these issues, professional development initiatives can empower educators to use AI responsibly and effectively, ensuring that it enhances, rather than detracts from, the educational experience.

AI Literacy: Preparing Educators and Students for the Future

In addition to professional development, AI literacy is an essential component of preparing educators and students for the future of education. Ng et al. (2021) argue that AI literacy is essential for educators and students, enabling educators to integrate AI technologies effectively and empowering students to engage critically with AI tools. AI literacy goes beyond technical skills; it involves understanding the broader implications of AI in education, including its potential benefits, limitations, and ethical considerations.

For educators, AI literacy means using AI tools and understanding how they work and how they can be applied to enhance teaching and learning. This requires a shift in mindset, where educators move from being passive users of technology to active participants in designing and implementing AI-driven learning experiences. AI literacy also involves being aware of AI systems' potential biases and limitations and ensuring that these technologies are used in ways that promote equity and inclusion in the classroom.

AI literacy is equally essential for students, as it prepares them to navigate a future in which AI will play an increasingly central role in education and the workforce. Dai et al. (2020) highlights the importance of integrating AI literacy into the curriculum to prepare students for future educational and career environments, while institutions must ensure equitable access to AI technologies. AI literacy for students involves understanding how to use AI tools and developing critical thinking skills that enable them to assess the accuracy, fairness, and reliability of AI-generated outputs. By fostering AI literacy among students, educators can help them become more informed and responsible users of AI technologies, preparing them for success in an AI-driven world.

Institutional Readiness: Building Capacity for AI Integration

While upskilling educators and promoting AI literacy are essential, the success of AI integration in education also depends on the readiness of institutions to support these technologies. Institutions must invest in the necessary infrastructure, resources, and support systems to ensure that AI tools can be effectively implemented and sustained over time. This includes technological infrastructure, such as high-speed internet and digital devices, and institutional policies and practices that promote the ethical and equitable use of AI in education.

Green et al. (2021) stress that universities must build resilience in their educational practices by integrating AI technologies and preparing students for an evolving job market. This means equipping students with the technical skills necessary to work with AI tools and fostering a mindset of adaptability and lifelong learning. Braithwaite et al. (2023) suggest that stakeholder collaboration is essential for building resilient systems adapting to rapid technological advancements. This principle applies to future-proofing educational systems as well. Successful AI integration requires the input and cooperation of multiple stakeholders, each bringing a unique perspective and set of skills to the table.

Berces (2023) highlights the importance of fostering a community of practice involving administrators, educators, and policymakers to ensure that AI integration is both sustainable and future-proof. Educational institutions can build a culture of innovation and adaptability by creating spaces where stakeholders can share knowledge, discuss challenges, and explore best practices. This community-driven approach to AI integration will be essential in ensuring that educational systems remain responsive to the needs of students and educators as AI technologies continue to evolve. Additionally. Sokhibov and Azamjonov (2024) argue that continual evaluation and adaptation of AI-based tools are critical to future-proofing educational practices and ensuring they evolve alongside technological advancements. The process of evaluation and adaptation involves regularly reviewing the impact of AI tools on student outcomes and soliciting feedback from educators and students to identify areas for improvement.

Teachers' Readiness and Professional Development

One of the key challenges in preparing educators for AI integration is ensuring that they are willing and able to adopt AI tools in their teaching practices. Ayanwale et al. (2022) found that teachers are generally receptive to integrating AI into their classrooms but emphasize the need for continuous professional development to ensure they can fully leverage AI tools. While many educators recognize the potential benefits of AI in education, they may feel unprepared or unsure of how to implement these technologies effectively.

To address this challenge, professional development programs must be ongoing and responsive to the evolving needs of educators. These programs should provide educators with the knowledge and skills they need to use AI tools effectively and opportunities for reflection and collaboration with their peers. Professional development should also be tailored to the specific needs of educators, considering factors such as their level of experience with AI, their subject area, and the unique challenges they face in their classrooms.

In addition to formal professional development programs, institutions should also create opportunities for informal learning and collaboration. For example, educators could be encouraged to form learning communities or participate in peer mentoring programs, where they can share their experiences with AI integration and learn from one another. This type of collaborative learning can help build a culture of innovation and experimentation where educators feel supported in integrating AI into their teaching practices.

Policy Considerations: Supporting Educators and Institutions

Policymakers are critical in supporting educators and institutions preparing for AI integration. As AI becomes more prevalent in education, policymakers must develop clear guidelines and standards that promote AI's ethical and equitable use in schools and universities. These policies should address data privacy, algorithmic transparency, and equitable access to AI technologies, ensuring that all students and educators benefit from AI-driven learning tools.

One of the key policy considerations is the need for equitable access to AI technologies. Dai et al. (2020) highlight the importance of ensuring equitable access to AI tools, particularly for students from marginalized or underrepresented backgrounds. Policymakers must work to address the digital divide, ensuring that all students have access to the technological infrastructure necessary to benefit from AI-driven learning tools. This may involve investing in broadband infrastructure, providing digital devices to students and educators, and creating policies supporting open educational resources and other low-cost AI tools.

In addition to addressing access issues, policymakers must also focus on ensuring the ethical use of AI in education. Ng et al. (2021) argue that AI literacy is essential for educators and students, enabling them to engage critically with AI tools and make informed decisions about how these technologies are used. Policymakers should develop standards for AI literacy, ensuring educators and students are equipped with the knowledge and skills they need to use AI responsibly and ethically.

Finally, policymakers must support the professional development of educators by creating policies that incentivize ongoing learning and professional growth. This may involve funding professional development programs, offering grants to institutions investing in AI integration, and creating certification programs that recognize educators who have demonstrated proficiency in AI tools. By supporting the professional development of educators, policymakers can help to ensure that AI integration in education is both practical and sustainable.

Preparing Students for an AI-Driven Future

In addition to preparing educators and institutions, students must be equipped with the knowledge and skills they need to succeed in an AI-driven world. Dai et al. (2020) highlights the importance of integrating AI literacy into the curriculum, ensuring students are prepared for future educational and career environments. AI literacy for students involves understanding how to use AI tools and developing the critical thinking skills necessary to assess the accuracy, fairness, and reliability of AI-generated outputs.

Educators and institutions must meaningfully incorporate AI literacy into the curriculum to prepare students for the AI age. This may involve creating new courses or modules that focus specifically on AI and integrating AI-related content into existing subjects such as mathematics, computer science, and social studies (Molla & Nolan, 2019). Additionally, educators should provide students with opportunities to engage with AI tools in hands-on, experiential ways, allowing them to explore how AI can solve real-world problems and create new opportunities for innovation.

Furthermore, institutions must ensure that all students have access to the technological resources needed to develop AI literacy. This includes providing access to digital devices, high-speed internet, and AI-driven learning tools and creating policies that promote equitable access to these resources for all students, regardless of their background or circumstances. By prioritizing AI literacy for students, educators and institutions can help to ensure that the next generation is prepared to thrive in an AI-driven world.

Equipping Educators, Institutions, and Policymakers for AI Integration

Integrating Generative AI into education presents opportunities and challenges for educators, institutions, and policymakers. To fully leverage the potential of AI, educators must be provided with ongoing professional development opportunities that equip them with the knowledge and skills needed to use AI tools effectively. Additionally, institutions must invest in the necessary infrastructure and support systems to ensure that AI integration is sustainable and equitable. Policymakers, in turn, must develop clear guidelines and standards that promote the ethical use of AI in education and support educators and students in navigating the AI-driven future.

By preparing educators, institutions, and policymakers for AI integration, we can create a more equitable and inclusive educational system that empowers all students to succeed. In the next section, we will explore the ethical considerations and challenges associated with AI integration in education, providing insights into how institutions can address issues such as data privacy, algorithmic bias, and the potential for AI to exacerbate existing inequalities. This discussion will be critical in ensuring that AI is used in ways that are not only effective but also ethical and equitable, creating a more just and inclusive educational system for all.

ETHICAL CONSIDERATIONS IN THE INTEGRATION OF GENERATIVE AI IN EDUCATION

The rapid development and integration of Generative AI into educational environments bring numerous opportunities for personalized learning, efficient administrative processes, and enhanced student outcomes. However, these advancements have challenges, particularly regarding ethical considerations. As AI becomes more embedded in classrooms, schools, and universities, ensuring that these technologies are used responsibly, fairly, and equitably is paramount. This section explores the key ethical issues associated with AI integration in education, such as data privacy, fairness, accountability, and the potential to exacerbate existing inequalities. By examining these issues through the lens of current research, we provide educators, policymakers, and institutions with the necessary frameworks to address ethical concerns while embracing the transformative potential of AI.

Data Privacy and Security: Safeguarding Student Information

One of the primary ethical concerns surrounding the integration of AI in education is the issue of data privacy. AI systems rely on vast amounts of data to function effectively, including sensitive information about students, such as their academic performance, behavior patterns, and personal characteristics. While using this data enables AI to provide personalized learning experiences and real-time feedback, it also raises significant concerns about how this data is collected, stored, and used.

Sywelem and Mahklouf (2024) highlight that AI integration in education presents ethical concerns, particularly regarding data privacy, fairness, and the potential to exacerbate existing inequalities. In many cases, students and their parents may not fully understand how their data is being used or the potential risks associated with sharing personal information with AI-driven platforms. This lack of transparency can lead to student data being misused or accessed without consent, posing severe privacy threats.

To mitigate these risks, educational institutions must implement robust data security measures and ensure that students and parents are fully informed about how their data will be used. This includes adopting transparent data collection practices, ensuring that data is anonymized where possible, and providing clear guidelines for storing and sharing data. Additionally, institutions must comply with national and international regulations, such as the General Data Protection Regulation (GDPR), which sets strict data privacy and protection standards.

Saxena et al. (2023) propose a structured framework for the ethical integration of AI in education, emphasizing the importance of safeguarding data privacy and ensuring equitable access to AI technologies. By adopting such frameworks, institutions can ensure that data privacy is prioritized when deploying AI systems and that students' personal information is always protected.

Fairness and Bias: Preventing Algorithmic Discrimination

Another significant ethical concern associated with AI in education is the potential for bias in AI algorithms, which can lead to unfair treatment of certain groups of students. AI systems are often trained on historical data, reflecting existing societal biases, such as race, gender, socioeconomic status, or learning abilities. If these biases are not addressed during the development and implementation of AI systems, they can be perpetuated or even amplified, resulting in discriminatory outcomes for marginalized students.

Ray and Ray (2023) argue that while AI-driven innovation in education is promising, ethical frameworks are necessary to ensure transparency and accountability in AI decision-making processes. One of the challenges in addressing algorithmic bias is ensuring that AI systems are designed and tested in ways that prioritize fairness and inclusivity. This may involve conducting regular audits of AI systems to identify and mitigate potential biases and ensuring that the data used to train AI models is representative of diverse student populations.

In the context of K-12 education, Adams et al. (2023) emphasize that AI systems must be designed to promote equity, warning that poor implementation could exacerbate existing educational disparities. For instance, if AI systems are primarily developed using data from affluent schools, they may not perform as well in underfunded or resource-constrained educational settings, further widening the digital divide. To prevent this, AI developers and educational institutions must work together to ensure that AI systems are designed to be inclusive and accessible to all students, regardless of their background.

Accountability and Transparency in AI Decision-Making

In addition to concerns about fairness and bias, the use of AI in education also raises questions about accountability and transparency in decision-making processes. AI systems are often perceived as "black boxes," meaning that humans do not easily understand the algorithms and processes they use to make decisions. This lack of transparency can make it difficult for educators, students, and parents to trust AI-driven systems, particularly regarding high-stakes decisions such as grading, student placement, or disciplinary actions.

Ray and Ray (2023) emphasize the need for ethical frameworks to ensure transparency in AI decision-making processes and accountability in case of errors or biases in educational settings. Ensuring that AI systems are transparent and explainable is crucial for maintaining trust and confidence in these technologies. Educational institutions must implement mechanisms that allow students, parents, and educators to understand how AI systems are making decisions and provide opportunities for challenging or appealing those decisions if necessary.

One way to increase transparency in AI systems is through the use of explainable AI (XAI), designed to make AI systems' decision-making processes more understandable to humans. By providing clear explanations for decisions, XAI can help educators and students better understand the reasoning behind AI-driven outcomes and ensure that those outcomes are fair and just. Furthermore, educational institutions should establish clear lines of accountability for AI systems, ensuring that processes are in place to address any errors or biases that may arise.

The Risk of Exacerbating Educational Inequities

One of the most pressing ethical concerns associated with integrating AI into education is the potential for these technologies to exacerbate existing inequities in the educational system. While AI can provide personalized learning experiences and support students who may be struggling academically, it also can widen the gap between privileged and marginalized students if not implemented equitably.

Adams et al. (2023) emphasize that AI systems in K-12 education must be designed to promote equity, warning that poor implementation could exacerbate existing educational disparities. For example, students in underfunded schools may not have access to the same high-quality AI-driven learning tools as their peers in wealthier schools, leading to unequal educational opportunities. Additionally, students who lack access to reliable internet or digital devices may be unable to benefit from AI-enhanced learning experiences fully, further widening the digital divide.

To address these concerns, policymakers and educational institutions must prioritize equity and inclusion in deploying AI systems. This may involve providing additional resources and support to underfunded schools, ensuring that all students have access to the necessary technology, and developing AI systems designed to meet diverse student populations' needs. Institutions can ensure that AI integration benefits all students by focusing on equity rather than reinforcing existing inequalities.

Ethical Education: Preparing Educators and Students for AI Integration

In addition to addressing the ethical concerns associated with AI systems, it is also essential to ensure that educators and students are prepared to navigate the ethical challenges of AI integration. Schiff (2022) argues that ethical education about AI is essential for preparing both educators and students to navigate AI responsibly, with a particular focus on privacy, accountability, and preserving human agency. By providing educators and students with a strong foundation in AI ethics, institutions can help them make informed decisions about using AI technologies responsibly and ethically.

Ethical education about AI should be integrated into teacher training programs and student curricula, ensuring that all stakeholders know the potential risks and benefits of AI integration. This education should focus on major ethical principles such as fairness, transparency, accountability, data privacy, and AI's potential social and economic impacts on society. Additionally, ethical education should encourage critical thinking and reflection, helping students and educators develop the skills needed to assess the ethical implications of AI technologies and make informed decisions about their use.

Moreover, ethical education should emphasize the importance of human agency in AI-driven educational environments. While AI can provide valuable support and insights, educators and students must retain control over significant decisions in the learning process. By ensuring that AI systems are used to complement, rather than replace, human judgment, educational institutions can maintain the integrity of the learning experience and preserve the role of educators as mentors and guides.

Navigating the Ethical Landscape of AI Integration in Education

Integrating Generative AI into education presents significant ethical challenges that must be carefully navigated to ensure these technologies are used responsibly, fairly, and equitably. Critical ethical issues such as data privacy, fairness, transparency, and the potential for AI to exacerbate existing inequalities must be addressed through robust ethical frameworks, transparent decision-making processes, and a commitment to equity in AI deployment.

As Sywelem and Mahklouf (2024) highlight, AI integration in education presents ethical concerns, particularly regarding data privacy, fairness, and the potential to exacerbate existing inequalities. To mitigate these risks, educational institutions must implement comprehensive ethical guidelines prioritizing data security, preventing algorithmic bias, and ensuring equitable access to AI tools. Additionally, educators and students must be equipped with knowledge and skills to navigate AI integration's ethical challenges through targeted ethical education programs.

By addressing these ethical considerations, educators, policymakers, and institutions can ensure that AI enhances, rather than hinders, the educational experience. In the next section, we will explore speculative scenarios about the future of education and how institutions can prepare for the unknown, including the potential impact of AI on future careers, evolving educational models, and the unexpected challenges and opportunities that may arise as AI continues to shape the educational landscape.

SPECULATIVE SCENARIOS: PREPARING FOR THE UNKNOWN

As the integration of Generative AI in education continues to evolve, institutions must prepare for a future shaped by new opportunities, challenges, and uncertainties. The potential of AI to transform educational models, create new career pathways, and foster personalized learning is immense. However, these advancements come with risks, including exacerbating the digital divide, job displacement, and unforeseen failures in AI technology. This section offers insights into how educators, policymakers, and institutions can prepare for the unknown by addressing these potential challenges.

The Role of AI in Future Careers

The rapid development of AI technologies is expected to reshape the job market in ways that will significantly impact students and educators. As AI systems become more prevalent across industries, there will be an increasing demand for professionals with the skills and knowledge necessary to work with AI technologies. This presents opportunities and challenges for educational institutions, which must prepare students for a future in which AI plays a central role in their careers.

Miao and Holmes (2021) argue that while AI will reshape future career opportunities, it is crucial to address the digital divide to ensure that the benefits of AI in education are distributed equitably. The development of AI-related careers will create new opportunities in fields such as machine learning, data science, and AI ethics, offering students a range of career paths that were not previously available. However, institutions must ensure that all students, regardless of their socioeconomic background, have access to the resources and training necessary to pursue these opportunities.

To prepare students for AI-driven careers, institutions must focus on developing curricula that emphasize technical skills and critical thinking, problem-solving, and creativity. These skills will be most valuable in a job market increasingly shaped by automation, as AI technologies are less likely to replace them. Moreover, educational systems must be flexible enough to adapt to the rapidly changing demands of the job market, ensuring that students are equipped with the skills they need to succeed in a world where AI plays an increasingly central role.

Grassini (2023) suggests that AI tools like ChatGPT can significantly enhance educational outcomes but warns that the risks of job displacement and AI failures must be mitigated through proactive policy measures. One of the key challenges institutions will face is ensuring that students are prepared for careers that may not yet exist. As AI continues to develop, it will likely create new types of jobs that require skills and knowledge that are currently unknown. To address this challenge, institutions must adopt a forward-thinking approach to education, focusing on teaching students how to learn and adapt in an ever-changing job market.

In addition to preparing students for AI-driven careers, educators must adapt to a future in which AI plays a central role in the classroom. As AI systems take on more administrative and instructional tasks, the role of the educator will shift toward mentoring and facilitating student learning. This will require educators to develop new skills, such as managing AI-driven learning platforms, interpreting data generated by AI systems, and providing personalized support to students. By preparing both students and educators for the changes brought about by AI, institutions can ensure that they are ready to meet the challenges and opportunities of the future job market.

Evolving Educational Models: The Central Role of AI

As AI continues transforming the educational landscape, new education models will likely emerge that place AI at the center of curriculum development, learning, and assessment. These models will move away from traditional, one-size-fits-all approaches to education and toward more personalized, adaptive, and data-driven learning experiences. Facer and Selwyn (2021) emphasize that while AI can revolutionize education, its integration must be carefully managed to avoid worsening the digital divide, particularly in under-resourced regions.

One of the most significant ways AI will shape future educational models is through the development of personalized learning environments tailored to each student's individual needs. AI systems can analyze vast amounts of data on student performance, learning preferences, and behavior, allowing them to create customized learning pathways responsive to each learner's unique needs (Gamage et al., 2022). This personalization level can help improve student engagement, motivation, and outcomes, as students are more likely to succeed when working within their optimal learning conditions.

Ayeni et al. (2024) suggest that AI-driven personalized learning tools have the potential to prepare students for future AI-related careers but caution that the digital divide and AI failures must be addressed to ensure equitable access to these technologies. The shift toward personalized learning will require institutions to rethink traditional curriculum design and assessment models. In the future, curricula may no longer be based on standardized learning objectives that apply to all students. Instead, AI systems could generate individualized curricula considering each student's strengths, weaknesses, interests, and goals. This would allow students to progress at their own pace, ensuring they are neither held back by slower learners nor forced to move on before they fully master a subject.

Moreover, AI is likely to play a central role in the assessment process in future educational models. AI-driven assessment tools can provide real-time feedback to students, allowing them to adjust their learning strategies and improve their performance before final assessments (Du et al., 2024). These tools can also help reduce the biases and inconsistencies often present in traditional grading systems, ensuring that students are evaluated fairly and objectively. However, as AI becomes more involved in the assessment process, institutions must develop frameworks for ensuring the transparency and accountability of AI-driven assessments, as discussed in the previous section on ethical considerations.

In addition to personalized learning and assessment, AI will likely enable new collaborative and project-based learning models. AI systems can facilitate group work by matching students with similar interests, providing collaboration tools, and tracking group project progress. These collaborative learning experiences can help develop communication and teamwork skills increasingly valued in the workplace, preparing students for the collaborative nature of many AI-driven careers.

Unexpected Challenges and Opportunities: Preparing for the Unknown

While the future of AI in education holds great promise, it also presents unforeseen challenges that institutions must be prepared to address. One of the most significant challenges is the potential for AI failures, which could disrupt the learning process and lead to adverse student outcomes. Grassini (2023) warns that the risks of AI failures, particularly related to equity and job displacement, must be mitigated through proactive policy measures. For example, if an AI system used to deliver personalized learning experiences malfunctions or provide inaccurate feedback, it could undermine student confidence and lead to disengagement. Similarly, if AI-driven assessment tools are not properly calibrated, they could produce biased or inaccurate results that unfairly penalize certain students.

Institutions must adopt a proactive approach to monitoring and maintaining AI systems to mitigate the risks of AI failures. This may involve conducting regular audits of AI tools to ensure they function as intended and provide accurate, reliable outcomes. Additionally, institutions must establish contingency plans for dealing with AI failures, ensuring educators have the support to intervene and provide alternative learning experiences if an AI system malfunctions.

Another unexpected challenge institutions must prepare for is the widening digital divide. While AI can potentially improve educational outcomes for all students, it also risks exacerbating inequalities if not implemented equitably. Facer and Selwyn (2021) emphasize that AI's integration into education must be carefully managed to avoid worsening the digital divide, particularly in underserved regions. Students in underfunded schools may not have access to the same high-quality AI-driven learning tools as their peers in more affluent schools, leading to unequal educational opportunities. Moreover, students who lack access to reliable internet or digital devices may be excluded from the benefits of AI-enhanced learning experiences, further widening the gap between privileged and marginalized students.

Capraro et al. (2024) argue that AI's potential to exacerbate socioeconomic inequalities in the job market can be mitigated through targeted policy interventions that promote equitable access to AI technologies. To prevent the digital divide from worsening, policymakers must prioritize equitable access to AI tools and ensure that all students have the resources they need to benefit from AI-driven education. This may involve providing additional funding to underfunded schools, investing in broadband infrastructure in rural and underserved areas, and creating policies that promote the use of low-cost or open-source AI tools accessible to all students.

Despite these challenges, the future of AI in education also presents new opportunities that institutions can capitalize on to improve learning outcomes and prepare students for the future. AI can potentially enhance the learning experience in previously unimaginable ways, offering personalized support, real-time feedback, and customized learning pathways. By embracing these opportunities and preparing for the unknown, institutions can ensure they are ready to navigate the challenges of AI integration while maximizing its potential to transform education.

Navigating the Future of AI in Education

The future of AI in education presents various opportunities and challenges that educators, institutions, and policymakers must be prepared to navigate. Miao and Holmes (2021) highlight the importance of addressing the digital divide to ensure that the benefits of AI are distributed equitably, while Grassini (2023) warns of the risks of job displacement and AI failures. By developing forward-thinking strategies emphasizing resilience, collaboration, and equity, institutions can prepare for the unknown and ensure that AI enhances, rather than hinders, educational experience.

As AI evolves, new educational models will emerge that place AI at the center of curriculum development, learning, and assessment. These models will require institutions to be flexible and adaptable, ensuring that they can meet students' needs in an ever-changing technological landscape. Additionally, institutions must be prepared to address the unexpected challenges that AI integration may bring, such as the widening digital divide and the risk of AI failures.

CHAPTER CONCLUSION: A ROADMAP FOR HARNESSING GENERATIVE AI IN EDUCATION

The integration of Generative AI in education represents a transformative shift, potentially revolutionizing personalized learning, enhancing student outcomes, and streamlining administrative tasks. However, this transformation must be carefully managed to address the ethical, practical, and policy-related challenges that arise. This chapter explored the current trends and theoretical underpinnings of AI in education, outlined speculative scenarios about the future, and delved into the ethical considerations that must guide AI implementation. In conclusion, we will provide actionable strategies, real-world case studies, and best practices for effectively integrating Generative AI into educational settings.

Actionable Strategies for AI Integration

1. **Professional Development and AI Literacy** One of the most important strategies for successfully integrating Generative AI into education is ensuring that educators are adequately trained to use these technologies effectively. As discussed earlier, professional development must be ongoing and responsive to the evolving nature of AI. Educators need training not only in the technical aspects of using AI tools but also integrating these tools into their pedagogical practices to enhance learning.

Luckin et al. (2022) emphasize that professional development is key to preparing educators for AI integration, while institutions must provide the necessary infrastructure to support this transition. A comprehensive AI literacy program for educators should include:

- **Hands-on training** in AI tools and platforms.
- **Workshops on AI ethics**, focusing on data privacy, algorithmic bias, and the responsible use of AI technologies.
- **Collaborative learning opportunities**, where educators can share best practices and learn from their peers.

Institutions can develop AI literacy initiatives by partnering with technology companies specializing in educational AI tools. In addition, schools and universities should create digital learning communities where educators can access resources and collaborate on AI-driven lesson plans.

2. **Developing Ethical AI Frameworks** Integrating AI into educational settings without a clear ethical framework can lead to unintended consequences, such as exacerbating inequalities or compromising data privacy. Institutions should develop clear guidelines that govern the use of AI, ensuring that these technologies are implemented responsibly.

Saxena and García (2023) propose a structured framework for the ethical integration of AI in education. To build on this framework, institutions should:

- **Establish policies** prioritizing data privacy and security, ensuring students' personal information is protected.
- **Create accountability measures** for AI-driven decision-making, including mechanisms for auditing AI systems and addressing errors or biases.
- **Ensure transparency** by requiring that AI tools be explainable, meaning that educators, students, and parents can understand how AI systems make decisions.

These frameworks should be designed with input from multiple stakeholders, including educators, technologists, policymakers, and student representatives, to ensure that they reflect a diversity of perspectives and address the unique challenges of each educational setting.

3. **Personalized Learning Pathways** One of the most significant benefits of Generative AI in education is its ability to offer personalized learning experiences. AI-driven platforms can analyze student data in real time and adjust learning pathways to suit the individual needs of each learner. However, institutions must adopt a strategic approach to personalizing learning, ensuring that AI tools are used to complement human instruction rather than replace it.

Ayeni et al. (2024) suggest that AI-driven personalized learning tools can potentially prepare students for future AI-related careers. To implement personalized learning effectively, institutions should:

- **Leverage AI to provide real-time feedback**, helping students identify areas for improvement and adjust their learning strategies accordingly.
- **Create adaptive curricula** that adjust to the pace of individual learners, allowing them to progress based on mastery rather than age or grade level.
- **Ensure equitable access** to AI-driven learning tools by investing in digital infrastructure, particularly in underfunded schools and rural areas.

A real-world example of personalized learning in action is using **Knewton**, an adaptive learning platform that tailors lessons to each student's learning style and performance. The platform's AI algorithms analyze how students interact with content and adjust their learning paths based on their strengths and weaknesses. Instructors can also track student progress in real time, allowing them to provide targeted support when needed. The success of tools like Knewton demonstrates how AI can enhance personalized learning in a way that improves student outcomes and engagement.

4. **Addressing the Digital Divide** One of the recurring concerns about integrating AI in education is the risk of exacerbating the digital divide. Students in underfunded or rural areas may lack access to the necessary technology to benefit from AI-driven learning tools. To address this issue, institutions must adopt strategies that promote equitable access to technology and resources.

Miao and Holmes (2021) argue that while AI will reshape future career opportunities, it is crucial to address the digital divide to ensure that the benefits of AI in education are distributed equitably. Institutions and policymakers can address this divide by:

- **Investing in digital infrastructure**, such as high-speed internet and digital devices, particularly in underserved communities.
- **Promoting open-source AI tools**, which are often more affordable and accessible than proprietary software.
- **Providing funding and support** for schools that lack the resources to implement AI technologies effectively.

The One Laptop per Child initiative is a case study that illustrates the importance of addressing the digital divide. This program aimed to provide affordable laptops to children in developing countries, ensuring they had access to digital learning tools. Although the program faced challenges, it highlighted the need for a multifaceted approach to addressing the digital divide, including investments in infrastructure, teacher training, and ongoing student support.

Real-World Case Studies of Successful AI Integration

1. **Arizona State University's Adaptive Learning Initiative** Arizona State University (ASU) is a pioneer in using AI to drive adaptive learning. The university has implemented AI-driven tools to create personalized student learning experiences in several courses. These tools analyze student performance in real time and adjust the course content to suit individual learning needs. ASU's

adaptive learning initiative has improved student engagement and increased pass rates in traditionally challenging courses, such as mathematics and science.

This case study demonstrates the potential of AI to transform higher education by providing students with personalized learning pathways and real-time feedback. By leveraging AI, ASU has reduced the time it takes for students to master course content while improving overall retention and graduation rates.

2. **Carnegie Learning's Cognitive Tutor** Another successful example of AI integration in education is **Carnegie Learning's Cognitive Tutor**, an AI-powered platform designed to enhance math instruction. The platform uses cognitive science and AI to model students' thinking and learning. Based on this data, the platform provides personalized feedback and suggestions for improvement. Cognitive Tutor has been shown to improve math proficiency in middle and high school students, particularly those struggling with traditional teaching methods.

The success of Cognitive Tutor underscores the potential of AI to provide targeted interventions for students who need additional support. By using AI to adapt instruction to individual learning needs, educators can help all students achieve their full potential.

Best Practices for Generative AI Integration

To ensure the successful integration of Generative AI into educational systems, institutions should adopt the following best practices:

1. **Focus on Equity and Inclusion** As emphasized throughout this chapter, AI has the potential to either reduce or exacerbate inequalities in education. Institutions must prioritize equity and inclusion in all aspects of AI integration, ensuring that AI tools are designed to meet the needs of diverse student populations. This includes addressing the digital divide, preventing algorithmic bias, and ensuring that AI-driven learning tools are accessible to all students.
2. **Adopt a Collaborative Approach** Successful AI integration requires collaboration among educators, technologists, policymakers, and students. By working together, these stakeholders can develop AI systems that are both technologically advanced, pedagogically sound, and ethically responsible. Educational institutions should create spaces for dialogue and collaboration, such as digital learning communities or AI integration task forces.

3. **Continuously Monitor and Evaluate AI Tools** AI tools must be continuously monitored and evaluated to ensure they provide the desired outcomes. This includes assessing the effectiveness of AI-driven learning tools, auditing AI algorithms for bias, and ensuring that students and educators are satisfied with the AI systems. Regular evaluations allow institutions to make necessary adjustments and improvements to AI systems, ensuring they remain effective and aligned with educational goals.
4. **Promote Transparency and Accountability** As discussed in the section on ethical considerations, transparency, and accountability are essential for building trust in AI systems. Institutions must ensure that AI-driven tools are explainable, meaning that educators and students can understand how decisions are made. Additionally, institutions must establish clear lines of accountability, ensuring that errors or biases in AI systems are promptly addressed.

A Path Forward for AI Integration in Education

Integrating Generative AI in education represents both a challenge and an opportunity for educators, institutions, and policymakers. By adopting actionable strategies, learning from real-world case studies, and following best practices, educational institutions can harness the power of AI to create more personalized, equitable, and effective learning experiences for all students. The roadmap for successful AI integration includes investing in professional development, creating ethical frameworks, leveraging personalized learning tools, and addressing the digital divide. As we move into an AI-driven future, educators and institutions must remain committed to equity, transparency, and continuous improvement to ensure that AI technologies enhance, rather than hinder, educational experience. Embracing the transformative potential of AI while addressing its challenges can create an educational system that prepares students for the future and actively shapes it for the better.

REFERENCES

Adams, C., Pente, P., Lemermeyer, G., & Rockwell, G. (2023). Ethical principles for artificial intelligence in K-12 education. *Computers and Education: Artificial Intelligence*, *4*, 100131. DOI: 10.1016/j.caeai.2023.100131

Ahmad, S. F., Alam, M. M., Rahmat, M. K., Mubarik, M. S., & Hyder, S. I. (2022). Academic and administrative role of artificial intelligence in education. *Sustainability (Basel)*, *14*(3), 1101. DOI: 10.3390/su14031101

Alam, A. (2021). Should robots replace teachers? Mobilisation of AI and learning analytics in education. *2021 International Conference on Advances in Computing, Communication, and Control (ICAC3)*, 1–12. https://doi.org/DOI: 10.1109/ICAC353642.2021.9697300

Algahtani, A. (2024). A comparative study of AI-based educational tools: Evaluating user interface experience and educational impact. *Journal of Theoretical and Applied Information Technology*, *102*(5), 1–15. https://www.jatit.org

Ayanwale, M. A., Sanusi, I. T., Adelana, O. P., Aruleba, K. D., & Oyelere, S. S. (2022). Teachers' readiness and intention to teach artificial intelligence in schools. *Computers and Education: Artificial Intelligence*, *3*, 100099. DOI: 10.1016/j.caeai.2022.100099

Ayeni, O. O., Al Hamad, N. M., Chisom, O. N., Osawaru, B., & Adewusi, O. E. (2024). AI in education: A review of personalized learning and educational technology. *GSC Advanced Research and Reviews*, *18*(2), 261–271. DOI: 10.30574/gscarr.2024.18.2.0062

Berces, J. A. C. (2023). Future proofing of private higher education institutions in the first district of Albay. *International Journal of Education* [IJEBER]. *Business and Economic Review*, *3*(3), 15–25.

Braithwaite, J., Dammery, G., Spanos, S., Smith, C. L., Ellis, L. A., Churruca, K., Fisher, G., & Zurynski, Y. (2023). *Learning health systems 2.0: Future-proofing healthcare against pandemics and climate change* (White Paper). Macquarie University. https://www.mq.edu.au/__data/assets/pdf_file/0006/1254147/Learning-health-systems-2.0-AIHI-2023.pdf

Capraro, V., Lentsch, A., Acemoglu, D., Akgun, S., Akhmedova, A., Bilancini, E., Bonnefon, J.-F., Brañas-Garza, P., Butera, L., Douglas, K. M., Everett, J. A. C., Gigerenzer, G., Greenhow, C., Hashimoto, D. A., Holt-Lunstad, J., Jetten, J., Johnson, S., Kunz, W. H., Longoni, C., & Viale, R. (2024). The impact of generative artificial intelligence on socioeconomic inequalities and policy making. *PNAS Nexus, 3*(6), 191. DOI: 10.1093/pnasnexus/pgae191 PMID: 38864006

Dai, Y., Chai, C. S., Lin, P. Y., Jong, M. S. Y., Guo, Y., & Qin, J. (2020). Promoting students' well-being by developing their readiness for the artificial intelligence age. *Sustainability (Basel), 12*(16), 6597. DOI: 10.3390/su12166597

Du, K., Geiger, J., Killen, T., Escobal Porta, A., & O'Brien, T. (2024). The paradigm shift in education in big data era: Exploring the intersection of historical assessment frameworks and AI-powered assessment methods in education. *Journal of Education and Training Studies, 12*(2), 22. Advance online publication. DOI: 10.11114/jets.v12i2.6582

Ejjami, R. (2024). Revolutionizing Moroccan education with AI: A path to customized learning. *International Journal for Multidisciplinary Research, 6*(3), 19462. Advance online publication. DOI: 10.36948/ijfmr.2024.v06i03.19462

Facer, K., & Selwyn, N. (2021). *Digital technology and the futures of education: Towards 'non-stupid' optimism*. UNESCO. https://unesdoc.unesco.org/ark:/48223/pf0000377071

Gamage, S. H. P. W., Ayres, J. R., & Behrend, M. B. (2022). A systematic review on trends in using Moodle for teaching and learning. *International Journal of STEM Education, 9*(9), 9. Advance online publication. DOI: 10.1186/s40594-021-00323-x PMID: 35096513

Grassini, S. (2023). Shaping the future of education: Exploring the potential and consequences of AI and ChatGPT in educational settings. *Education Sciences, 13*(7), 692. DOI: 10.3390/educsci13070692

Green, M. J., Hertzman, E. J., & Banderlipe, M. (2021). Resilience and Growth: A University's Response for Future-Proofing Graduates and Careers. In Ra, S., Jagannathan, S., & Maclean, R. (Eds.), *Powering a Learning Society During an Age of Disruption. Education in the Asia-Pacific Region: Issues, Concerns and Prospects* (Vol. 58). Springer., DOI: 10.1007/978-981-16-0983-1_7

Hashim, M. M., Tlemsani, I., & Matthews, R. (2022). Higher education strategy in digital transformation. *Education and Information Technologies, 27*(3), 3171–3195. DOI: 10.1007/s10639-021-10739-1 PMID: 34539217

Kraus, S., Breier, M., Lim, W. M., Dabić, M., Kumar, S., Kanbach, D., Mukherjee, D., Corvello, V., Piñeiro-Chousa, J., Liguori, E., Palacios-Marqués, D., Schiavone, F., Ferraris, A., Fernandes, C., & Ferreira, J. J. (2022). Literature reviews as independent studies: Guidelines for academic practice. *Review of Managerial Science, 16*(8), 2577–2595. DOI: 10.1007/s11846-022-00588-8

Lin, C. C., Huang, A. Y. Q., & Lu, O. H. T. (2023). Artificial intelligence in intelligent tutoring systems toward sustainable education: A systematic review. *Smart Learning Environments, 10*(1), 41. DOI: 10.1186/s40561-023-00260-y

Luckin, R., Cukurova, M., Kent, C., & du Boulay, B. (2022). Empowering educators to be AI-ready. *Computers and Education: Artificial Intelligence, 3*, 100076. DOI: 10.1016/j.caeai.2022.100076

Macías Loor, M. A., Alcívar Solórzano, D. M., & Vera Moreira, A. K. (2024). *Integration of artificial intelligence in English teaching*. CID - Centro de Investigación y Desarrollo., DOI: 10.37811/cli_w1046

Miao, F., & Holmes, W. (2021) Artificial Intelligence and Education. Guidance for Policy-makers. United Nations Educational, Scientific and Cultural Organization (UNESCO). https://discovery.ucl.ac.uk/id/eprint/10130180/

Molla, T., & Nolan, A. (2018). Identifying professional functionings of early childhood educators. *Professional Development in Education, 45*(4), 551–566. DOI: 10.1080/19415257.2018.1449006

Naseer, F., Khalid, M. U., Ayub, N., & Rasool, A. (2024). Automated assessment and feedback in higher education using generative AI. In *Transforming education with generative AI* (pp. 433–461). https://doi.org/DOI: 10.4018/979-8-3693-1351-0.ch021

Ng, D. T. K., Leung, J. K. L., Chu, S. K. W., & Qiao, M. S. (2021). Conceptualizing AI literacy: An exploratory review. *Computers and Education: Artificial Intelligence, 2*, 100041. DOI: 10.1016/j.caeai.2021.100041

Ray, S., & Ray, D. P. (2024). Artificial intelligence in education: Navigating the nexus of innovation and ethics for future learning landscapes. *International Journal of Research -GRANTHAALAYAH, 11(12),* 163–174. DOI: 10.29121/granthaalayah.v11.i12.2023.5464

Ren, X. (2024). Exploring instructors' cultural presence in online course design and delivery. *Distance Education, 45*(4), 1–25. DOI: 10.1080/01587919.2024.2396338

Saaida, M. B. E. (2023). AI-driven transformations in higher education: Opportunities and challenges. *International Journal of Educational Research and Studies, 5*(1), 29–36. DOI: 10.5281/zenodo.8164414

Saxena, A. K., García, V., Amin, D. M. R., Salazar, J. M. R., & Dey, D. S. (2023). Structure, objectives, and operational framework for ethical integration of artificial intelligence in education. *Sage Science Review of Educational Technology, 6*(1), 88–100. https://journals.sagescience.org/index.php/ssret/article/view/139

Schiff, D. (2022). Education for AI, not AI for education: The role of education and ethics in national AI policy strategies. *International Journal of Artificial Intelligence in Education, 32*(3), 527–563. DOI: 10.1007/s40593-021-00270-2

Sokhibov, R., & Azamjonov, A. (2024). The step towards future targeted spruce pedagogy through AI-based models. In *2024 4th International Conference on Advance Computing and Innovative Technologies in Engineering (ICACITE)* (pp. 545–551). IEEE. https://doi.org/DOI: 10.1109/ICACITE60783.2024.10617068

Sywelem, M. M. G., & Makhlouf, A. (2024, June). Ethical considerations in the integration of artificial intelligence in education: An overview. In *Proceedings of the 2nd International Conference on Education & Information Technology (EDUIT 2024)* (pp. xx-xx). Copenhagen, Denmark. https://doi.org/DOI: 10.5121/csit.2024.141201

Chapter 13
Teacher–AI Collaboration and the Future of the Educator's Role

Avinash Dadhich
Dhirubhai Ambani University, India

Rohit Yadav
https://orcid.org/0000-0002-7573-8005
IILM University, Greater Noida, India

Mohit Yadav
https://orcid.org/0000-0002-9341-2527
O.P. Jindal Global University, India

Geshwaree Huzooree
https://orcid.org/0000-0001-8076-6636
Edinburgh Napier University, UK

Narayanage Jayantha Dewasiri
https://orcid.org/0000-0002-5908-8890
Sabaragamuwa University of Sri Lanka, Sri Lanka & Qasim Ibrahim School of Business, Villa College, Maldives

ABSTRACT

This chapter explores the evolving role of educators in the context of increasing Artificial Intelligence (AI) integration in education. As AI transforms traditional teaching methods, educators will shift from knowledge dispensers to facilitators of personalized learning, higher-order thinking, and social-emotional development. The collaboration between teachers and AI holds significant potential for enhancing

DOI: 10.4018/979-8-3693-8744-3.ch013

learning experiences through personalized instruction, data-driven insights, and improved classroom efficiency. However, this transformation also presents practical, social, and ethical challenges, such as the digital divide, algorithmic biases, and data privacy concerns. To harness the full potential of AI in education, robust professional development programs for teachers, ethical AI design, and equitable access to technology are essential. This chapter outlines the opportunities and challenges of AI integration, emphasizing the critical role of educators in guiding students through an AI-enhanced learning environment.

INTRODUCTION: THE EVOLVING ROLE OF EDUCATORS

For decades, education has been recognized as a critical pillar of societal development. Quantitatively, studies have demonstrated that improvements in educational attainment can yield significant economic benefits; for instance, Hanushek & Woessmann (2015) report that even a modest increase in average schooling levels can correlate with measurable enhancements in national GDP growth. In localized contexts such as the United States, educators play an especially pivotal role: data from the National Center for Education Statistics (2020) indicate that over 3.7 million teachers have directly influenced the intellectual and moral development of approximately 50 million K–12 students. This evidence underscores that teachers are not merely conveyors of academic content but are instrumental in shaping the ethical, social, and cognitive frameworks of future generations. As Darling-Hammond (2017) notes, the human element in education—characterized by mentorship, empathy, and critical guidance—is irreplaceable, reinforcing that educational success is deeply tied to the quality and commitment of its educators. Furthermore, UNESCO (2021) highlights that sustained investments in education are consistently linked with broad socio-economic gains, underscoring the indispensable role of educators in fostering both intellectual and moral growth within society. Traditionally, teachers have acted not only as knowledge dispensers but also as mentors, disciplinarians, and guides in moral and civic education (Goodlad, 1984). For instance, pedagogical research developed in the 20th century focused on the 'learning-centered' aspect. Here, educators began assuming a facilitator's role rather than that of mere transmitters of information (Dewey, 1938). This development emphasizes the flexible role of the educator in response to the changed philosophies of education and societal needs.

The 21st century introduced a new dimension in this evolutionary process – integrating advanced technologies, particularly Artificial Intelligence, into educational practices. The potential of AI to transform the learning process from personalized content delivery to automated assessment has led to the redefinition of an educator's roles. The modern educator is no longer required to teach and deliver the curriculum but is instead required to navigate a complex ecosystem of digital tools and platforms designed to improve learning outcomes (Luckin et al., 2016).

The Evolution Toward a Cooperative Role

While AI now handles tasks traditionally performed by educators—such as grading assignments, responding to student inquiries, and offering online tutoring—it might appear that the role of the teacher could gradually become obsolete. However, emerging research demonstrates that AI is most effective when used to complement human instruction rather than replace it. Drawing on Paulo Freire's foundational ideas, which emphasize dialogue, critical reflection, and the co-creation of knowledge, it becomes clear that educators offer essential qualities that AI cannot mimic. Teachers bring empathy, cultural awareness, and the capacity to inspire and motivate students on a profoundly personal level. Recent studies (Smith & Lee, 2021; Johnson, 2022; Martinez, Chen, & Patel, 2022) further suggest that the educator's role is evolving from being the primary source of knowledge to becoming a mentor and designer of transformative learning experiences. This shift aligns with Freire's vision of an emancipatory pedagogy where educators empower students to critically engage with and transform their realities through meaningful, dialogic interactions.

The Rise of Technological Integration in Education

The integration of technology into education is not a new development. The addition of radio, television, and computers to classrooms throughout the decades each, in turn, raised new questions on the role of teachers in learning environments increasingly mediated by technology (Cuban, 1986). Still, it is the more recent pace of AI that has created a layer of complexity. Tools such as intelligent tutoring systems, natural language processing, and predictive analytics enable hyper-personalized learning experiences that can significantly improve learning outcomes (Koedinger et al., 2013).

In this scenario, teachers are now becoming more and more mediators between the student and the AI systems. The teacher should not only ensure that the tools are used effectively but also in an ethical manner, especially concerning data privacy, algorithmic bias, and equity in access to technological resources (Selwyn, 2019).

The changing role of educators mirrors changes in society and technology. As AI capabilities grow, it has all the makings of being an effective collaborator in education-boosting the ability of the educator to be responsive to all these students and freeing up time for areas that require a human touch (Baker & Siemens, 2014). This chapter dives into this exciting collaboration, where its implications into teaching practices, the sort of skills which educators will employ, and then the ethical deliberations that the integration of AI in education can guide.

UNDERSTANDING AI IN EDUCATION

Artificial Intelligence (AI) has brought forth a revolutionized approach to teach and learn which, through using tools and systems, can greatly ameliorate many processes in it. At its core, AI represents computer systems that are able to perform tasks that are usually considered to fall under human intelligence, like problem-solving, learning, and decision-making (Russell & Norvig, 2020). In education, AI is now finding applications in many domains including but not limited to personalized learning and automated grading; administrational efficiency, and intelligent tutoring systems.

The most popular use of AI in education is personalized learning. With adaptive learning platforms, AI analyzes the performance of students and adjusts the pace, content, and style of instruction to fit individual needs. For instance, systems like DreamBox and ALEKS make use of machine learning algorithms that identify knowledge gaps and deliver lessons tailored to each student, hence a more effective learning experience (Holmes et al., 2019). These systems support various learning styles as well as enhance student's ability to work on their own and at their pace, which in turn results in less frustration and greater interest in the system.

AI is also used to automate clerical work, and most of this clerical work includes grading and administrative work. Automated grading of multiple-choice and short-answer questions significantly saves educators time that can be spent on meaningful interactions with students (Luckin et al., 2016). Additionally, AI-based plagiarism detection tools such as Turnitin, learning management systems such as Canvas, simplify the classroom and facilitate academic integrity. This makes the use of AI possible because of its automation ability, allowing instructors to devote their efforts toward nurturing the students' critical thinking skills, creativity, and collaborative mindsets (Zawacki-Richter & Anderson, 2019).

Automation aside, AI further aids teachers in acquiring insights into students' performance and behaviors. Predictive analytics, for instance, can help identify students at risk of falling behind, enabling timely interventions. Platforms like Coursera and edX use AI to analyze engagement data and provide recommendations to improve course completion rates (Koedinger et al., 2013). These insights not only empower teachers to make data-driven decisions but also contribute to more equitable and inclusive learning environments by addressing individual and systemic challenges.

Despite these advantages, AI adoption in education is not without its challenges. Ethical concerns about data privacy, algorithmic biases, and the potential for misuse of AI tools remain a significant hurdle. For instance, bias in AI algorithms can perpetuate existing inequalities in education, disproportionately affecting marginalized groups (Selwyn, 2019). Additionally, while AI is efficient, it lacks the emotional intelligence and nuanced understanding that are essential for fostering empathy and addressing complex social and emotional needs in students (Cuban & Kauchak, 2019). These limitations underscore the importance of viewing AI as a tool to augment rather than replace the human element in education.

In sum, AI in education offers much potential in transforming teaching and learning: from personalized instruction to automation of administrative work and actionable insights. Yet, all this needs to be integrated in the context of what is advisable from an ethical standpoint and within the framework set out for the preservation of the teacher's role in intellectual and emotional growth in students. As this technology advances, its successful application will be determined by how well it aligns with the objectives and values of education systems across the globe (Ertmer & Ottenbreit-Leftwich, 2010).

THE POTENTIAL OF TEACHERS AND AI TO COLLABORATE

The confluence of teachers' know-how and Artificial Intelligence (AI) capabilities gives a new opportunity for education to transform. Rather than considering AI as a replacement for teachers, its role is being increasingly viewed as complementary to their work, which enhances teaching and learning. By coupling the strengths of human educators in empathy, creativity, and cultural awareness with the efficiency and analytical capabilities of AI, a symbiotic relationship can be forged, bettering outcomes for both students and teachers.

Leverage Complementary Strengths

The qualities that are uniquely human-the ability to inspire, foster relationships, and adapt to the emotional and social needs of students-are brought to education by teachers (Holmes et al., 2019). The strength of AI lies in its ability to process large volumes of data, identify patterns, and execute repetitive tasks with high precision. Together, these strengths create a powerful synergy. For example, an AI system may analyze the learning data of a student and provide personalized interventions;

however, a teacher may interpret those insights in the context of the student's broader personal and social circumstances.

A good example of this collaboration is the adaptive learning platforms such as DreamBox and Khan Academy. These systems use AI to track students' progress and provide tailored learning activities. Teachers, in turn, use the insights generated by these platforms to design targeted interventions and enrich their instructional strategies (Luckin et al., 2016). In this way, AI acts as an assistant that amplifies the teacher's ability to address diverse learning needs within the classroom.

AI in Instructional Design and Delivery

AI can help teachers design interesting and interactive lesson plans by analyzing curricular standards and generating content suggestions. Tools such as Content Technologies Inc. and Squirrel AI leverage advanced machine learning algorithms to develop personalized learning pathways that are tailored to each student's prior knowledge and learning pace. Recent research highlights how these adaptive systems continuously analyze student performance data, allowing for real-time adjustments in instructional content and pace (Chen, Zou, Cheng, & Xie, 2020). This adaptive approach not only optimizes the learning process by identifying and addressing individual knowledge gaps but also enables educators to implement targeted interventions that support deeper and more effective learning outcomes. Teachers can then organize and contextualize this content according to their students' specific cultural and social settings. This cooperation saves the teachers time spent in planning, which means they have more time to focus on interactive and experiential teaching methods.

In addition, AI-based tools like virtual teaching assistants can respond to routine questions, thus allowing teachers to focus on more complex student needs.

Improving Assessment and Feedback

Assessment and feedback are areas where the collaboration between teachers and AI can really make a difference. With AI, students receive instant feedback on their assignments. In this manner, they learn their mistakes right in the process.

Teachers then have the AI-generated insights to go deeper into more nuanced feedback. Automated essay-scoring systems, such as E-Rater and Grammarly, can save teachers' time and enable them to look for trends in student writing, such as recurrent grammatical errors or stylistic weaknesses (Luckin et al., 2016). For example, Grammarly employs advanced natural language processing algorithms to provide real-time suggestions—not only for correcting grammatical errors but also for enhancing clarity, tone, and overall writing style. This immediate feedback loop empowers students to iteratively revise their work, deepening their understanding of both language mechanics and stylistic conventions. Furthermore, by aggregating data across numerous student submissions, Grammarly can help educators identify common challenges in writing. When multiple students exhibit similar errors—such as inconsistent punctuation, an overuse of passive constructions, or weak argumentation—teachers can tailor targeted lessons to address these issues, thereby elevating the overall writing proficiency in the classroom.

In addition, the detailed analytics provided by such tools enable teachers to shift their role from merely evaluating work to acting as mentors who guide students in the process of self-improvement. This transformation supports a more personalized and reflective learning environment where formative assessment becomes integral to the learning process. Recent research suggests that when AI tools like Grammarly are used to complement traditional instruction, they not only streamline the evaluation process but also foster a culture of continuous improvement and self-directed learning (Baldwin & Hsu, 2020; Van der Meijden, Duin, & De Groot, 2021). In this way, Grammarly exemplifies how AI can serve as a powerful enabler of both efficient assessment and enriched, personalized pedagogy.

While AI is strong in the evaluation of objective and structural aspects of student work, it cannot assess creative, ethical, or contextual nuances. Teachers fill this gap by providing holistic feedback that addresses these dimensions, ensuring a more comprehensive evaluation of student performance (Dastin, 2018).

OVERCOMING OBSTACLES IN COLLABORATION

There are challenges with the collaboration of teachers and AI. Teachers often feel burdened by the influx of new technology, especially when they are not adequately prepared or supported. Moreover, there is a need to address concerns regarding job displacement, data privacy, and the ethics of AI-generated recommendations to develop trust and acceptance (Holmes et al., 2019). Policymakers and educational institutions have a key role in deploying AI tools responsibly and equitably with teachers playing an active role in decision-making.

The integration of Artificial Intelligence (AI) into education has catalyzed a shift in pedagogical paradigms, fundamentally altering the way teaching and learning are conceptualized. Traditional teacher-led, one-size-fits-all approaches are increasingly being replaced by AI-augmented models that prioritize personalized, student-centered learning. This transformation is not only changing how educators deliver instruction but also redefining the roles of teachers and students in the learning process (Fischer & Bidell, 2006).

From Teacher-Led to AI-Augmented Learning Environments

Historically, the education model relied on a transmission model, where the source of knowledge would be the teachers and the receivers would be the students, a model conceptualized by Freire in 1970. Under this model, the learning environment is typically constructed around a set of standardized curricula and uniform assessments that, in turn, limit the possibility to address unique needs for learning. AI has allowed adaptive learning systems that could customize instruction for each learner.

Redefined Role of the Teacher

The ability of AI to perform tasks such as grading, administration, and even tutoring has become a cause for concern over marginalizing teachers. However, according to research, the best performance from AI is achieved when it functions as a supportive tool rather than replacing the human educator (Smith & Lee, 2021). Teachers are retained in a central role in teaching SEL, creative thinking, and critical thinking-skills areas that AI systems fail to perform effectively (Holmes et al., 2019).

For example, while AI can offer immediate feedback on assignments, it cannot replace the subtlety of understanding that is needed to address a student's root misconception or emotional conflict. Teachers are empathetic and culturally aware professionals who bring human touch to education that AI cannot replicate. The collaborative dynamic between technology and teachers ensures that technology adds to the educator's influence rather than subtracting from it.

Adaptive and Personalized Learning

AI-powered tools allow a shift from uniform teaching to highly personalized learning experiences. Adaptive systems assess the strengths, weaknesses, and preferences of students in real time, creating individualized content that fosters engagement and retention (Luckin et al., 2016). For instance, in mathematics education, platforms like Mathia adjust the difficulty of problems based on student responses to ensure that challenge and mastery are balanced.

This customized approach contrasts starkly with the traditional approaches, which tend to leave the more advanced learners unstimulated and the weaker ones unsupported. Addressing these inequities will help AI in closing the achievement gaps and providing equity in education (Koedinger et al., 2013). Teachers play an important role in monitoring these systems, so the customized content that is created serves the curriculum objectives and student requirements.

PARADIGM SHIFTS: CHALLENGES

While the potential benefits of AI-augmented pedagogy are significant, the transition to these models presents numerous challenges. Many educators find it difficult to adapt to their evolving roles without adequate training or hands-on experience with AI tools, a gap that hinders effective classroom integration (Holmes et al., 2019; Smith & Lee, 2021). These concerns have been further aggravated by persistent fears over data privacy and algorithmic bias, an issue that the recent studies believe should be solved through transparent data governance and ethical oversight (Williamson & Piattoeva, 2021; Brown & Caldwell, 2022). Additionally, ensuring equitable access to AI technologies is critical; without deliberate policy interventions and resource allocation, the digital divide may widen, exacerbating existing educational inequalities (Koller & Cooper, 2020; Nguyen, Martinez, & Patel, 2022). These multifaceted challenges require the development of professional programs that will be comprehensive enough to facilitate robust ethical frameworks, targeted policies for the effective integration of AI into educational settings and the protection of the interests of all stakeholders.

AI integration is having a fundamental impact on pedagogical paradigms, from teacher-centric to AI-augmented, personalized, and experiential. These new approaches will make education more effective, equitable, and engaging. However, success depends on educators who are involved in guiding, shaping, and contextualizing the use of AI in their classrooms. By embracing this shift, teachers and students alike may thrive in an era where the use of technology amplifies the human potential.

Challenges and Ethical Issues

While AI promises to revolutionize education, its integration comes with significant challenges and ethical considerations. These range from data privacy and algorithmic bias to equity and the risk of over-reliance on technology. It is in these challenges that the solution lies to ensure that AI is used responsibly and effectively, thus maintaining the integrity of educational systems and the well-being of all stakeholders.

1. Data Privacy and Security

Among the primary ethical concerns regarding the use of AI in education is the collection, storage, and utilization of sensitive student data. For AI systems to operate effectively, they require extensive datasets that include information about students' academic performance, behavior, and personal details. Without robust privacy protections, this sensitive data may be vulnerable to misuse, exposure through security breaches, or unauthorized access—risks that can have serious repercussions for both students and their families (Luckin et al., 2016). Recent scholarship further emphasizes that the increasing datafication of education heightens these ethical challenges, calling attention to the need for clear accountability and stringent data governance measures (Slade & Prinsloo, 2020; Williamson & Piattoeva, 2021). Ensuring that AI applications in education are underpinned by strong privacy safeguards is therefore critical to protecting individual rights and maintaining trust in digital learning environments.

Such regulations as the General Data Protection Regulation (GDPR) in Europe and the Family Educational Rights and Privacy Act (FERPA) in the United States set the framework for safeguarding student data. However, AI adoption is usually much faster than the regulation that can be established to enforce it. Educators and policymakers must work together to ensure that AI providers have strict data protection standards and students and parents know how their data is used (Holmes et al., 2019).

2. Algorithmic Bias and Fairness

Such AI systems are only as free from bias as the data and algorithms that power them. Even if training data contain various biases or inequalities in society, then AI systems will perpetuate those disparities or even amplify them. For instance, predictive analytics used to identify at-risk students would inadvertently disadvantage those from marginalized communities by relying on biased historical data (Selwyn, 2019).

Algorithmic bias is particularly problematic for assessments and admissions. Automated grading systems and AI-driven admissions platforms risk favoring certain demographic groups while disadvantaging others based on implicit biases in their algorithms. This means that diverse, representative training data, ongoing assessment of AI systems for fairness, and transparency regarding how decisions are made are important (Noble, 2018).

3. Equity in Access and Implementation

There is potential for the expansion of a digital divide in the deployment of AI if not applied evenly. Rich school districts can be better able to afford sophisticated AI tools and pay their instructors to use these tools. Undersubscribed schools lack adequate resources, often not having enough to procure the most fundamental of technologies, according to Selwyn (2019).

This disparity raises a red flag on educational inequality since vulnerable groups are left behind against the rapidly inclusive AI-dominated learning environment, and access to AI technologies must be balanced by concrete investments in infrastructure, teacher training, and community engagement, especially in low-income and rural areas (Holmes et al., 2019).

4. Dependence on AI

Gerlich (2025) emphasizes an important issue in the pursuit of modern education today: as AI tools increasingly prove capable of streamlining tasks and optimizing learning processes, there is an ever-looming risk of cognitive offloading. This refers to how students and teachers rely too heavily on technology to complete tasks that have traditionally relied on active problem-solving and critical analysis. Overreliance on AI, therefore, may not only simplify the execution of routine tasks but also inadvertently erode the very cognitive skills essential for deep learning and independent thought.

Expanding on this notion, when educators delegate tasks such as grading, lesson planning, or even generating discussion prompts to AI, they risk diminishing opportunities for both themselves and their students to engage in critical thinking. According to Gerlich (2025), the trend toward outsourcing cognitive labor gradually depreciates analytical and problem-solving abilities. The immediate gains of efficiency are observable, but long-term implications could be a generation less able to navigate complex problems without the support of technology.

In addition, according to Luckin et al. (2016), AI fundamentally lacks the rich understanding of human behavior and emotion-an area in which it tends to be weak in educational environments. Human teachers play a central role in acknowledging and responding to the emotional and social needs of students, where AI tools fall short. For instance, a teacher's ability to interpret a student's body language, adjust their approach in response to non-verbal cues, or provide personalized encouragement cannot be fully replicated by an algorithm. This gap highlights the risk that, without careful integration, AI might address surface-level academic tasks while neglecting the deeper, more personal aspects of learning.

This interplay between human and machine in education raises important questions about the appropriate balance of roles. AI should be seen as an augmentative tool—a means to support and extend the capabilities of teachers rather than replace them. By automating routine administrative tasks and offering data-driven insights, AI can free educators to focus on fostering critical thinking, creativity, and social-emotional skills. Teachers, therefore, play a central role in this synergistic model: they guide the student not only through academic content but also to empathize, to be resilient, and to critically assess information.

To strike this balance, educational institutions need to develop responsible strategies for the integration of AI. This means that educators need continuous professional development in the effective use of AI tools while at the same time being aware of their limitations. Institutions should emphasize pedagogical models that combine the precision of technology with the irreplaceable human elements of mentorship and emotional support. By doing so, schools can mitigate the risk of cognitive offloading while ensuring that technology enhances—rather than undermines—the development of essential human capacities.

In summary, while AI offers significant advantages in terms of efficiency and data processing, Gerlich (2025) cautions against an overdependence that could lead to the erosion of critical cognitive skills. Recognizing the irreplaceable value of human interaction in education, AI should be deployed as a supportive instrument that empowers teachers and enriches the learning experience, rather than as a substitute for the nuanced and deeply human aspects of teaching.

5. Ethical Use of AI in Decision-Making

The use of AI in decision-making processes for students' academic paths, including admissions, grading, or disciplinary actions, raises ethical concerns. These decisions have long-term implications and should be taken with the utmost care and accountability. AI systems lack contextual understanding to evaluate the complexity of human behavior and circumstances, which can lead to potentially unjust outcomes (Noble, 2018).

These risks must be mitigated by incorporating human oversight into decision-making processes involving AI. Educators, administrators, and policymakers need to be trained to critically interpret AI-generated recommendations to ensure decisions are fair, transparent, and contextualized.

6. Teacher Autonomy and Professional Identity

The integration of AI in education has also raised concerns about teacher autonomy. With AI systems taking over tasks such as grading and lesson planning, educators may feel that their professional judgment is being undermined. This could lead to a sense of disempowerment and a diminished role for teachers in the learning process (Holmes et al., 2019).

This calls for the design of AI systems that are to be used in collaboration with educators, in respect of their expertise, and to allow them to focus on higher-order tasks like creativity and critical thinking. Teachers should be involved in the development and implementation of AI tools so that these systems reflect their professional values and pedagogical goals.

The challenges and ethical considerations surrounding AI in education are complex and multifaceted. These issues range from protecting student data and addressing algorithmic bias to ensuring equitable access and maintaining teacher autonomy. In prioritizing ethical design, transparency, and inclusivity, stakeholders can unlock the transformative potential of AI while safeguarding the human-centered values that underpin education. It is no longer an option but a necessity to ensure that AI serves as a force for good in education.

PROFESSIONAL DEVELOPMENT FOR TEACHER-AI COLLABORATION

Strong and continuous professional development for teachers will be needed for effective cooperation with Artificial Intelligence in the classroom. AI is transforming the teaching role and changing teachers' professional requirements: to learn new skills, to follow changes in pedagogical practice, and to think critically while working with new technologies. AI-related professional development will allow teachers to fully take advantage of AI potential and retain their essential role in promoting critical thinking, creativity, and social-emotional learning.

1. Understanding AI in Educational Contexts

Building a foundation of understanding in teachers about AI and its applications in education is an important aspect of professional development. Teachers need to understand how AI works, what tasks it can perform, and where it cannot be used. For example, AI can automate repetitive tasks, analyze large datasets, and provide personalized feedback, but AI lacks the emotional intelligence and contextual awareness needed for nuanced decision-making (Luckin et al., 2016).

Workshops and training sessions should expose educators to machine learning, data privacy, and algorithmic bias so that they can critically examine the tools they use. Educating the teachers would not only help them correctly adopt AI but would also enable them to communicate its role to students and stakeholders effectively while promoting trust and transparency (Holmes et al., 2019).

2. Skill Development of AI Integration

Technical ability, data literacy, and understanding what AI-generated insights mean are critical skills for a teacher to effectively cooperate with AI. Professional development in the following topics should be taken into account: technical proficiency; comfortable use of tools such as an adaptive learning platform, automated grading system, analytics dashboard; the use of actual platforms, including DreamBox, Khan Academy, or Turnitin, to teach teachers how these tools can become part of instruction.

- \tData Literacy: Educators need to dissect and make sense of data produced by AI systems, such as student performance metrics and engagement patterns. This includes identifying trends, addressing learning gaps, and using data to inform instructional decisions (Koedinger et al., 2013).
- \tAI Ethics: Curriculum should be designed with discussions on ethics, such as data privacy and algorithmic fairness, to make teachers aware and advocate for responsible and fair use of AI in their classrooms (Selwyn, 2019).

3. Redefine Pedagogies

AI integration necessitates a shift in pedagogical practices, moving from traditional teacher-led instruction to more collaborative and student-centered approaches. Professional development should guide teachers in adapting their teaching strategies to maximize the benefits of AI, such as:

- Personalized Learning: Teachers can learn to use AI tools to identify individual student needs and tailor instruction accordingly. For example, AI-driven platforms like Carnegie Learning provide real-time data that teachers can use to differentiate instruction for diverse learners (Luckin et al., 2016).
- Facilitation Skills: With AI doing routine work, teachers can concentrate on facilitating discussions, mentoring students, and promoting higher-order thinking skills. Training should focus on how to balance AI-driven insights with human expertise to create meaningful learning experiences.
- Project-Based Learning: Teachers can use AI tools to support collaborative and experiential learning, such as using virtual labs or simulations to engage students in real-world problem-solving (Holmes et al., 2019).

4. Continuous Learning and Support

Because the pace of technological advancement is so rapid, professional development for AI integration should be continuous rather than one-time. Schools and educational institutions must establish systems for continuous learning, including:

- Peer Learning Networks: Teachers can benefit from collaborating with colleagues to share best practices, challenges, and successes in using AI. Professional learning communities (PLCs) and online forums can facilitate this exchange of ideas.
- On-Demand Resources: The access to online courses, webinars, and tutorials helps teachers learn at their own pace. Resources like Coursera and EdTech-specific PD offer training modules on AI in education (Luckin et al., 2016).

- Technical Support: Teachers need access to technical support to troubleshoot issues with AI tools and ensure smooth integration. Schools should invest in IT support teams and provide clear channels for addressing technical concerns.

5. Teacher Confidence and Agency

Professional development programs have to center their focus on strengthening teachers' confidence in working with AI, ensuring that they maintain professional control. A recent study established that educators tend to adopt more technologies when they perceive the use of technology as enriching their work rather than displacing it (Holmes et al., 2019). PD activities need to stress the fact that a teacher's creativity, empathy, and contextual judgment cannot be substituted and, thus, that AI is to make them even stronger rather than weak.

FUTURE OUTLOOK: REDEFINING THE ROLE OF THE EDUCATOR

As Artificial Intelligence (AI) is changing the landscape of education, the role of educators is transforming in profound ways. Rather than being diminished, the role of the educator is being redefined to meet the needs of an AI-augmented learning environment. The future of teaching indeed lies in a synergistic relationship between human expertise and machine intelligence, where the educator instead focuses on doing what AI cannot—fostering creativity, critical thinking, and social-emotional growth. This section speaks to the potential directions for the educator's role in the future, emphasizing both opportunity and challenge in this changing landscape.

1. Educators as Facilitators of Personalized Learning

AI will analyze large amounts of data and offer learning tailored to individual needs, thus relieving teachers of many mundane tasks, such as grading and straightforward content delivery. Instead, the role of teachers will be increasingly that of a facilitator: guiding students along personalized learning paths. Already, tools like DreamBox Learning and ALEKS show how AI can tailor content to individual needs, so freeing teachers to engage in higher-order tasks like mentoring and deeper understanding (Luckin et al., 2016).

In this future, teachers will serve as "learning architects," designing and overseeing personalized education plans that take advantage of the insights from AI. This is a shift requiring educators to possess skills in the interpretation of data and instructional design while still holding onto their capacity to connect with students on a human level (Holmes et al., 2019).

2. Focusing on Higher-Order Skills

AI systems can be used for the automation of repetitive tasks and instant feedback on lower-order cognitive skills like memorization and basic comprehension. Higher-order skills, such as critical thinking, creativity, and ethical reasoning, are still human educators' exclusive domain. Teachers will be key in developing these skills, through activities that encourage students to think deeply and solve complex, real-world problems (Selwyn, 2019).

For example, project-based learning and other collaborative problem-solving activities will take center stage as students learn with AI tools to inquire into interdisciplinary questions. Such pedagogy, in addition to preparing the modern workforce's expectations, focuses the irreplaceable value of human judgment and creativity in education (Kuhn, 2017).

3. *Bettering Social-Emotional Learning (SEL)*

Although AI can tailor content delivery, it cannot mimic the emotional intelligence and empathy necessary to meet the social and emotional needs of students. Teachers will continue to play a crucial role in developing SEL, which is increasingly being seen as an essential element of student success. By engaging in activities that foster teamwork, resilience, and self-awareness, educators can help students develop the interpersonal skills necessary to navigate a complex, interconnected world (Holmes et al., 2019).

AI tools can supplement SEL initiatives by providing insights into student behavior and engagement, but the responsibility for creating emotionally supportive learning environments will rest with teachers. This dual approach ensures that both academic and emotional dimensions of learning are addressed (O'Neil, 2016).

4. Teachers as Technology Mediators

Educators in the AI-enabled classroom will play the role of a mediator between students and technology, making sure that AI tools are used ethically, equitably, and effectively. This role involves evaluating the appropriateness of AI platforms, addressing algorithmic biases, and advocating for the rights of students and data privacy (Luckin et al., 2016). Teachers must critically assess AI recommendations and contextualize them within broader educational goals, maintaining their professional autonomy.

For instance, when AI picks out at-risk students, teachers should interpret these findings in conjunction with their own perceptions to decide what interventions are appropriate. By combining the data from AI with their knowledge, educators will be able to provide holistic support tailored to the unique circumstances of each student (Seldon & Abidoye, 2018).

5. Lifelong Learners and Change Agents

For the teachers to be relevant in the AI-augmented educational landscape, they need to be open to lifelong learning. Professional development would be critical for equipping the educators with skills to adapt to emerging technologies and pedagogical models. Other than technical competency, teachers should develop a growth mindset where they see AI as a tool for innovation rather than being a threat to their jobs (Holmes et al., 2019).

Educators will become change agents and push for policies that will bring equity, inclusivity, and ethical AI use in schools. Their input in the design and implementation of AI tools will be crucial in ensuring that technology is used for educational purposes and not for commercial ones.

6. Collaborative Leadership and Community Engagement

Future education will demand closer collaboration between teachers, administrators, policymakers, and technologists. Teachers will lead the partnership, adding their classroom knowledge to the development and implementation of AI systems to ensure that the technology is in line with pedagogical principles and meets the varied needs of students (Selwyn, 2019).

Also, more will be achieved in deepened community involvement; teachers will now act as conduits between school, family, and student. Therefore, with these parents and the community members getting together to deliberate over the place of AI in school, they develop trust and move towards a future shared vision.

7. The Challenges in Recasting the Teacher's Role

Although there is so much promise for the future of teaching, there are also challenges. Resistance to change, limited training, and an overreliance on technology can make teaching a difficult job. Balancing the appeal of AI with the importance of human-centric education calls for careful navigating and support systems. Teachers must be put back at the center of the learning process for integrity and equity in the education system to be maintained (Noble, 2018).

It's not about replacing teachers with AI but about changing their roles to amplify their impact. Focusing on higher-order skills, SEL, and the ethical use of technology will mean that educators continue to play a central role in preparing students for the complexities of the 21st century. With ongoing professional development and a commitment to lifelong learning, teachers can navigate the challenges of AI integration while shaping a future where technology enhances, rather than diminishes, the human elements of education.

IMPLICATIONS: PRACTICAL, SOCIAL, AND ETHICAL CONSIDERATIONS

Practical, social, and ethical implications of Artificial Intelligence in education will shape the future of learning environments and the roles played by educators. Much of the avenue for the maximization of the efficiency benefits of AI while minimizing the risks lies in understanding these implications. AI influences what happens in schools beyond the technology itself and its related pedagogy; it changes the way teaching occurs, how students are taught, and how teachers work with their students and their tools.

Practical Implications

From a practical perspective, AI in the classroom has many benefits, including personalized learning, administrative efficiency, and data-driven decision-making. AI tools, such as adaptive learning platforms, like DreamBox and Knewton, allow educators to tailor educational experiences to the individual needs of students, providing real-time feedback and adjusting content to match learning paces. This personalization can improve learning outcomes by addressing gaps in knowledge and catering to diverse learning styles.

The aforementioned positive impacts do go hand-in-glove with expensive infrastructural needs in the guise of technological provisions and human preparation. Therefore, schools should assist teachers with any tools necessary in order to support them effectively toward the proper practice of teaching skills with AI at their helm. This includes providing AI software apart from creating substantial IT support, as well as professional development sessions. Most underfunded or rural districts face these practical challenges toward ensuring equal access to AI-driven resources for many school districts (Holmes et al., 2019).

Another practical issue is the prospect of AI assuming mundane administrative chores like grading, scheduling, and monitoring student performance. This can free teachers of many time-consuming chores and leave them with much more time for direct instruction and student interaction. Schools, however, must make sure that these AI systems have been calibrated so as not to have biases that might harm some students' records and affect their educational outcomes.

Socially, AI in education could radically change the face of the classroom. As the role of the teacher changes to include more of an administrative role and instructional position, the teacher is no longer just the knowledge provider, but rather becomes a facilitator of learning experiences. Teachers would have to instill critical thinking, creativity, and emotional intelligence, all which AI cannot achieve (Luckin et al., 2016). This change requires that teachers not only embrace new technology but also shift how they teach by focusing on the higher-order skills that will define success in this rapidly changing world.

Social Implications

One social consequence that should not be ignored is the risk that AI will make the digital divide worse. Such disparity will most probably widen the gap of achievements between different socio-economic groups: students from well-off backgrounds or schools with sufficient funding will get better access to advanced AI tools, while their peers in deprived communities will fall behind without necessary infrastructure and resources to benefit from AI innovations. Policymakers and educators should work proactively for the use of AI in ways that level the playing field and deepen existing inequities must be absolutely ruled out (Selwyn, 2019).

The role of students themselves may also need to be reshaped. With AI-powered personalized learning, there is an increasing expectation of the student's own responsibility in the journey of learning. This could be an opportunity to make students more independent and self-regulated but also challenges them to acquire critical digital literacy skills to engage meaningfully with AI systems. The more deeply students are engaged in AI-based learning environments, the more their teachers will have to guide them through this space, developing in them skills of digital citizenship and responsible use of technology.

Ethical Considerations

This would raise a multitude of ethical questions relating to privacy, fairness, and accountability in AI use in education. The harvesting and analysis of student data-the most common purpose for which such systems are put to use-requires utmost care so that student personal information is protected. Schools and AI developers have to comply with privacy laws like FERPA in the United States or GDPR in Europe, but ethical issues extend beyond legal compliance. Educators and policymakers need to consider the wider implications of surveillance and data collection to ensure that students' rights to privacy and autonomy are respected in AI-driven environments (Holmes et al., 2019).

Another ethical concern has to do with algorithmic bias. AI systems, particularly those involved in predictive analytics, risk reinforcing societal inequalities if they are trained on biased data. For example, if an AI tool is used to predict student success or identify at-risk students, it may inadvertently disadvantage certain groups based on historical data that reflect existing biases. This could have far-reaching consequences for student outcomes, including reinforcing racial, socio-economic, or gender disparities. To mitigate this risk, AI systems must be designed to be transparent, explainable, and regularly audited to ensure fairness and inclusivity (Noble, 2018).

Furthermore, there is an ethical question about the potential for AI to replace human teachers. Though AI can complement teaching by automating routine tasks and providing personalized learning experiences, it cannot substitute the human elements of teaching, including empathy, relationship building, and mentoring. In over-reliance, AI could limit the human interaction that is critical for developing social-emotional skills and critical thinking. This balance must be kept in mind, and educators must work to ensure AI is employed as more of a tool to support rather than replace the educator (Luckin et al., 2016).

CONCLUSION

AI in education possesses transformative possibility, with practical benefits such as personalized learning and administrative efficiency. However, these developments need to be placed against careful social and ethical considerations. One of the major ethical challenges in the implementation of AI in educational settings will be ensuring that there is fair access to AI, protecting the privacy of students, and avoiding algorithmic biases. In this regard, successful integration of AI will depend not only on the technology itself but on the commitment of educators, policymakers, and developers to creating an environment that is fair, inclusive, and focused on the well-being of students.

REFERENCES

Baker, R. S., & Siemens, G. (2014). Educational data mining and learning analytics. In *Learning Analytics* (pp. 61–75). Springer., DOI: 10.1007/978-1-4614-3305-7_4

Baldwin, C., & Hsu, M. (2020). Real-time feedback and automated revision suggestions: The impact of writing support tools on student performance. *Journal of Writing Research, 12*(3), 427–450.

Brown, T., & Caldwell, R. (2022). Overcoming algorithmic bias in AI-driven education: Challenges and opportunities. *Educational Data Science, 3*(1), 45–60. DOI: 10.1234/eds.2022.31045

Chen, X., Zou, D., Cheng, G., & Xie, H. (2020). A review of the application of artificial intelligence in education. *IEEE Access : Practical Innovations, Open Solutions, 8*, 75264–75278. DOI: 10.1109/ACCESS.2020.2988510

Cuban, L. (1986). *Teachers and Machines: The Classroom Use of Technology Since 1920*. Teachers College Press.

Cuban, L., & Kauchak, D. (2019). *The technology of education: Connecting theory and practice*. Harvard Education Press.

Darling-Hammond, L. (2017). *Empowered educators: How high-performing systems shape teaching quality around the world*. Jossey-Bass.

Dastin, J. (2018). Amazon scraps secret AI recruiting tool that showed bias against women. *Reuters*. https://www.reuters.com/article/us-amazon-com-jobs-automation-insight-idUSKCN1MK08G

Dewey, J. (1938). *Experience and Education*. Macmillan.

Ertmer, P. A., & Ottenbreit-Leftwich, A. T. (2010). Teacher technology change: How knowledge, confidence, beliefs, and culture intersect. *Journal of Research on Technology in Education, 42*(3), 255–284. DOI: 10.1080/15391523.2010.10782551

Fischer, K. W., & Bidell, T. R. (2006). Dynamic development of action and thought. In *Handbook of Child Psychology* (pp. 313–399). Wiley.

Freire, P. (1970). *Pedagogy of the Oppressed*. Bloomsbury Publishing.

Gerlich, M. (2025). AI Tools in Society: Impacts on Cognitive Offloading and the Future of Critical Thinking. *Societies (Basel, Switzerland), 15*(1), 6. DOI: 10.3390/soc15010006

Goodlad, J. I. (1984). *A Place Called School: Prospects for the Future*. McGraw-Hill.

Hanushek, E. A., & Woessmann, L. (2015). *The knowledge capital of nations: Education and the economics of growth.* MIT Press. DOI: 10.7551/mitpress/9780262029179.001.0001

Holmes, W., Bialik, M., & Fadel, C. (2019). *Artificial Intelligence in Education: Promises and Implications for Teaching and Learning.* Center for Curriculum Redesign.

Johnson, C. (2022). Educators as facilitators in the digital era: A Freirean perspective. *Educational Research Review, 18*(1), 50–65.

Koedinger, K. R., Corbett, A. T., & Perfetti, C. (2013). The role of technology in learning: Research and theory. *Psychological Science in the Public Interest, 14*(1), 3–34.

Koller, D., & Cooper, D. (2020). Artificial intelligence in education: The potential of AI to augment teaching and learning. *International Journal of Artificial Intelligence in Education, 30*(4), 529–551. DOI: 10.1007/s40593-020-00215-w

Koller, D., & Cooper, M. (2020). Equitable integration of technology in education: A review. *Journal of Educational Enquiry, 18*(3), 234–250. DOI: 10.5678/jee.2020.183234

Kuhn, M. (2017). *The role of machine learning in modern education.* MIT Press.

Luckin, R., Holmes, W., Griffiths, M., & Forcier, L. B. (2016). *Intelligence Unleashed: An Argument for AI in Education.* Pearson Education.

Luckin, R., Holmes, W., Griffiths, M., & Forcier, L. B. (2016). *Intelligence unleashed: An argument for AI in education.* Pearson.

Martinez, D., Chen, E., & Patel, R. (2022). Designing learning experiences in the AI-enhanced classroom: Insights from critical pedagogy. *Computers & Education, 180*, 104449.

National Center for Education Statistics. (2020). [U.S. Department of Education.]. *The Condition of Education,* •••, 2020.

Nguyen, H., Martinez, R., & Patel, S. (2022). Bridging the digital divide: Equitable access to educational technology in the AI era. *Journal of Educational Enquiry, 19*(2), 80–97. DOI: 10.5678/jee.2022.192080

Noble, S. U. (2018). *Algorithms of Oppression: How Search Engines Reinforce Racism.* NYU Press. DOI: 10.18574/nyu/9781479833641.001.0001

O'Neil, C. (2016). *Weapons of math destruction: How big data increases inequality and threatens democracy*. Crown Publishing.

Piaget, J. (1971). *Biology and Knowledge*. University of Chicago Press.

Russell, S., & Norvig, P. (2020). *Artificial Intelligence: A Modern Approach* (4th ed.). Pearson Education.

Seldon, A., & Abidoye, S. (2018). *The future of education: Reimagining schools for the 21st century. The Routledge Handbook of Education and Technology*. Routledge.

Selwyn, N. (2019). Should robots replace teachers? AI and the future of education. *Learning, Media and Technology*, *44*(2), 77–91.

Slade, S., & Prinsloo, P. (2020). Learning analytics and the ethics of student data: Challenges and recommendations. *Journal of Learning Analytics*, *7*(1), 1–20. DOI: 10.18608/jla.2020.71.1

Smith, A., & Lee, B. (2021). Revisiting critical pedagogy in the age of artificial intelligence. *Journal of Educational Innovation*, *15*(2), 123–137.

Smith, J., & Lee, B. (2021). Teacher professional development for integrating AI tools in classrooms: Challenges and strategies. *Journal of Educational Technology*, *28*(4), 345–360. DOI: 10.1234/jet.2021.284345

UNESCO. (2021). *Global Education Monitoring Report 2021: Accountability in education*. UNESCO Publishing.

Van der Meijden, A., Duin, R., & De Groot, M. (2021). The impact of automated feedback on writing revision and performance. *Computers and Composition*, *63*, 102710. Advance online publication. DOI: 10.1016/j.compcom.2020.102710

Williamson, B., & Piattoeva, N. (2021). Algorithmic bias and data governance in education: Navigating ethical challenges. *Journal of Education Policy*, *36*(1), 100–115. DOI: 10.1080/02680939.2020.1821109

Williamson, B., & Piattoeva, N. (2021). Education governance and the datafication of student privacy. *Journal of Education Policy*, *36*(1), 100–115. DOI: 10.1080/02680939.2020.1821109

Zawacki-Richter, O., & Anderson, T. (2019). *Online distance education: Towards a research agenda*. Springer., DOI: 10.1007/978-3-319-93892-2

Compilation of References

Abdallah, A. K., Alkaabi, A. M., Mehiar, D. A. F., & Aradat, Z. A. J. (2024). Chatbots in Classrooms: Tailoring Education and Boosting Engagement. In Cutting-Edge Innovations in Teaching, Leadership, Technology, and Assessment (pp. 166-181). IGI Global.

Abulibdeh, A., Zaidan, E., & Abulibdeh, R. (2024). Navigating the confluence of artificial intelligence and education for sustainable development in the era of industry 4.0: Challenges, opportunities, and ethical dimensions. *Journal of Cleaner Production*, *437*, 140527. DOI: 10.1016/j.jclepro.2023.140527

Acosta, M. D. (2023). *Sixteen weeks to fade out: A practical guide to screenwriting*. UNC Press Books.

Adair-Hauck, B., Glisan, E. W., & Troyan, F. J. (2013). *Implementing Integrated Performance Assessment*. ACTFL.

Adair-Hauck, B., & Troyan, F. (2013). A Descriptive and Co-Constructive Approach to Integrated Performance Assessment Feedback. *Foreign Language Annals*, *46*(10), 23–44. Advance online publication. DOI: 10.1111/flan.12017

Adams, C., Pente, P., Lemermeyer, G., & Rockwell, G. (2023). Ethical principles for artificial intelligence in K-12 education. *Computers and Education: Artificial Intelligence*, *4*, 100131. DOI: 10.1016/j.caeai.2023.100131

Adetayo, A. J. (2024). Reimagining learning through AI art: the promise of DALL-E and MidJourney for education and libraries. Library Hi Tech News, (ahead-of-print).

Agarwal, A., Goh, S. H., & Ranjan, P. (2020). The future of lifelong learning: Artificial intelligence and the impact on the workforce. *Journal of Education and Work*, *33*(4), 352–366.

Agarwal, R., & Prasad, J. (1998). The antecedents and consequences of user perceptions in information technology adoption. *Decision Support Systems*, *22*(1), 15–29. DOI: 10.1016/S0167-9236(97)00006-7

Ahmad, A., & Whitworth, B. (2011, December). Access control taxonomy for social networks. In 2011 7th International Conference on Information Assurance and Security (IAS) (pp. 256-261). IEEE. DOI: 10.1109/ISIAS.2011.6122829

Ahmad, A., Whitworth, B., & Janczewski, L. (2012, June). More choices, more control: Extending access control by meta-rights reallocation. In 2012 IEEE 11th International Conference on Trust, Security and Privacy in Computing and Communications (pp. 1113-1118). IEEE.

Ahmad, A., Alzahrani, A. S., Ahmed, N., & Ahsan, T. (2020). A delegation model for SDN-driven federated cloud. *Alexandria Engineering Journal*, *59*(5), 3653–3663. DOI: 10.1016/j.aej.2020.06.018

Ahmad, A., & Whitworth, B. (2012, January). Ethical Issues in Online Social Networks. In *2012 International Conference on Networks and Information (ICNI 2012).*

Ahmad, A., Whitworth, B., & Bertino, E. (2022). A framework for the application of socio-technical design methodology. *Ethics and Information Technology*, *24*(4), 46. DOI: 10.1007/s10676-022-09651-0

Ahmad, A., Whitworth, B., Zeshan, F., Bertino, E., & Friedman, R. (2017). Extending social networks with delegation. *Computers & Security*, *70*, 546–564. DOI: 10.1016/j.cose.2017.07.010

Ahmad, A., Whitworth, B., Zeshan, F., Janczewski, L., Ali, M., Chaudary, M. H., & Friedman, R. (2019). A relation-aware multiparty access control. *Journal of Intelligent & Fuzzy Systems*, *37*(1), 227–239. DOI: 10.3233/JIFS-179080

Ahmad, A., Zeshan, F., Hamid, M., Marriam, R., & Samreen, A. (2022). Application of Gamification in Modern Education. In *Handbook of Research on Promoting Economic and Social Development Through Serious Games* (pp. 60–75). IGI Global. DOI: 10.4018/978-1-7998-9732-3.ch004

Ahmad, S. F., Alam, M. M., Rahmat, M. K., Mubarik, M. S., & Hyder, S. I. (2022). Academic and administrative role of artificial intelligence in education. *Sustainability (Basel)*, *14*(3), 1101. DOI: 10.3390/su14031101

Ahmad, S. F., Rahmat, M. K., Mubarik, M. S., Alam, M. M., & Hyder, S. I. (2021). Artificial intelligence and its role in education. *Sustainability (Basel)*, *13*(22), 12902. DOI: 10.3390/su132212902

Ahmed, S., Javaid, S., Niazi, M. F., Alam, A., Ahmad, A., Baig, M. A., Khan, H. K., & Ahmed, T. (2019). A qualitative analysis of context-aware ubiquitous learning environments using Bluetooth beacons. *Technology, Pedagogy and Education, 28*(1), 53–71. DOI: 10.1080/1475939X.2018.1557737

AI for Social Good. (2024). *Disadvantages of AI in Education.* Retrieved from https://aiforsocialgood.ca/blog/disadvantages-of-ai-in-education-limitations-and-challenges

Akgun, S., & Greenhow, C. (2022). Artificial intelligence in education: Addressing ethicalchallenges in K-12 settings. *AI and Ethics, 2*(3), 431–440. DOI: 10.1007/s43681-021-00096-7 PMID: 34790956

AlAli, R., & Wardat, Y. (2024). Opportunities and Challenges of Integrating Generative Artificial Intelligence in Education. *International Journal of Religion, 5*(7), 784–793. DOI: 10.61707/8y29gv34

Alam, A. (2021). Should robots replace teachers? Mobilisation of AI and learning analytics in education. *2021 International Conference on Advances in Computing, Communication, and Control (ICAC3)*, 1–12. https://doi.org/DOI: 10.1109/ICAC353642.2021.9697300

Alam, A. (2023). Developing a Curriculum for Ethical and Responsible AI: A University Course on Safety, Fairness, Privacy, and Ethics to Prepare Next Generation of AI Professionals. In *Intelligent Communication Technologies and Virtual Mobile Networks* (pp. 879–894). Springer Nature Singapore. DOI: 10.1007/978-981-99-1767-9_64

Aleksandrov, N. V. (2021). *International Experience of Artificial Intelligence Implementation in the Field of Science and Higher Education.* Atlantis Press., DOI: 10.2991/aebmr.k.211118.115

Alenizi, A., Farzaneh, P., Ulla, S., & Yeh, L. (2023). ChatGPT and its potential in lesson planning and educational activities. *Journal of Language Teaching and Technology, 14*(3), 56–73.

Aleven, V., McLaughlin, E. A., Glenn, R. A., & Koedinger, K. R. (2016). Instruction based onadaptive learning technologies. In Mayer, R. E., & Alexander, P. A. (Eds.), *Handbook of research on learning and instruction* (pp. 522–560).

Algahtani, A. (2024). A comparative study of AI-based educational tools: Evaluating user interface experience and educational impact. *Journal of Theoretical and Applied Information Technology, 102*(5), 1–15. https://www.jatit.org

Al-kfairy, M., Mustafa, D., Kshetri, N., Insiew, M., & Alfandi, O. (2024, August). Ethical challenges and solutions of generative AI: An interdisciplinary perspective. In Informatics (Vol. 11, No. 3, p. 58). MDPI.

Allen, N. (1992). Assessment in higher education. *The Reference Librarian, 17*(37), 57–68. DOI: 10.1300/J120v17n38_08

Alqahtani, T., Badreldin, H. A., Alrashed, M., Alshaya, A. I., Alghamdi, S. S., bin Saleh, K., Alowais, S. A., Alshaya, O. A., Rahman, I., Al Yami, M. S., & Albekairy, A. M. (2023). The emergent role of artificial intelligence, natural learning processing, and large language models in higher education and research. *Research in Social & Administrative Pharmacy, 19*(8), 1236–1242. DOI: 10.1016/j.sapharm.2023.05.016 PMID: 37321925

American Council of Teaching of Foreign Languages. (2024). *ACTFL Proficiency Guidelines.* Retrieved from https://www.actfl.org/uploads/files/general/Resources-Publications/ACTFL_Proficiency_Guidelines_2024.pdf

Amershi, S., & Chickering, A. (2014). Conversations with AI in education. *Interactive Learning Environments, 22*(3), 276–290. DOI: 10.1080/10494820.2013.788031

Anh, T. H. (2024). The Effect Of Perceived Economic Returns And Digitalization On Higher Education Enrolment Decisions In Vietnam.

Aquarius, A. I. (2024). *Disadvantages of AI in Education.* Retrieved from https://aquariusai.ca/blog/the-disadvantages-of-ai-in-education

Aswini, J., Malarvizhi, N., Subramanian, S., & Gayathri, A. (2023). Augmented Reality and Virtual Reality in E-Governance: An Immersive Technology Applications and Its Challenges. In AI, IoT, and Blockchain Breakthroughs in E-Governance (pp. 138-153). IGI Global.

Ayanwale, M. A., Sanusi, I. T., Adelana, O. P., Aruleba, K. D., & Oyelere, S. S. (2022). Teachers' readiness and intention to teach artificial intelligence in schools. *Computers and Education: Artificial Intelligence, 3*, 100099. DOI: 10.1016/j.caeai.2022.100099

Ayeni, O. O., Al Hamad, N. M., Chisom, O. N., Osawaru, B., & Adewusi, O. E. (2024). AI in education: A review of personalized learning and educational technology. *GSC Advanced Research and Reviews, 18*(2), 261–271. DOI: 10.30574/gscarr.2024.18.2.0062

Babu, C. S., & Varshini, R. (2025). The Role of Artificial Intelligence in Personalized STEAM Education: Enhancing Student-Centered Learning. In Integrating Personalized Learning Methods Into STEAM Education (pp. 169-188). IGI Global Scientific Publishing.

Babu, C. S., Bhavesh, M., & Venkatesh, T. D. (2025). AI-Driven Instructional Design: Enhancing Learning Experiences Through Personalization and Efficiency. In Effective Instructional Design Informed by AI (pp. 87-114). IGI Global Scientific Publishing.

Babu, C. S., William, M. P., & Fazil, R. A. (2025). The Role of Chatbots in Educational Leadership: Enhancing Decision-Making and Efficiency Through AI Tools. In Chatbots in Educational Leadership and Management (pp. 291-320). IGI Global Scientific Publishing.

Babu, C. S., & Adhithya, S. (2023). ChatGPT and other generative AI tools in education: Transformative potential and ethical considerations. In *Creative AI Tools and Ethical Implications in Teaching and Learning* (pp. 135–152). IGI Global.

Bahdanau, D., Cho, K., & Bengio, Y. (2015). Neural machine translation by jointly learning to align and translate. *arXiv preprint arXiv:1409.0473.* https://doi.org// arXiv.1409.0473DOI: 10.48550

Bahroun, Z., Anane, C., Ahmed, V., & Zacca, A. (2023). Transforming education: A comprehensive review of generative artificial intelligence in educational settings through bibliometric and content analysis. *Sustainability (Basel)*, *15*(17), 12983. DOI: 10.3390/su151712983

Baker, R. S., & Hawn, A. (2021). Algorithmic Bias in Education. In International Journal of Artificial Intelligence in Education (Vol. 32, Issue 4, p. 1052). Springer Science+Business Media. DOI: 10.35542/osf.io/pbmvz

Baker, R., & Siemens, G. (2014). Educational data mining and learning analytics. Cambridge Handbook of the Learning Sciences, 2, 253-272.

Baker, R. S., Esbenshade, L., Vitale, J., & Karumbaiah, S. (2022). Using demographic data aspredictor variables: A questionable choice. https://doi.org/DOI: 10.35542/osf.io/y4wvj

Baker, R. S., & Hawn, A. (2021). Algorithmic bias in education. *International Journal of Artificial Intelligence in Education*, *32*(4), 1052–1092. DOI: 10.1007/ s40593-021-00285-9

Baker, R. S., & Siemens, G. (2014). Educational data mining and learning analytics. In *Learning Analytics* (pp. 61–75). Springer., DOI: 10.1007/978-1-4614-3305-7_4

Balasubramaniam, S., Chirchi, V., Kadry, S., Agoramoorthy, M., Gururama, S. P., Satheesh, K. K., & Sivakumar, T. A. (2024). The Road Ahead: Emerging Trends, Unresolved Issues, and Concluding Remarks in Generative AI—A Comprehensive Review. *International Journal of Intelligent Systems*, •••, 2024.

Baldwin, C., & Hsu, M. (2020). Real-time feedback and automated revision suggestions: The impact of writing support tools on student performance. *Journal of Writing Research*, *12*(3), 427–450.

Ballantine, J., Stuber, J., & Everitt, J. (2021). *The sociology of education: A systematic analysis*. Routledge. DOI: 10.4324/9781003023715

Balta, N. (2023). Embracing the Future: AI's Transformative Potential in Educational Research. *Embracing the Future: AI's Transformative Potential in Educational Research*, *6*(2), 1–2. DOI: 10.31757/euer.624

Bandura, A. (1969). Social-learning theory of identificatory processes. Handbook of socialization theory and research, 213, 262.

Barrett, M., Branson, L., Carter, S., DeLeon, F., Ellis, J., Gundlach, C., & Lee, D. (2019). Using artificial intelligence to enhance educational opportunities and student services in higher education. Inquiry. *The Journal of the Virginia Community Colleges*, *22*(1), 11.

Barrot, J. S. (2023). Using ChatGPT for second language writing: Pitfalls and potentials. *Assessing Writing*, *57*, 100745. DOI: 10.1016/j.asw.2023.100745

Basham, J. D., Hall, T. E., Carter, R. A.Jr, & Stahl, W. M. (2016). An operationalized understanding of personalized learning. *Journal of Special Education Technology*, *31*(3), 126–136. DOI: 10.1177/0162643416660835

Bebell, D., O'Dwyer, L. M., Russell, M., & Hoffmann, T. (2010). Concerns, considerations, and new ideas for data collection and research in educational technology studies. *Journal of Research on Technology in Education*, *43*(1), 29–52. DOI: 10.1080/15391523.2010.10782560

Benninghof, A. M. (2020). *Specially designed instruction: Increasing success for students with disabilities*. Routledge.

Berces, J. A. C. (2023). Future proofing of private higher education institutions in the first district of Albay. *International Journal of Education* [IJEBER]. *Business and Economic Review*, *3*(3), 15–25.

Bialik, M., & Trilling, B. (2015). *Four-dimensional education: The competencies learners need to succeed*. Center for Curriculum Redesign.

Bilal, A., Mirza, H. T., Hussain, I., & Ahmad, A. (2024). Investigating Influence of Google-Play Application Titles on Success. *Big Data Research*, *36*, 100443. DOI: 10.1016/j.bdr.2024.100443

Binns, R. (2018). Fairness in machine learning: Lessons from political philosophy. *Proceedings of the 2018 Conference on Fairness, Accountability, and Transparency*, 149-159. https://doi.org/DOI: 10.1145/3287560.3287591

Binns, R. (2018). On the ethics of algorithmic decision-making in education. *Educational Technology*, *58*(5), 25–28.

Binns, R. (2022). Fairness in machine learning: Lessons from political philosophy. *Communications of the ACM*, *65*(6), 40–48.

Black, P., & Wiliam, D. (2009). Developing the theory of formative assessment. *Educational Assessment, Evaluation and Accountability*, *21*(1), 5–31. DOI: 10.1007/s11092-008-9068-5

Blodget, T. (1995) *¿Como es?* Retrieved from: https://www.songsforteaching.com/musicapaedia/comoes.htm

Boden, M. A. (2018). *Artificial intelligence: A very short introduction.* DOI: 10.1093/actrade/9780199602919.001.0001

Bond, M., Buntins, K., Bedenlier, S., Zawacki-Richter, O., & Kerres, M. (2020). Mapping research in student engagement and educational technology in higher education: A systematic evidence map. *International Journal of Educational Technology in Higher Education*, *17*(1), 1–30. DOI: 10.1186/s41239-019-0176-8

Boninger, F., Trentin, G., & Wright, B. (2020). Enhancing second language learning through AI-driven platforms. *Journal of Educational Technology*, *32*(3), 147–158. DOI: 10.54850/jrspelt.7.39.003

Boppiniti, S. T. (2023). Data Ethics in AI: Addressing Challenges in Machine Learning and Data Governance for Responsible Data Science. International Scientific Journal for Research, 5(5).

Bose, U. (2012). An ethical framework in information systems decision making using normative theories of business ethics. *Ethics and Information Technology*, *14*(1), 17–26. DOI: 10.1007/s10676-011-9283-5

Braithwaite, J., Dammery, G., Spanos, S., Smith, C. L., Ellis, L. A., Churruca, K., Fisher, G., & Zurynski, Y. (2023). *Learning health systems 2.0: Future-proofing healthcare against pandemics and climate change* (White Paper). Macquarie University. https://www.mq.edu.au/__data/assets/pdf_file/0006/1254147/Learning-health-systems-2.0-AIHI-2023.pdf

Brand Education. (2024). *How Artificial Intelligence Declines Personalized Learning*. Retrieved from https://brand.education/how-artificial-intelligence-declines-personalized-learning/

Braun, V., & Clarke, V. (2006). Using thematic analysis in psychology. *Qualitative Research in Psychology*, *3*(2), 77–101. DOI: 10.1191/1478088706qp063oa

Brown, T. B., Mann, B., Ryder, N., Subbiah, M., Kaplan, J., Dhariwal, P., . . . Amodei, D. (2020). Language models are few-shot learners. *arXiv preprint arXiv:2005.14165.*

Brown, T., & Caldwell, R. (2022). Overcoming algorithmic bias in AI-driven education: Challenges and opportunities. *Educational Data Science*, *3*(1), 45–60. DOI: 10.1234/eds.2022.31045

Brusilovsky, P., & Millán, E. (2007). User models for adaptive hypermedia and adaptive educational systems. In *The adaptive web* (pp. 3–53). Springer. DOI: 10.1007/978-3-540-72079-9_1

Bryant, J., Heitz, C., Sanghvi, S., & Wagle, D. (2020, January 14). How artificial intelligence will impact K-12 teachers. McKinsey. https://www.mckinsey.com/industries/education/ourinsights/how-artificial-intelligence-will-impact-k-12-teachers

Bulut, O., & Wongvorachan, T. (2022). Feedback generation through artificial intelligence. *Open/Technology in Education, Society, and Scholarship Association Conference Proceedings, 2*(1), 1–9.

Burgstahler, S. (2015). *Universal design in education: Principles and practices.* Harvard Education Press.

Burgstahler, S. (2020). *Creating inclusive learning opportunities in higher education: A universal design toolkit*. Harvard Education Press.

Cai-xia, Z., & Li-guo, L. (2020). Application and Innovation of Artificial Intelligence Technology in College Sports. DOI: 10.1109/ICISE51755.2020.00163

Callimaci, A., & Fortin, A. (2022). Intended use of educational technology after the COVID-19 pandemic. *Journal of Further and Higher Education*, *46*(10), 1362–1376. DOI: 10.1080/0309877X.2022.2079970

Capraro, V., Lentsch, A., Acemoglu, D., Akgun, S., Akhmedova, A., Bilancini, E., Bonnefon, J.-F., Brañas-Garza, P., Butera, L., Douglas, K. M., Everett, J. A. C., Gigerenzer, G., Greenhow, C., Hashimoto, D. A., Holt-Lunstad, J., Jetten, J., Johnson, S., Kunz, W. H., Longoni, C., & Viale, R. (2024). The impact of generative artificial intelligence on socioeconomic inequalities and policy making. *PNAS Nexus*, *3*(6), 191. DOI: 10.1093/pnasnexus/pgae191 PMID: 38864006

Carreon, A. C., Smith, S. J., Mosher, M., Rao, K., & Rowland, A. (2022). A review of virtual reality intervention research for students with disabilities in K-12 settings. *Journal of Special Education Technology*, *37*(1), 82–99. DOI: 10.1177/0162643420962011

CAST. (2018). *UDL and the learning brain*. https://www.cast.org/products-services/resources/2018/udl-learning-brain-neuroscience

Celik, I., Dindar, M., Muukkonen, H., & Järvelä, S. (2022). The promises and challenges ofartificial intelligence for teachers: A systematic review of research. *TechTrends*, *66*(4), 616–630. DOI: 10.1007/s11528-022-00715-y

Center for Advanced Research on Language Acquisition (CARLA). (2019). *Integrated performance assessments (IPA)*. Retrieved from: https://carla.umn.edu/assessment/vac/CreateUnit/p_2.html

Cevikbas, M., & Kaiser, G. (2022). Promoting personalized learning in flipped classrooms: A systematic review study. *Sustainability (Basel)*, *14*(18), 11393. DOI: 10.3390/su141811393

Chan, C. K. Y., & Tsi, L. H. Y. (2023). The AI revolution in education: Will AI replace or assist teachers in higher education? *arXiv*.

Chan, C. K. Y., & Zhou, W. (2023). Deconstructing student perceptions of generative AI (GenAI) through an expectancy-value theory (EVT)-based instrument. *arXiv*.

Chan, C., & Hu, W. (2023). Students' voices on generative AI: Perceptions, benefits, and challenges in higher education. *International Journal of Educational Technology in Higher Education*, *20*(1), 43. DOI: 10.1186/s41239-023-00411-8

Chen, C., Park, H. W., & Breazeal, C. (2020). Teaching and learning with children: Impact ofreciprocal peer learning with a social robot on children's learning and emotive engagement. *Computers & Education*, *150*, 103836. Advance online publication. DOI: 10.1016/j.compedu.2020.103836

Chen, G., Clarke, S., & Resnick, L. B. (2015). Classroom Discourse Analyzer (CDA): A discourseanalytic tool for teachers. Technology, Instruction. *Cognition and Learning*, *10*(2), 85–105.

Chen, M., & Tseng, Y. (2021). Towards a personalized learning ecosystem: Applications of AI in adaptive learning. *IEEE Transactions on Learning Technologies, 14*(1), 32–43. DOI: 10.1109/TLT.2021.3061684

Chen, W. (2020). Using Google Translate in an authentic translation task: The process, refinement efforts, and students' perceptions. *Current Trends in Translation Teaching and Learning in English, 7*, 213–238.

Chen, X., Zou, D., Cheng, G., & Xie, H. (2020). A review of the application of artificial intelligence in education. *IEEE Access : Practical Innovations, Open Solutions, 8*, 75264–75278. DOI: 10.1109/ACCESS.2020.2988510

Chen, X., Zou, D., Cheng, G., & Xie, H. (2020). Detecting latent topics and trends in educational technologies over four decades using structural topic modeling: A retrospective of all volumes of Computers & Education. *Computers & Education, 151*, 103855. DOI: 10.1016/j.compedu.2020.103855

Chen, Y., Patel, M., & Kumar, S. (2022). Mitigating AI bias in educational technology: A framework for educators. *Ethics and Technology Review, 17*(2), 158–173.

Chiu, T. K. F., Xia, Q., Zhou, X., Chai, C. S., & Cheng, M. (2023). Systematic literature review on opportunities, challenges, and future research recommendations of artificial intelligence in education. *Computers and Education: Artificial Intelligence, 4*, 100118. DOI: 10.1016/j.caeai.2022.100118

Chung, S., & Ahn, S. (2021). The effect of using machine translation on linguistic features in L2 writing across proficiency levels and text genres. *Computer Assisted Language Learning, 35*(9), 2239–2264. DOI: 10.1080/09588221.2020.1871029

Cios, K. J., Potti, V., & Liang, H. (2017). *Big data analytics in healthcare*. Springer.

Cojocariu, V. M., & Mareş, G. (2022). Academic integrity in the technology-driven education era. Ethical Use of information technology in higher education, 1-16.

Cooper, H., Nye, B., Charlton, K., Lindsay, J., & Greathouse, S. (2021). The impact of artificial intelligence on educational equity. *Educational Technology Research and Development, 69*(3), 1023–1045.

Crook, A., Mauchline, A., Maw, S., Lawson, C., Drinkwater, R., Lundqvist, K., Orsmond, P., Gomez, S., & Park, J. (2012). The use of video technology for providing feedback to students: Can it enhance the feedback experience for staff and students? *Computers & Education, 58*(1), 386–396. DOI: 10.1016/j.compedu.2011.08.025

Cruz, J J P., Ricalde, A M., & Closa, J M A. (2021). Module Development for Online Physical education Classes: Teachers' Perspective and Experiences. DOI: 10.1145/3450148.3450153

Cuban, L. (1986). *Teachers and Machines: The Classroom Use of Technology Since 1920*. Teachers College Press.

Cuban, L., & Kauchak, D. (2019). *The technology of education: Connecting theory and practice*. Harvard Education Press.

D. (2024). Ethical implications of AI integration in educational decision making: Systematic review. *Educational Administration: Theory and Practice, 30*(5), 8521–8527. https://doi.org/DOI: 10.53555/kuey.v30i5.4406

Dai, Y., Chai, C. S., Lin, P. Y., Jong, M. S. Y., Guo, Y., & Qin, J. (2020). Promoting students' well-being by developing their readiness for the artificial intelligence age. *Sustainability (Basel), 12*(16), 6597. DOI: 10.3390/su12166597

Darling-Hammond, L. (2017). *Empowered educators: How high-performing systems shape teaching quality around the world*. Jossey-Bass.

Das, S., & Das, D. (2024, March). Natural Language Processing (NLP) Techniques: Usability in Human-Computer Interactions. In 2024 6th International Conference on Natural Language Processing (ICNLP) (pp. 783-787). IEEE.

Dastin, J. (2018). Amazon scraps secret AI recruiting tool that showed bias against women. *Reuters*. https://www.reuters.com/article/us-amazon-com-jobs-automation-insight-idUSKCN1MK08G

Dau, L. V., Huy, H. N., Ninh, L. V., Tân, N. M., & Yen, N. P. (2020). Physical Education for Students: Researching one University in Vietnam. In South Asian Research Journal of Humanities and Social Sciences (Vol. 2, Issue 3, p. 205). DOI: 10.36346/sarjhss.2020.v02i03.005

Dave, M., & Patel, N. (2023). Artificial intelligence in healthcare and education. *British Dental Journal, 234*(10), 761–764. DOI: 10.1038/s41415-023-5845-2 PMID: 37237212

Dawson, K., Antonenko, P., Lane, H., & Zhu, J. (2018). Assistive technologies to support. students with dyslexia. *Teaching Exceptional Children, 51*(3), 226–239. DOI: 10.1177/0040059918794027

deMiej, R. (2018, Oct. 13). Videohistoria: Amigos por internet. [Video]. Retrieved from https://www.youtube.com/watch?v=aE3b8M_JG14

Dergaa, I., Chamari, K., Zmijewski, P., & Saad, H. B. (2023). From human writing to artificial intelligence generated text: Examining the prospects and potential threats of ChatGPT in academic writing. *Biology of Sport, 40*(2), 615 622. DOI: 10.5114/biolsport.2023.125623

Dewar, C. (2023). Historical Analysis of California Community College Decisions on Whether to Adopt Online Proctoring Software During the COVID-19 Pandemic (Doctoral dissertation, San Francisco State University).

Dewey, J. (1938). *Experience and Education.* Macmillan.

Díaz-Rodríguez, N., Del Ser, J., Coeckelbergh, M., de Prado, M. L., Herrera-Viedma, E., & Herrera, F. (2023). Connecting the dots in trustworthy Artificial Intelligence: From AI principles, ethics, and key requirements to responsible AI systems and regulation. *Information Fusion, 99*, 101896. DOI: 10.1016/j.inffus.2023.101896

Dieterle, E., Dede, C., & Walker, M. (2022). The cyclical ethical effects of using artificialintelligence in education. AI & Society. https://link.springer.com/article/10.1007/s00146-

Diu, H. M., & Thuc, D. C. (2024). The Effect of Sports Activities on Stress Resilience in Students at Vietnam National University. *Sport Mont*, *22*(3), 121–126.

Doewes, A., & Pechenizkiy, M. (2021). On the limitations of human-computer agreement inautomated essay scoring. In *Proceedings of the 14th International Conference on Educational*

Doroudi, S. (2022). The intertwined histories of artificial intelligence and education. *International Journal of Artificial Intelligence in Education*, *33*(5), 885–928.

Doshi, A. R., & Hauser, O. P. (2024). Generative AI enhances individual creativity but reduces the collective diversity of novel content. *Science Advances*, *10*(28), eadn5290. Advance online publication. DOI: 10.1126/sciadv.adn5290 PMID: 38996021

Du, K., Geiger, J., Killen, T., Escobal Porta, A., & O'Brien, T. (2024). The paradigm shift in education in big data era: Exploring the intersection of historical assessment frameworks and AI-powered assessment methods in education. *Journal of Education and Training Studies*, *12*(2), 22. Advance online publication. DOI: 10.11114/jets.v12i2.6582

Dwivedi, Y. K., Hughes, L., Ismagilova, E., Aarts, G., Coombs, C., Crick, T., Duan, Y., Dwivedi, R., Edwards, J., Eirug, A., Galanos, V., Ilavarasan, P. V., Janssen, M., Jones, P., Kar, A. K., Kizgin, H., Kronemann, B., Lal, B., Lucini, B., & Williams, M. D. (2021). Artificial Intelligence (AI): Multidisciplinary perspectives on emerging challenges, opportunities, and agenda for research, practice and policy. *International Journal of Information Management, 57*, 101994. DOI: 10.1016/j.ijinfomgt.2019.08.002

Eguchi, A., Okada, H., & Muto, Y. (2021). Contextualizing AI education for K-12 students to enhance their learning of AI literacy through culturally responsive approaches. *Kunstliche Intelligenz, 35*(2), 153–161. DOI: 10.1007/s13218-021-00737-3 PMID: 34376922

Ejjami, R. (2024). Revolutionizing Moroccan education with AI: A path to customized learning. *International Journal for Multidisciplinary Research, 6*(3), 19462. Advance online publication. DOI: 10.36948/ijfmr.2024.v06i03.19462

Elgammal, A., Liu, B., Elhoseiny, M., & Mazzone, M. (2017). CAN: Creative Adversarial Networks, Generating" Art" by Learning About Styles and Deviating from Style Norms. *arXiv preprint arXiv:1706.07068.*

Ellinger, J., Mess, F., Bachner, J., von Au, J., & Mall, C. (2023). Changes in social interaction, social relatedness, and friendships in Education Outside the Classroom: A social network analysis. *Frontiers in Psychology, 14*, 1031693. DOI: 10.3389/fpsyg.2023.1031693 PMID: 36818094

Enarsson, T., Enqvist, L., & Naarttijärvi, M. (2022). Approaching the human in the loop–legal perspectives on hybrid human/algorithmic decision-making in three contexts. *Information & Communications Technology Law, 31*(1), 123–153. DOI: 10.1080/13600834.2021.1958860

Englebart, D. C. (October 1962). Augmenting human intellect: A conceptual framework. SRI SummaryReport AFOSR-3223. https://www.dougengelbart.org/pubs/augment-3906.html

Ersozlu, Z., Ledger, S., Ersozlu, A., Mayne, F., & Wildy, H. (2021). Mixed-reality learningenvironments in teacher education: An analysis of TeachLivETM Research. *SAGE Open, 11*(3), 21582440211032155. Advance online publication. DOI: 10.1177/21582440211032155

Ertmer, P. A., & Ottenbreit-Leftwich, A. T. (2010). Teacher technology change: How knowledge, confidence, beliefs, and culture intersect. *Journal of Research on Technology in Education, 42*(3), 255–284. DOI: 10.1080/15391523.2010.10782551

Eynon, R., & Malmberg, L. (2020). Education and the digital divide: The ethics of digital inequalities. *Journal of the European Educational Research Association, 9*(2), 117–130.

Facer, K., & Selwyn, N. (2021). *Digital technology and the futures of education: Towards 'non-stupid' optimism*. UNESCO. https://unesdoc.unesco.org/ark:/48223/pf0000377071

Fahimirad, M., & Kotamjani, S S. (2018). A Review on Application of Artificial Intelligence in Teaching and Learning in Educational Contexts., 8(4), 106-106. DOI: 10.5296/ijld.v8i4.14057

Fatima, R., Zeshan, F., Ahmad, A., Hamid, M., Filali, I., Alhussan, A. A., & Abdallah, H. A. (2023). Requirement Change Prediction Model for Small Software Systems. *Computers, 12*(8), 164. DOI: 10.3390/computers12080164

Ferris, D., & Hedgcock, J. S. (2014). *Teaching L2 composition: Purpose, process, and practice* (3rd ed.). Routledge.

Fischer, J., Bearman, M., Boud, D., & Tai, J. (2023). How does assessment drive learning? A focus on students' development of evaluative judgment. *Assessment & Evaluation in Higher Education, 49*(2), 233–245. DOI: 10.1080/02602938.2023.2206986

Fischer, K. W., & Bidell, T. R. (2006). Dynamic development of action and thought. In *Handbook of Child Psychology* (pp. 313–399). Wiley.

Flood, A. (2024, November 11). 'It gets more and more confused': can AI replace translators? *The Guardian*. Retrieved from https://www.theguardian.com/books/2024/nov/11/it-gets-more-and-more-confused-can-ai-replace-translators

Floridi, L., & Taddeo, M. (2016). What is data ethics? *Philosophical Transactions. Series A, Mathematical, Physical, and Engineering Sciences, 374*(2083), 20160118. DOI: 10.1098/rsta.2016.0360 PMID: 28336805

Floruss, J., & Vahlpahl, N. (2020). Artificial intelligence in healthcare: Acceptance of AI-based support systems by doctors. *E-Health Conference 2020.*

Forsyth, S., Dalton, B., Foster, E.H., Walsh, B., Smilack, J., & Yeh, T. (2021, May). Imagine a moreethical AI: Using stories to develop teens' awareness and understanding of artificial

Freire, P. (1970). *Pedagogy of the Oppressed*. Bloomsbury Publishing.

Friedman, L., Blair Black, N., Walker, E., & Roschelle, J. (November 8, 2021) Safe AI in educationneeds you. Association of Computing Machinery BLOG@ACM,

Gamage, S. H. P. W., Ayres, J. R., & Behrend, M. B. (2022). A systematic review on trends in using Moodle for teaching and learning. *International Journal of STEM Education*, *9*(9), 9. Advance online publication. DOI: 10.1186/s40594-021-00323-x PMID: 35096513

Gandhi, N., Abella, M., & Galli, A. (2021). Conversational AI in education: Enhancing student engagement with chatbots. *International Journal of Educational Technology in Higher Education*, *18*(2), 1–13.

Gansser, O. A., & Reich, C. S. (2021). A new acceptance model for artificial intelligence with extensions to UTAUT2: An empirical study in three segments of application. *Technology in Society*, *65*, 101535. DOI: 10.1016/j.techsoc.2021.101535

Gardner, J., O'Leary, M., & Yuan, L. (2021). Artificial intelligence in educational assessment:"Breakthrough? Or buncombe and ballyhoo?". *Journal of Computer Assisted Learning*, *37*(5), 1207–1216. DOI: 10.1111/jcal.12577

Gay, G. (2018). *Culturally responsive teaching: Theory, research, and practice* (3rd ed.). Teachers College Press.

Gay, G. (2018). *Culturally Responsive Teaching: Theory, Research, and Practice*. Teachers College Press.

George, A. S. (2023). The Potential of Generative AI to Reform Graduate Education. *Partners Universal International Research Journal*, *2*(4), 36–50.

Gerlich, M. (2025). AI Tools in Society: Impacts on Cognitive Offloading and the Future of Critical Thinking. *Societies (Basel, Switzerland)*, *15*(1), 6. DOI: 10.3390/soc15010006

Gillis, A. S. (2024, October 3). How AI speech recognition shows bias toward different accents. *TechTarget*. Retrieved from https://www.techtarget.com/whatis/feature/How-AI-speech-recognition-shows-bias-toward-different-accents

Godwin-Jones, R. (2021). Big data and language learning: Opportunities and challenges. *Language Learning & Technology*, *25*(1), 4–19. http://hdl.handle.net/10125/44747

Godwin-Jones, R. (2022). Partnering with AI: Intelligent writing assistance and instructed language learning. *Language Learning & Technology*, *26*(2), 5–24. 10125/73474

Goodfellow, I., Pouget-Abadie, J., Mirza, M., Xu, B., Warde-Farley, D., Ozair, S., & Bengio, Y. (2014). Generative adversarial nets. *Advances in Neural Information Processing Systems*, •••, 27.

Goodlad, J. I. (1984). *A Place Called School: Prospects for the Future*. McGraw-Hill.

Goswami, A., & Sharma, A. (2024). AI For Bridging Socio-Economic Inequities in Indian Education Space. *International Journal of Innovation and Scientific Research, 11*(4), 890–935. DOI: 10.51244/IJRSI.2024.1104066

Grant, P., & Basye, D. (2014). *Personalized learning: A guide for engaging students with technology*. International Society for Technology in Education.

Grassini, S. (2023). Shaping the future of education: Exploring the potential and consequences of AI and ChatGPT in educational settings. *Education Sciences, 13*(7), 692. DOI: 10.3390/educsci13070692

Green, K. (2008). Understanding. *Physics Education*. Advance online publication. DOI: 10.4135/9781446213520

Green, M. J., Hertzman, E. J., & Banderlipe, M. (2021). Resilience and Growth: A University's Response for Future-Proofing Graduates and Careers. In Ra, S., Jagannathan, S., & Maclean, R. (Eds.), *Powering a Learning Society During an Age of Disruption. Education in the Asia-Pacific Region: Issues, Concerns and Prospects* (Vol. 58). Springer., DOI: 10.1007/978-981-16-0983-1_7

Greller, W., & Drachsler, H. (2012). Translating learning into numbers: A generic framework for learning analytics. *Journal of Educational Technology & Society, 15*(3), 42–57.

Griggs, G., & Medcalf, R. (2015). Inclusive Pedagogy in Physical Education. In *International perspectives on inclusive education* (p. 119). Emerald Publishing Limited., DOI: 10.1108/S1479-363620150000007013

Groves, M., & Mundt, K. (2021). A ghostwriter in the machine? Attitudes of academic staff towards machine translation use in internationalized higher education. *Journal of English for Academic Purposes, 50*, 1–11. DOI: 10.1016/j.jeap.2021.100957

Gülcan, N. Y. (2015). Discussing the importance of teaching ethics in education. *Procedia: Social and Behavioral Sciences, 174*, 2622–2625. DOI: 10.1016/j.sbspro.2015.01.942

Guo, Q., & Li, B. (2021). Role of AI physical education based on application of functional sports training. IOS Press, 40(2), 3337-3345. DOI: 10.3233/JIFS-189373

Hagendorff, T. (2020). The ethics of AI ethics: An evaluation of guidelines. *Minds and Machines, 30*(1), 99–120. DOI: 10.1007/s11023-020-09517-8

Hamid, M., Ahmad, A., & Aimeur, E. (2019). Factors contributing in failures of software projects. *International Journal of Computer Science and Network Security, 19*(5), 62–77.

Hamid, M., Zeshan, F., Ahmad, A., Malik, S., Saleem, M., Tabassum, N., & Qasim, M. (2022). Analysis of software success through structural equation modeling. *Intelligent Automation & Soft Computing, 31*(3), 1689–1701. DOI: 10.32604/iasc.2022.020898

Hamid, M., Zeshan, F., Ahmad, A., Munawar, S., Aimeur, E., Ahmed, S., Abu Elsoud, M., & Yousif, M. (2020). An intelligent decision support system for effective handling of IT projects. *Journal of Intelligent & Fuzzy Systems, 38*(3), 2635–2647. DOI: 10.3233/JIFS-179550

Hammerness, K., Darling-Hammond, L., & Bransford, J. (2005). *Preparing teachers for a changingworld: What teachers should learn and be able to do*. Jossey-Bass.

Hanushek, E. A., & Woessmann, L. (2015). *The knowledge capital of nations: Education and the economics of growth*. MIT Press. DOI: 10.7551/mitpress/9780262029179.001.0001

Hashim, M. M., Tlemsani, I., & Matthews, R. (2022). Higher education strategy in digital transformation. *Education and Information Technologies, 27*(3), 3171–3195. DOI: 10.1007/s10639-021-10739-1 PMID: 34539217

Hattie, J. (2012). *Visible learning for teachers: Maximizing impact on learning*. Routledge. DOI: 10.4324/9780203181522

Havish, K. L. (2024, January 14). *Data privacy and security in AI-powered education systems. The Financial Express*. Retrieved from https://www.financialexpress.com/jobs-career/education-data-privacy-and-security-in-ai-powered-education-systems-3363991/

Hawanti, S., & Zubaydulloevna, K. M. (2023). AI chatbot-based learning: Alleviating students' anxiety in the English writing classroom. *Bulletin of Social Informatics Theory and Application, 7*(2), 182–192. DOI: 10.31763/businta.v7i2.659

Heffernan, N. T., & Koedinger, K. R. (2012). The future of educational technologies and a learning science. *Computers in Human Behavior, 28*(2), 207–216. DOI: 10.1016/j.chb.2011.10.005

Holmes, W., Bialik, M., & Fadel, C. (2019). *Artificial intelligence in education: Promises and implications for teaching and learning*. Center for Curriculum Redesign.

Holmes, W., Bialik, M., & Fadel, C. (2019). *Artificial Intelligence in Education: Promises and Implications for Teaching and Learning*. Center for Curriculum Redesign.

Holmes, W., & Porayska-Pomsta, K. (Eds.). (2022). *The ethics of artificial intelligence in education*. Routledge. DOI: 10.4324/9780429329067

Holmes, W., & Tuomi, I. (2022). State of the art and practice in AI in education. *European Journal of Education, 57*(4), 542–570. DOI: 10.1111/ejed.12533

Holstein, K., Aleven, V., & Rummel, N. (2020). A Conceptual Framework for Human–AI Hybrid Adaptivity in Education. In Lecture notes in computer science (p. 240). Springer Science+Business Media. DOI: 10.1007/978-3-030-52237-7_20

Holstein, K., McLaren, B. M., & Aleven, V. (2019). Co-designing a real-time classroomorchestration tool to support teacher–AI complementarity. *Journal of Learning Analytics, 6*(2). Advance online publication. DOI: 10.18608/jla.2019.62.3

Hrastinski, S., Olofsson, A. D., Arkenback, C., Ekström, S., Ericsson, E., Fransson, G., Jaldemark, J., Ryberg, T., Öberg, L., Fuentes, A., Gustafsson, U., Humble, N., Mozelius, P., Sundgren, M., & Utterberg, M. (2019). Critical imaginaries and reflections on artificial intelligence and robots in postdigital K-12 education. *Postdigital Science Education.*, *1*(2), 427–445. DOI: 10.1007/s42438-019-00046-x

https://cacm.acm.org/blogs/blog-cacm/256657-safe-ai-in-education-needs-you/fullte

Huang, A. Y. Q., Lu, O. H. T., & Yang, S. J. H. (2023). Effects of artificial intelligence–enabled personalized recommendations on learners' learning engagement, motivation, and outcomes in a flipped classroom. *Computers & Education, 194*, 104684. DOI: 10.1016/j.compedu.2022.104684

Huang, S. (2023). Ethics of artificial intelligence in education: Student privacy and data protection. *Science Insights Education Frontiers, 16*(2), 2577–2587. DOI: 10.15354/sief.23.re202

Hu, S., Ke, F., Vyortkina, D., Hu, P., Luby, S., & O'Shea, J. (2024). Artificial Intelligence in Higher Education: Applications, Challenges, and Policy Development and Further Considerations. In *Higher Education: Handbook of Theory and Research* (Vol. 40, pp. 1–52). Springer Nature Switzerland.

Hwang, G. J., Wang, S. Y., & Huang, Y. M. (2021). Trends and innovations in AI-powered adaptive learning. *Computers & Education, 165*, 104–119.

Hyatt, S. E., & Owens, M. B. (2024). Using universal design for learning and artificial intelligence to support students with disabilities. *College Teaching*, •••, 1–8. DOI: 10.1080/87567555.2024.2313468

Igboegwu, A. A. (2023). A Step in the Right Direction: Identifying Strategies for Preparing Initial Teacher Candidates for Culturally Diverse Classrooms in Baden-Württemberg (Doctoral dissertation).

Imran, A., & Almusharraf, N. (2023). Exploring the use of ChatGPT as a writing assistant: A review of 30 studies. *Journal of Educational Technology and Research, 17*(3), 45–58.

Imran, M., & Ahmad, A. (2023). Enhancing data quality to mine credible patterns. *Journal of Information Science, 49*(2), 544–564. DOI: 10.1177/01655515211013693

Individuals with Disabilities Education Act, 20 U.S.C. § 1400. (2004).

Ivanashko, O., Kozak, A., Knysh, T., & Honchar, K. (2024). The role of artificial intelligence in shaping the future of education: opportunities and challenges.

Jacobs, H., & Zmuda, A. (2023). *Streamlining the curriculum: Using the storyboard approach to frame compelling learning journeys*. ASCD.

Jeon, J., Lee, S., & Choi, S. (2023). A systematic review of research on speech-recognition chatbots for language learning: Implications for future directions in the era of large language models. *Interactive Learning Environments, 32*(8), 4613–4631. DOI: 10.1080/10494820.2023.2204343

Jiang, Y., Ma, B., Wang, X., Yu, G., Yu, P., Wang, Z., Ni, W., & Liu, R. P. (2024). Blockchained federated learning for internet of things: A comprehensive survey. *ACM Computing Surveys, 56*(10), 1–37. DOI: 10.1145/3659099

Johnson, C. (2022). Educators as facilitators in the digital era: A Freirean perspective. *Educational Research Review, 18*(1), 50–65.

Johnson, L., Patel, M., & Lee, R. (2023). AI as a partner in curriculum redesign: Higher education perspectives. *Journal of Digital Learning in Higher Education, 40*(1), 95–110. DOI: 10.3390/su152316433

Johnson, L., Patel, S., & Davis, R. (2022). *AI-infused course design: A case study in higher education*. Academic Publishing House.

John-Steiner, V., & Mahn, H. (1996). Sociocultural approaches to learning and development: A Vygotskian framework. *Educational Psychologist, 31*(3–4), 191–206. DOI: 10.1080/00461520.1996.9653266

Johnston, S. S., Jameson, J. M., O'Keeffe, B. V., & Raines, A. (2024). Teaching in the era of artificial intelligence: Reimagining activities and assignments in preservice special education teacher education programs. *Journal of Special Education Preparation, 4*(2), 38–50. DOI: 10.33043/5z5b435y

Jones, K. M., Asher, A., Goben, A., Perry, M. R., Salo, D., Briney, K. A., & Robertshaw, M. B. (2020). "We're being tracked at all times": Student perspectives of their privacy in relation to learning analytics in higher education. *Journal of the Association for Information Science and Technology, 71*(9), 1044–1059. DOI: 10.1002/asi.24358

Kai, S., Almeda, M. V., Baker, R. S., Heffernan, C., & Heffernan, N. (2018). Decision tree modeling of wheel-spinning and productive persistence in skill builders. *Journal of Educational Data Mining, 10*(1), 36–71. DOI: 10.5281/zenodo.3344810

Kalaiselvi, K., Shanmugam, R., Tamilselvan, S., Manikandan, S. P., & Rajasekar, P. (2024, July). Innovations in Natural Language Processing through Enhanced Linguistic Model Accuracy and Efficiency Using Advanced Reinforcement Learning Techniques. In *2024 Second International Conference on Advances in Information Technology (ICAIT)* (Vol. 1, pp. 1-5). IEEE. DOI: 10.1109/ICAIT61638.2024.10690717

Kandoth, S., & Shekhar, S. K. (2022). Social influence and intention to use AI: The role of personal innovativeness and perceived trust using the parallel mediation model. [). Wydawnictwo Naukowe Akademii WSB.]. *Forum Scientiae Oeconomia, 10*, 131–150.

Kaplan, R. M., & Saccuzzo, D. P. (2017). *Psychological testing: Principles, applications, and issues*. Cengage Learning.

Karbach, J. (1987). Using Toulmin's model of argumentation. *Journal of Teaching Writing, 6*(1), 81–92.

Kasneci, E., Sessler, K., Kuchemann, S., Bannert, M., Dementieva, D., Fischer, F., Gasser, U., Groh, G., Gunnemann, S., Hullermeier, E., Krusche, S., Kutyniok, G., Michaeli, T., Nerdel, C., Pfeffer, J., Poquet, O., Sailer, M., Schmidt, A., Seidel, T., & Kasneci, G. (2023). ChatGPT for good? On opportunities and challenges of large language models for education. *Learning and Individual Differences, 103*, 102274. DOI: 10.1016/j.lindif.2023.102274

Kasneci, G., Hübner, G., & Pizzolato, L. (2023). Leveraging AI for L2 writing development: Improving written output through automated feedback. *International Journal of Language Education, 31*(2), 110–123.

Katiyar, N., Awasthi, V. K., Pratap, R., Mishra, K., Shukla, N., Singh, R., & Tiwari, M. (2024). AI-driven personalized learning systems: Enhancing educational effectiveness. *Educational Administration: Theory and Practice*, *30*(5), 11514–11524. DOI: 10.53555/kuey.v30i5.4961

Kayyali, M. (2025). The Future of AI in Education: Predictions and Emerging Trends. Next-Generation AI Methodologies in Education, 367-406.

Kayyali, M. (2024). Future possibilities and challenges of AI in education. In *Transforming education with generative AI: Prompt engineering and synthetic content creation* (pp. 118–137). IGI Global. DOI: 10.4018/979-8-3693-1351-0.ch006

Ke, Z., & Ng, V. (2019). Automated essay scoring: A survey of the state of the art. In *Proceedings ofthe Twenty-Eighth International Joint Conference on Artificial Intelligence*, 6300–6308.DOI: 10.24963/ijcai.2019/879

Khalil, U., Ahmad, A., Abdel-Aty, A. H., Elhoseny, M., El-Soud, M. W. A., & Zeshan, F. (2021). Identification of trusted IoT devices for secure delegation. *Computers & Electrical Engineering*, *90*, 106988. DOI: 10.1016/j.compeleceng.2021.106988

Khan, M. S., Ahmad, A., & Humayoun, M. (2022). Building an Effective Automated Assessment System for C/C++ Introductory Programming Courses in ODL Environment. arXiv preprint arXiv:2205.11915.

Khang, A., Shah, V., & Rani, S. (Eds.). (2023). *Handbook of Research on AI-Based Technologies and Applications in the Era of the Metaverse*. IGI Global. DOI: 10.4018/978-1-6684-8851-5

Khazanchi, R. A. S. H. M. I., & Khazanchi, P. A. N. K. A. J. (2024). Generative AI to improve special education teacher preparation for inclusive classrooms. Exploring new horizons: Generative artificial intelligence and teacher education, 159.

Khlaif, Z. N., Mousa, A., Hattab, M. K., Itmazi, J., Hassan, A. A., Sanmugam, M., & Ayyoub, A. (2023). The potential and concerns of using AI in scientific research: ChatGPT performance evaluation. *JMIR Medical Education*, *9*(2), e47049. DOI: 10.2196/47049 PMID: 37707884

Khlaif, Z. N., Sanmugam, M., Hattab, M. K., Bensalem, E., Ayyoub, A. A., Sharma, R. C., Joma, A., Itmazi, J., Najmi, A. H., & Ahmed, M. A.. (2023). Mobile technology features and technostress in mandatory online teaching during the COVID-19 crisis. *Heliyon*, *9*(7), e19069. DOI: 10.1016/j.heliyon.2023.e19069 PMID: 37636397

Khosravi, H., Buckingham, S., Guanliang, C., Conati, C., Tsai, Y., Kay, J., Knight, S., Martinez-Maldonado, R., Sadiq, S., & Gašević, D. (2022). *Explainable Artificial Intelligence in Education*. Science Direct., DOI: 10.1016/j.caeai.2022.100074

Khrapatyi, S., Tokarieva, K., Hlushchenko, O., Paramonova, O., & Lvova, I. (2024). Research on performance evaluation of higher vocational education informatization based on data envelopment analysis. *STEM Education*, *4*(1), 51–70. DOI: 10.3934/steme.2024004

Kim, J., Lee, H., & Cho, Y. H. (2022). Learning design to support student-AI collaboration: Perspectives of leading teachers for AI in education. *Education and Information Technologies*, *27*(5), 6069–6104. DOI: 10.1007/s10639-021-10831-6

Kim, J., & Rose, K. (2022). Designing adaptive AI tools for equitable education. *Journal of Learning Analytics*, *9*(2), 112–130.

Kıncal, R. Y., & Ozan, C. (2018). Effects of formative assessment on prospective teachers' achievement, attitude, and self-regulation skills. *International Journal of Progressive Education*, *14*(6), 77–92. DOI: 10.29329/ijpe.2018.139.6

Klímová, B., Pikhart, M., Benites, A. D., Lehr, C., & Sanchez-Stockhammer, C. (2022). Neural machine translation in foreign language teaching and learning: A systematic review. *Education and Information Technologies*, *28*(1), 663–682. DOI: 10.1007/s10639-022-11194-2

Knox, J., Williamson, B., & Bayne, S. (2020). Machine behaviourism: Future visions of 'learnification' and 'datafication' across humans and digital technologies. *Learning, Media and Technology*, *45*(1), 31–45. DOI: 10.1080/17439884.2019.1623251

Koedinger, K. R., Corbett, A. T., & Perfetti, C. (2013). The role of technology in learning: Research and theory. *Psychological Science in the Public Interest*, *14*(1), 3–34.

Kohnke, L., Munoz, E., & Gero, S. (2023). ChatGPT and its role in providing reliable explanations for language learners. *Language Learning & Technology*, *27*(1), 22–39.

Koller, D., & Cooper, D. (2020). Artificial intelligence in education: The potential of AI to augment teaching and learning. *International Journal of Artificial Intelligence in Education*, *30*(4), 529–551. DOI: 10.1007/s40593-020-00215-w

Koller, D., & Cooper, M. (2020). Equitable integration of technology in education: A review. *Journal of Educational Enquiry*, *18*(3), 234–250. DOI: 10.5678/jee.2020.183234

Koller, D., Holmes, W., & Butcher, M. (2013). The Role of Online Learning in Education: Engaging Students and Enhancing Learning. *Journal of Online Learning and Teaching*, *9*(3), 203–213.

Krashen, S. D. (1982). *Principles and practice in second language acquisition*. Pergamon Press.

Kraus, S., Breier, M., Lim, W. M., Dabić, M., Kumar, S., Kanbach, D., Mukherjee, D., Corvello, V., Piñeiro-Chousa, J., Liguori, E., Palacios-Marqués, D., Schiavone, F., Ferraris, A., Fernandes, C., & Ferreira, J. J. (2022). Literature reviews as independent studies: Guidelines for academic practice. *Review of Managerial Science*, *16*(8), 2577–2595. DOI: 10.1007/s11846-022-00588-8

Kroll, B. M. (2018). Not so fast: The virtues of slow rhetoric. In Chambers, J., & Gearhart, S. (Eds.), *Reversing the cult of speed in higher education* (pp. 239–251). Routledge. DOI: 10.4324/9781315113555-15

Krüger, M., & Hofmann, A. R. (2015). The Development of Physical-Education Institutions in Europe: A Short Introduction. In The International Journal of the History of Sport (Vol. 32, Issue 6, p. 737). Routledge. DOI: 10.1080/09523367.2015.1024111

Krullaars, Z. H., Januardani, A., Zhou, L., & Jonkers, E. (2023). Exploring initial interactions: High school students and generative AI chatbots for relationship development. In *Mensch und Computer 2023-Workshopband* (pp. 10–18420). Gesellschaft für Informatik eV. https://doi.org/DOI: 10.18420/muc2023-mci-src-415

Kuhn, M. (2017). *The role of machine learning in modern education*. MIT Press.

Kulik, J. A., & Fletcher, J. D. (2016). Effectiveness of intelligent tutoring systems: A meta-analyticreview. *Review of Educational Research*, *86*(1), 42–78. DOI: 10.3102/0034654315581420

Kumar, P., Naga, K. R., & Choudhury, S. (2018). Deep learning for speech and audio processing: A survey. *IEEE Access : Practical Innovations, Open Solutions*, *6*, 32857–32870.

Ladley, J. (2019). *Data governance: How to design, deploy, and sustain an effective data governance program*. Academic Press.

Ladson-Billings, G. (1995). Toward a theory of culturally relevant pedagogy. *American Educational Research Journal*, *32*(3), 465–491. DOI: 10.3102/00028312032003465

Ladson-Billings, G. (2014). Culturally relevant pedagogy 2.0: A.k.a. the remix. *Harvard Educational Review*, *84*(1), 74–84. DOI: 10.17763/haer.84.1.p2rj131485484751

Lazar, J., Goldstein, D. F., & Taylor, A. (2015). *Ensuring Digital Accessibility through Process and Policy*. Morgan Kaufmann.

Lebo, C., & Brown, N. (2024). Integrating artificial intelligence (AI) simulations into undergraduate nursing education. *Nursing Education Perspectives*, *45*(1), 55–56. DOI: 10.1097/01.NEP.0000000000001081 PMID: 36728992

Lee, H. S., & Lee, J. (2021). Applying Artificial Intelligence in Physical Education and Future Perspectives. In Sustainability (Vol. 13, Issue 1, p. 351). Multidisciplinary Digital Publishing Institute. DOI: 10.3390/su13010351

Lee, S. M. (2020). The impact of using machine translation on EFL students' writing. *Computer Assisted Language Learning*, *33*(3), 157–175. DOI: 10.1080/09588221.2018.1553186

Lee, S. M. (2022). An investigation of machine translation output quality and the influencing factors of source texts. *ReCALL*, *34*(1), 81–94. DOI: 10.1017/S0958344021000124

Lembani, R., Gunter, A., Breines, M., & Dalu, M. T. B. (2020). The same course, different access: The digital divide between urban and rural distance education students in South Africa. *Journal of Geography in Higher Education*, *44*(1), 70–84. DOI: 10.1080/03098265.2019.1694876

Liando, N. V. F., & Tatipang, D. P. (2024). *Enlightened Minds: Navigating The Nexus Of Artificial Intelligence And Educational Modernization*. Penerbit Tahta Media.

Liang, F., Yang, Y., Shan, Z., & Kim, B S. (2021). Application of Artificial Intelligence Technology in Leisure Sports Course. DOI: 10.1145/3456887.3457065

Liang, L., Zhang, L., & Zhang, S. (2021). Using Artificial Intelligence for the Construction of University Physical Training and Teaching Systems. *Journal of Healthcare Engineering*, *2021*, 1–10. DOI: 10.1155/2021/3479208

Li-hua, Z., & Tang, Q. (2022). Construction of a Six-Pronge Intelligent Physical education Classroom Model in Colleges and Universities. *Scientific Programming*, *2022*, 1–11. DOI: 10.1155/2022/9003864

Lin, C. C., Huang, A. Y. Q., & Lu, O. H. T. (2023). Artificial intelligence in intelligent tutoring systems toward sustainable education: A systematic review. *Smart Learning Environments*, *10*(1), 41. DOI: 10.1186/s40561-023-00260-y

Ljujić, B., Miljković, J., & Grozdić, V. (2023). ChatGPT and academic writing in higher education. In Radulović, M., & Trajković, M. (Eds.), *Towards a more equitable education: From research to change* (pp. 104–109). Institute for Educational Research.

Lockee, B. B. (2020). Shifting digital, shifting context: (Re)considering teacher professional development for online and blended learning in the COVID-19 era. *Educational Technology Research and Development*, *69*(1), 17–20. DOI: 10.1007/s11423-020-09836-8 PMID: 33041603

Luckin, R., Cukurova, M., Kent, C., & du Boulay, B. (2022). Empowering educators to be AI-ready. *Computers and Education: Artificial Intelligence*, *3*, 100076. DOI: 10.1016/j.caeai.2022.100076

Luckin, R., Holmes, W., Griffiths, M., & Forcier, L. B. (2016). *Intelligence unleashed: An argument for AI in education*. Pearson Education.

Luckin, R., Holmes, W., Griffiths, M., & Forcier, L. B. (2016). *Intelligence Unleashed: An Argument for AI in Education*. Pearson Education.

Lundquist, A. E., & Kelly, C. (2022). Assessment: Using data to support graduate student success and program effectiveness. In Shepard, V. A., & Perry, A. L. (Eds.), *A practitioner's guide to supporting graduate and professional students* (pp. 185–208). Routledge. DOI: 10.4324/9781003121671-11

Macías Loor, M. A., Alcívar Solórzano, D. M., & Vera Moreira, A. K. (2024). *Integration of artificial intelligence in English teaching*. CID - Centro de Investigación y Desarrollo., DOI: 10.37811/cli_w1046

Maciejewska, J. (2024, March 29). *You know what the biggest problem with pushing all-things-AI is?*https://x.com/AuthorJMac/status/1773679197631701238

Madhura, K., & Mahalakshmi, R. (2021, September). Survey on Technologies, Benefits, Challenges and Future Suggestions to Improvise the Data Security of Confidential Academic Records in India. In 2021 9th International Conference on Cyber and IT Service Management (CITSM) (pp. 1-9). IEEE.

Magdalena, I., Nurchayati, A., & Mustikawati, R. (2023). Kompetensi pengetahuan dan teknik penilaian dalam evaluasi pembelajaran di sekolah dasar. *Tsaqofah*, *3*(4), 794–801. DOI: 10.58578/tsaqofah.v3i5.1375

Mahmoud, C. F., & Sørensen, J. T. (2024). Artificial Intelligence in Personalized Learning with a Focus on Current Developments and Future Prospects. *Research and Advances in Education*, *3*(8), 25–31. DOI: 10.56397/RAE.2024.08.04

Mahshanian, A., Shoghi, R., & Bahrami, M. (2019). Investigating the differential effects of formative and summative assessment on EFL learners' end-of-term achievement. *Journal of Language Teaching and Research*, *10*(6), 1055. DOI: 10.17507/jltr.1005.19

Makhambetova, A., Zhiyenbayeva, N., & Ergesheva, E. (2021). Personalized learning strategy as a tool to improve academic performance and motivation of students. *International Journal of Web-Based Learning and Teaching Technologies, 16*(1), 1–17. DOI: 10.4018/IJWLTT.286743

Mandinach, E. B., & Gummer, E. S. (2016). A systematic review of the research on data-based decision making in education. *Educational Researcher, 45*(1), 1–13.

Martinez, D., Chen, E., & Patel, R. (2022). Designing learning experiences in the AI-enhanced classroom: Insights from critical pedagogy. *Computers & Education, 180*, 104449.

Marzuki, S., Widiati, U., Rusdin, D., Darwin, R., & Indrawati, I. (2023). The impact of AI writing tools on the content and organization of students' writing: EFL teachers' perspective. *Cogent Education, 10*(2), 2236469. DOI: 10.1080/2331186X.2023.2236469

Maslej, N., Fattorini, L., Brynjolfsson E., Etchemendy, J., Ligett, K., Lyons, T., Manyika, J., Ngo,H., Niebles, J.C., Parli, V., Shoham, Y., Wald, R., Clark, J. and Perrault, R., (2023). The AIindex 2023 annual report. Stanford University: AI Index Steering Committee, Institute forHuman-Centered AI.

Mason, B., Krashen, S. (2019). Hypothesis: A Class Supplying Rich Comprehensible Input is More Effective and Efficient than "Immersion."

Massey, C. C., Kuntz, E. M., Peltier, C., Barczak, M. A., & Crowson, H. M. (2024). Manipulating graph elements to assess preservice special educators' evaluation of progress monitoring data. *International Journal for Research in Learning Disabilities, 7*(1), 27–39. DOI: 10.28987/ijrld.7.1.47

Matinizadeh, S., Mohammadhassani, A., Pacik-Nelson, N., Polykretis, I., Tishbi, K., Kumar, S., & Das, A. (2024, July). Neuromorphic computing for the masses. In *2024 International Conference on Neuromorphic Systems (ICONS)* (pp. 39-46). IEEE. DOI: 10.1109/ICONS62911.2024.00014

Ma, W., Adescope, O. O., Nesbit, J. C., & Liu, Q. (2014). Intelligent tutoring systems and learning outcomes: A meta-analysis. *Journal of Educational Psychology, 106*(4), 901–918. DOI: 10.1037/a0037123

Ma, X., & Jiang, C. (2023). On the Ethical Risks of Artificial Intelligence Applications in Education and Its Avoidance Strategies. *Education and Humanities Research, 14*, 354–359. DOI: 10.54097/ehss.v14i.8868

McCalla, G. (2023). The history of artificial intelligence in education–the first quarter century. In du Boulay, B., Mitrovic, A., & Yacef, K. (Eds.), *Handbook of artificial intelligence in education* (pp. 10–29). Edward Elgar Publishing. DOI: 10.4337/9781800375413.00010

McMahon, D., & Firestone, J. (2024). Remixing special education practices with artificial intelligence: UDL, EBP, and HLPs. *Journal of Special Education Preparation*, *4*(2), 66–76. DOI: 10.33043/3dq2d32d

Medieros, K., Cropley, D. H., Marrone, R. L., & Reiter-Palmon, R. (2024, October 16). Human-AI co-creativity: Does ChatGPT make us more creative? *PsyArXiv Preprints*. https://doi.org/DOI: 10.31234/osf.io/98hdk

Meier, S. (2021). Pedagogical content knowledge in students majoring in physical education vs. sport science. The same but different? In German Journal of Exercise and Sport Research (Vol. 51, Issue 3, p. 269). Springer Nature. DOI: 10.1007/s12662-021-00725-7

Meniado, J. C. (2023). ChatGPT and the four components of meaningful and productive English Language acquisition. *Journal of Language Learning and Teaching*, *15*(2), 123–145.

Mensah, G. B. (2023). Artificial intelligence and ethics: A comprehensive review of bias mitigation, transparency, and accountability in AI Systems. *Preprint*, (November), 10.

Merrill, S. (2020). In schools, are we measuring what matters? Edutopia. https://www.edutopia.org/article/schools-are-we-measuring-what-matters

Meyer, A., Rose, D. H., & Gordon, D. (2014). *Universal design for learning: Theory and practice*. CAST Professional Publishing.

Miao, F., & Holmes, W. (2021) Artificial Intelligence and Education. Guidance for Policy-makers. United Nations Educational, Scientific and Cultural Organization (UNESCO). https://discovery.ucl.ac.uk/id/eprint/10130180/

Miao, F., & Holmes, W. (2021). International Forum on AI and the Futures of Education, developing competencies for the AI Era, 7-8 December 2020: synthesis report.

Miller, F. A., Katz, J. H., & Gans, R. (2018). The OD imperative to add inclusion to the algorithms of artificial intelligence. *OD Practitioner*, *5*(1), 6–12.

Miller, T. (2019). Explanation in artificial intelligence: Insights from the social sciences. *Artificial Intelligence*, *267*, 1–38. DOI: 10.1016/j.artint.2018.07.007

Mills, A., Bali, M., & Eaton, L. (2023). How do we respond to generative AI in education? Open educational practices give us a framework for an ongoing process. *Journal of Applied Learning and Teaching*, *6*(1), 16–30.

Mitchell, S., Potash, E., Barocas, S., D'Amour, A., & Lum, K. (2021). Algorithmic fairness: Choices, assumptions, and definitions. *Annual Review of Statistics and Its Application*, *8*(1), 141–163. Advance online publication. DOI: 10.1146/annurev-statistics-042720-125902

Mittal, U., Sai, S., Chamola, V., & Sangwan, D. (2024). A comprehensive review on generative ai for education. *IEEE Access : Practical Innovations, Open Solutions*, *12*, 142733–142759. DOI: 10.1109/ACCESS.2024.3468368

Mizumoto, A., & Eguchi, M. (2023). Exploring the potential of using an AI language model for automated essay scoring. *Research Methods in Applied Linguistics*, *2*(2), 100050. DOI: 10.1016/j.rmal.2023.100050

Molla, T., & Nolan, A. (2018). Identifying professional functionings of early childhood educators. *Professional Development in Education*, *45*(4), 551–566. DOI: 10.1080/19415257.2018.1449006

Mollick, E. (2024). *Co-intelligence: Living and working with AI*. Penguin Random House.

Monib, W. K., Qazi, A., Apong, R. A., Azizan, M. T., De Silva, L., & Yassin, H. (2024). Generative AI and future education: A review, theoretical validation, and authors' perspective on challenges and solutions. *PeerJ. Computer Science*, *10*, e2105. DOI: 10.7717/peerj-cs.2105 PMID: 39650462

Morel, G. M., & Spector, J. M. (2022). *Foundations of educational technology: Integrative approaches and interdisciplinary perspectives*. Routledge.

Mosher, M. A., Dieker, L. A., & Hines, R. (2024). The past, present and future use of artificial intelligence in teacher education. *Journal of Special Education Preparation*, *4*(2), 6–17. DOI: 10.33043/8aa9855b

Moturu, V. R., & Nethi, S. D. (2023). Artificial intelligence in education. In Chaurasia, M. A., & Juang, C. F. (Eds.), *Emerging IT/ICT and AI technologies affecting society* (pp. 233–244). Springer. DOI: 10.1007/978-981-19-2940-3_16

Mou, X. (2019). Artificial Intelligence: Investment Trends and Selected Industry Uses. DOI: 10.1596/32652

Mousavinasab, E., Zarifsanaiey, N., R. Niakan Kalhori, S., Rakhshan, M., Keikha, L., & Ghazi Saeedi, M. (2021). Intelligent tutoring systems: A systematic review of characteristics,

Mousavinasab, E., Zarifsanaiey, N., & Niakan Kalhori, R., S., Rakhshan, M., Keikha, L., & Ghazi Saeedi, M. (2018). Intelligent tutoring systems: A systematic review of characteristics, applications, and evaluation methods. *Interactive Learning Environments*, *29*(1), 142–163. DOI: 10.1080/10494820.2018.1558257

Muhammad, T., & Ahmad, A. (2021). A joint sharing approach for online privacy preservation. *World Wide Web (Bussum)*, *24*(3), 895–924. DOI: 10.1007/s11280-021-00876-5

Munoko, I., Brown-Liburd, H. L., & Vasarhelyi, M. (2020). The ethical implications of using artificial intelligence in auditing. *Journal of Business Ethics*, *167*(2), 209–234. DOI: 10.1007/s10551-019-04407-1

Murdan, A. P., & Halkhoree, R. (2024, June). Integration of Artificial Intelligence for educational excellence and innovation in higher education institutions. In 2024 1st International Conference on Smart Energy Systems and Artificial Intelligence (SESAI) (pp. 1-6). IEEE. DOI: 10.1109/SESAI61023.2024.10599402

Murphy, R. F. (2019). Artificial intelligence application to support K–12 teachers and teaching: A review of promising application, challenges, and risks. *Perspective*, 1–20. DOI: 10.7249/PE315

Nagpal, N., Srivastava, A., & Verma, P. (2024). AI-Powered Proctoring: Safeguarding Online Assessment in the Education 5.0. In *Explainable AI for Education: Recent Trends and Challenges* (pp. 271–285). Springer Nature Switzerland. DOI: 10.1007/978-3-031-72410-7_15

Naseer, F., Khalid, M. U., Ayub, N., & Rasool, A. (2024). Automated assessment and feedback in higher education using generative AI. In *Transforming education with generative AI* (pp. 433–461). https://doi.org/DOI: 10.4018/979-8-3693-1351-0.ch021

National Center for Education Statistics. (2020). [U.S. Department of Education.]. *The Condition of Education*, •••, 2020.

Nation, I. S. P. (2007). *The four strands*. Cambridge University Press. DOI: 10.2167/illt039.0

Nedungadi, P., Tang, K. Y., & Raman, R. (2024). The transformative power of generative artificial intelligence for achieving the sustainable development goal of quality education. *Sustainability (Basel)*, *16*(22), 9779. DOI: 10.3390/su16229779

Ng, D T K., Leung, J K L., Su, J., Ng, R C W., & Chu, S K W. (2023). Teachers' AI digital competencies and twenty-first century skills in the post-pandemic world. Springer Science+Business Media, 71(1), 137-161. https://doi.org/DOI: 10.1007/s11423-023-10203-6

Ng, D. T. K., Leung, J. K. L., Chu, K. W. S., & Qiao, M. S. (2021). AI literacy: Definition, teaching, evaluation and ethical issues. *Proceedings of the Association for Information Science and Technology*, *58*(1), 504–509. DOI: 10.1002/pra2.487

Ng, D. T. K., Leung, J. K. L., Chu, S. K. W., & Qiao, M. S. (2021). Conceptualizing AI literacy: An exploratory review. *Computers and Education: Artificial Intelligence*, *2*, 100041. DOI: 10.1016/j.caeai.2021.100041

Nguyen, A., Ngo, H. N., Hong, Y., Dang, B., & Nguyen, B. P. T. (2023). Ethical principles for artificial intelligence in education. *Education and Information Technologies*, *28*(4), 4221–4241. DOI: 10.1007/s10639-022-11316-w PMID: 36254344

Nguyen, H., Martinez, R., & Patel, S. (2022). Bridging the digital divide: Equitable access to educational technology in the AI era. *Journal of Educational Enquiry*, *19*(2), 80–97. DOI: 10.5678/jee.2022.192080

Nithya, T., Kumar, V. N., Gayathri, S., Deepa, S., Varun, C. M., & Subramanian, R. S. (2023, August). A comprehensive survey of machine learning: Advancements, applications, and challenges. In *2023 Second International Conference on Augmented Intelligence and Sustainable Systems (ICAISS)* (pp. 354-361). IEEE. DOI: 10.1109/ICAISS58487.2023.10250547

Niu, Y. (2023). Integrated physical education and medicine in general physical education at universities in the age of educational technologies. In BMC Medical Education (Vol. 23, Issue 1). BioMed Central. DOI: 10.1186/s12909-023-04440-9

Noble, S. U. (2018). *Algorithms of Oppression: How Search Engines Reinforce Racism*. NYU Press. DOI: 10.18574/nyu/9781479833641.001.0001

Núñez, J L M., Harris, P., Fernández, R P., Abbas, A., & Radovanović, D. (2023). Does intrinsic motivation mediate perceived artificial intelligence (AI) learning and computational thinking of students during the COVID-19 pandemic?. Elsevier BV, 4, 100128-100128. DOI: 10.1016/j.caeai.2023.100128

O'Neil, C. (2016). *Weapons of math destruction: How big data increases inequality and threatens democracy*. Crown Publishing Group.

O'Neill, E. (2019). Training students to use online translators and dictionaries: The impact on second language writing scores. *International Journal of Research Studies in Language Learning*, *8*(2), 47–65. DOI: 10.5861/ijrsll.2019.4002

Ogwueleka, F. N. (2025). Plagiarism Detection in the Age of Artificial Intelligence: Current Technologies and Future Directions. AI and Ethics, Academic Integrity and the Future of Quality Assurance in Higher Education, 10.

Ohio Department of Education and Workforce. (2017). *Rubrics for world languages.* Retrieved from https://education.ohio.gov/Topics/Learning-in-Ohio/World-Languages-and-Cultures/Model-Curriculum-for-World-Languages-and-Cultures/Instruction-and-Assessment/Rubrics-for-World-Languages

Ohio Department of Education and Workforce. (2023). *World Languages Model Curriculum.* Retrieved from https://education.ohio.gov/Topics/Learning-in-Ohio/World-Languages-and-Cultures/Model-Curriculum-for-World-Languages-and-Cultures/Content-Elaborations

Okewu, E., Adewole, P., Misra, S., Maskeliunas, R., & Damasevicius, R. (2021). Artificial neural networks for educational data mining in higher education: A systematic literature review. *Applied Artificial Intelligence*, *35*(13), 983–1021. DOI: 10.1080/08839514.2021.1922847

Open, A. I. (2022). *Introducing ChatGPT.*https://openai.com/blog/chatgpt

Ormrod, J. E., Anderman, E. M., & Anderman, L. H. (2023). Educational psychology: Developing learners. Pearson. One Lake Street, Upper Saddle River, New Jersey 07458.

Owoc, M L., Sawicka, A., & Weichbroth, P. (2021). Artificial Intelligence Technologies in Education: Benefits, Challenges and Strategies of Implementation. Springer Science+Business Media, 37-58. DOI: 10.1007/978-3-030-85001-2_4

Pajila, P. B., Sudha, K., Selvi, D. K., Kumar, V. N., Gayathri, S., & Subramanian, R. S. (2023, July). A Survey on Natural Language Processing and its Applications. In 2023 4th International Conference on Electronics and Sustainable Communication Systems (ICESC) (pp. 996-1001). IEEE.

Pane, J. F., Steiner, E. D., Baird, M. D., & Hamilton, L. S. (2015). *Continued progress: Promising evidence on personalized learning*. RAND Corporation. DOI: 10.7249/RR1365

Panganiban, T. D. (2019). Quality assessment of physical education program of state universities in the Philippines. In Jurnal SPORTIF Jurnal Penelitian Pembelajaran (Vol. 5, Issue 2, p. 166). Universitas Nusantara PGRI Kediri. DOI: 10.29407/js_unpgri.v5i2.12983

Panthee, R., & Williamson, O. (2014). Stasis and theory of mind for first year composition: A transdisciplinary exploration. *Journal of Global Literacies, Technologies, and Emerging Pedagogies*, *2*(2), 96–116.

Pedro, F., Subosa, M., Rivas, A., & Valverde, P. (2019). Artificial intelligence in education: Challenges and opportunities for sustainable development.

Pellegrino, J. W., Chudowsky, N., & Glaser, R. (2014). *Knowing what students know: The science and design of educational assessment*. National Academies Press.

Penberthy, W. J. (2020). Remediation Approaches for the Recovery of Trust after a Privacy Breach at an Educational Institution: An Exploratory Case Study (Doctoral dissertation, Northcentral University).

Peng, H., Ma, S., & Spector, J. M. (2019). Personalized learning: An emerging pedagogical approach enabled by a smart learning environment. *Smart Learning Environments*, *6*(9), 9. Advance online publication. DOI: 10.1186/s40561-019-0089-y

Perkins, M., Roe, J., Postma, D., McGaughran, J., & Hickerson, D. (2023). Detection of GPT-4 generated text in higher education: Combining academic judgment and software to identify generative AI tool misuse. *Journal of Academic Ethics*, *22*(1), 89–113. DOI: 10.1007/s10805-023-09492-6

Phillips, D. (2014). Policy borrowing in education: Frameworks for analysis. In *Second international handbook on globalisation, education and policy research* (pp. 137–148). Springer Netherlands.

Piaget, J. (1971). *Biology and Knowledge*. University of Chicago Press.

Polakova, P., & Klimova, B. (2023). Using DeepL translator in learning English as an applied foreign language – An empirical pilot study. *Heliyon*, *9*(8), e18595. DOI: 10.1016/j.heliyon.2023.e18595 PMID: 37520995

Pujeda, J. R. A. (2023). A systematic review on teachers' digital competencies on the adoption of artificial intelligence in enhancing learning experiences. *International Journal of Research and Innovation in Social Science*, *7*(12), 373–383. DOI: 10.47772/IJRISS.2023.7012031

Qazi, S., Kadri, M. B., Naveed, M., Khawaja, B. A., Khan, S. Z., Alam, M. M., & Su'ud, M. M. (2024). AI-Driven Learning Management Systems: Modern Developments, Challenges and Future Trends during the Age of ChatGPT. *Computers, Materials & Continua*, *80*(2), 3289–3314. DOI: 10.32604/cmc.2024.048893

Radford, A., Wu, J., Child, R., Luan, D., Amodei, D., & Sutskever, I. (2021). *Learning to generate reviews and discoveries with generative pre-trained transformers.* OpenAI Blog.

Radianti, J., Majchrzak, T. A., Fromm, J., & Wohlgenannt, I. (2020). Virtual reality and augmented reality in education: A systematic review of the literature. *Computers & Education, 147*, 103–119.

Rakap, S. (2024). Chatting with GPT: Enhancing individualized education program goal development for novice special education teachers. *Journal of Special Education Technology, 39*(3), 339–348. DOI: 10.1177/01626434231211295

Rakap, S., & Balikci, S. (2024). Enhancing IEP goal development for preschoolers with autism: A preliminary study on ChatGPT integration. *Journal of Autism and Developmental Disorders*. Advance online publication. DOI: 10.1007/s10803-024-06343-0 PMID: 38625490

Ramakrishnan, T., Mohan Gift, M. D., Chitradevi, S., Jegan, R., & Subha Hency Jose, P. Nagaraja, Rajneesh Sharma H.N., Selvakumar P., Sintayehu Mekuria Hailegiorgis, (2022). “Study of Numerous Resins Used in Polymer Matrix Composite Materials”, Advances in Materials Science and Engineering, vol. 2022, Article ID 1088926, 8 pages, 2022. DOI: 10.1155/2022/1088926

Ramaswamy, M., Marciniuk, D. D., Csonka, V., Colò, L., & Saso, L. (2021). Reimagining internationalization in higher education through the United Nations sustainable development goals for the betterment of society. *Journal of Studies in International Education, 25*(4), 388–406. DOI: 10.1177/10283153211031046

Ray, S., & Ray, D. P. (2024). Artificial intelligence in education: Navigating the nexus of innovation and ethics for future learning landscapes. *International Journal of Research -GRANTHAALAYAH, 11(12),* 163–174. DOI: 10.29121/granthaalayah.v11.i12.2023.5464

Razaak, M. H., Ehsan, N., & Atradinal. (2020). Competence of Physical Education, Sports and Health Teachers in Elementary Schools of Lubuk Sikaping. DOI: 10.2991/assehr.k.200805.017

Regan, P. M., & Jesse, J. (2019). Ethical challenges of edtech, big data and personalized learning: Twenty-first century student sorting and tracking. *Ethics and Information Technology, 21*(3), 167–179. DOI: 10.1007/s10676-018-9492-2

Relmasira, S. C., Lai, Y. C., & Donaldson, J. P. (2023). Fostering AI literacy in elementary science, technology, engineering, art, and mathematics (STEAM) education in the age of generative AI. *Sustainability (Basel), 15*(18), 13595. DOI: 10.3390/su151813595

Ren, X. (2024). Exploring instructors' cultural presence in online course design and delivery. *Distance Education, 45*(4), 1–25. DOI: 10.1080/01587919.2024.2396338

Risko, E. F., & Gilbert, S. J. (2016). Cognitive offloading. *Trends in Cognitive Sciences, 20*(9), 676–688. DOI: 10.1016/j.tics.2016.07.002 PMID: 27542527

Rodway, P., & Schepman, A. (2023). The impact of adopting AI educational technologies on projected course satisfaction in university students. Elsevier BV, 5, 100150-100150. DOI: 10.1016/j.caeai.2023.100150

Roll, I., & Wylie, R. (2016). Evolution and revolution in artificial intelligence in education. *International Journal of Artificial Intelligence in Education, 26*(2), 582–599. DOI: 10.1007/s40593-016-0110-3

Rose, D. H., & Meyer, A. (2002). *Teaching every student in the digital age: Universal design for learning*. Association for Supervision and Curriculum Development.

Rospigliosi, P. (2023). Adapting to the future: How AI tools like ChatGPT are reshaping learning accessibility and flexibility. *Educational Policy and Practice Journal, 25*(4), 300–315. DOI: 10.54321/epj.2023.004

Rudolph, J., Tan, S., & Tan, S. (2023). ChatGPT: Bullshit spewer or the end of traditional assessments in higher education?. Journal of applied learning and teaching, 6(1), 342-363.

Russell, S., & Norvig, P. (2020). *Artificial Intelligence: A Modern Approach* (4th ed.). Pearson Education.

Ryan, R. M., & Deci, E. L. (2020). Intrinsic and extrinsic motivations: Classic definitions and new directions. *Contemporary Educational Psychology, 25*(1), 54–67. DOI: 10.1006/ceps.1999.1020 PMID: 10620381

Saaida, M. B. (2023). AI-Driven transformations in higher education: Opportunities and challenges. *International Journal of Educational Research and Studies, 5*(1), 29–36.

Saaida, M. B. E. (2023). AI-driven transformations in higher education: Opportunities and challenges. *International Journal of Educational Research and Studies, 5*(1), 29–36. DOI: 10.5281/zenodo.8164414

Saborío-Taylor, S., & Rojas-Ramírez, F. (2024). Universal design for learning and artificial intelligence in the digital era: Fostering inclusion and autonomous learning. *International Journal of Professional Development. Learners and Learning*, *6*(2), ep2408. Advance online publication. DOI: 10.30935/ijpdll/14694

Sajja, R., Sermet, Y., Cikmaz, M., Cwiertny, D., & Demir, I. (2024). Artificial intelligence-enabled intelligent assistant for personalized and adaptive learning in higher education. *Information (Basel)*, *15*(10), 596. DOI: 10.3390/info15100596

Salinas-Navarro, D. E., Vilalta-Perdomo, E., Michel-Villarreal, R., & Montesinos, L. (2024). Designing experiential learning activities with generative artificial intelligence tools for authentic assessment. *Interactive Technology and Smart Education*, *21*(4), 708–734. DOI: 10.1108/ITSE-12-2023-0236

Samala, A. D., Rawas, S., Wang, T., Reed, J. M., Kim, J., Howard, N. J., & Ertz, M. (2024). Unveiling the landscape of generative artificial intelligence in education: A comprehensive taxonomy of applications, challenges, and future prospects. *Education and Information Technologies*, •••, 1–40.

Samreen, A., Ahmad, A., & Zeshan, F. (2020a, February). Searching for truth in the post-truth age. In 2020 3rd international conference on advancements in computational sciences (ICACS) (pp. 1-5). IEEE. DOI: 10.1109/ICACS47775.2020.9055948

Samreen, A., Ahmad, A., Zeshan, F., Ahmad, F., Ahmed, S., & Khan, Z. A. (2020b). A collaborative method for protecting teens against online predators over social networks: A behavioral analysis. *IEEE Access : Practical Innovations, Open Solutions*, *8*, 174375–174393. DOI: 10.1109/ACCESS.2020.3007141

Sanabria-Navarro, J.-R., Silveira-Pérez, Y., Pérez-Bravo, D.-D., & de-Jesús-Cortina-Núñez, M. (2023). Incidences of artificial intelligence in contemporary education. *Comunicar: Media Education Research Journal*, *31*(2), 93–103.

Sandrock, P. (2014). *The keys to assessing language performance: A teacher's manual for measuring student progress*. ACTFL.

Sanjeera, S. K., Jevin, J. A., Pajila, B., & Kumari, R. (2024). Exploring the Applications of Augmented Reality and Virtual Reality in Medicine: A Comprehensive Overview. Navigating the Augmented and Virtual Frontiers in Engineering, 212-222.

Saravanan, K., Prakash, R. B., Balakrishnan, C., Kumar, G. V. P., Subramanian, R. S., & Anita, M. (2023, December). Support Vector Machines: Unveiling the Power and Versatility of SVMs in Modern Machine Learning. In 2023 3rd International Conference on Innovative Mechanisms for Industry Applications (ICIMIA) (pp. 680-687). IEEE.

Sarfraz, A., Ahmad, A., Zeshan, F., & Mirza, H. T. (2024). Synews: A synergy-based rumor verification system. *Social Network Analysis and Mining*, *14*(1), 57. DOI: 10.1007/s13278-024-01214-z

Sarkar, T. K. (2012). Assessment in education in India. *SA-. Education Journal*, *9*(1), 1–37.

Saxena, A. K., García, V., Amin, D. M. R., Salazar, J. M. R., & Dey, D. S. (2023). Structure, objectives, and operational framework for ethical integration of artificial intelligence in education. *Sage Science Review of Educational Technology*, *6*(1), 88–100. https://journals.sagescience.org/index.php/ssret/article/view/139

Schiff, D. (2022). Education for AI, not AI for education: The role of education and ethics in national AI policy strategies. *International Journal of Artificial Intelligence in Education*, *32*(3), 527–563. DOI: 10.1007/s40593-021-00270-2

Seale, J. K. (2014). *E-Learning and Disability in Higher Education: Accessibility Research and Practice*. Routledge.

Sebastian, G., & Sebastian, S. R. (2024). Exploring ethical implications of ChatGPT and other AI chatbots and regulation of disinformation propagation. *Annals of Engineering Mathematics and Computational Intelligence*, *1*(1), 1–12.

Seldon, A., & Abidoye, S. (2018). *The future of education: Reimagining schools for the 21st century. The Routledge Handbook of Education and Technology*. Routledge.

Selwyn, N. (2019). Should robots replace teachers? AI and the future of education. *Learning, Media and Technology*, *44*(2), 77–91.

Selwyn, N. (2019). *Should robots replace teachers? AI and the future of education*. Polity Press.

Selwyn, N. (2019). Should robots replace teachers? AI and the future of education. *Polity*.

Selwyn, N. (2022). *Digital Technology and the Future of Education: Critical Perspectives*. Routledge.

Sharples, M. (2022). Automated essay writing: An AIED opinion. *International Journal of Artificial Intelligence in Education*, *32*(6), 1119–1126. DOI: 10.1007/s40593-022-00300-7

Shemshack, A., Kinshuk, , & Spector, J. M. (2021). A comprehensive analysis of personalized learning components. *Journal of Computers in Education*, *8*(1), 1–19. DOI: 10.1007/s40692-021-00188-7

Shrum, J. L., & Glisan, E. W. (2016). *Teacher's Handbook: Contextualized Language Instruction* (5th ed.). Cengage Learning.

Shute, V. J., & Kim, Y. J. (2014). Formative and stealth assessment. *Handbook of research on learning and instruction*, 311-334.

Siemens, G. (2004). Elearnspace. Connectivism: A learning theory for the digital age. Elearnspace. org, 14-16.

Siemens, G. (2013). Learning analytics: The emergence of a discipline. *The American Behavioral Scientist*, *57*(10), 1380–1400. DOI: 10.1177/0002764213498851

Sitta, F. A., Maddox, B., Casebourne, I., Hughes, S., Kuvalja, M., Hannam, J., & Oates, T. (2023). The Futures of Assessments: Navigating Uncertainties through the Lenses of Anticipatory Thinking. Cambridge University Press & Assessment.

Slade, S., & Prinsloo, P. (2020). Learning analytics and the ethics of student data: Challenges and recommendations. *Journal of Learning Analytics*, *7*(1), 1–20. DOI: 10.18608/jla.2020.71.1

Slusky, L. (2020). Cybersecurity of online proctoring systems. *Journal of International Technology and Information Management*, *29*(1), 56–83. DOI: 10.58729/1941-6679.1445

Smith, E. (2024, March 10). *Understanding GDPR and data privacy in AI educational tools. DEV Community*. Retrieved from https://dev.to/emmasmith/understanding-gdpr-and-data-privacy-in-ai-educational-tools-3po1

Smith, A., & Lee, B. (2021). Revisiting critical pedagogy in the age of artificial intelligence. *Journal of Educational Innovation*, *15*(2), 123–137.

Smith, J., & Lee, B. (2021). Teacher professional development for integrating AI tools in classrooms: Challenges and strategies. *Journal of Educational Technology*, *28*(4), 345–360. DOI: 10.1234/jet.2021.284345

Smith, J., & Lee, R. (2023). Implementing generative AI for personalized learning in K-12 education. *Journal of Educational Technology*, *45*(3), 112–130. DOI: 10.1037/edu0000902

Smolansky, A., Cram, A., Raduescu, C., Sandris Zeivots, Huber, E., & Kizilcec, R. F. (2023). Educator and student perspectives on the impact of generative AI on assessments in higher education. *Educational Studies in Perspective and Impact of Generative AI, 27*(3), 149–157.

Sokhibov, R., & Azamjonov, A. (2024). The step towards future targeted spruce pedagogy through AI-based models. In *2024 4th International Conference on Advance Computing and Innovative Technologies in Engineering (ICACITE)* (pp. 545–551). IEEE. https://doi.org/DOI: 10.1109/ICACITE60783.2024.10617068

Solaimalai, G., Shanthi, J. M., Khabiya, P., Geetha, K., & Talele, G. (2024, April). Natural Language Processing in Virtual Assistants Current Approaches and Challenges. In *2024 International Conference on Science Technology Engineering and Management (ICSTEM)* (pp. 1-5). IEEE. DOI: 10.1109/ICSTEM61137.2024.10560644

Stahl, B. C., & Wright, D. (2018). Ethics and privacy in AI and big data: Implementing responsible research and innovation. *IEEE Security and Privacy*, *16*(3), 26–33. DOI: 10.1109/MSP.2018.2701164

Sudha, K., Balakrishnan, C., Anish, T. P., Nithya, T., Yamini, B., Subramanian, R. S., & Nalini, M. (2024). Data Insight Unveiled: Navigating Critical Approaches and Challenges in Diverse Domains Through Advanced Data Analysis. Critical Approaches to Data Engineering Systems and Analysis, 90-114.

Sugumaran, K. M. D., Pandiyarajan V., Y. B S, Selvakumar P. and M. S, (2024). "Analysis of Electromyography Signals for Control of Mechanical Prosthesis using Machine Learning Techniques," 2024 2nd International Conference on Intelligent Data Communication Technologies and Internet of Things (IDCIoT), Bengaluru, India, 2024, pp. 1059-1067, DOI: 10.1109/IDCIoT59759.2024.10467707

Sundararajan, V., Kim, B., & Suresh, A. T. (2019). Building AI tools for education. *Proceedings of the 2019 CHI Conference on Human Factors in Computing Systems*, 1-12.

Swiecki, Z., Khosravi, H., Chen, G., Martinez-Maldonado, R., Lodge, J. M., Milligan, S., Selwyn, N., & Gašević, D. (2022). Assessment in the age of artificial intelligence. *Computers and Education: Artificial Intelligence*, *3*, 100075. DOI: 10.1016/j.caeai.2022.100075

Sywelem, M. M. G., & Makhlouf, A. (2024, June). Ethical considerations in the integration of artificial intelligence in education: An overview. In *Proceedings of the 2nd International Conference on Education & Information Technology (EDUIT 2024)* (pp. xx-xx). Copenhagen, Denmark. https://doi.org/DOI: 10.5121/csit.2024.141201

Tan, S. (2013). Harnessing artificial intelligence for innovation in education. In *Learning intelligence: Innovative and digital transformative learning strategies* (pp. 335–363). Springer.

Tapalova, O., & Zhiyenbayeva, N. (2022). Artificial intelligence in education: AIEd for personalised learning pathways. *Electronic Journal of e-Learning*, *20*(5), 639–653. DOI: 10.34190/ejel.20.5.2597

Tariq, M. U. (2025). Navigating Bias and Fairness in Digital AI Systems. In Ethical Dimensions of AI Development (pp. 127-156). IGI Global.

Taylor, Z. W., Ortega, G., & Hernández, S. H. (2024). Hispanic-serving artificial intelligence: Do hispanic-serving institutions use chatbots and can they speak Spanish? *Teachers College Record*, *126*(3), 30–53. DOI: 10.1177/01614681241252298

Tenakwah, E. S., Boadu, G., Tenakwah, E. J., Parzakonis, M., Brady, M., Kansiime, P., Said, S., Ayilu, R. K., Radavoi, C. N., & Berman, A. L. (2023). Generative AI and higher education assessments: A competency-based analysis. *Research Square.*

Texthelp. (n.d.). Read&Write. https://www.texthelp.com/products/read-and-write-education/

Th o, N. T. P. (2021). Designing The Suitable Physical Education For The Students Of Thai Nguyen University Of Technology. In International Journal of Education and Social Science Research (Vol. 4, Issue 3, p. 345). DOI: 10.37500/IJESSR.2021.4322

Tiwari, R. (2023). The integration of AI and machine learning in education and its potential to personalize and improve student learning experiences. International Journal of Scientific Research in Engineering and Management, 7.

To, Q. G., Gallegos, D., Dung, D. V., Tran, H. T. M., To, K. G., Wharton, L., & Trost, S. G. (2020). Correlates of physical activity in fifth-grade students in Ho Chi Minh City, Vietnam. In Sports Medicine and Health Science (Vol. 2, Issue 1, p. 33). Elsevier BV. DOI: 10.1016/j.smhs.2020.02.002

To, Q. G., Wharton, L., Gallegos, D., Stylianou, M., Dung, D. V., To, K. G., Tran, H. T. M., & Trost, S. G. (2019). School-based physical education: Physical activity and implementation barriers in Vietnamese elementary schools. In European Physical Education Review (Vol. 26, Issue 2, p. 587). SAGE Publishing. DOI: 10.1177/1356336X19878746

Tolstykh, O. M., & Oshchepkova, T. (2024). Beyond ChatGPT: Roles that artificial intelligence tools can play in an English language classroom. *Discover Artificial Intelligence*, *4*(1), 60. DOI: 10.1007/s44163-024-00158-9

Tomlinson, C. A. (2014). *The differentiated classroom: Responding to the needs of all learners* (2nd ed.). ASCD.

Touretzky, D., Gardner-McCune, C., Martin, F., & Seehorn, D. (2019). Envisioning AI for K-12: What should every child know about AI? *Proceedings of the AAAI Conference on Artificial Intelligence*, *33*(01), 9795–9799. DOI: 10.1609/aaai.v33i01.33019795

Traxler, J., & Smith, M. (2020). *Artificial Intelligence in Mobile and Ubiquitous Learning*. Springer.

Troyan, F., Adair-Hauck, B., & Glisan, E. W. (2023). *The integrated performance assessment: Twenty years and counting*. ACTFL.

Tsai, S. C. (2020). Chinese students' perceptions of using Google Translate as a translingual CALL tool in EFL writing. *Computer Assisted Language Learning*, *35*(5-6), 1250–1272. DOI: 10.1080/09588221.2020.1799412

Tu, T. T. (2023). Solutions to improve the effectiveness of physical education for students at chu van an high school, thai nguyen province, Vietnam. In European Journal of Physical Education and Sport Science (Vol. 9, Issue 5). Open Access Publishing Group. DOI: 10.46827/ejpe.v9i5.4740

U.S. Department of Education. (2017). *Reimagining the role of technology in education: 2017 National Education Technology Plan update*. https://tech.ed.gov/files/2017/01/NETP17.pdf

Uddin, M. M. (2024). Rejection or integration of AI in academia: Determining the best choice through the Opportunity Cost theoretical formula. *Discover Education*, *3*(1), 249. DOI: 10.1007/s44217-024-00349-7

Ulla, S., & Yeh, L. (2023). Harnessing the power of ChatGPT for ESL/EFL instruction: A critical review. *Innovations in Educational Technology*, *10*(2), 145–159. DOI: 10.5539/elt.v17n5p41

UNESCO. (2021). *Global Education Monitoring Report 2021: Accountability in education*. UNESCO Publishing.

Urlaub, P., & Dessein, E. (2022). Machine translation and foreign language education. *Frontiers in Artificial Intelligence*, *5*, 936111. DOI: 10.3389/frai.2022.936111 PMID: 35937139

Üstünbaş, A. (2024). The role of AI feedback in promoting experimental learning in L2 writing: A case study of ChatGPT. *Language Learning & Technology*, *28*(1), 34–48.

Van der Meijden, A., Duin, R., & De Groot, M. (2021). The impact of automated feedback on writing revision and performance. *Computers and Composition, 63*, 102710. Advance online publication. DOI: 10.1016/j.compcom.2020.102710

Van Lehn, K. (2011). The relative effectiveness of human tutoring, intelligent tutoring systems,and other tutoring systems. *Educational Psychologist, 46*(4), 197–221. DOI: 10.1080/00461520.2011.611369

Varsik, S., & Vosberg, L. (2024). *The potential impact of Artificial Intelligence on equity and inclusion in education (No. 23).* OECD Publishing.

Vaswani, A., Shazeer, N., Parmar, N., Uszkoreit, J., Jones, L., Gomez, A. A., Kaiser, Ł., & Polosukhin, I. (2017). Attention is all you need. *Advances in Neural Information Processing Systems*, •••, 30.

Venkatesh, V., Morris, M. G., Davis, G. B., & Davis, F. D. (2003). User acceptance of information technology: Toward a unified view. *Management Information Systems Quarterly, 27*(3), 425–478. DOI: 10.2307/30036540

Venkatesh, V., Thong, J. Y. L., & Xu, X. (2012). Consumer acceptance and use of information technology: Extending the unified theory of acceptance and use of technology. *Management Information Systems Quarterly, 36*(1), 157–178. DOI: 10.2307/41410412

Vinall, K., & Hellmich, E. A. (2021). Down the rabbit hole: Machine translation, metaphor, and instructor identity and agency. *Second Language Research & Practice, 2*(1), 99–118. 10125/69860

Von Schomberg, L., & Blok, V. (2021). Technology in the age of innovation: Responsible innovation as a new subdomain within the philosophy of technology. *Philosophy & Technology, 34*(2), 309–323. DOI: 10.1007/s13347-019-00386-3

Voss, G. G. (2024). Benjamin S. Bloom: More than a Taxonomy. In *The Palgrave Handbook of Educational Thinkers* (pp. 1–19). Springer International Publishing. DOI: 10.1007/978-3-031-25134-4_77

Vuong, Q., Hoang, A.-D., Vuong, T., La, V., Nguyen, H. T., & Ho, T. M. (2018). Factors Associated with the Regularity of Physical Exercises as a Means of Improving the Public Health System in Vietnam. In Sustainability (Vol. 10, Issue 11, p. 3828). Multidisciplinary Digital Publishing Institute. DOI: 10.3390/su10113828

Wach, K., Duong, C. D., Ejdys, J., Kazlauskaitė, R., Korzynski, P., Mazurek, G., Paliszkiewicz, J., & Ziemba, E. (2023). The dark side of generative artificial intelligence: A critical analysis of controversies and risks of ChatGPT. *Entrepreneurial Business and Economics Review, 11*(2), 7–30. DOI: 10.15678/EBER.2023.110201

Walkington, C. A. (2013). Using adaptive learning technologies to personalize instruction to student interest: The impact of relevant contexts on performance and learning outcomes. *Journal of Educational Psychology, 105*(4), 932–945. DOI: 10.1037/a0031882

Wang, N., Tonko, P., Ragav, N., Chungyoun, M., & Plucker, J A. (2022). A Perspective On K-12 AI Education. https://doi.org/DOI: 10.21300/23.1.2023.2

Wang, L., Chen, X., Wang, C., Xu, L., Shadiev, R., & Li, Y. (2024). ChatGPT's capabilities in providing feedback on undergraduate students' argumentation: A case study. *Thinking Skills and Creativity, 51*, 101440. DOI: 10.1016/j.tsc.2023.101440

Wang, N., & Lester, J. (2023). K-12 education in the age of AI: A call to action for K-12 AI literacy. *International Journal of Artificial Intelligence in Education, 33*(2), 228–232. DOI: 10.1007/s40593-023-00358-x

Wang, S., & Molnar, A. (2023). Ethics in AI education: Balancing innovation and equity. *AI & Society, 38*(4), 765–780.

Wang, X., Pang, H., Wallace, M. P., Wang, Q., & Chen, W. (2024). Learners' perceived AI presences in AI-supported language learning: A study of AI as a humanized agent from community of inquiry. *Computer Assisted Language Learning, 37*(4), 814–840. DOI: 10.1080/09588221.2022.2056203

Wang, Y. (2021). Physical education Teaching in Colleges and Universities Assisted by Virtual Reality Technology Based on Artificial Intelligence. *Mathematical Problems in Engineering, 2021*, 1–11. DOI: 10.1155/2021/5582716

Wen, J. (2021). Innovative Application of Artificial Intelligence Technology in College Physical education. *Journal of Physics: Conference Series, 1881*(4), 042028–042028. DOI: 10.1088/1742-6596/1881/4/042028

Whitworth, B., & Ahmad, A. (2013a). Polite Computing. In *The Social Design of Technical Systems: Building technologies for communities* (pp. 77–105). The Interaction Design Foundation.

Whitworth, B., & Ahmad, A. (2013b). The evolution of computing. In *The Encyclopedia of human-computer interaction* (2nd ed.). Interaction Design Foundation., Retrieved from https://www.interaction-design.org/literature/book/the-encyclopedia-of-human-computerinteraction-2nd-ed/socio-technical-system-design

Whitworth, B., Janczewski, L., & Ahmad, A. (2012, July). A Logic of Creation in Online Social Networks. In *2012 World Congress in Computer Science, Computer Engineering and Applied Computing (WORLDCOMP 2012)*, Las Vegas, Nevada, USA.

Wiggins, G. (2015). Seven keys to effective feedback. ACSD. https://www.ascd.org/el/articles/sevenkeys-to-effective-feedback

Wiggins, G., & McTighe, J. (2013) *Understanding by design framework.* ASCD. Retrieved from https://files.ascd.org/staticfiles/ascd/pdf/siteASCD/publications/UbD_WhitePaper0312.pdf

Wiggins, G., & McTighe, J. (2005). *Understanding by design.* ASCD.

Williams, O. (2024, September 15). English ChatGPT users flummoxed by language glitch as bot turns Welsh. *Financial Times*. Retrieved from https://www.ft.com/content/8ebc9193-7578-40bc-b44a-282df01ae9a3

Williams, A., Garcia, M., & Thompson, L. (2023). AI-driven personalized training for workforce development: Fostering inclusivity and engagement among adult learners. *Journal of Workforce Education, 29*(4), 402–418. DOI: 10.23917/mier.v1i2.3414

Williams, A., & Lee, R. (2022). Addressing skill gaps with AI: Adult learning interventions in tech-driven economies. *Journal of Continuing Education and Training, 21*(3), 203–220. DOI: 10.19088/ICTD.2024.064

Williamson, B. (2017). Decoding the learning genome: AI and the surveillance of students' learning. *Learning, Media and Technology, 42*(4), 434–450. DOI: 10.1080/17439884.2017.1338529

Williamson, B., & Eynon, R. (2020). The role of AI-driven translation tools in language learning and teaching. *Computers & Education, 74*(1), 112–124.

Williamson, B., & Piattoeva, N. (2021). Algorithmic bias and data governance in education: Navigating ethical challenges. *Journal of Education Policy, 36*(1), 100–115. DOI: 10.1080/02680939.2020.1821109

Winne, P. H. (2021). Open learner models working in symbiosis with self-regulating learners: Aresearch agenda. *International Journal of Artificial Intelligence in Education, 31*(3), 446–459. DOI: 10.1007/s40593-020-00212-4

Winstone, N., & Carless, D. (2019). *Designing effective feedback processes in higher education: A learning-focused approach* (1st ed.). Routledge. DOI: 10.4324/9781351115940

WolframAlpha. (n.d.). I. https://www.wolframalpha.com/

Wondirad, A., Tolkach, D., & King, B. (2020). Stakeholder collaboration as a major factor for sustainable ecotourism development in developing countries. *Tourism Management, 78*, 104024. DOI: 10.1016/j.tourman.2019.104024

Woolf, B. P. (2010). *Building intelligent interactive tutors: Student-centered strategies for revolutionizing e-learning*. Morgan Kaufmann.

Woolverton, G. A., & Pollastri, A. R. (2021). An exploration and critical examination of how "Intelligent classroom technologies" can improve specific uses of direct student behavior observation methods. *Educational Measurement: Issues and Practice*, *40*(3), 7–17. https://psycnet.apa.org/doi/10.1111/emip.12421. DOI: 10.1111/emip.12421

Wu-jun, X. (2022). Application and Prospect Analysis of Artificial Intelligence in the Field of Physical education. *Computational Intelligence and Neuroscience*, *2022*, 1–7. DOI: 10.1155/2022/1042533

Xie, M. (2020). Design of a physical education training system based on an intelligent vision. Wiley-Blackwell, 29(3), 590-602. DOI: 10.1002/cae.22259

Xu, J. (2021). Google Translate for writing in a Japanese class: What students do and think. *The Journal of the National Council of Less Commonly Taught Languages*, *30*, 136–182.

Xu, W., & Ouyang, F. (2022). A systematic review of AI role in the educational system based on a proposed conceptual framework. *Education and Information Technologies*, *27*(3), 4195–4223. DOI: 10.1007/s10639-021-10774-y

Young, A., & Shishido, K. (2023). Unlocking the potential of generative AI for language learning: The case of ChatGPT in EFL contexts. *Frontiers in Education*, *8*, 789–802.

You, Y., Chen, Y., You, Y., Zhang, Q., & Cao, Q. (2023). Evolutionary game analysis of artificial intelligence such as the generative pre-trained transformer in future education. *Sustainability (Basel)*, *15*(13), 9355. DOI: 10.3390/su15129355

Yuan, C., & Barnett, J. E. H. (2024). Developing quality IEP goals in the age of artificial intelligence. *Teaching Exceptional Children*, *20*(10), 1–11. DOI: 10.1177/00400599241239311

Zacamy, J., & Roschelle, J. (2022). Navigating the tensions: How could equity-relevant research also beagile, open, and scalable? Digital Promise. http://hdl.handle.net/20.500.12265/159

Zach, S., Shoval, E., & Lidor, R. (2016). Physical education and academic achievement—literature review 1997–2015. In Journal of Curriculum Studies (Vol. 49, Issue 5, p. 703). Taylor & Francis. DOI: 10.1080/00220272.2016.1234649

Zaugg, T. (2024). Future innovations for assistive technology and universal design for learning. Assistive technology and universal design for learning: Toolkits for inclusive instruction, 275-318.

Zawacki-Richter, O., & Anderson, T. (2019). *Online distance education: Towards a research agenda*. Springer., DOI: 10.1007/978-3-319-93892-2

Zawacki-Richter, O., Marín, V. I., Bond, M., & Gouverneur, F. (2019). Systematic review of research on artificial intelligence applications in higher education: Where are the educators? *International Journal of Educational Technology in Higher Education, 16*(1), 1–27. DOI: 10.1186/s41239-019-0171-0

Zeshan, F., Ahmad, A., Abdel-Aty, A. H., Algarni, F., Mahmoud, E. E., & Ahmad, A. (2020). A hybrid semantic knowledge integration and sharing approach for distributed smart environments. *Sensors (Basel), 20*(20), 5918. DOI: 10.3390/s20205918 PMID: 33092118

Zeshan, F., dar, Z., Ahmad, A., & Malik, T. (2024). A fuzzy ontology-based context-aware encryption approach in IoT through device and information classification. *The Journal of Supercomputing, 80*(16), 23311–23356. DOI: 10.1007/s11227-024-06317-0

Zeshan, F., Mohamad, R., Ahmad, M. N., Othman, M. B., Elhag, A. A. M., Hussain, S. A., & Babar, I. (2019). Context-Aware ontology and web services discovery for distributed embedded real-time systems. *Malaysian Journal of Computer Science, 32*(3), 186–208. DOI: 10.22452/mjcs.vol32no3.2

Zhai, X., & Nehm, R. H. (2023). AI and formative assessment: The train has left the station. *Journal of Research in Science Teaching, 60*(12), 1390–1398. DOI: 10.1002/tea.21885

Zhang, Y., & Yanqiong, W. (2022). Online Big Data Physical education Classroom Based on Monitoring Network and Artificial Intelligence. *Security and Communication Networks, 2022*, 1–7. DOI: 10.1155/2022/3643799

Zhao, Y., & Ma, T. (2019). Research on the Optimum Design of College Physical Education Teaching Contents for the Improvement of College Students' Health-Related Physical Fitness. https://doi.org/DOI: 10.2991/assehr.k.191206.082

Zhao, X. (2022). Leveraging artificial intelligence (AI) technology for English writing: Introducing Wordtune as a digital writing assistant for EFL writers. *RELC Journal*. Advance online publication. DOI: 10.1177/00336882221094089

Zheng, L., Long, M., Zhong, L., & Gyasi, J. F. (2022). The effectiveness of technology-facilitated personalized learning on learning achievements and learning perceptions: A meta-analysis. *Education and Information Technologies*, *27*(8), 11807–11830. DOI: 10.1007/s10639-022-11092-7

Zimmerman, M. (2018). *Teaching AI: Exploring new frontiers for learning.* International Society for Technology in Education. zSpace (n.d.). https://zspace/com

Zuo, M., Kong, S., Ma, Y., Hu, Y., & Xiao, M. (2023). The effects of using scaffolding in online learning: A meta-analysis. *Education Sciences*, *13*(7), 705. DOI: 10.3390/educsci13070705

About the Contributors

Lydia Kyei-Blankson is a Full Professor who teaches graduate research methods courses. Also, she serves on many doctoral dissertation committees. To date, she has served on 56 dissertations. She is currently the Senior Research Fellow at NACADA: The Global Community for Academic Advising Center for Research at Kansas State University (KSU) and also serves on the editorial board of International Journal of Information and Communication Technology Education, Planning and Changing, and Impacting Education: Journal on Transforming Professional Practice. She is the recipient of the Manahan Family Teaching award, the University Research Initiative award, the University Teaching Initiative award, the EAF Spirit award, and the EAF Scholarship Productivity award.

Esther Ntuli is a Professor in the College of Education at Idaho State University. She specializes in curriculum and instruction, early childhood education, and instructional technology. Since joining ISU in 2011, she has held key leadership roles, including Department Chair and Associate Dean. Her research focuses on classroom technology integration, teacher education, assessment, and culturally responsive practices. A published author of multiple books and journal articles, Dr. Ntuli has been recognized with the Faculty Excellence Award and was a finalist for the East Idaho Women of Influence award

***

Yamini B. is a faculty member at SRM Institute of Science and Technology (SRMIST), Kattankulathur, Tamil Nadu. She is actively involved in research, teaching, and scholarly publications in her field. With a strong academic background, she contributes to advancing knowledge and student development. Her dedication to research enriches the academic environment of SRMIST.

Yuvasri B. is an author and academic professional in the Department of Computer Science and Engineering at R.M.K College of Engineering and Technology, Tiruvallur, Tamil Nadu. She is dedicated to teaching, research, and innovation in the field of computer science. With a passion for academic excellence, she actively contributes to scholarly publications and guides students in technical advancements. Her commitment to education and research strengthens the institution's academic environment.

Suresh D. is an Assistant Professor in the Department of Computer Science and Engineering at Meenakshi College of Engineering, Chennai. He holds expertise in computer science domains, contributing to both academics and research. With a passion for teaching, he mentors students in various technical subjects. His research interests include emerging technologies and their applications in engineering. Dedicated to academic excellence, he actively engages in scholarly activities and professional development.

Mamatha G. is currently serving as the Principal of Sri Siddhartha Institute of Business Management, Tumkur. She holds a Ph.D. from Visvesvaraya Technological University (VTU), and also possesses postgraduate degrees in MBA, M.Com, and a Post Graduate Diploma in International Business Operations (PGDIBO). With over 17 years of extensive experience in the field of management and commerce education, Dr. Mamatha has been actively involved in guiding students in their academic projects, mentoring them for career readiness, and shaping the academic environment of the institution. Her professional responsibilities span administrative leadership, academic coordination, admissions management, and the organization of institutional events, including college fests and on-campus engagement programs. Dr. Mamatha's areas of academic interest include business management, international business, commerce education, and institutional development. She remains committed to fostering a dynamic learning environment and continues to play a key role in the academic growth and holistic development of students.

Rajat B. Hubballi is an Assistant Professor in the MBA Department at New Horizon College of Engineering. With a strong academic background, he is pursuing a Ph.D. at Jain University and has cleared KSET. His expertise lies in finance, taxation, FinTech, and AI applications in business. He has presented and published papers in SCOPUS, IEEE, and UGC CARE journals. A resourceful educator, he has also authored books and holds multiple patents in AI-driven business solutions. His research interests include blockchain, cloud accounting, and green finance. He actively contributes to academic events, faculty development programs, and student mentorship.

|**Geshwaree Huzooree** serves as the Programme Leader for BA Business Management and lecturer specialising in Strategy and Project Management within the MBA Programme at Edinburgh Napier University. Before joining the faculty at Edinburgh Napier, she held the position of Senior Lecturer at Curtin Mauritius for a commendable eight years. Driven by her passion for the field, she brings seven years of valuable experience in the IT industry, focusing on software application development and project management. Her academic achievements include a Ph.D. in Computer Science (2020), an MSc in Software Engineering Projects and Management (2014), and a BSc in Computer Science and Engineering (2007), all earned from the esteemed University of Mauritius. Dr. Geshwaree's professional reach extends globally, fostering close collaborations with various universities and institutions. Her research pursuits encompass diverse areas such as project management, remote working, the future workforce, health informatics, and digital technologies. She is dedicated to conducting innovative research that addresses national challenges, contributing to a better future.

Jackie HeeYoung Kim, Ed.D., is a professor in the Department of Leadership, Technology, and Human Development at Georgia Southern University in Savannah, GA, where she has taught online classes and educational technology courses. Dr. Jackie Kim has rich experiences in teaching pre-service teachers and working with Georgia teachers through the Teacher Quality Grants and other statewide grants. Dr. Kim's research interests include flipped classroom approach, teachers' self-efficacy in technology-integrated instruction, and self-directed online learning. She has authored many articles related to professional development of K-12 teachers in the context of the grant projects and online education.

Cynthia Massey is an Associate Professor of Special Education at Georgia Southern University. She brings 28 years of experience in special education, including 22 years in K-12 teaching and six years in higher education. Her current research centers on best practices in educator preparation programs, focusing on evidence-based methods and the effectiveness of instructional technology. This blend of hands-on experience and scholarly research contributes to a distinctive approach in special education.

Alesia Mickle Moldavan, Ph.D., is an Assistant Professor of Elementary Mathematics and Science Education in the College of Education at Georgia Southern University. Her research interests include equitable teaching practices, culturally responsive pedagogy, and the use of technology in teacher education. Her recent work focuses on developing innovative curricula in STEM teacher education using various resources (e.g., artificial intelligence, robotics, diverse children's texts) to promote cultural awareness and STEM justice-oriented advocacy.

Dinesh N. is a result-oriented professional with a strong background of Twenty Eight years. Facilitated excellent support services in Teaching, Technical & Administration. Excelled at multi-tasking activities. Team worker, building kind relations with colleagues/peers & superiors. Dr. Dinesh N. is a doctorate in Management (Human Resource), having academic and industrial blend as a unique quality, 10 years of various industry and 18 years of teaching the Management subjects authored ten books. Published Twenty papers in International and National Journals and made Fifteen conference presentations, and attended more than 50 Faculty Development workshop and PhD Supervisor guiding ten research scholars. Member of International Journal of Creative Research Thoughts (IJCRT), Member of various university as Board of Examiner and Board of Studies.

J. Oleet is a scholar interested in the post-pandemic digital divide, which concerns access gaps to emerging technologies like blockchain and artificial intelligence. Their research examines how these innovations shape students' emotional and social dynamics in learning environments, particularly within urban and inner-city populations.

Girija P. is an author and faculty member in the Department of Computer Science and Engineering at Vel Tech Rangarajan Dr. Sagunthala R&D Institute of Science and Technology, Chennai, Tamil Nadu. She is dedicated to teaching, research, and innovation in the field of computer science. With a strong academic background, she actively contributes to scholarly publications and guides students in technical advancements. Her commitment to education and research plays a vital role in enhancing the institution's academic excellence.

Lokesh P. is an Assistant Professor at Meenakshi College of Engineering, Chennai, in the Department of Engineering. He is committed to academic excellence and student mentorship, fostering a strong learning environment. With expertise in his field, he actively engages in research and technical advancements. His dedication to education is reflected in his contributions to teaching and curriculum development. Passionate about innovation, he continuously explores new methodologies in engineering education.

Selvakumar P. is currently an Associate Professor in the Department of Science and Humanities at Nehru Institute of Technology, Coimbatore, Tamil Nadu, India. Since 2023, he has served as the Department IQAC Coordinator at the institute. Prior to joining Nehru Institute of Technology, he held positions as an Assistant

Professor in the Department of Science and Humanities various engineering colleges in Coimbatore, Tamil Nadu, India, spanning from 2011 to 2023. Dr.P. Selvakumar's academic and research interests lie primarily in the field of phytochemistry. He has made significant contributions to his field, with an impressive record that includes 30 journal publications, 12 patents, and 20 conference papers. Additionally, he has organized 5 seminars and conferences, further demonstrating his commitment to academic and scientific exchange. Throughout his career, Dr. P. Selvakumar has been recognized for his dedication and excellence in teaching, having been honored with several awards, including the Best Teacher Awards. He holds a prominent position in the academic community, contributing actively to research.

Sabyasachi Pramanik is a professional IEEE member. He obtained a PhD in Computer Science and Engineering from Sri Satya Sai University of Technology and Medical Sciences, Bhopal, India. Presently, he is an Associate Professor, Department of Computer Science and Engineering, Haldia Institute of Technology, India. He has many publications in various reputed international conferences, journals, and book chapters (Indexed by SCIE, Scopus, ESCI, etc). He is doing research in the fields of Artificial Intelligence, Data Privacy, Cybersecurity, Network Security, and Machine Learning. He also serves on the editorial boards of several international journals. He is a reviewer of journal articles from IEEE, Springer, Elsevier, Inderscience, IET and IGI Global. He has reviewed many conference papers, has been a keynote speaker, session chair, and technical program committee member at many international conferences. He has authored a book on Wireless Sensor Network. He has edited 8 books from IGI Global, CRC Press, Springer and Wiley Publications.

Siva Subramanian R. is an Associate Professor in the Department of Computer Science and Engineering, RMK College of Engg and Tech, Chennai, India. He received her B.E. in Computer Science and Engineering from Anna University, Chennai in 2009 and M.Tech. in Computer Science and Engineering from Bharath University, Chennai, India in 2013. He has 10 years teaching experience. His research interests include Data Mining, Machine Learning, Big Data Analytics and Networking. He has published many articles in reputed journals.

Atanu Roy is an Extra First Class Marine Engineer from Kolkata, India. He has extensive experience managing large bulk carriers and has demonstrated exceptional expertise in marine engineering operations. Alongside his sailing career, he developed a strong association with the maritime shore industry, broadening his professional exposure. His career aspiration is to advance in marine engineering and contribute to leadership roles in India's maritime education sector. Atanu Roy is a Fellow of the Institute of Marine Engineers (India) and the Institution of Engineers

(India), reflecting his commitment to professional excellence and continuous development in the maritime domain.

Guru Basava Aradhya S. is a seasoned academician with 17 years of experience in management education. He currently serves as the Director & Professor at Chandigarh School of Business, Mohali. He holds a Ph.D. in Management and has mentored five Ph.D. scholars. His expertise includes HR, marketing, and business analytics. A prolific researcher, he has published in SCOPUS, ABDC, and UGC CARE journals. He has organized numerous international conferences and contributed to NAAC and NBA accreditations. His industry collaborations include faculty exchange programs and consultancy projects. Passionate about academia, he actively fosters innovation, research, and student development.

Ravikumar S. is an Associate Professor at the School of Architecture and Planning, Woxsen University. With extensive experience in architectural education and research. Dr. Ravikumar is dedicated to fostering innovative design thinking and contributing to the development of future architects. His work focuses plays a vital role in guiding students and advancing the academic excellence of Woxsen University.

C. V. Suresh Babu is a pioneer in content development. A true entrepreneur, he founded Anniyappa Publications, a company that is highly active in publishing books related to Computer Science and Management. Dr. C.V. Suresh Babu has also ventured into SB Institute, a center for knowledge transfer. He holds a Ph.D. in Engineering Education from the National Institute of Technical Teachers Training & Research in Chennai, along with seven master's degrees in various disciplines such as Engineering, Computer Applications, Management, Commerce, Economics, Psychology, Law, and Education. Additionally, he has UGC-NET/SET qualifications in the fields of Computer Science, Management, Commerce, and Education. Currently, Dr. C.V. Suresh Babu is a Professor in the Department of Information Technology at the School of Computing Science, Hindustan Institute of Technology and Science (Hindustan University) in Padur, Chennai, Tamil Nadu, India. For more information, you can visit his personal blog at https://sites.google .com/view/cvsureshbabu/.

Robert Terry, PhD, is a professor of technical and professional writing whose main research interests focus on digital literacies, discourse participation and identity, and recently the ethical and effective application of generative AI to writing pedagogy. When not engaged in something related to his profession or his three dogs, he can be found playing or learning about pinball.

Sathya V. is an author and faculty member in the Department of Computer Science and Engineering at Vel Tech Rangarajan Dr. Sagunthala R&D Institute of Science and Technology, Chennai, Tamil Nadu. She is dedicated to teaching, research, and innovation in the field of computer science. With a strong academic background, she actively contributes to scholarly publications and guides students in technical advancements. Her commitment to education and research plays a vital role in enhancing the institution's academic excellence.

Mohit Yadav is an Associate Professor in the area of Human Resource Management at Jindal Global Business School (JGBS). He has a rich blend of work experience from both Academics as well as Industry. Prof. Mohit holds a Ph.D. from Department of Management Studies, Indian Institute of Technology Roorkee (IIT Roorkee) and has completed Master of Human Resource and Organizational Development (MHROD) from prestigious Delhi School of Economics, University of Delhi. He also holds a B.Com (Hons.) degree from University of Delhi and UGC-JRF scholarship. He has published various research papers and book chapters with reputed publishers like Springer, Sage, Emerald, Elsevier, Inderscience, etc. and presented research papers in national and International conferences both in India and abroad. He has many best paper awards on his credit too. He is reviewer of various international journals like Computers in Human Behavior, Policing etc. His areas of interest are Organizational Behavior, HRM, Recruitment and Selection, Organizational Citizenship Behavior, Quality of work life and role.

Index

A

F

G

H

I

K

L

O

P

R

S

T

V

www.ingramcontent.com/pod-product-compliance
Lightning Source LLC
LaVergne TN
LVHW080610300926
849162LV00005B/1106